Governance Feminism

AN INTRODUCTION

Janet Halley, Prabha Kotiswaran,
Rachel Rebouché, and Hila Shamir

 University of Minnesota Press
Minneapolis
London

The University of Minnesota Press gratefully acknowledges the generous assistance provided for the publication of this book by the Margaret S. Harding Memorial Endowment, honoring the first director of the University of Minnesota Press.

Small portions of chapter 4 were published as Prabha Kotiswaran, "A Bittersweet Moment: Indian Governance Feminism and the 2013 Rape Law Reforms," *Economic & Political Weekly* 52, nos. 25–26 (2017): 78–87. Small portions of chapter 6 were published as Rachel Rebouché, "Testing Sex," *University of Richmond Law Review* 49 (2015): 519–77, and as Rachel Rebouché, "Abortion Rights as Human Rights," *Social and Legal Studies* 25 (2016): 765–82.

Published by the University of Minnesota Press
111 Third Avenue South, Suite 290
Minneapolis, MN 55401-2520
http://www.upress.umn.edu

Printed in the United States of America on acid-free paper

The University of Minnesota is an equal-opportunity educator and employer.

Library of Congress Cataloging-in-Publication Data

Names: Halley, Janet E., author.
Title: Governance feminism : an introduction / Janet Halley, [and three others].
Description: Minneapolis : University of Minnesota Press, [2018] |
    Includes bibliographical references and index. |
Identifiers: LCCN 2017018693 (print) | ISBN 978-0-8166-9845-5 (hc) |
    ISBN 978-0-8166-9847-9 (pb)
Subjects: LCSH: Feminism—Political aspects.
Classification: LCC HQ1236 .H274 2018 (print) | DDC 320.56/22—dc23
LC record available at https://lccn.loc.gov/2017018693

UMP BmB 2018

In memory of Helen Reece

Contents

Introducing Governance Feminism

JANET HALLEY

Feminists now walk the halls of power. By no means all feminists: some forms of feminism disqualify their proponents from inclusion in the power elite. But you can get a job in the United Nations, the World Bank, the International Criminal Court, the local prosecutor's office, and the child welfare bureaucracy for espousing various strands of feminism. Exactly what forms of feminism "make sense" to power elites as they gradually let women in? What happens when feminists and feminist ideas find their way into legal institutions and change legal thought and legal operations? Whose nongovernmental organizations get funding from international aid and development agencies and from ideologically driven private donors? Once feminists gain a foothold in governance, what do they *do* there and which particular legal forms are they most heavily invested in? What are the distributive consequences of the partial inclusion of some feminist projects? Who benefits and who loses? Can feminism foster a critique of its own successes?

The four authors of this book have dubbed our topic Governance Feminism (GF). By that we[1] mean every form in which feminists and feminist ideas exert a governing will within human affairs: to follow Michel Foucault's definition of governmentality, every form in which feminists and feminist ideas "conduct the conduct of men."[2] And of course that does not include only male human beings but all of us, and not only all human affairs but also human-inflected processes like knowledge formation, technology, and even the weather. We wish this book could address the full range of GF efforts, but—because we intend it merely as an introduction to the idea that feminism has engaged in governance—we have granted ourselves license to address only a subset of them: here, we concentrate on efforts feminists have made to become incorporated into *state, state-like, and state-affiliated* power.[3]

Though we think it is useful to generalize so far as to claim that GF *exists,* the category encompasses highly heterogeneous elements. GF is not one single thing; it does not have a life of its own. It is a useful heuristic category, but only that. We keep discovering how differentiated various GF projects are. When we speak of governance feminist projects *doing* something, therefore, we will speak not of GF but of GFeminists.

Feminism is by aspiration an emancipatory project, and GF is one kind of feminists' effort to discover pathways to human emancipation. In the process, GFeminists have been, in some cases, highly successful in changing laws, institutions, and practices, very often remarkably for the better. Just scan the canonical first-wave manifesto for change, the 1848 Seneca Falls Declaration of Sentiments,[4] for once-impossible, now well-established changes in the legal status of U.S. women: the right to vote; the rights of married women to form contracts, to sue and be sued, to acquire and manage separate property, to select their place of residence, to be criminally and civilly responsible for their own actions, to seek a divorce and to seek child custody on formally equal footing with husbands and fathers, and other powers formerly denied to them by coverture; to formally equal access to paid employment; to formally equal access to "wealth and distinction"[5] and to the professions; and to access to education. These are all basic elements of a liberal feminist agenda for women. Women have devoted entire lifetimes to achieving them. None of them came easily. They are not complete emancipation, surely. But compared with lack of all franchise, coverture, and categorical exclusion from the public sphere and all but the most grinding and ill-paid work, they are immense achievements attributable almost entirely to GFeminist efforts. One reason to describe GF is to be clear about its immense emancipatory achievements.

But in our view it has also done some damage: some GF projects strike us as terrible mistakes; others have unintended consequences that are or should be contested within feminist political life. As some

GF projects become part of established governance, we find ourselves worrying about them more, or differently, than we did when they were unorthodox, "outsider" ideas. We are, therefore, inviting a robust discussion within feminism and between feminism and its emancipatory allies about which elements are emancipatory and which may, after all, be mistakes.

Many feminist visions of emancipation have been left at the station when various governance trains took off: what Kerry Rittich calls the "selective engagement" of feminist ideas into governmental power has left some diamonds in the dust.[6] Sometimes selectivity so overwhelms engagement, or defeat so swamps success, that—despite feminists' best efforts—a governance project simply should not be described as feminist at all. Sometimes the result will be vaguely recognizable but so alien, so transformed by adverse political forces, that the best possible term for it might be Nancy Fraser's designation of feminism's "strange shadowy version," its "uncanny double."[7] Figuring this out without evading responsibility is one reason to study GF. It is an invitation precisely to take stock of the inclusions and exclusions—and the upsides and the downsides—across their full range.

Let us suppose for a moment that the only intended beneficiaries of feminism are women. Of course this is not true, but let us just posit that for a moment. GF has produced immense changes, most of them positive, in the lives of women, who enjoy more equality, more autonomy, and a greater share of the world's wealth because of feminism in power. But there are costs: women benefit differentially, some are harmed, and transforming a feminist idea into a law can prematurely settle productive conflicts among feminists about what worlds to imagine. Merging into the mainstream can efface the feminist fingerprints on important governance projects and preclude intrafeminist politics about them. It can consolidate a particularistic identity-based project, sometimes at the expense of alternative affiliations. It can respond to more general discursive or strategic demands making victimization and identity the prerequisites for legal intelligibility and leave behind questions about the costs of these formations. Some of the best things within and about feminism get left out. For all these reasons, recovering the specifically feminist ideas that animate various GF projects strikes us as an urgent undertaking—but one that, we think, should be approached with scholarly care and political vision.

As we have advanced the idea that GF now exists and tried out different ways of assessing it, we have often encountered feminist resistance. Much of Part I of this book is devoted to responses to that resistance. The first and most persistent form of resistance we have encountered is based on an idea that governance is per se bad, often expressed as an understanding that our *describing* GF is identical with *denouncing* it. **We do not think it is a gotcha to say that feminism rules.** We think GF simply does exist, and that naming and describing it are almost always empowering for feminists, and more empowering for them than their opponents. We also think that the question of normative assessment is highly situational, various, and necessarily—even more than descriptive work—politically motivated in distinct ways for differently situated feminists. We do not pretend to have a lock on normative assessments of GF: our goal here, instead, is to make them possible and to place them in a rich discussion among feminists and their Left allies. And of course we do not think feminists shoulder *more* responsibility than other aspirational projects focused on governance. This book focuses on feminism because it matters so much to us, not because its will to power is more suspect than that of, say, LGBT politics or movements to reframe ability and disability.

Meanwhile, we think that foreclosing the space between *describing* and *assessing* the consequences of feminist engagement with law, and with governance more broadly, is a gravely disabling position for a politically and legally engaged emancipatory movement to adopt. Taking the stance that describing GF is so dangerous that it cannot and should not be undertaken, or the stance that merely describing it is condemning it, forecloses precisely that space.

Feminists seek to rule for emancipatory purposes, and the tools they find in governance are among their best guesses as to how to move toward an emancipatory future. Understanding how this is working seems crucial to deciding how it should proceed going forward. We think that describing GF is a prerequisite for assessing it—and that our assessments can be affirmative as well as troubling and even alienating. We predict that they will most often be riven between affirmation and alienation. We propose that inhabiting that engaged ambivalence is hard work, morally challenging, and deeply at odds with a rhetorical renunciation of all feminist will to power.

We are completely open to—but ourselves right now do not take—the conclusion that involvement in governance is intrinsically bad and therefore to be avoided. Pure outsiderism was once a hallmark of radical politics in the United States, including radical feminism. Alice Echols's gripping historical account, based on interviews with dozens of feminists who had been active in the movement in the late 1960s and early 1970s, makes it clear that radical feminism then was radical in two quite different senses of the word: it stood radically outside the political settlement of its time, demanding wholesale transformation by acts of acute resistance and sometimes even violence; and it rejected class, race, and other axes of oppression to focus solely and exclusively on male domination and female subordination.[8] It shared the former with many Left movements of the time, but it embraced the latter as a cause of schism from them. The animus against seeking any change inside the state was acute. When 5,000 women, organized as the Jeannette Rankin Brigade, demonstrated on Capitol Hill in January 1968, demanding to present a petition to Congress calling for immediate withdrawal of U.S. forces from Vietnam, the feminist movement split: younger militant women denounced the brigade not only for the arguments it used but also for its very turn to the state—for "petitioning the U.S. Congress rather than talking to the people about taking power."[9] When Ti-Grace Atkinson resigned from the board of the National Organization for Women's New York chapter in 1968, she did so in the name of a "division . . . between those who want to empower women to have the opportunity to be oppressors, too, and those who want to destroy oppression itself."[10] In 1970, radical feminists *opposed* the Equal Rights Amendment, arguing that it threatened to repeat the damage that the fight for the vote had done to first-wave feminism, co-opting it, buying it out, individualizing it, and deradicalizing it. Their denunciation: "We are aware that the system will try to appease us with their paper offerings. We will not be appeased. Our demands can only be met by a total transformation of society, which you cannot legislate, you cannot co-opt, you cannot *control.*"[11] It was militancy, radical transformation, and the struggle to purify feminist theory and to prefigure emancipation in the life of feminist organizations (all then, among radical feminists, terms of praise) against reformism, collaboration, incrementalism, bourgeoisification, and selling out (all equivalently terms of condemnation).

As we write this, the United States and the world brace for the tenure of Donald J. Trump as president of the United States. It is very possible that the shock of his policies will once again turn feminists away from the state and back to the search for modes of pure resistance. But until that happens, if it does, we think the contrast between the current stance of many feminists vis-à-vis the state and that of radical feminism of the late 1960s is so stark as to throw a bright light on a background assumption that engagement with the state is a good feminist practice. Adamant outsider positions have not been visible in U.S. feminism since the collapse of the radical feminism of the late 1960s and early 1970s into the cultural and liberal feminism of the mid-1970s. Indeed, the turn of radical feminism to the state over the course of the 1970s—abandoning the first sense of the term "radical" but keeping the second—is one of the miracles of feminist creativity. And even if some feminists go back to militancy on a radically redrawn political map, others will refuse that path, and feminism will live on inside the GF projects developed so far.

More likely, significant feminist energy will be devoted to defending and, where possible, advancing the role of feminism in the state and state-like apparatuses. For those who acknowledge and even seek to own and expand these efforts, we urge a turn from what Max Weber, in his famous essay "Politics as a Vocation," called an "ethics of conviction" to an "ethics of responsibility."[12]

As Weber distinguishes these ethical attitudes from each other, the former is the will to do what is right *ruat coelom*—to preserve the purity of one's intentions no matter the damage they occasion—while to inhabit the latter "you must answer for the . . . *consequences* of your actions."[13] To engage governance, Weber reminds us, is to make use of force; to do so responsibly is to acknowledge that this is so whether one uses law to justify a bombing raid or merely tilts legal institutions as they engage in the *"daily grind."*[14] Figuring out consequences even in retrospect is hard work; calling it "cost–benefit analysis" makes it sound easy. Even dubbing it "a distributional analysis"—which sounds a lot harder—does not quite capture the challenge. But we use those terms because they describe the process that we think must come before we can decide *how* to answer for the consequences of our actions—and how to continue to act.

This book asks: how do we, as feminists, understand our feminism once we acknowledge our immersion in the uncontainably complex dynamics of law and its sister institutions? Weber asks us to *own*—rather than renounce—the power we lay hands on:

> Anyone who wishes to engage in politics at all, and particularly anyone who wishes to practice it as a profession, must become conscious of these ethical paradoxes and of his own responsibility for what may become *of him* under the pressure they exert. For, I repeat, he is entering into relations with the satanic powers that lurk in every act of violence.[15]

An ethics of conviction can lead us to political engagement, Weber argues, but—once we are there—can abandon us to our sense of inner virtue. No problem with that if the goal is the salvation of individual souls; but if it is political transformation, we face "quite different tasks, tasks that can only be accomplished with the use of force."[16]

Weber provides a very chilling warning here that engagement in politics can be fully responsible only if one is willing to look down and behold the blood on one's own hands. This can take the form he specifies—of involving one's self in the use of force—and in many others, especially what you could call the five C's: collaboration, compromise, collusion, complicity, and co-optation. Political work is work in struggle with one's opponents and often requires one to accept their victories as the price of one's own. And the five C's can change you: existentially, you can be transformed into a person who accepts and even loves a settlement that, once, you would have resisted.

For all his acknowledgment that being politically engaged cuts off retreat to "clean hands" stances, Weber suggests that the turn toward an ethics of responsibility can lead back to ethical conviction—chastened now by a conscious effort to become aware of the unknowable complexity of cause and effect, of collaboration and resistance, and of power and powerlessness in a world of proliferating consequences:

> I find it immeasurably moving when a *mature* human being—whether young or old in actual years is immaterial—who feels the responsibility he bears for the consequences of his own actions with his entire soul and who acts in harmony with an ethics of responsibility reaches the point where he says, "Here I stand, I can do no other." That is authentically human and cannot fail to move us. For this is a situation that *may* befall *any* of us at some point, if we are not inwardly dead. In this sense an ethics of conviction and an ethics of responsibility are not absolute

antitheses but are mutually complementary, and only when taken together do they constitute the authentic human being who *is capable* of
having a "vocation for politics."[17]

This book invites feminists to engage our involvement in actual, real-
world governance with an attitude imbued with this ethics of responsibility, in the hope that—as we confront our involvement not only
in the big decisions but in the daily grind—we can sometimes find
that disenchanted conviction that can say " 'Nevertheless!' despite
everything."[18]

The book proceeds as follows. Part I asks: which halls of power do
feminists walk? Which elements of feminism have had the most success in gaining access to those halls of power as of this moment? And
how have feminists modeled various feminist ways of relating to this
power? Part I aims to convince readers that GF does now exist and has
already acquired distinct ideological and institutional traditions that
influence its engagements with power. It closes with examples of feminists grappling with the ethical challenges and dilemmas that come
with engagement inside governmental power.

Part II presents three case studies of GF. In chapter 4, Prabha Kotiswaran analyzes an intensely productive period in the life of Indian
feminism, opened by the rape, mutilation, and murder of Jyoti Pandey
(given the posthumous honorific Nirbhaya, or "the fearless one") and
culminating in significant reform of rape law. In chapter 5, Hila Shamir
examines a transformative moment in anti-trafficking enforcement
in Israel, motivated in part by dominance feminist ambitions to advance the neo-abolitionist project through trafficking law, in which the
state deported virtually all the illegal migrants from Eastern Europe
working in Israeli prostitution markets. And in chapter 6, Rachel
Rebouché shows how U.S. feminists engaged two rhetorically and legally
linked but contradictory arguments for reproductive rights: one promoting women's unfettered choice to select abortion, and the other
seeking to delegitimate and regulate sex-selective abortion of female
fetuses.

These case studies bear out the observation made in Part I that GF
is alive and well in many legal forms, from the national to the transnational, and showcase very different roles for U.S. feminist thought
in non-U.S. settings. Kotiswaran (chapter 4) demonstrates that the

Indian women's movement (IWM) was sufficiently deep and strong, with a long though frustrated history of advocacy for broadly sweeping rape law reform that, in the crisis produced by the immense public outrage over the Nirbhaya case, its leaders could step into GF roles immediately. Shamir (chapter 5), on the other hand, shows how the U.S. dominance feminist equation of prostitution with trafficking managed to get installed into the lead U.S. anti-trafficking statute and to enlist the administration of George W. Bush to threaten the Israeli government with the loss of nonhumanitarian, non-trade-related aid if it did not suppress immigrant prostitution in Israel. She also shows how the Israeli government's action in response to this threat was channeled and managed in part by Israeli feminists influenced, to a large extent, by U.S. dominance feminism. Her story is thus one of the transmissions of U.S. feminist ideas both by force and by charisma, and their very local manifestations in the context of a strong security state. Put side by side, these two chapters make a compelling case that national feminism in the global South is strong enough to get into governance and make a big difference, and that U.S. feminist influence can transform local law far away from U.S. shores.

Rebouché (chapter 6) demonstrates a third point about the transnational span of GF: she examines the commitment of U.S. and international feminists focused on reproductive rights, particularly abortion, to establish themselves within international legal institutions. International agreements became the transmission system for a conflict within U.S. feminism. Liberal feminists, attempting to hold the line protecting women's reproductive choice under U.S. constitutional law, resisted social conservatives' and religious conservatives' efforts to install bans on particular abortions, including those motivated by particular reasons, while dominance feminists sought to restrict sex-selective abortion around the world, and particularly in the global South. These two projects collided because both policies had found expression in language that feminists had installed in international treaties and because religious and social conservatives pushed for bans on sex-selective abortion in countries such as India, China, and South Korea. In the United States, anti-abortion movements could cite feminists against feminists. GF became a transmission vehicle for conflict within feminism, both at the transnational level and in diverse locales, from the United States to India.

In addition, these three chapters showcase the power of distributional analysis to give feminists choices about how to assess and deploy their engagements with law. As Janet Halley shows in the Conclusion, doing a distributional analysis is a critical practice that exposes the distributional stakes of law reform in complex social interactions involving multiple social actors with complex and conflicting motivations. The Conclusion collects many of the discrete steps involved in distributional analysis and describes them in what we hope is a user-friendly, how-to way. In Part II, however, we offer instead three concrete distributional analyses. Though short and by no means exhaustive, they provide ways of thinking in realistic, consequentialist terms about the results of GF efforts.

In chapter 4, Kotiswaran examines the likely uses of the post-Nirbhaya rape law reforms by actual social interests that are alive and well in India. Indian law allows third parties to initiate criminal prosecutions, has increased the age of consent to eighteen, and has broadened the definitions of rape and sexual assault, including an affirmative consent rule that puts the defendant in the position of needing positive proof that consent was given. Kotiswaran observes that, given these changes, not only may rape prosecutions become more numerous and more effective in securing convictions (the intended consequences, from a feminist point of view), but families can now prosecute men who have had entirely consented-to and indeed avidly welcomed sex with their daughters and secure convictions (an unintended consequence). She argues that the latter use of the reforms will strengthen the hand of heteropatriarchal and caste-based control over women's sexuality. She also shows that, even if feminists had managed to abrogate spousal immunity for rape, the combined result of a marital rape offense and domestic violence crimes that wives can bring against husbands would have differential effects depending on how severe the violence is and on whether the women seek to exit their marriages—distributional consequences *among women* that strengthen the bargaining power of some but weaken that of others. And in both analyses, Kotiswaran highlights the possibility that innocent men will go to jail for extended sentences—the sex partners of young women whose families object to their consensual relationships and men married to women willing to use exaggerated and even bad-faith domestic violence accusations to intensify their leverage in divorce.

In chapter 5, Shamir asks what the deportation of immigrant women engaged in prostitution in Israel did, distributively, for them, for Israeli women involved in the sex sector, and for policy choices that had to be strengthened in order to make this transformation possible. Strikingly, no one knows what happened to the immigrants after they were repatriated as victims of trafficking to their countries of origin. Shamir indicates, however, that some, perhaps many, of them experienced their return home as a bad outcome. Meanwhile, prostitution in Israel was taken back over by Israeli women, with complex results: the possibility of extreme exploitation declined precipitously, the entire sector was subjected to newly invasive forms of police harassment, and a sex workers movement began to take shape and to compete with dominance feminists for the ear of the state. Shamir also observes a series of "discursive costs" to the intensification of anti-trafficking enforcement in Israel, for instance, the ratification of the border control enterprises of one of the strongest security states in the world. And she observes that most of the costs she identifies can be articulated only outside the dominance feminist vocabulary that motivated the reform.

In chapter 6, Rebouché steps down from the lofty heights of constitutional law and moral certainty that so pervade conflicts over abortion to ask: what would it *really mean* to ban sex-selective abortion? The genetic screening that can identify the sex—and other genetic characteristics—of a fetus early in pregnancy have entered clinical use and are about to become cheap to do at home. Women can have these tests performed in one physician's office and then obtain an abortion from a different provider. A regulatory system that would effectively ban access to the tests or ban their use for sex-selective abortion would reach deep into what are now open-textured markets. However unlikely that may be, Rebouché examines the distribution of *costs and benefits* to women—alternatively framed out of dominance feminist and liberal feminist accounts of the practice—if states adopted regulatory structures capable of restricting it. For example, the rise of female births in South Korea after it adopted a ban was supported by women's fertility decisions in a complexly neoliberalizing economy: Did the ban cause it, or was the rising economic value of women workers in play? Like Shamir, Rebouché looks to discursive costs as well, particularly to the tensions between liberal feminists and disability rights advocates, on the one hand, and between dominance feminists and postcolonial critique, on the other. These movements—not necessarily feminist—register costs and benefits of their own, differing substantially from those measurable on a feminist yardstick. A full distributional analysis, Rebouché argues, would reach out to take them into account.

Kotiswaran, Shamir, and Rebouché refrain from determining whether the distributions that they observe, with all their diverse costs and benefits, are *worth it.* But they pose the question in a trenchant, realist, and critical way. Each analysis opens the path to GFeminists involved in projects on rape, prostitution, and women's fertility—and on GF projects more generally—to engage them anew, with an ethic of responsibility.

Finally, the Conclusion provides a road map for doing a distributional analysis.

We also wish to point to our second book in this two-book series, *Governance Feminism: Notes from the Field,* which will provide case studies describing and assessing national, international, and transnational GF projects by a range of feminists deeply engaged in building and critiquing them. We hope the two books together will energize feminists—and allies in related social movements—to think anew about engaging directly with power.

Notes

1. Though authored by Janet Halley, this Preface, Part I, and the Conclusion often speak as "we." Those passages express the collected thinking of all four authors of this book.

2. Michel Foucault, *The Birth of Biopolitics: Lectures at the Collège de France, 1978–79,* trans. Graham Burchell (Basingstoke, U.K.: Palgrave Macmillan, 2008), 186.

3. For an assessment of the ways in which feminism has become a driving force in consumer culture, see Andi Zeisler, *We Were Feminists Once: From Riot Grrrl to Covergirl®, the Buying and Selling of a Political Movement* (New York: PublicAffairs, 2016).

4. "Seneca Falls Declaration of Sentiments," in *History of Woman Suffrage,* vol. 1, ed. Elizabeth Cady Stanton, Susan B. Anthony, and Matilda Joslyn Gage (Rochester, N.Y.: Charles Mann, 1887), 70–71.

5. Ibid.

6. Kerry Rittich, "The Future of Law and Development: Second Generation Reforms and the Incorporation of the Social," *Michigan Journal of International Law* 26, no. 1 (2004): 223.

7. Nancy Fraser, "Feminism, Capitalism, and the Cunning of History," *New Left Review* 56 (2009): 114. For a comment on this issue, see Diane Otto, "Constructing Feminism's Institutional Doubles: Troubling the Security Council's Women, Peace and Security Agenda," in *Governance Feminism: Notes from the Field,* ed. Janet Halley, Prabha Kotiswaran, Rachel Rebouché, and Hila Shamir (Minneapolis: University of Minnesota Press, forthcoming); see also Karen Engle, "Feminist Governance and International Law: From Liberal to Carceral Feminism," in Halley et al., *Governance Feminism: Notes from the Field.*

8. Alice Echols, *Daring to Be Bad: Radical Feminism in America, 1967–75* (Minneapolis: University of Minnesota Press, 1989).

9. Ibid., 54–59.

10. Ibid., 168–69, quoting Ti-Grace Atkinson, "Resignation from NOW," in Atkinson, *Amazon Odyssey* (New York: Links Books, 1974), 10.

11. Ibid., 200, quoting "Women's Liberation Testimony," *off our backs* 1, no. 5 (May 1970): 7.

12. Max Weber, "Politics as a Vocation," in *The Vocation Lectures,* ed. David Owen and Tracy B. Strong, trans. Rodney Livingstone (Indianapolis: Hackett Publishing Company, 2004), 83.

13. Ibid.

14. Ibid., 90.

15. Ibid.

16. Ibid.

17. Ibid., 92 (citation omitted).

18. Ibid., 94.

Abbreviations

ACLU	American Civil Liberties Union
AIDWA	All India Democratic Women's Association
APLO	Anti-Prostitution Loyalty Oath
BBA	Bachpan Bachao Andolan
BWS	battered women's syndrome
CEDAW	Convention on the Elimination of All Forms of Discrimination against Women
CLA	Criminal Law (Amendment) Act
CLS	critical legal studies
CRPD	Convention on the Rights of Persons with Disabilities
CRR	Center for Reproductive Rights
D&E	dilation and evacuation
DOE OCR	Department of Education Office for Civil Rights
ERA	Equal Rights Amendment
FIR	first information report
FSU	Former Soviet Union
GF	Governance Feminism
ICPD	International Convention on Population and Development
ICTY	International Criminal Tribunal for the Former Yugoslavia
IEA	Indian Evidence Act
IGLP	Institute for Global Law and Policy
IPC	Indian Penal Code
IWM	Indian women's movement
LCI	Law Commission of India

LGBT	lesbian, gay, bisexual, and transgender
MRM	men's rights movement
MWCD	Ministry of Women & Child Development
NAPAWF	National Asian Pacific American Women's Forum
NCW	National Commission for Women
NGOs	nongovernmental organizations
OPT	Occupied Palestinian Territories
PIL	public interest litigation
PPFA	Planned Parenthood Federation of America
PRENDA	Prenatal Nondiscrimination Act
PROFAM	Programa de Promoción del Fortalecimiento de la Familia y el Capital Social
PTSD	posttraumatic stress disorder
PWDVA	Protection of Women from Domestic Violence Act
SH Act	Sexual Harassment of Women at Workplace (Prevention, Prohibition and Redressal) Act
SOGI	sexual orientation and gender identity
TIP	Trafficking in Persons
TVPA	Trafficking Victims Protection Act
UNFPA	United Nations Population Fund
UNIFEM	UN Development Fund for Women
UN Women	UN Entity for Gender Equality and the Empowerment of Women
USAID	U.S. Agency for International Development
WCGJ	Women's Caucus for Gender Justice
WHO	World Health Organization

PART I

VARIETIES OF GOVERNANCE FEMINISM

CHAPTER 1

Where in the Legal Order Have Feminists Gained Inclusion?

JANET HALLEY

Many terms have been invented to describe particular phases of GF: state feminism, carceral feminism, femocrats, female policy entrepreneurs, the "special advisors on gender violence" who dot the international legal landscape . . . the list is long.[1] Each of them focuses on a specific governmental form that feminists have found to be at least somewhat hospitable—in the list we just gave, the state, the penal state, state bureaucracy, "civil society," and legally authorized experts, respectively. We have selected as an overarching term "Governance Feminism" in order to embrace them all: *any* form of state, state-like, or state-affiliated power is, we presuppose, capable of being influenced and guided by feminists and feminist ideas, and many have been. Where has this possibility become reality?

Like many other students of the contemporary legal order,[2] we are struck by the real-world proliferation of forms of organized power that break the bounds of the classically imagined state, and like them we find the term "governance" useful to describe the resulting expansion of institutional forms and social practices that govern. These forms of power operate immanently as well as top-down, facilitate and inherit state power from outside the state, and shimmer back and forth across every private/public distinction. Much of transnational law has this interstitial character, however much it mimes the trappings of state power. For instance, the reporting system that most treaty bodies substitute for adjudication has produced an immense discursive network of text exchange in which an array of players manage, mediate, and struggle over treaty-based norms. When states appoint commissions to examine and report on controversial problems, hire private contractors to execute governmental functions, and incorporate—sometimes even "certifying" as superlegitimate—so-called nongovernmental organizations (NGOs) to do work on human conduct, they govern through formally nongovernmental entities. And those nongovernmental entities, we consider, are also government.

But there is still more to our term "governance." We turn to it to signal an effort to defetishize the state as the sole source of governmental power—the dark star of the power firmament, to be longed for and feared with equal fervor. Here, we draw on a series of frame-breaking moves from Michel Foucault's genealogy of modern forms of governmental knowledge/practice in his Collège de France lectures of 1977–78 and 1978–79.[3] Especially now, as feminism accedes to the halls of power, we value efforts to resist taking the state on its own terms, whether as indispensable avenger or "cold monster"—a mystifying collaboration that, as Foucault repeatedly observes in these lectures, arouses almost instantly a "fear of the state."[4]

> The state, no more today than in the past, does not have this unity, individuality, and rigorous functionality, nor, I would go so far as to say, this importance. After all, maybe the state is just a composite reality and a mythicized abstraction whose importance is much less than we think. Maybe. What is important . . . is not then the state's takeover (*étatisation*) of society, so much as what I would call the "governmentalization" of the state.[5]

Not only the sovereign, and not only the monopoly over the legitimate use of force, and not only the vox populi on the scale of the nation-state: Foucault's governmentality frames the full range of power relations attentive to the "way in which one conducts the conduct of men."[6] The master of a ship governs it and all that rides within it; so does the single mom raising her kids in a slum or a suburb. A school administrator hired to manage sexual assault complaints within the institution is as much a governor as the U.S. Supreme Court installing into law a feminist theory of sexual harassment: "The analysis of micro-powers, or of procedures of governmentality, is not confined by definition to a precise domain determined by a sector of the scale, whatever its size."[7]

Indeed, at the level of definition this "is not a question of scale" at all[8]—though of course scale becomes crucial within any particular engagement.

Normatively, widening the frame along these dimensions asks for a suspension of paranoia not only about the state but also about power. When feminists have objected to our proposal that GF exists, we sometimes hear them saying not only that feminism remains *very small* but also that the state looms *immensely large, immensely threatening, and impervious to change.* We are the more worried about this image because it was initially fully ours. At first we thought that the flagship GF successes were all concentrated on sexual violence and envisioned law as primarily punitive[9] (the carceral feminism disclosed by Elizabeth Bernstein).[10] This is, to be sure, the dimension of GF that we collectively find most problematic. And indeed this formulation describes a great deal of national and international GF; the appetite of many strands of feminism for government through prohibition and punishment is one of the most striking features of GF today. Male sexual wrongdoing—sometimes exemplified by rape, sometimes by prostitution—is often understood to be primarily *crime.*

But even the carceral state is not a monolithic top-down power that—in itself—warrants a unilateral and a priori moral rejection. Some human actions *should* be crimes, we think. Calling feminism carceral is no more a gotcha than saying GF exists: describe it first, we think, and then assess its effects with particularity. Moreover, punishment requires bureaucracy and shades into everyday, minute forms of social pressure that we all exert on each other constantly. Striving toward an ethic of responsibility in confronting the punitive ambitions of feminist projects is a central aspect of this book.

Moreover, the subjects of GF vastly exceed the use of criminal enforcement to address sexual wrongdoing: they include women in the workplace, women seeking to have children or to end pregnancies, women in the family, women on corporate boards, and women in the public sphere. We have feminist norms that govern our everyday gendered courtesies (who opens the door for whom?); during the 2016 U.S. presidential campaign our ideas about what Hillary Clinton should wear and what Donald Trump could and should not say about her were very often *feminist* ideas. Across this range, GF accommodates a myriad of *feminisms,* and GF appears in the form of every governmental tool imaginable. So we are interested in how feminists select their governmental tools, and how those with control over access to those tools select among feminist aspirations, taking some on board and leaving others out.

Finally, as these feminist governmentalities become legal, social, cultural, and/or ideological *common sense,* they disappear into the light of common day. Studying them is like watching a drop of water hitting the larger pool of water below: at first we see ripples, but soon the surface is perfectly smooth and the drop dissolves into the whole. The specifically *feminist* character of the cultural or legal intervention can and often does disappear. This effect is particularly strong in GF projects aimed at law: many legal orders demand a neutrality in exchange for legitimacy. Like other political actors, feminist judges, feminist policymakers, and feminist experts find they must obey the rituals of the rule of law, objectivity, and legal rationality to enter into many possible, productive relationships with legal power. Sometimes participating in power requires passionate feminists to deny their "partiality," to declare that they are not feminists at all, or to argue for feminist-inspired changes on the basis of nonfeminist rationales. As all three case studies addressed in this book and many included in *Governance Feminism: Notes from the Field* demonstrate, entering into law as policy and as political struggle requires finding, working with, and tacitly advancing the cause of alien bedfellows. Sometimes a legal rule with feminist origins is applied by someone indifferent or even actively malign to women or feminist ideals. Collaboration, compromise, collusion, complicity, and co-optation: the five C's.[11] We are treading here into morally fraught territory that can make calling a legal reform "feminist" a tendentious move. Studying GF that has reached these stages of incorporation and performativity can be challenging—but all the more necessary as it brings us to places of moral inquiry.

For all that, we think it is glaringly clear that GF does exist. In the following pages, we marshal examples.

Bad Sex

In 2009, Charlotte Bunch nominated sexual violence as the preeminent GF success: "No issue better illustrates how the women's movement can and has moved a concern . . . to the tables of power."[12] Bad sex has been a focus of feminist reform for more than thirty years now.

Here are some examples. I start with reforms in the United States because, given its superpower status, many legal ideas that gain a purchase in state institutions there are sure to spread throughout the world. What happens as they encounter feminist ideas on the same subject developed elsewhere is a large preoccupation of this book.

Rape

U.S. feminists have worked hard to make rape charges easier to prove; to motivate police, prosecutors, and inquisitors to open proceedings and to pursue charges energetically; to protect the complaining witness from impeachment based on her sexual history or conduct before the alleged rape; and to promote severe sentences. In many jurisdictions, they have made significant progress in these efforts. For instance, rape at common law was sexual intercourse achieved by force *and* without the woman's consent. Now, the threat of force or the subjective experience of being threatened with force suffices, and in some places force is no longer part of the crime. At common law, the woman had to resist to the utmost or attempt to flee; that requirement is gone. Before, if the woman consented in the face of force, there was no rape; now, force vitiates any consent given. Sexual intercourse is no longer a requirement of rape—touching the genitals or anus now is enough; and a new, slightly lesser crime of sexual assault includes unconsented kissing and fondling. Sexual crimes departments have opened up in police departments and prosecutors' offices to concentrate institutional will to make the prosecution of rape and other sexual assaults a consistent priority and to ensure that the people who handle them share the mission.

This is not at all to say that the reform effort is completed. Controversies and political pressure campaigns continue: rape-kit backlogs, statutes of limitations, and defendant rights that expose the complainant to scrutiny are just some of the issues that remain of concern to many feminists in the United States and around the world. A cadre of feminists is proposing—to significant feminist opposition—the further extension of rape and/or sexual assault to include any sexual contact achieved without the woman's "affirmative consent." The project is ongoing. But it is clear even to its most ardent supporters that it has gained significant traction in the rules and in the institutional apparatus.

Sexual Harassment

Unwanted sexual attention that is sufficiently severe or pervasive to harm a worker's or student's engagement in the workplace or at school is a civil wrong in the United States, and both employers and educational institutions are responsible for preventing and redressing it. Expanded definitions of the wrong and expanded institutional roles in addressing it are giving both private and public institutions quite broad enforcement and prevention obligations. A for-profit industry of investigatory and juridical experts has emerged to help corporations and schools build the institutional infrastructure needed to run these procedures and discipline wrongdoers.[13] At the time of this writing, sexual harassment has encompassed "campus sexual violence"— exemplified by rape but extending to variously defined sexual misconduct. Under threat of loss of government funding across the board, colleges and universities have installed new student discipline policies and procedures. Those new rules are jumping the fence from education to the employment relationship. Feminists are deeply engaged in this institutional transformation.

Domestic Violence

Domestic violence law stands out as a body of law reform that was developed by feminists and that found institutional form almost entirely by dint of feminist advocacy. At common law, husbands had a right of reasonable correction over their wives; women could not testify against husbands who abused this right, and police and courts looked away when women complained. Now, domestic violence is a crime; a protection order system requires the defendant to keep away from the home and the victim on pain of criminal penalties; special evidentiary standards apply when women kill their batterers and seek to prove that they acted in self-defense; a state-supported shelter system is in place to house and support at least some women escaping from violent homes; and in some states victims can sue the state if it fails to enforce a protection order and the victim is injured because of its inaction.

Some elements of this effort are highly carceral: feminist reforms in the United States include mandatory arrest and "no drop" policies, for instance, overriding the default rule giving police and prosecutors discretion to decide which cases to pursue. Other times, what feminists have built far more closely resembles social services, as in the shelter system.

Anti-prostitution

Prostitution is so controversial among feminists that it forms a case study of intrafeminist struggle *within* national, international, and transnational governance. Some strands of U.S. feminism classify all prostitution as rape for pay, as sexual violence, and as slavery: for them, prostitution is per se coercive. To them, criminalization of all participants except the "prostituted woman" herself is the primary legal remedy. They are often called neo-abolitionists in an analogy with slavery abolitionists of the nineteenth century. Other strands of U.S. feminism disagree, instead regarding prostitution as a sale of services of a particularly intimate kind and thus as a legitimate activity that should be regulated for the benefit of the weaker party—but, in this, not much different from other forms of vulnerable and usually low-wage labor. They seek social services, market regulation, and organization rights for "sex workers." These two feminist cadres fight hard against each other for every small victory in criminal law, in international/transnational trafficking law, and in social service provision. The victories of the first strand, often achieved in alliance with social and religious conservative forces, include criminal law "end demand" dragnets that arrest johns, publicize their humiliation, dole out long sentences, and route them into re-education programs. In many jurisdictions around the world, the first strand has persuaded legislators that any purchase of sexual services from, or employment hierarchy over, a prostituted woman is trafficking, a classification that increases penalties, draws funding to the criminalization enterprise, motivates rescue efforts, and requires governments to devote resources to criminal enforcement. Meanwhile, the second strand pushes back against these reforms and has helped labor leftists and workplace advocates divert some of the trafficking system's attention and resources to abuses in the non-sex sector. Feminists who engage prostitution as a social issue enter a landscape in which the state is a virtually inevitable dance partner and in which they must struggle against other feminists to achieve their governance goals.

The Family and the Market

Before the rise of industrial capitalism in the United States (and around the world), the household was the site of production, reproduction, and consumption. Now, architecture, ideology, and educational institutions—our very roads, modes of work, and cultural surround—along with myriad elements in the legal order tell us that the family and the market are vastly different, opposite, and complementary domains, with the former housing reproduction (of new human beings, of the continued productive capacity of existing ones, and of care for those with dependency needs), with production churning out of the market (where most people work for a wage to support the family's internal economy), and with family consumption of market-acquired goods linking the two in an endless cycle of exchange. As Frances Olsen taught us in her classic article, "The Family and the Market: A Study of Ideology and Law Reform," feminists have engaged deeply on both sides of this divide, seeking to improve women's lives in the market in order to strengthen their position in the home and vice versa.[14] And though it is glaringly obvious that their goals have been only partially achieved, they have a long history of lawmaking and influence on policy in this vast project.

The Economics of Marriage and Parenthood

Feminists have had immense influence on Western family law in the last thirty-five years. The changes they have achieved have transformed the policy vision of marriage from a male-dominant economic unit to an economic partnership: however much reality has failed to conform to this vision, its ascendancy in law and governance is unmistakable. Along with these changes came feminist ideas of spouses' mutual dependency, the importance of women's unpaid care work, and the injustice of allocating few to no marital assets to divorced and widowed homemaker wives.

Before, in most states, the breadwinner husband owned all the earnings of the marriage and walked off with them at the time of divorce.

Indeed, the husband and the wife appeared in statutory law and in courts as distinct legal persons with dramatically different rights and duties: he with a duty of support, she with a duty of obedience. Constitutional attacks on this regime as *unequal*—attacks in which feminists have played the leading role—have retired this version of marriage from positive law. Now, the law must formally treat the spouses as equals. Every formerly unequal rule that is now formally equal is a feminist victory. Such rules are littered all over the landscape of family law.

That leaves a large, durable, de facto inequality unsolved—the problem of women's unpaid labor in the home. What feminists have actually achieved is pretty remarkable: now, if a marriage breaks up through divorce, the homemaker wife (and the working wife who successfully claims she bore a disproportionate share of household labor) has a direct claim on about half of the marital assets. These assets are regarded not only as social insurance and private responsibility for dependency needs but also as returns on investment: women's unpaid labor in the home has finally found significant monetary meaning in law. Every divorce that tilts away from the husband-takes-all outcome of yore is an achievement we can chalk up to GF. To be sure, feminists disagree about whether the main constituency is the working mom or the stay-at-home mom, and whether going further to compensate the latter will relieve her of ancient stereotypes or entrench her in them.

Work in the Marketplace

Feminists have fought for more than a century for the right to work in the marketplace on an equal footing with men, and for actual employment, compensation, and working conditions that are equal to those of men. When "sex" was added to the list of prohibited grounds of employer action in the flagship federal employment statute—Title VII—the proponents thought it was a joke and even hoped it would sink the statute because of its sheer absurdity. Now the idea that women should be equal in the workplace permeates education and employer policy, sustains an important (if shrinking) role for litigation in protecting women workers, and has produced a large constituency for the view that "shattering the glass ceiling" for elite women workers will benefit all women.

Partly because law has opened women's opportunities in the workplace and raised their compensation, and partly because the market was hungry for new workers—especially new service workers doing not only traditionally women's work but men's jobs too—women have poured en masse into paid employment. Married households are vastly predominantly dual-earner. Single women raise children and hold down jobs, sometimes multiple jobs. This immense social change and the rules that encouraged, enabled, and sustain it have many causes, among them feminist advocacy and policy work.

Employers have always had family and gender policy. Now these forms of governance show signs of feminist advocacy. The law commands equal treatment of men and women at work, and while unequal treatment has by no means disappeared, men now appear in nursing and primary school teaching and women in law partnerships, in judgeships, as doctors, and on corporate boards. Employers who fail to redress sexual harassment by supervisors and coworkers can face heavy legal penalties and powerful public shaming campaigns. Again, feminists disagree about remedies for durable differences between men and women in the workplace. Some seek mandated accommodation of pregnancy and child-rearing duties; others prefer to see them packaged as "parental leave." Legally mandated care accommodations are minimal in the United States compared with social democratic welfare systems, but the few that do exist can be partially if not largely credited to the political labors of feminists. Employers seeking to remain competitive in higher-wage labor markets have "work/life" policies designed to help employees—largely women—balance employment and home-based responsibilities.

The campaign that led to the election of Trump to the U.S. presidency showed Gretchen Carlson, a former Fox News anchor, suing Roger Ailes, CEO and board chairman of Fox News—who was one of the most powerful men in American media—for sexual harassment.[15] Immediately afterward several other women told the press that they had been harassed by Ailes and by other men at the media giant. Within days of Carlson's suit going public, Ailes stepped down from his job.[16] Law played a role here: Ailes's exit from Fox News started with a claim of legal right. The media played a role too. And so did the assumption among the political and media elites—one that feminists worked for decades to build—that quid pro quo sexual harassment is beyond the pale. That was power. When Trump was exposed, in a surreptitiously captured videotape, joking that he had assaulted women, grabbing their "pussies" and getting away with it because he was a star,[17] those elites assumed he would lose the election on the force of women voters' sharing that assumption. It did not turn out that way. Women voters were a large and important constituency leading to Trump's Electoral College victory.[18] The norm against sexual harassment is not all the power feminists want and are seeking, but it is power nevertheless.

Modes of Governance

Feminists seeking to wield governmental power have been highly adaptable about the modes of power that they seek to master. Crime and punishment have been central, especially for bad sex, but much "softer" forms of power have been useful too.

Constitutionalism, to take but one example, is a major mode of GF and a key transmission device for feminist ideals and ideas for how to govern. Feminists in the United States, seeking to update a constitution adopted when women's social, political, economic, and cultural inequality was cemented into the legal order, waged a major effort in the 1970s through the early 1980s to pass an Equal Rights Amendment to the Constitution.[19] This effort failed but left feminists with a large, national political infrastructure. They used their know-how and institutional capacity not only to elect women to public office (and thus to make change through legislation and public policy) but also to generate constitutional litigation. They have also fought political resistance to their legislative- and executive-branch efforts, resisting opponents who claim that their reforms violate constitutional rights. Constitutional thinking in the United States is an ingrained element of public sentiment, and feminists have worked to build an unspoken assumption that women should be voters, holders of public office, men's equals in the family and the workplace, and able to determine their own reproductive fates.

Feminists around the world have taken advantage of the massive spread of constitutionalism as the first-order means of organizing national governments that attended decolonization in the global South after World War II, and that continues to this day. Here, they have fought to get to the drafting table and have worked hard to insert feminist language into constitutions worldwide. And they have often succeeded: the

2010 Kenyan constitution, for instance, bars sex discrimination (a concept that has constitutional force in the United States only because judges adopted it) and stipulates the minimum number of women who must be elected or appointed to various governmental bodies.[20] A recent global survey of constitutions around the world concludes that women's rights have enjoyed "particularly dramatic surges" in "popularity" in postwar constitutionalism.[21]

What connects U.S. feminist constitutionalism and the constitutional activism of feminists around the world is a complex network that could be called feminist comparative constitutionalism. The end of the Cold War and the rise of the United States as the sole superpower mean that U.S. legal ideas—including U.S. GF ideas—have unprecedented global reach. This extends way beyond constitutional ideas, but certainly includes them. Sometimes this export project is carried by the force of military arms and the will of the U.S. government to hold sway abroad. As Hila Shamir shows in chapter 5 in this book, following U.S.-based anti-trafficking rules, including some installed in legislation by U.S. feminists, was effectively obligatory for the government of Israel if it was to keep U.S. aid flowing. And U.S. influence travels by the myriad means of nonviolent transmission that depend on charisma rather than force. These range from the export of American films and other cultural products to the enrollment of foreign students in degree programs throughout American higher—and increasingly secondary—education. Shamir shows this as well: a robust dominance feminist activist network in Israel was formed and is led by Israeli women who came to the United States for graduate training and learned feminist chops in the process. They became strong enough in Israeli anti-trafficking debates, working in conjunction with U.S. influence that also carried significant dominance-feminist influence, to push dominance feminist ideas into state practice.

And wherever U.S. legal thought goes—including U.S. feminist legal thought—it enters into interactions with the thinking of feminists throughout the world (and their opponents) with their own rich local, international, and transnational traditions of thought and action on power and justice in a gendered world. As Rachel Rebouché shows in chapter 6, feminists in the United States have opinions about what feminists in India should want law to do for them. And as Prabha Kotiswaran shows in chapter 4, feminists in India have their own feminist milieu with its own historical momentum and internal tensions and projects. Rebouché shows how a dense network of influence and counterinfluence, carried by the specific legal technology afforded by the ideas of a constitutional right to abortion or to life, forms a frame within which feminists work on reproductive rights at home and transnationally. Making these circuits of influence and resistance visible is one of the main reasons we have isolated GF as an important object of study.

In the rest of this subsection, I set out a few of the newest, most distinctive ways that feminists have organized this transnational life of GF.

Gender Mainstreaming / Gender Specialists

No matter how often you remind them, some people forget that sex, sexuality, gender, and the family matter the minute you stop talking. Feminists in governance invented gender mainstreaming to deal with this problem. Mainstreaming stipulates that gender must be "an integral dimension of the design, implementation, monitoring and evaluation of policies and programs in all political, economic, and societal spheres."[22] It is a bureaucratic mandate that every decision-making process at a given level of authority within an institution *must* include a review of its gender implications. The need for this review and its procedures are both bureaucratized.

Gender mainstreaming has located feminists in many organizations, from the UN to college administrations, almost always as bureaucrats. Here they wield not judicial power, not the sword of punishment, but the more fine-grained power of *administration*.

Gender mainstreaming, which aims to universalize feminist ideas in governance and convert every governmental entity into a branch of GF, paradoxically produces gender specialists. It ensures that we have people certified as capable of producing feminist analyses that are at least intelligible and perhaps even authoritative in an institution vested with some kind of legal power. Indeed, gender specialists were the vanguard who argued for gender mainstreaming and then carried on to monitor it. The specialist can be anything from a single person carrying the gender portfolio to an entire agency. In part because the UN committed itself to gender mainstreaming, it now has a top-level bureau, UN Women, reporting directly to the secretary general and focused across the entire range of UN activities—but exclusively on women's and gender issues. This has given rise to a surprising new situation: people who have not been feminists before have feminist jobs, giving rise to the term "9-to-5 feminists."

Gender mainstreaming in the UN, in turn, required member states in the global South to develop "national machineries" devoted to gender issues, and these machineries are in turn funded by the UN to network among themselves. National machineries are one of the most important places to study the interaction of Western and non-Western feminist agendas.

One consequence of the gender mainstreaming project is that the gender specialist becomes a *professional*. The things that she is a professional *of* become an officially sanctioned feminist knowledge. It is not a long way from there to standardization of a set of GF commitments that appear routinely in the work of the gender specialists and that are normally modifiable not through feminist consciousness raising, blogging, activism, or pedagogy, but through shifts in feminist ideology among the cadre of professionals.

NGOs and Networking

The rise of GF came at the same time as the expansion and fragmentation of the international legal order. Starting in the early 1990s, international legal institutions of all kinds—human rights, financial, trade, criminal enforcement, population, environmental—grew and proliferated. As they did, they extended their reach into civil society by fostering partnerships with NGOs. This would have happened even without the rise of GF, but feminists saw it happening from the start and enthusiastically entered into it. International/transnational GF and the NGO-sphere coinvented each other.

Take the UN Conferences on Women: Mexico City (1975), Copenhagen (1980), Nairobi (1985), and Beijing (1995). Each of them was preceded by large UN preparatory conferences, and each of those by further preparatory meetings. The initial idea, conventional in the early days of this process, was that these meetings would bring together representatives of states.[23] But soon, thousands of women's (read: feminist) NGOs clamored for inclusion. Beijing was the last time they could be relegated to a conference of NGOs at a site remote from the official meeting. From then on, NGOs could apply for certification to participate in the meeting and take part in the proceedings as insiders.

It would be a mistake, however, to see GF in the NGO form as entirely focused on high centers of power. Equally distinctive of the first decades of GF has been the ability of feminists to create organizational networks that engage the local and are at times led and informed by it. Feminists helped generate the dispersed network of NGOs now operating at the subnational, national, and regional levels all over the world but especially in the developing world. Funded by the UN, the U.S. Agency for International Development, and European and large donor foundations, these NGOs form networks of feminists that build relationships, gather local input, disseminate policy, and coordinate with the next-higher-up level of feminist networking NGOs. They professionalize their members in much the same way that the job of gender specialist does within the UN. Though these funding streams provide large opportunities for feminist activism, they also confront feminists with prerequisites of ideological and, increasingly, legal compliance. Donors require deliverables, and those deliverables are always ideologically laden. And sometimes they displace rather than empower local activism. As polygamy and so-called female genital mutilation, for instance, got reframed not as culture but as sexual violence, local feminists who could join the international program to criminalize and eradicate these practices gained funding and organizational capacity, while those with different priorities worked at a relative disadvantage.[24]

Expertise

Often, feminist ideas can join in governance only if they cease looking political and become neutral, objective, and simply *right*. When they successfully do this, they become common sense and can even disappear. But they can also become the technical, ornate, elite, authorized, and credentialed version of common sense. Either way, feminism becomes a form of expertise.[25]

Sometimes feminism as expertise is embodied in an expert. The battered women's movement in the United States saw this in the 1980s. Defending women who had killed their batterers, movement activists needed to defeat the assumption, shared by judges and juries, that these women could have saved themselves, without killing anyone, simply by moving out. They developed a (controversial) psychological syndrome, battered women's syndrome (BWS), and identified experts who could gain expert-witness status in court cases and testify that the dead man had psychologically disabled his victim from acting in her own interest in any other way. BWS as expertise upheld a defense of self-defense, or sought a legal excuse.[26]

In the mid-1990s, international feminists adapted a distinctive UN role, the "special rapporteur," to feminist ends. Special rapporteurs report to the Human Rights Council (formerly the Human Rights Commission) and occasionally the General Assembly; they are charged with a single mandate like torture or the right to food. Special rapporteurs produce reports about an officially recognized problem that can circulate as factual truth in policy debates and that move existing policy statements forward in incremental ways. They are automatically included in many policy processes, and more recently can even take complaints and forward them up to the Council. They are not paid by the UN, a set-aside that supposedly removes them from bureaucratic politics. The Human Rights Council established the Special Rapporteur on Violence against Women, Its Causes and Consequences in 1994; since then the office has produced volumes of material, ranging from general policy statements to detailed country reports. Then, in 2009, the Security Council established a Special Representative of the Secretary General on Sexual Violence in Conflict. The evolving domain that these offices oversee—note the transition from "violence against women" to "sexual violence"—manifests constant savvy maneuvering of feminists within the UN to dedicate one of its expert roles for feminist priorities.

As David Kennedy argues in *A World of Struggle,* the world is governed by experts struggling for influence and control over the course of events and their meaning. For all its supposed neutrality and objectivity, feminist expertise—like other forms of expertise—plays deeply ritualized and strategic power politics. Feminists are important partners in this often unseen but pervasive mode of governing.

Notes

1. For the specific terms we mention, see, for instance, Joyce Outshoorn and Johanna Kantola, eds., *Changing State Feminism* (Basingstoke, U.K.: Palgrave Macmillan, 2007); Elizabeth Bernstein, "The Sexual Politics of the 'New Abolitionism,'" *Differences: Journal of Feminist Cultural Studies* 18, no. 3 (2007): 128–51; Hester Eisenstein, *Inside Agitators: Australian Femocrats and the State* (Philadelphia:

Temple University Press, 1996); Kate Bedford, "Introduction," in *Developing Partnerships: Gender, Sexuality, and the Reformed World Bank* (Minneapolis: University of Minnesota Press, 2009), xvii; Rome Statute of the International Criminal Court, art. 42(9), July 17, 1998, 2187 U.N.T.S. 3, http://www.un.org/law/icc/index.html (provision authorizing the International Criminal Court prosecutor to appoint experts on sexual violence, eventually institutionalized as the Office of the Special Advisor to the Prosecutor on Gender Violence).

For other studies of what we are calling GF, see Victoria Bernal and Inderpal Grewal, eds., *Theorizing NGOs: States, Feminisms, and Neoliberalism* (Durham, N.C.: Duke University Press, 2014); Kristin Bumiller, *In an Abusive State: How Neoliberalism Appropriated the Feminist Movement against Sexual Violence* (Durham, N.C.: Duke University Press, 2008); Gülay Caglar, Elisabeth Prügl, and Susanne Zwingel, eds., *Feminist Strategies in International Governance* (New York: Routledge, 2013); Sara R. Farris, *In the Name of Women's Rights: The Rise of Femonationalism* (Durham, N.C.: Duke University Press, 2017); Leela Fernandes, *Transnational Feminism in the United States: Knowledge, Ethics, and Power* (New York: New York University Press, 2013); Nancy Fraser, *Fortunes of Feminism: From State-Managed Capitalism to Neoliberal Crisis* (New York: Verso, 2013); Dorothy L. Hodgson, ed., *Gender and Culture at the Limit of Rights* (Philadelphia: University of Pennsylvania Press, 2011); Karen Knop, ed., *Gender and Human Rights* (Oxford: Oxford University Press, 2004); Nivedita Menon, *Recovering Subversion: Feminist Politics beyond the Law* (Urbana: University of Illinois Press, 2004); Sally Engle Merry, *Human Rights and Gender Violence: Translating International Law into Local Justice* (Chicago: University of Chicago Press, 2006); Shirin M. Rai and Kate Bedford, eds., "Feminists Theorize International Political Economy," special issue, *Signs* 36, no. 1 (Autumn 2010); Shirin M. Rai and Georgina Waylen, *Global Governance: Feminist Perspectives* (Basingstoke, U.K.: Palgrave Macmillan, 2008); Annelise Riles, *The Network Inside Out* (Ann Arbor: University of Michigan Press, 2000); Anna Yeatman, *Bureaucrats, Technocrats, Femocrats: Essays on the Contemporary Australian State* (Sydney: Allen & Unwin, 1990).

2. See, e.g., Orly Lobel, "The Renew Deal: The Fall of Regulation and the Rise of Governance in Contemporary Legal Thought," *Minnesota Law Review* 89, no. 2 (2004): 342–470; John Ruggie, "Global Governance," syllabus, Harvard Kennedy School, Cambridge, Mass., Fall 2013, http://www.hks.harvard.edu/syllabus/IGA -103.pdf; Benedict Kingsbury, Nico Krisch, and Richard B. Stewart, "The Emergence of Global Administrative Law," *Law and Contemporary Problems* 68, nos. 3–4 (2005): 15. For a critical assessment of new governance, see Amy J. Cohen, "Negotiation, Meet New Governance: Interests, Skills, and Selves," *Law and Social Inquiry* 33, no. 2 (2008): 503–62.

3. Michel Foucault, *Security, Territory, Population: Lectures at the Collège de France 1977–78*, trans. Graham Burchell (Basingstoke, U.K.: Palgrave Macmillan, 2007); Michel Foucault, *The Birth of Biopolitics: Lectures at the Collège de France, 1978–79*, trans. Graham Burchell (Basingstoke, U.K.: Palgrave Macmillan, 2008); Alexandria Jayne Innes and Brent J. Steele, "Governmentality in Global Governance," in *Oxford Handbook of Governance*, ed. David Levi-Faur (Oxford: Oxford University Press, 2012), 716–29.

4. Foucault, *The Birth of Biopolitics,* 75–100.

5. Foucault, *Security, Territory, Population,* 109.

6. Foucault, *The Birth of Biopolitics,* 186.

7. Ibid.

8. Ibid.

9. Janet Halley, Prabha Kotiswaran, Hila Shamir, and Chantal Thomas, "From the International to the Local in Feminist Legal Responses to Rape, Prostitution / Sex Work, and Sex Trafficking: Four Studies in Contemporary Governance Feminism," *Harvard Journal of Law and Gender* 29, no. 2 (2006): 335–423.

10. Bernstein, "The Sexual Politics of the 'New Abolitionism,'" 143.

11. See the Preface, xv.

12. Charlotte Bunch, "Listen Up: UN Must Hear Women on Sexual Violence," *On the Issues Magazine,* Spring 2009, http://www.ontheissuesmagazine.com/2009spring/2009spring_11.php.

13. Vicki Schultz, "The Sanitized Workplace," *Yale Law Journal* 112, no. 8 (2003): 2061–193.

14. Frances E. Olsen, "The Family and the Market: A Study of Ideology and Legal Reform," *Harvard Law Review* 96, no. 7 (1983): 1497.

15. John Koblin, "How Gretchen Carlson Took On the Chief of Fox News," *New York Times,* July 6, 2016, http://www.nytimes.com/2016/07/07/business/media/gretchen-carlson-files-sex-harassment-suit-against-roger-ailes-of-fox-news.html.

16. Jim Rutenberg, Emily Steel, and John Koblin, "At Fox News, Kisses, Innuendo, Propositions, and Fears of Reprisal, *New York Times,* July 23, 2016, http://www.nytimes.com/2016/07/24/business/at-fox-news-kisses-innuendo-propositions-and-fears-of-reprisal.html; John Koblin, Emily Steel, and Jim Rutenberg, "Roger Ailes Leaves Fox News, and Rupert Murdoch Steps In," *New York Times,* July 21, 2016, http://www.nytimes.com/2016/07/22/business/media/roger-ailes-fox-news.html.

17. "Transcript: Donald Trump's Taped Comments about Women," *New York Times,* October 8, 2016, https://www.nytimes.com/2016/10/08/us/donald-trump-tape-transcript.html.

18. Susan Chira, "'You Focus on the Good': Women Who Voted for Trump, in Their Own Words," *New York Times,* January 14, 2017, https://www.nytimes.com/2017/01/14/us/women-voters-trump.html; Clare Malone, "Clinton Couldn't Win Over White Women," *FiveThirtyEight,* November 9, 2016, https://fivethirtyeight.com/features/clinton-couldnt-win-over-white-women/.

19. Jane J. Mansbridge, *Why We Lost the ERA* (Chicago: University of Chicago Press, 1986).

20. Kenya Constitution of 2010, art. 27(4) (prohibits sex discrimination); ibid., art. 97(1)(b) (provides that the National Assembly shall include forty-seven elected women).

21. David S. Law and Mila Versteeg, "The Evolution and Ideology of Global Constitutionalism," *California Law Review* 99, no. 5 (2011): 1163–57, 1200.

22. Rep. of the Economic and Social Council for 1997, U.N. Doc. A/52/3, at 27 (September 18, 1997). For a feminist assessment of mainstreaming, see Hilary Charlesworth, "Not Waving but Drowning: Gender Mainstreaming and Human Rights in the United Nations," *Harvard Human Rights Journal* 18, no. 2 (2005): 1–18.

23. Two ethnographies provide, respectively, optimistic and grim accounts of this process: Merry, *Human Rights and Gender Violence*; Riles, *The Network Inside Out.*

24. See, for instance, Dorothy L. Hodgson, "'These Are Not Our Priorities': Maasai Women, Human Rights, and the Problem of Culture," in Hodgson, *Gender and Culture*, 138–57 (internationally funded feminist NGOs and Maasai women with differing agendas for "female genital mutilation"); Ousseina D. Alidou, "Muslim Women, Rights Discourse, and the Media in Kenya," in Hodgson, *Gender and Culture*, 180–99 (Kenyan women's organizations supporting sexual violence bill including criminalization of domestic violence contested by a Muslim woman with a one-woman activist model). For a more positive assessment of the rise of sexual violence as the primary framework for feminist transnational organizing, see S. Laurel Weldon and Mala Htun, "Feminist Mobilisation and Progressive Policy Change: Why Governments Take Action to Combat Violence against Women," *Gender and Development* 21, no. 2 (2013): 231–47.

25. David Kennedy, *A World of Struggle: How Power, Law, and Expertise Shape Global Political Economy* (Princeton, N.J.: Princeton University Press, 2016). For an account of the rise of gender-based or sexual violence as a key priority in international and transnational law—an account in which the development of feminist-inspired expertise about rape and trauma became an institutional force and required an elaborate range of institutional and documentary practices—see Carol Harrington, *Politicization of Sexual Violence: From Abolitionism to Peacekeeping* (Burlington, Vt.: Ashgate, 2010).

26. For a critical reflection on these efforts by a feminist who had herself engaged in them, see Elizabeth M. Schneider, *Battered Women and Feminist Lawmaking* (New Haven, Conn.: Yale University Press, 2000), 8–86, 113–47.

CHAPTER 2

Which Forms of Feminism Have Gained Inclusion?

JANET HALLEY

Feminist ideas and feminists *travel*. The remarkable installation of feminist policy ideas in international organizations such as the UN and the World Bank, in the Rome Statute establishing the International Criminal Court, and in treaty commitments such as the Convention on the Elimination of Discrimination against Women and the Palermo Protocol against Human Trafficking means that law itself is a transmission vehicle for GF and thus for feminism. Also the NGO-sphere, powered by government grants, deep-pocketed private donors, and Internet activism, moves feminist norms and practices around the world, from many centers of feminist production to innumerable local sites of feminist engagement. And in locales across the world, local feminisms thrive while welcoming, ignoring, grudgingly accommodating, and resisting other feminisms coming from "outside." The study of GF is necessarily a comparative project, tracing genealogies of transmission—of production and reception—from the international to the local and back again, from center to periphery and back again, from the ivory tower to the street and back again. And because feminism now takes governance forms, the struggle over production, transmission, and reception of feminist people, ideas, and practices is achieved not only through their intrinsic charisma but sometimes at the end of a gun.

For all that we emphasize local sites of feminist production all over the world, chapters 1 and 2 focus on feminism in the United States. The ascendancy of the United States in the post-Soviet era means that, within GF, U.S. feminisms have a salience and transportability that feminisms emerging elsewhere do not enjoy. Indeed, U.S. feminism, like U.S. citizens, has a passport that can travel almost everywhere without applying for an entry visa: this very salience and transportability have made U.S. feminism a little deaf to its own limits and to the intense resistance it has provoked among some non-U.S.-based feminists. What this chapter is about to describe is thus both a model and an anti-model. Still, we think it worthwhile, right at the outset, to sketch the tools available within U.S. feminism pretty starkly. At certain points, this examination necessarily tracks alliances between U.S. feminists and those from elsewhere. At others, it notices resistances.

Feminism is a sustained disagreement about sex, sexuality, gender, and the family among people who share a central, sometimes pivotal or indispensable commitment to the emancipation of things F—women, femininity, female or feminine genders, mothers, daughters, girls.[1] But patterns are discernible. Feminisms that accentuate power hierarchies differ from those that see cultural values as the key; and feminisms that discern inequality rather than domination speak very differently about injustice and emancipation from feminisms that attend to maldistribution. Each of these emphases comes in various radical and mild forms. Feminisms that see men, male domination, or masculinist values as the problem differ from those that see *everyone's gender* as the problem. Feminisms that emphasize sex and sexuality as the problem read different traditions and identify different realities than those emphasizing reproduction, the family, and work. And feminisms that can take on board that there are other problems in the world than M/F gender, or their variants—which are just as committed to working on race or colonialism or global warming—are very different from those whose basic thought rule is that all "intersecting" power or cultural bad things must ultimately be understood as part of the problem and of the solution proposed *by feminism.* To make it even more complicated, American feminists often carry all these ideas in their consciousness as ambivalences and contradictions that they see no need to resolve into logical purity. And finally, feminist internal critique flourishes—in some zones more than in others—giving some feminists critical distance from their own most deeply felt projects.

Nevertheless, distinct traditions of thought and practice thrive in U.S. feminism. They are different enough to come into conflict, and many are sufficiently animated by a will to governmental power that they come into conflict *within* and *about* governance.[2] We see the following as the key players on the GF landscape: liberal feminism, dominance feminism, feminist investments in the sexual orientation and gender identity (SOGI) movement, critical-race feminism, postcolonial feminism, and materialist feminism.

Of these, the two that have had the largest purchase on law are liberal and dominance feminism. This chapter asks why they have been so eager to emerge within legal pronouncements and practices, why they have had relatively good uptake there, and why—despite the large differences between them—they have so often been able to work together in governance projects. The argument, in short, is this: both liberal and dominance feminism have harmonics with basic tenets in American liberal legalism, and—moreover—their compatibilities with American legal legalism, though different, overlap. They can work together on a broad range of social-control projects and can make sense to social conservative, liberal, and neoliberal forms of American legal thought when they do so. And because of the distinct pathways by which they found this sweet spot for entry into governmentality, especially punitive, carceral, and tort-based reforms, their success has also created and ratified the conditions for the opposite fate for materialist, socialist feminism in its efforts to rule. Liberal and dominance feminism have formed a coalition that makes it harder to think distributively, from the Left, within U.S. GF.

In the chapters to follow, and in the companion volume to this book, *Governance Feminism: Notes from the Field,* we further develop this line of analysis with respect to feminism in international and transnational law, and its implications for the ways in which feminist ideas travel the globe, in part through their emergence in governmental practice.[3]

Liberal Feminism

U.S. liberal feminism focuses on three basic ideals of liberalism: freedom, equality, and democratic participation in government through the vote and through elected and appointed office. Much could be and has been said about the U.S. feminist campaign to ensure that candidates heed the "gender gap" between men and women voters and that women are represented in government at every level. Here, though, I focus on freedom and equality.

U.S. liberal feminism is an immensely rich fund of critiques and ideas, centuries old: in a very incisive and detailed way, John Locke was a feminist.[4] It is difficult to study precisely because all U.S. feminists are liberal feminists at least some of the time. Still, liberal feminism as it emanates from the United States is different enough from its counterparts around the world that sketching its main commitments, however difficult, seems necessary here.[5]

American liberal feminism spans a wide spectrum from Left to center and indeed can be understood as a series of Left/Right tensions in which an aspiration for social-justice-oriented redistribution and criticism of classic center-liberal positions causes Left-liberal feminists to move leftward away from their more centrist sisters and toward socialist feminism, and in which faith in liberal individualism, faith in equal opportunity, and a general desire to separate themselves from their leftist sisters cause other feminists to shift toward the political center.[6] Liberal feminists halt these trends before they cause an embrace of revolutionary leftism, on the one hand, or of hardline right-wing thinking, on the other. It is a dynamic, almost hydraulic process, mediated across the range of center positions by feminists who share the ideas of the mainstream or who are, at least, committed to audibility within the mainstream.

Freedom and equality in American liberal-centrist feminism are recurrently understood to inhere in rights. This brings into the project a constitutive legal formalism and a willingness to rely on the state. It also structures in, at the foundation, an emphasis on the individual rather than the collective as the primary subject of moral and political concern. Left-liberal feminists take issue with these emphases: for New Deal feminists, for instance, building a robust social-welfare state and mobilizing labor, tenants, consumers, and so on, to push back against capital are core commitments.

The feminist equality/freedom and Left/center conflicts inhere in one of the most important victories of liberal feminism and its sequel in the U.S. Supreme Court: *Roe v. Wade* (1973) and *Harris v. McRae* (1980).[7] *Roe* established the (limited) constitutional right of a woman to *choose* to terminate a pregnancy. *Harris v. McRae* exposed the market-liberal logic of that right by holding that women on federally supported public assistance via the Medicaid program fully enjoyed that right, even though Congress had barred the use of federal funds to subsidize even medically necessary abortions; the sole exceptions were abortion needed to save the life of the woman and termination of pregnancies originating in rape or incest. A woman who fell outside these narrow exceptions could choose to have an abortion; after that it was up to the woman herself and market forces to provide her with the means to obtain one. Feminists of course decried this outcome, but it was a far more trenchant problem for New Deal feminists than for their centrist sisters. By 1993, when President Bill Clinton's promise to "end welfare as we know it" was enacted as law, this split within U.S. liberal feminism had widened, pushing some feminists further toward the center and even the Right on the issue of public benefits for the poor, and others further toward the Left. Here we encounter a genuine antagonism between liberal-leftist feminism, which regards the market as the site of chronic maldistribution, and liberal-centrist feminism, which looks primarily to individual self-reliance on the classic liberal model for women's progress.

Working this tension out within American liberal legalism has meant that the centrist versions of the feminist agenda win more often. This is partly because those versions make more sense to more actual feminists; it is also because they make more sense to the people whom feminists can form alliances with, persuade, and do deals with. There is more money, a greater ability to use the state to "make up people"[8] who agree with the agenda, and thus more actual feminists who think this way.

But the tension endures, and, as a result, American feminism is consistently marked by chronic ambivalences about what freedom and equality mean. The liberal-centrist version of freedom is the freedom to choose. The *decision* of an individual actor must be free and so must be respected. Choice must be free from constraint; from force, fraud, or coercion; and from violence. Traditional gender roles, whether they are imposed by the state or social forces, have long been the primary form in which American liberal feminism envisions constraint that the state must remove to guarantee women freedom. Genuine freedom as imagined in American liberal feminism is thus almost never libertarian; it takes aim not only at governmental but also at social sources of constraint and harbors a large will to use the state to make social conditions more favorable to women. A long-running critique of the private/public distinction equips American liberal feminism to dismiss claims that freedom has been secured when the state alone refrains from imposing constraints: feminists argue that social actors depend on legal support in innumerable ways, and that when the state abandons women to them, it either permits and indirectly structures social dominance of men over women (the more centrist version) or directly does so in ways that are hidden only ideologically and fictionally by the private/public distinction (the more Left version).

But traditional gender roles are also often precisely what women *do* choose. The project of unburdening motherhood, marriage, and the work of care from social constraints that prevent women from exercising their free choice not to avoid them but to engage in them recurrently threatens to involve feminists not in dismantling but in perpetuating traditional gender roles. Many liberal feminists seem to have assumed that permitting women to join the workforce and to be as self-determining as the men in their lives would unleash their pent-up desire to do these things: socially transformative change can come, on this expectation, from a market-clearing ban on sex discrimination at work and the formal freedom of women from legal commands, like those of traditional marriage law, to accept a subordinate role. The failure of actual women to perform these social changes has been a daunting reality for liberal feminists. It puts them into a direct confrontation with—and a possible role in promoting—the traditional choices *of women*. Immense feminist energy goes into working out the meaning of this paradox for middle-class and professional women.[9] And again, the Right/Left spectrum plays a tension-creating role here: many women *are* social conservatives.

A further tension within American liberal feminism emerges at the intersection between the characteristic commitment of liberalism to freedom and feminist critiques of oppressive social conditions faced by women. The former comes with a will to use the state to protect freedom from force, fraud, and coercion. This is the contract/crime paradigm:[10] it supports a state project of promoting freedom in markets and civil society while punishing and deterring—often through criminal enforcement—acts that directly undermine that freedom. A parallel form, less focused on the market, derives from John Stuart Mill's harm principle: the state must leave citizens free until and unless they harm one another, and then it can step in to change social conditions.[11]

Working within these models has meant, for American liberal feminists, accepting a free/coerced distinction in which male/female hierarchy is coercion or harm. Ushered along by this logic, issue by issue, as they managed to achieve this translation, and abetted by an alliance with dominance feminism (more on this below), liberal feminists joined the general U.S. turn to criminalization. For many feminists on many issues, punishment became the remedy of choice for any social wrong that they could describe as coercive or as harm.

The criminal turn in feminism has been controversial among feminists for decades now, in debates that form yet another Left/center/Right dynamic within and at the margins of American liberal feminism.[12] Left-leaning liberal feminists have had repeated opportunities to notice with dismay the ease with which feminist criminal-enforcement and social-control projects attract alliances with social conservatives. They observe that these were often not merely marriages of convenience: the social and legal visions of fellow feminists had begun to look, feel, and taste socially conservative in substance. Feminists harkening from critical race theory noticed that the criminal projects were likely to tolerate harms to Black women while imposing ever-more-rigorous criminal control on Black men.[13] As U.S. social opinion has woken up to the vast incarceration of Black men and other men of color produced by the wars on drugs and on crime—and as Black Lives Matter has mobilized an expanding critique of the U.S. approach to crime—this critique has increasingly distanced Left-liberal feminists from center liberal feminists. And civil libertarian feminists have noticed that many feminists express a will to use the legal system as harshly as possible, bypassing due process and other general fairness constraints, when harm to women is at stake.

Many of the tensions that appear among liberal feminists seeking freedom reappear when they seek equality. Here, the ideal alternatives are formal and substantive equality. Formal equality is equal treatment: men and women get equally good or equally bad treatment at the hands of the state. In its ideal form, it is substantively empty. If male soldiers get on-base housing for their families, so do women soldiers; but if the rules deny this benefit to the men, it is fine to withhold it from the women too. The socially "thicker" alternative, substantive equality, looks for equal *outcomes*. Substantive equality requires an account of social distributions and some socially oriented judgments about what is fair and unfair about them. In its most robust forms, it favors remedies that affirmatively take from the haves in order to give to the have-nots.

Liberal feminists disagree about which pole on the equality map they should steer to. Substantive equality is far more receptive to the feminist critique of social hierarchy, for obvious reasons. But formal equality is closer to the heart of center-liberal visions of the proper role of the state in individuals' lives. Preferring formal equality is often a matter of strategy. Judges are much more likely to rule in your favor if you can frame your case as a formal equality claim; their political, intellectual, and affective orientation to judicial restraint often counsels them that they are staying well within the judicial role when they rule in favor of plaintiffs seeking formal equality and that they will stray far outside it—way into legislative territory—when they are mandating substantive equality.[14] Affirmative action for racial minorities has become the paradigm substantive-equality project in U.S. constitutional debate, and feminists are well aware of the intense blowback this substantive (if actually quite minor in the grand scheme of things) redistributive project has met. They do not want to see it transposed, across the well-slicked rails of constitutional analogy, into the discourses and doctrines of sex discrimination.[15]

But center-liberal feminists often love formal equality "for itself." It accords with their commitment to individual autonomy and self-reliance. They identify the traditional rules of marriage and legislation restricting women's access to traditionally male employment as false stereotypes, outmoded conventions, and paternalist interferences with women's autonomy that modern equality law must sweep away: once this work is done, and women are free to live the lives they choose, the state should keep out of their lives—classic centrist liberalism in a feminist form.

A major tension arises when feminists rediscover the limits of this solution and return to substantive equality. The problem (again) is that so many feminist substantive equality arguments seek socially redistributive equality for pregnant women, women as mothers, women as caregivers, and women as affectively altruistic.[16] From a New Deal feminist perspective, using equality law to accommodate these differences between men and women will make up for women's forced or chosen altruism and place them in a market economy with something approaching equal opportunity. From a cultural feminist perspective (more on this below), these differences also mark women's positive moral value: compensating them, and even rewarding them, for shining the light of care and altruism in an individualist market-driven world honors women's moral stature, values their crucial contributions, and infuses equality into a world permeated not with sameness but with difference. Whatever the value of the social claims underlying these motives, they often provoke strong resistance from centrist liberal feminists, whom they strike as paternalistic, a return to outmoded conventions and false stereotypes, an entrenching social bribe that will keep women bound to care, and a bid for redistribution from working women to homemakers. They also trouble leftist feminists, who see the war on traditional gender roles faltering and women accepting social vulnerability they could avoid. Once again, these feminists think it is no accident that feminists seeking these forms of substantive equality can form alliances with social conservatives: the progressive movement was rich in repressive social-control projects, including the protection of women's care roles, they will recall. And perhaps the alliances are not just strategic. Maybe, they wonder, there is something conservative *in* American feminism.

Dominance Feminism

One of the great puzzles of American legal feminism, in our view, is the hospitality that liberal feminists have offered to *some* of their radical sisters—specifically, those emerging from dominance feminism. I turn now to those sisters and then spell out the terms of this uneasy alliance.

Many of the big new ideas boasted by American feminism since the beginning of the third wave came from radical, structural feminists. We call them radical, again, for two reasons. First, because their vision of human emancipation demands a complete transvaluation of all values, a complete upheaval of all power, change must be root and branch, from each human's inner consciousness to the highest courts, from the minute details of everyday life to the world constitution. As we have indicated, when contemporary radical feminism was aborning in the late 1960s, this transform-everything emancipatory vision required a corresponding strategy of clean, categorical opposition to mere reformism.[17] Alice Echols shows how radical feminists then actively scorned and trashed feminists who turned toward the state and state-like institutions, while the strategic commitment to prefiguring emancipation inside the beloved community turned radical feminism into a hotbed of GF efforts seeking to purify the conduct of fellow feminists. Radical feminism in the United States for several decades now has almost reversed these commitments: by the early 1980s it turned its emancipatory vision into a state-centered reform program while relaxing most expectations that feminists would live out the maxim "the personal is the political" in perfectionist feminist cells racked by rituals of self-criticism, purges, and schism. Radical feminism became an agenda for law reform.

But dominance feminism was radical for a second reason, also stemming from its origins in late-1960s U.S. radical Left politics. As Echols again shows in astonishingly rich detail, radical feminists then shared outsiderism with the movement against the Vietnam War and the draft, with the Black power movement then breaking off from the civil rights movement, and with an active Marxist/socialist movement opposed to capitalism.[18] All of these movements were "against the system" and took radical action, not progressive and incremental reform, as the premise of collective political life. Radical feminists shared that. But step by step, renunciation by renunciation, schism by schism, radical feminism was born as some feminists determined that the war, race, and class were incorrectly framed as *male* problems and that the primary—indeed, in the last analysis, the only—oppression was male domination. Male domination *subsumed* war, racial domination, and class exploitation. What made the radical feminists "radical" on the radical U.S. Left was their willingness to commit themselves to male domination alone as the deep structure of the entire oppressive system, and to feminism alone as the necessary political response. This commitment became structural: the problem that feminism confronts is a deep structure, the hidden (and not-so-hidden) driver of everything.

When Catharine A. MacKinnon synthesized these commitments in a major theoretical statement published in *Signs* in 1982 and 1983,[19] she conjoined the radical emancipatory vision and the structuralist foundationalist commitment to male domination and female subordination that had been hammered out years before on the anvil of radical feminist politics, with a critique of the state as male. But at the same time that she was writing those articles, in her work on sexual harassment, she pivoted in a decisive *turn to the state* that reflected a strategic redirection of radical feminist political energy.[20] Once turned *against* the state, radical feminism was now directed *into* it.

Two distinct strands of American radical feminism have mattered most for the engagements of American feminism with the state. One, which I have called power feminism[21] and which is exemplified by MacKinnon's work, holds that male domination and female subordination constitute gender, sexuality, reproduction, and the family as power hierarchies; in its most radical form, this strand of feminism claims that this power creates our consciousnesses and our desires so profoundly that only a radical break in the fabric of reality itself could ever change it. The other, widely known as cultural feminism, holds that male values (logic, reason, abstract justice) have held sway and erroneously sidelined female ones (feeling, care, sensitivity to context); in its most radical form, this strand of feminism holds that emancipation will come when the female values reverse this hierarchy and basically take over.[22]

Both power feminism and cultural feminism emerged as radical theories and continue to draw from their radical sources, even as both of them have turned to the state, to incrementalism, to reform, and even to working within the system—all terms of opprobrium in late-1960s U.S. radicalism but now political common sense. For instance, power feminism, as it turned toward engagement with the state as a path to emancipation, broke with its apocalyptic visions and latched onto the freedom/force paradigm and the harm principle for rights-based and criminalization projects founded on the idea that women experience pervasive sexual violence—framed as force and as harm—because of the pervasively coercive conditions of male domination and female subordination.[23] Meanwhile, radical cultural feminism made an uneasy transit into liberal feminism in part by envisioning not a takeover by women's altruistic values but a harmonious marriage between them and reason, abstract justice, and rights to autonomy.[24]

Power and cultural feminism often meld into each other or appear side by side, but they also have a long history of mutual antagonism.[25] Together they are frequently dubbed *dominance* feminism, and we will hew to that practice. Dominance feminism finds male domination in two distinct forms: in the false superiority of male values and male *culture,* and in the domination of all things F by all things M *as sexuality.*

Cultural Feminism

Some of the surprising harmonies between dominance and liberal American feminisms are specific to cultural feminism. Cultural feminism can take milder and stronger forms, the latter being an important fount of dominance feminist ideas. The milder cultural feminisms can endorse proceduralist and "democratic" governmental programs for participation, sometimes emphasizing the inclusion of women in power institutions as a necessary first step to democratic reform. Stronger cultural feminism, however, seeks to put women in power because they came from a specific standpoint, the standpoint of an "ethic of care": only women could see what, and how bad, injustice really is. Whenever you hear an argument that women are the disproportionate victims of war but never its promoters, an argument that women suffer but never promote traditional familial practices, an argument that development energy should be concentrated on women because—unlike men, who spend anything they earn on beer and cigarettes—they will spend their gains on children's welfare, you are hearing an argument formed in the crucible of cultural feminist thought. Cultural feminism has thus worked well with social-conservative views of armed conflict as men's business, with the idea that humanitarian efforts in wartime should focus on women and children first, and with an ideology in which the home is a haven in a heartless world—even while it pushes for reform that mainstreams women into military roles, regards men's sexual injury as feminization, and makes the workplace, as Frances Olsen put it, "more like the ideal family."[26] And it has coincided comfortably with neoliberal efforts to entrepreneurialize women: liberal feminists knew well that equal access to employment was one of the most important keys to women's emancipation, but cultural feminism helped this large project along in development policy by arguing that women, having better values than men, would spend their earnings more altruistically and thus be better vectors for economic growth.

Pregnancy and motherhood are central foci in cultural feminism, and they have produced a conceptual ambivalence that is both a weakness and a strength of this mode of feminist legalism. Drawing from early-second-wave feminist anthropology, feminists distinguished sex from gender: the former was natural and unavoidable sexual difference, while the latter comprised all the cultural meanings given to sexual difference, often coercively and often through law.[27] The idea was that sex, as a natural characteristic, was a given that had to be respected; and that gender, as an element of culture, was an artifact and could be changed. This matrix (pun intended) gave rise to a heady but contradictory mix of prescriptive formulae: pregnancy and motherhood are cultural and saturated with malign male imperatives, *and* they form the natural source of women's morally superior experience. The contradiction here: culture is a historical accident and can be changed *and* women's biological experience forms the natural basis for their emancipatory role in producing that change. The origins of a protracted struggle in feminism over social-constructionism and essentialism lie in contradictory commitments like these.

Cultural feminism operating in these legal frameworks helped push liberal feminists toward pregnancy rights, accommodations for caregivers, remuneration of the homemaker wife, and so on—all of them substantive rather than formal equality ideas. As international human rights took its turn from formal equality to all manner of outcome-driven, women-specific rights—from rights to be free from political abuse at state hands to rights to social outcomes—cultural feminism was ready to go transnational.

Power Feminism

With its focus on male domination and female subordination *in and as sexuality,* the power branch of dominance feminism has always been a class theory of women. For many years at the beginning of the second wave in the United States, seeking a class theory of women required feminists to draw simultaneously from Marxism and feminism, to seek theoretical and political synthesis of their critique of patriarchy or male domination and economic class exploitation. The systematic workings of "capitalist patriarchy" would be exposed, Marxist feminists argued, only when the exploitation of labor by capital and of women by men could be understood in a seamless analysis. As Echols details, however, in the late 1960s radical feminism broke off from Marxist feminism by abandoning the effort to understand the relations between labor and capital in favor of a single form of domination, sexuality, and a single object of emancipation, women.

MacKinnon's rightfully famous 1982–83 two-part article in *Signs* mentioned above, tellingly titled "Feminism, Marxism, Method, and the State," ensured that dominance feminism entered into its direct confrontation with state power quite self-consciously as a *successor* to Marxism.[28] For MacKinnon, at that time, feminism was destined to become the overarching theory of power and emancipation, subsuming the critique of capital within it. This theoretical frame had large consequences in the thought of MacKinnon and other power feminists: from then on, they could develop their critique of sexuality and their law reform agenda about sexuality without sustained attention to class or other social dominations and without the need for much attention to material distribution. The MacKinnon/Dworkin antipornography ordinance, for instance, defined pornography as male domination even when it was hidden away in a drawer—not because it necessarily degraded the women depicted in it, or the women who had sex with the men who consumed it, but because it degraded all women by existing.[29] Long lists of wrongs done to women could be compiled, each item a mere reiteration of the others. Rape, pornography, domestic violence, prostitution: they could all become the paradigm of the single same thing, male domination and female subordination. The differences between them, and the different ways that they actually played out for women in different racial, economic-class, generational, and national settings; the different ways they distributed resources; the many ways they affected men—none of these registered.[30] This dovetailed perfectly with the cultural feminist substantive-equality priority put on women's pregnancy, motherhood, and caregiver roles: increasingly, unless a feminist leaned Left, these issues could be discussed without reference to the class differences between women. The class-based, race-based, or colonial/postcolonial suffering of poor men dropped out of view. Feminists working within these logics could join conservative and neoliberal projects without worrying too much about the strangeness of their bedfellows: their theoretical priors led them to put a small price on the social-conservative and market-liberal consequences of their alliances.

Nowhere is this tendency more apparent than in the power feminist analysis of prostitution. Kathleen Barry, long a radical feminist voice, rebuilt radical feminism around a critique of the market for sex but without a critique of class or material maldistribution.[31] In 1979, in a book titled *Female Sexual Slavery,* Barry posited that sexual exchange between women and men *from which women could exit* was off-limits to feminist critique.[32] Women in heterosexual life with no exit, on the other hand, were enslaved. In 1995, Barry had had an aha: calling male sexual domination of women slavery implied that, when it ended, women were *free*; and this ratified the freedom/force distinction on which liberal and neoliberal commodification and exploitation of women's sexuality was based and which it mystified and justified. She replaced her keystone term "slavery" with "prostitution": prostitution could be the exemplar of male domination because it included women's *willing* sale of sexual access that encapsulated all of male domination in a single example.[33]

According to Barry in 1995, liberal feminists who thought noncoerced prostitution was possible and could be meaningfully chosen, and "proprostitution" feminists—that is, feminists who saw prostitution as a form of labor—were not just complicit with neoliberal and social conservative forces; they were virtually identical in that they all endorsed the commodification of women's sexuality.

The subtitle of Barry's 1995 book is *The Global Exploitation of Women.* This signals that feminism has become a theory of *exploitation*. Like a Marxist feminist, Barry thus has a critique of rights: rights were individual solutions for exceptionally victimized women, not collective ones for all women; they were instrumentally focused on fostering market exchange, not ends in themselves as instantiations of human well-being and dignity. She had a critique of consumerism, competition, and above all consent to sexual abuse, including, paradigmatically, prostitution. But what she did *not* have is an account of economic stratification that includes, as part of the problem, poverty and market exploitation that do not end in sexual abuse.

This generated some pretty serious blind spots in her account. Consider Barry's treatment of marriage. In it, women with abusive husbands who stay in their relationships, often even defending their husbands, are just like prostitutes who do the same with their pimps. But marriage itself comes in for no criticism—only sexually abusive marriages do.[34] That marriage is a richly redistributive institution, with myriad legal and social rules shifting powers and resources between husbands and wives, parents and children, employers and workers, the tax base and welfare systems, drops out of the picture entirely.

Or consider her analysis of the Human Development Index, a measure issued by the United Nations Development Programme that aggregates data on longevity and health, education levels, and income on a country-by-country basis to comparatively rank the countries of the world, from the lowest developed to the highest developed.[35] Consulting the 1992 *Human Development Report* exposed Barry to an avalanche of statistics about social life. Out of this avalanche, Barry extracted a supposed correlation of low, middle, and high development levels among contemporary countries and her "stages" of prostitution (in which prostitution takes the form of "trafficking" in premodern, family-based economies; industrialization in industrialized economies; and normalization in post-Fordist economies).[36] You would think that the only problem affecting human welfare in Nepal and Bangladesh—countries with per capita GNPs, according to Barry's chart, fully 1/116 of the per capita GNP of the United States—was that parents and relatives moved girls from their natal homes to population centers for forced marriage and prostitution. The economic desperation that would drive them to this miserable expedient drops out of the picture entirely.

American dominance feminism is a top-down, bottom-up model of M/F relations: there are perpetrators (men) and victims (women); people with an individualist ethic (men) and people with an ethic of care (women); people feminists advocate for (women) and people they accuse (men). This model of right and wrong is highly assimilable to criminal law and tort law frameworks. Thus the very visible elements of GF that use the penal powers of the state to "end" sexual violence in all its forms are saturated with dominance feminist ideas. Especially where power feminism makes its influence felt, it makes *sexuality* the core of the problem: dominance feminist thinking places *sexual* wrongs front and center, and assimilates other seemingly nonsexual wrongs to sexual ones.

This is, we think, a manifestly narrow, crabbed, and even paranoid view of the gender order in the United States, and it is hospitable to quite ethnocentric, neocolonial construals of the gender order prevailing in the global South. It is remarkably indifferent to distributional consequences. Why does it play such a large role in GF today?

At the turn of the twenty-first century, if you went to any gender and sexuality studies program at a U.S. university and tried to start a conversation about key dominance feminist ideas, you got a blank stare. Students and teachers alike would ask, "Why are you still thinking about those debunked models of feminism?"[37] But if you went to a *law* school, students flocked all around you, some because these ideas make sense to them as they prepare to move (or to move into) the legal system, others because they know they have to be literate in them to resist them. As we survey the GF landscape as this book goes to press, dominance feminist ideas have migrated out of the law schools to emerge all over the campus. For years now, undergraduate feminist life has been animated by a dominance-feminist / liberal-feminist outrage over campus "rape culture." This trend, again, reflects the ready absorbability of dominance feminism into liberal and neoliberal modes of governance. It has helped sexual violence displace social and economic rights, and a fortiori explicit redistributional aims, through its hold on human rights institutions and rhetorics. Dominance feminism travels on the wingspread of American power far more readily than its contestant theories and politics of sexuality. Why?

We think there are two answers to this question. First, liberal and dominance feminism have found powerful ways to work together within the framework of legal liberalism. And second, Marxist, socialist, and materialist traditions in U.S. feminism have been pushed to the side by a battery of forces, feminist and nonfeminist, effectively de-skilling feminists when it comes to economic distribution. This chapter turns now to genealogical accounts of these two processes.

The Uneasy but Effective Alliance of Liberal Feminism with Dominance Feminism

Liberal and dominance feminisms are often expressly antagonistic; sometimes they make a grudging alliance. Sometimes they simply do not intersect at all, and sometimes the ideas and commitments of dominance feminism *become* the beating heart of liberal feminist reform.

Instances of antagonism abound. Liberal feminists, for instance, formed a crucial part of the feminist resistance to MacKinnon and Andrea Dworkin's antipornography ordinance[38]—a decision to move intrafeminist disagreement front and center that led to the American feminist "sex wars." Liberal feminist Martha Nussbaum, after a short dalliance with dominance feminist ideas, broke with them by publishing a classically liberal takedown of the idea that prostitution was worse for women than other forms of low-paid bodily service work.[39]

Unhappy strategic alliances are also possible. As Rachel Rebouché demonstrates in chapter 6, liberal and dominance feminists have reached a fragile détente in their disagreement about how to approach sex-selective abortion in the United States. Rather than break up a feminist coalition opposing the piecemeal reversal of *Roe v. Wade* (that threatened bastion of liberal-feminist choice), dominance feminists export their opposition to sex-selective abortion to the developing world but mute it at home. And as Amy Cohen, Aya Gruber, and Kate Mogulescu have shown, dominance feminists and feminists who see prostitution as a hard but legitimate choice for women work together in New York City's new prostitution courts because the former loves the end-demand policy giving shape to the courts, and the equation of prostitution with trafficking that underlies the diversion remedy, while the former cannot find any substitute for the social services that sex workers can get there.[40]

And sometimes ships pass in the night without anyone noticing. Dominance feminists just do not show up when liberal feminists participate in the formation of technocratic neoliberal economic policy. They are not seeking a place at the table in the World Trade Organization, in regional trade associations, or in legislative microdesign of the neoliberal welfare-replacement programs. Liberal feminists donate money and time to systematic efforts to elect women to Congress. You will not find many dominance feminists doing this.

But often dominance and liberal feminists merge together so smoothly that it is impossible to tell them apart. These convergences often promote a crime-and-punishment model for conduct described as sexual violence as coercion or harm. Let us look at some examples.

Governance feminists in the Obama Department of Education Office for Civil Rights (DOE OCR) threatened officials at the University of Montana with a cutoff of all federal funds unless they adopted a rule defining sexual harassment as unwanted sexual conduct, full stop, and abandoned any inquiry into whether the complainant's say-so on unwantedness was reasonable.[41] This is a purely subjective test; it includes a lot more conduct within the definition of wrongful conduct than you would get with a reasonableness test. MacKinnon has advocated it for years.[42] The Supreme Court's definition of sexual harassment makes prominent display of a reasonableness requirement.[43] Presumably you had to be a liberal in some important way to become a top administrator in the Obama-era DOE OCR, but this is a certifiably dominance-feminist idea. Without a dominance feminist / liberal feminist fusion, it could not have happened.

Another example emerged in feminist advocacy for a crime of sexual slavery at the Rome Conference, where the Rome Statute establishing the International Criminal Court was negotiated. Feminists participated in this conference in full insider GF mode, especially as the Women's Caucus for Gender Justice (WCGJ), which was included in the top leadership of the pro-Court NGOs in the conference. The WCGJ's goal throughout months of intense activism in the lead-up to the conference and at it was to move rape into the center of this new body of international law addressing wrongs committed in armed conflict. Valerie Oosterveld, a WCGJ leader and an experienced Canadian GFeminist, grounded her liberal-feminist case for the criminalization of rape on women's "bodily integrity and autonomy."[44] But she also supported the WCGJ's structuralist position on the broad scope of gender violence. And she argued for adding sexual slavery as a new crime because, in her view, it would preclude any consent defense:

> By definition, an exercise of . . . [the powers attaching to the right of ownership] involves a negation of consent, which is why the Special Rapporteur on systematic rape, sexual slavery and slavery-like practices in armed conflict stated: "[A] person cannot, under any circumstances, consent to be enslaved or subjected to slavery. Thus, it follows that a person accused of slavery cannot raise consent of the victim as a defense." If a judge finds that the actions of the perpetrator fall within

the first element of the crime of slavery, an evaluation of whether a defence of consent can apply to the sexual acts of the second element is not necessary . . . The fact that consent cannot serve as a defense to the crime of sexual slavery is another advance in international law.[45]

Oosterveld thus adopted as her own the WCGJ December 1997 position on sexual slavery: "Under international law, it does not matter whether a slave-like status was initiated by an 'agreement' or involved some exchange."[46]

Oosterveld's position was extreme along the range of positions adopted by feminists working on rape in armed conflict. It was an update of the hard-line structuralist feminist position on rape in the International Criminal Tribunal for the Former Yugoslavia (ICTY), which had been that there should be no consent defense *at all.* The argument was that women who had sex with combatants from the other side of an armed conflict were operating in coercive circumstances, and any consent they gave was meaningless. Evidence of consent should be inadmissible because no valid inference of meaningful consent could be drawn from it.[47] The ICTY very briefly adopted the no-consent-defense position, only to shift rapidly to a complex of rules that presume nonconsent from the coercive circumstances and that allow defendants to offer their proof on the issue only after it had been found to be probative in an in-camera hearing and to be devoid of any admissions by the complaining witness.[48] Rhonda Copelon, a leader in that phase of international feminist activism, promoted the tribunal's compromise position, arguing publicly that it would make the ICTY's rules easier to download into national law.[49] Based on personal communication, I believe she was also motivated by her knowledge that some women living in war zones really do want to maintain sexual alliances with combatants on the "other" side. That is, she wanted a carve-out from the strict no-consent-defense position because she respected women's autonomy to decide whom they would take as sexual partners. Probably because it was the most they could argue for, the official WCGJ position was to advocate the ICTY's compromise position on rape.[50] And this is why sexual slavery was an important innovation when it showed up on the WCGJ's and Oosterveld's agendas at Rome: sexual slavery was an end run around this concession. Oosterveld and the

WCGJ sought to define sexual slavery so that prosecutors could charge it instead of rape and foreclose all inquiry into consent. But remember, Oosterveld is a liberal feminist.

Why, given the vast differences between them, have liberal feminism and dominance feminism been so willing to merge? Each instance is its own story, but there is also a general framework making it possible again and again. Liberal feminism converts dominance feminism's super-capacious understandings of domination into *coercions* and uses them *within the liberal legal paradigm* to justify feminist social-control initiatives and to build them out into highly punitive GF projects. Only constraint justifies legal intervention in the supposedly free exchanges and relations of liberalism; in response, liberal and dominance feminism collaborated to argue that the social field is permeated by constraint of women by men. Though they may disagree about whether to promote minimalist or maximalist definitions of coercion, and about whether to use criminal law or "softer" legal tools to address the problems of domination, liberal and dominance feminisms have fallen in together on making this accommodation to liberal legalism.

All of this has led to a paradox in the relationship between American feminism and its governmental successes globally and stateside. Power and cultural feminisms are seriously contested within American feminist politics, but highly translatable into GF.

The contests are many. In the mid-1980s this conflict burst into life as the sex wars mentioned above, in which the wall-to-wall dysphoric view of sexuality propounded by dominance feminists encountered a pleasure-affirmative alliance of feminists, homosexuals, and—an emerging trend—post-identitarian queer theory. The power and cultural feminists' obsessively heterosexual view of gender came in for criticism from the same array of emerging voices. Their unremittingly pejorative view of men and masculinity and their reified populations of men and women proved unusable for women who had a more fluid view of power in gender relations, women who thought they had balls, and indeed everyone in the burgeoning youth culture of gender transitivity. Their laundry-list approach to "other differences"—that is, their half-hearted effort to account for race, class, postcolonial, age, and other gradients by reciting them as an afterthought—was flatly rejected by people focused on those forms of power and ethical concern.

Their analysis and their law reform agenda were part of the problem for Third World–affiliated feminists who did not appreciate the aptitude of dominance feminism for demonizing the men of the global South and setting themselves up to rescue brown women from brown men in the name of universal sisterhood.

Another example: in the United States, the religious-conservative / neo-abolitionist-feminist alliance achieved federal legislation called the Anti-Prostitution Loyalty Oath (APLO) barring any grant of federal aid to NGOs until they declare their unwavering refusal to promote prostitution. Feminists opposing them helped obtain a Supreme Court ruling saying that this rule was an unconstitutional interference with protected free speech—but only within U.S. borders.[51] Sex worker organizations in the global South, staggering to their feet under U.S. policy requiring them to sign the APLO in order to qualify for aid, encountered U.S. dominance feminism in the zombielike form of NGOs formed by their national sisters that were eager or willing to sign the oath.[52]

In the process, dominance feminism has begun to test the rightward limits of liberal feminism and to morph into a new strand of American *conservative* thought and action. Here are some characteristics of social conservatism that now appear in dominance feminist carceral projects: a commitment to social order and social control as the preeminent goals, an understanding of human sexuality as a profound challenge to social order requiring repression and delegitimation, a classification of the state as a protector and of women as a pervasively vulnerable social group in need of its protection (more like children than like men), a belief in the logic of repressive criminalization as the primary legal tool for dealing with social problems, and a profound distrust of women's choices when they diverge from this agenda. The danger for dominance feminism today seems not to be losing its edge in an alliance with liberal feminists, but losing its Left-liberal credentials entirely as it emerges as a new form of conservatism and situates itself in an expanding institutionalization of crime control.

The Multiply Determined Blindspotting of Materialist Feminism

Many strands of U.S. feminism draw, directly or indirectly, on the work of Karl Marx and the socialist critique of class exploitation. Here, economic class relations and processes are hypothesized to be of equal importance to sex, sexuality, and gender; capitalism matters as much as patriarchy; and redistribution is considered a far more powerful step in the direction of emancipation than rights. In their radical forms these feminisms intend revolution; in variously progressive and conservative forms they favor the social state; and always they are highly suspicious of liberal individualism and market ideology. Pending the revolution, people who draw their social theory from this conflicting and complex set of traditions gravitate to work on behalf of exploited labor, the poor, tenants and the homeless, immigrants, and those accused and convicted of crimes. Their strategy usually requires them to find advocacy roles that oppose the state, but even those—criminal defense work, labor union work—become incorporated within state governance broadly construed. The most "insider" places for them to be are probably the welfare system, immigration and labor regulation, governmental sectors that restrain the exploitative power of corporations, and, if they can get there, monetary and financial policymaking. New Deal and other leftists carry the commitments of socialism in a liberal direction toward the state and strive to redistribute using law.

Socialist feminism inherits an embattled legacy that is specific to the United States and that differentiates the spectrum of possibility for U.S. feminists from that faced by feminists in other historical contexts. It shares some causes of its marginality with socialism generally; others are specific to the genealogies of contemporary feminism.

Marxism and socialism in the United States never fully recovered from the Cold War role of the United States as the world leader of anticommunism or the McCarthy-era equation of leftism with treason. They suffered a second disabling brain drain when news of the Gulag emerged. With the fall of the wall, socialist thought and activism were widely deemed "proven wrong." Alliances in organized labor became stressed, first in the late 1960s by the conflicts between the New Left and the established labor movement, and then in the 1980s as neoliberal economic policy got a grip and shrank the unions to a vanishing fraction of their former strength.

The specifically feminist piece of this history takes us back to the late 1960s and the split of radical feminism from feminists participating more broadly in U.S. radical movements addressed to the war, to racial hierarchy, and to class domination. A New Left driven by young activists split from Old Left socialists. Repelled by their seniors' doctrinaire Marxist line, the New Left welcomed and fomented new intellectual and political trends flooding in from every direction. "Politico" feminists helped to produce this schism but committed themselves to working within the New Left. They invented a dual-systems (class and sex) radical politics and struggled with the male chauvinism of men running the movement. *It was from these politico feminists that radical feminists split* to form a new feminist movement focused solely on women's oppression. Dropping class analysis was a defining move for radical feminism.[53]

Socialist feminism continued to thrive well into the 1980s, largely as a theoretical project centered in the social sciences and in radical book series and journals. Consistently, these feminists wedged their Archimedes lever under the sexual division of labor. For some, the key was women's common relationship to the capitalist industrialist mode of production as unpaid producers of use values, reproducers of the workforce, and factors for consumption in the home. For others, the central issue was the economic organization of the home itself: a radical home economics. And for others, the participation of women in the paid workforce was crucial: prostitution and its relationship to heterosexual marriage; pink-collar and industrial labor; the dependence of capital on women's double day.[54]

But in a large and growing series of trends inside and outside feminism, the socialist feminists became increasingly marginal in U.S. feminist movements. The Althusserian turn away from (what was criticized as) simple base/superstructure analysis led American socialists, feminists included, to concentrate on ideology and culture as productive forces in human organization, and on psychology, semiotics, aesthetics, and ethnography as ways to examine the epistemic rather than the market-economic forces in generating social hierarchy. "The personal is the political" became the hypothesis, and Left political energy turned to understand the production not of economic systems but of subjectivities. Postmodernism emerged within feminism as well as outside it, suggesting to some leftists, feminists included, that fragmented processes rather than class antagonisms arranged in a resolutely over/under pattern characterized economic exploitation. Inside feminism, the turn to sexuality as the core structure produced a new conflict that absorbed feminist energy: Was human sexuality (nearly) pure danger, or the site of pleasure and danger both? Answers to that question could be fully engaged within U.S. feminism without referring even once to class.

All these processes facilitated the marginalization of economic-class analysis within feminism. Nancy Fraser, seeking to keep the socialist feminist flame alive, offers an arresting account of what happened then. As feminism became but one of many elements of a rising Left-multicultural politics of identity in the late 1980s and early 1990s, liberal and dominance feminism turned away from economic-systemic remedies toward recognition remedies, equality rights, and crime control—all articulated without reference to the economic system. Fraser sees the feminist embrace of identity politics as an unwitting but uncanny abandonment of the economic barricades, one that effectively cleared feminist resistance out of the path of the neoliberal historical steamroller. My own sense is that—however accurately she tells the story of socialist feminists drawn into the vortex of the rise of identity-based politics in the 1980s and 1990s—she elides the active role of radical feminism and, later, dominance feminism, in affirmatively dropping class analysis and making peace with rising neoliberalism.

She and many other feminists lament this turn from material distribution and leftist class analysis; we do too.[55] The materialist flame still burns, small but bright, in work by intellectuals,[56] intellectual collectives and networks,[57] and grassroots activists inventing and commandeering small-scale institutions.[58] It has been an important part of the renewed vitality of the Left in the mid-to-late 2010s, and all signs point to its continued, renewed energy in the Trump era. They can occasionally infiltrate mainstream organizations and divert their energies leftward,[59] but the Trump era has also created the political will for more outsider, resistance styles of engagement. We offer this book as one pathway back to a robust engagement with the distributive critique and redistributive projects of materialist feminism.

Notes

1. Sometimes the clientele of feminist advocacy includes transgender and gender-transitive projects; sometimes feminists adamantly refuse to admit T to the golden circle of concern. See Judith Butler, *Gender Trouble: Feminism and the Subversion of Identity* (New York: Routledge, 1990), for a foundational text extending feminism to gender as performance, and Janice G. Raymond, *The Transsexual*

Empire: The Making of the She-Male (Boston: Beacon Press, 1979), for a classic argument restricting feminist concern to "genetic women." This tension reappears when transgender politics turns to law. The primary form of G-trans to date—transgender politics assuming governance form—is "sexual orientation and gender identity" (SOGI), which splices gay and transgender projects onto each other. The transnational legal manifestations of the SOGI project are many; they include the Yogyakarta Principles: International Commission of Jurists, "The Yogyakarta Principles," March 2007, http://www.yogyakartaprinciples.org/, and the appointment of a SOGI special rapporteur to the UN Human Rights Council: UN Human Rights Council, Resolution 32/2, "Protection against Violence and Discrimination Based on Sexual Orientation and Gender Identity," June 30, 2016, para. 3, http://www.un.org/en/ga /search/view_doc.asp?symbol=A/HRC/RES/32/2. In the United States, a conflict over whether transgender students can use the bathroom that conforms with their gender identity went to the U.S. Supreme Court before the end of the Obama administration. G.G. v. Gloucester County School Board, 822 F.3d 709 (4th Cir. 2016), cert. granted, 137 S. Ct. 369 (2016), vacated and remanded, 137 S. Ct. 1239 (2017), and has produced intense Left/Right polarized dynamics under Trump. Feminists sometimes support and sometimes oppose these governance "successes," some because they seek to preserve the distinct identity of biological women (Brief of Amicus Curiae Women's Liberation Front in Support of Petitioner, G.G. v. Gloucester County School Board, No. 16-273 [U.S. Sept. 26, 2016]), and others because they resist the strong tendency to ratify strong forms of gender identity that emerge as SOGI takes legal form (Coalition of African Lesbians, "Activists Brief: Coalition of African Lesbians Says NO to a Special Rapporteur on Sexual Orientation, Gender Identity," May 29, 2016, http:// sxpolitics.org/activists-brief-coalition-of-african-lesbians-says-no-to-a-special -rapporteur-on-sexual-orientation-gender-identity/14809). As important as these developments are to GF, we think they deserve sustained separate attention.

2. We thus leave out many important forms of contemporary feminism that work in culture and pay little attention to state-based and state-like power. Feminism thrives in fashion, Internet and social media, art, literary criticism, religion, journalism, food politics, wellness and healing, and pedagogy. For an account of "marketplace feminism"—the media adoption of feminism as an immensely profitable commodity and commodity-enhancer—see Andi Zeisler, *We Were Feminists Once: From Riot Grrrl to Covergirl®, the Buying and Selling of a Political Movement* (New York: PublicAffairs, 2016).

3. In particular, see Karen Engle, "Feminist Governance and International Law: From Liberal to Carceral Feminism," in *Governance Feminism: Notes from the Field,* ed. Janet Halley, Prabha Kotiswaran, Rachel Rebouché, and Hila Shamir (Minneapolis: University of Minnesota Press, forthcoming).

4. Nancy J. Hirschmann and Kirstie M. McClure, *Feminist Interpretations of John Locke* (University Park: Pennsylvania State University Press, 2007).

5. For philosophical and political-theoretical elaborations of liberal feminism and feminist liberalism, see Amy R. Baehr, *Varieties of Feminist Liberalism* (Lanham, Md.: Rowman & Littlefield, 2004).

6. For Left/Right spectrumization projects, see Duncan Kennedy, *A Critique of Adjudication: Fin de Siècle* (Cambridge, Mass.: Harvard University Press, 1997), 46–56 (rights claims and courts in the United States); Gary Peller, "Race

Consciousness," *Duke Law Journal* 1990, no. 4 (1990): 758–847 (movements for racial emancipation in the United States); Lama Abu-Odeh, "Modernizing Muslim Family Law: The Case of Egypt," *Vanderbilt Journal of Transnational Law* 37, no. 4 (2004): 1043–146 (family law reform in Egypt).

7. Roe v. Wade, 410 U.S. 113 (1973); Harris v. McRae, 448 U.S. 297 (1980).

8. Ian Hacking, "Making Up People," in *Reconstructing Individualism: Autonomy, Individuality, and the Self in Western Thought*, ed. Thomas C. Heller, Morton Sosna, and David E. Wellbery (Stanford, Calif.: Stanford University Press, 1986), 222–36.

9. See, e.g., Judith Warner, "The Opt-Out Generation Wants Back In," *New York Times Magazine*, August 7, 2013, http://www.nytimes.com/2013/08/11/magazine /the-opt-out-generation-wants-back-in.html; Lisa Belkin, "The Opt-Out Revolution," *New York Times Magazine*, August 7, 2013, http://www.nytimes.com/2013/08/11 /magazine/the-opt-out-revolution.html?_r=0 (a republication of the article that appeared in print on October 26, 2003); Ann Marie Slaughter, *Unfinished Business: Women, Men, Work, Family* (New York: Random House, 2015); Sheryl Sandberg, *Lean In: Women, Work, and the Will to Lead* (New York: Alfred A. Knopf, 2013); Mary Anne Case, "How High the Apple Pie—A Few Troubling Questions about Where, Why, and How the Burden of Care for Children Should Be Shifted," *Chicago-Kent Law Review* 76, no. 3 (2001): 1753–86.

10. On the contract/crime paradigm, we turn to the work of our 2006 coauthor, Chantal Thomas, "Disciplining Globalization: International Law, Illegal Trade, and the Case of Narcotics," *Michigan Journal of International Law* 24, no. 2 (Winter 2003): 563–68 (exploring the concept of market "normalcy" as a basis for mediating the tension between liberalism and prohibitionism); "Undocumented Migrant Workers in a Fragmented International Order," *Maryland Journal of International Law* 25, no. 1 (2010): 188 (describing the Illegal Markets Project); "International Law against Sex Trafficking, in Perspective," Cornell Legal Studies Research Paper No. 13-85 (June 4, 2013): 29–30, http://ssrn.com/abstract=2274095 (manuscript presented at the Wisconsin–Harvard Workshop on International Economic Law and Transnational Regulation). See also Janet Halley, Prabha Kotiswaran, Hila Shamir, and Chantal Thomas, "From the International to the Local in Feminist Legal Responses to Rape, Prostitution / Sex Work, and Sex Trafficking: Four Studies in Contemporary Governance Feminism," *Harvard Journal of Law and Gender* 29, no. 2 (2006): 335–423. For a homologous account of how John Stuart Mill's harm principle drew liberal legal feminists to characterize the wrongs of gender as *harmful*—producing the politics of *injury* that supplements domination and constraint with a distinctively *affective* component—see Janet Halley, *Split Decisions: How and Why to Take a Break from Feminism* (Princeton, N.J.: Princeton University Press, 2006), 320–40.

11. Halley, *Split Decisions*, 323–26.

12. See, for instance, Kristen Bumiller, *In an Abusive State: How Neoliberalism Appropriated the Feminist Movement against Sexual Violence* (Durham, N.C.: Duke University Press, 2008) for resistance to the feminist turn to crime in the United States; and Alice M. Miller and Mindy Jane Roseman, eds., *Beyond Virtue and Vice: International Human Rights and the Criminal Regulation of Sexuality, Gender, and Reproduction* (Philadelphia: University of Pennsylvania Press, forthcoming) for

similarly critical assessments of its salience in international and transnational feminist projects.

13. For a classic treatment, see Angela P. Harris, "Race and Essentialism in Feminist Legal Theory," *Stanford Law Review* 42, no. 3 (1990): 581–616. For more recent interventions, see Mimi Kim, "Dancing the Carceral Creep: The Anti–Domestic Violence Movement and the Paradoxical Pursuit of Criminalization, 1973–1986" (working paper, Institute for the Study of Societal Issues, UC Berkeley, California, 2015); INCITE! Women of Color against Violence, *Color of Violence: The INCITE! Anthology* (Cambridge, Mass.: South End Press, 2016).

14. Libby Adler, *Gay Priori: A Queer Critical Legal Studies Approach to Law Reform* (Durham, N.C.: Duke University Press, 2018).

15. Janet E. Halley, "Like-Race Arguments," in *What's Left of Theory?*, ed. Judith Butler, John Guillory, and Kendall Thomas (New York: Routledge, 2000), 40–74.

16. In chapter 6 of this book, Rachel Rebouché argues that the same thing happened in international human rights argumentation. When the emphasis there shifted from formal equality toward substantive equality, from negative to positive rights—toward outcome-driven, women-specific rights assertion—women as mothers and caregivers came immediately to the fore.

17. See Preface, xiii.

18. Alice Echols, *Daring to Be Bad: Radical Feminism in America, 1967–75* (Minneapolis: University of Minnesota Press, 1989), 3–202.

19. Catharine A. MacKinnon, "Feminism, Marxism, Method, and the State: An Agenda for Theory," *Signs* 7, no. 3 (1982): 515–44; "Feminism, Marxism, Method, and the State: Toward Feminist Jurisprudence," *Signs* 8, no. 4 (1983): 635–58. (Note: further references to these works appear as "Feminism," followed by the subtitle.)

20. Catharine A. MacKinnon, *Sexual Harassment of Working Women: A Case of Sex Discrimination* (New Haven, Conn.: Yale University Press, 1979).

21. Halley, *Split Decisions,* 41–79.

22. See, e.g., Mary Daly, *Gyn/Ecology: The Metaethics of Radical Feminism* (Boston: Beacon Press, 1978).

23. MacKinnon, "Feminism: Toward Feminist Jurisprudence." For a discussion, see Halley, *Split Decisions,* 41–58.

24. Robin West, *Caring for Justice* (New York: New York University, 1997). For a discussion, see Halley, *Split Decisions,* 60–76.

25. Ellen C. DuBois, Mary C. Dunlap, Carol J. Gilligan, Catharine A. MacKinnon, and Carrie J. Menkel-Meadow, "Feminist Discourse, Moral Values, and the Law—A Conversation," *Buffalo Law Review* 34, no. 1 (Winter 1985): 11–87 (discussion held on October 19, 1984, at the law school of the State University of New York in Buffalo as part of the James McCormick Mitchell Lecture Series).

26. Frances E. Olsen, "The Family and the Market: A Study of Ideology and Legal Reform," *Harvard Law Review* 96, no. 7 (1983): 1497–578.

27. Gayle Rubin, "The Traffic in Women: Notes on the 'Political Economy' of Sex," in *Toward an Anthropology of Women,* ed. Rayna R. Reiter (New York: Monthly Review Press, 1975), 157–210. Major developments in queer theory, feminist and otherwise, undermined both the descriptive and prescriptive components of this distinction, and Rubin eventually stepped back from it. Gayle Rubin and Judith Butler, "Sexual Traffic, Interview," in *Feminism Meets Queer Theory,* ed. Elizabeth Weed and

Naomi Schor (Bloomington: Indiana University Press, 1997), 68–108. It nevertheless is a staple of international feminist law reform.

28. MacKinnon, "Feminism: An Agenda for Theory"; "Feminism: Toward Feminist Jurisprudence."

29. The Indianapolis ordinance defined pornography as "the graphic sexually explicit subordination of women, whether in pictures or in words, that also includes one or more of the following: (1) Women are presented as sexual objects who enjoy pain or humiliation; or (2) Women are presented as sexual objects who experience sexual pleasure in being raped; or (3) Women are presented as sexual objects tied up or cut up or mutilated or bruised or physically hurt, or as dismembered or truncated or fragmented or severed into body parts; or (4) Women are presented as being penetrated by objects or animals; or (5) Women are presented in scenarios of degradation, injury, abasement, torture, shown as filthy or inferior, bleeding, bruised, or hurt in a context that makes these conditions sexual; or (6) Women are presented as sexual objects for domination, conquest, violation, exploitation, possession, or use, or through postures or positions of servility or submission or display." Indianapolis Code. § 16–3(q) (1984), quoted in American Booksellers Ass'n. Inc., v. Hudnut, 771 F.2d 323, 324 (7th Cir. 1985), *aff'd*, 475 U.S. 1001 (1986).

30. Halley, *Split Decisions*, 192–207.

31. See Prabha Kotiswaran, "Revisiting the Material: Recasting the Sex Work Debates" and "Theorizing the Lumpen Proletariat: A Genealogy of Materialist Feminism on Sex Work," in *Dangerous Sex, Invisible Labor: Sex Work and the Law in India* (Princeton, N.J.: Princeton University Press, 2011), 24–49, 50–82, for an excellent genealogy.

32. Kathleen Barry, *Female Sexual Slavery* (Englewood Cliffs, N.J.: Prentice-Hall, 1979), 40.

33. Kathleen Barry, "Sexual Power," in *The Prostitution of Sexuality: The Global Exploitation of Women* (New York: New York University Press, 1995), 90 (the "aha" moment); Barry, "Human Rights and Global Feminist Action," in *Prostitution of Sexuality*, 276–320 (spinning out consequences of a Proposed Convention Against Sexual Exploitation).

34. Barry, "Sexual Power."

35. United Nations Development Programme, *Human Development Report 1992* (New York: Oxford University Press, 1992).

36. Barry, *Prostitution of Sexuality*, 175–78.

37. For example, see Suzanna Danuta Walters, "Introduction: The Dangers of a Metaphor—Beyond the Battlefield of the Sex Wars," *Signs* 42, no. 1 (2016): 1–9.

38. "Brief Amici Curiae of Feminist Anti-censorship Taskforce, et al.," in American Booksellers Ass'n. v. Hudnut, 771 F.2d 323, 475 U.S. 1001, reprinted in Nan D. Hunter and Sylvia A. Law, "Brief Amici Curiae of Feminist Anti-censorship Taskforce, et al., in *American Booksellers Association v. Hudnut*," *Michigan Journal of Law Reform* 21, nos. 1 and 2 (1987–88): 69–136.

39. Martha C. Nussbaum, "Whether from Reason or Prejudice: Taking Money for Bodily Services," *Journal of Legal Studies* 27, no. 2 (June 1998): 693–724.

40. Aya Gruber, Amy Cohen, and Kate Mogulescu, "Penal Welfare and the New Human Trafficking Intervention Courts," *Florida Law Review* 68, no. 5 (2016): 1333–402; Amy Cohen and Aya Gruber, "Governance Feminism in New York's Human

Trafficking Intervention Courts," in Halley, Kotiswaran, Rebouché, and Shamir, *Governance Feminism: Notes from the Field.*

41. U.S. Department of Justice, "University of Montana Findings Letter," https:// www.justice.gov/sites/default/files/opa/legacy/2013/05/09/um-ltr-findings.pdf (letter from the Department of Justice, Civil Rights Division, and DOE Office for Civil Rights to President Royce Engstrom and University Counsel Lucy France of the University of Montana, dated May 9, 2013).

42. See, e.g., Catharine A. MacKinnon, *Women's Lives, Men's Laws* (Cambridge, Mass.: Harvard University Press, 2005), 244.

43. For some of the Supreme Court's holdings requiring, for a finding of liability, that the unwanted sexual conduct be not merely subjectively but reasonably sufficiently severe or pervasive to harm the victim's educational or workplace performance, see Davis v. Monroe Co. Bd. of Ed., 526 U.S. 629, 681 (1999); Harris v. Forklift Systems, Inc., 510 U.S. 17, 21–22 (1993); Oncale v. Sundowner Offshore Services, Inc., 523 U.S. 75, 81 (1998). For a discussion, see Janet Halley, "The Move to Affirmative Consent," *Signs* 42, no. 1 (2016): 257–79.

44. Valerie Oosterveld, "Sexual Slavery and the International Criminal Court: Advancing International Law," *Michigan Journal of International Law* 25, no. 3 (2004): 605–51.

45. Ibid., 640 (all deletions and ellipses mine).

46. Women's Caucus for Gender Justice in the International Criminal Court, *Recommendations and Commentary for December 1997 PrepCom on the Establishment of an International Criminal Court United Nation Headquarters,* part III, recommendation 5 (1997) (on file with the author).

47. Janet Halley, "Rape in Berlin: Reconsidering the Criminalisation of Rape in the International Law of Armed Conflict," *Melbourne Journal of International Law* 9, no. 1 (2008): 86–91.

48. Rules of Procedure and Evidence of the International Criminal Tribunal for the Former Yugoslavia, U.N. Doc. IT/32/Rev.41 (March 8, 2008), Rule 96.

49. Halley, "Rape in Berlin," 99.

50. Women's Caucus for Gender Justice in the International Criminal Court, *Gender Justice and the International Criminal Court,* 45 (1998) (on file with the author).

51. Agency for Int'l Dev. v. Alliance for Open Soc'y Int'l, Inc., 133 S. Ct. 2321 (2013).

52. Debolina Dutta, "Rethinking Care and Economic Justice with Third-World Sexworkers," in *The Palgrave Handbook of Gender and Development: Critical Engagements in Feminist Theory and Practice,* ed. Wendy Harcourt (Basingstoke, U.K.: Palgrave Macmillan, 2016), 196–98.

53. Echols, *Daring to Be Bad,* 51–202.

54. Pat Armstrong et al., eds., *Feminist Marxism or Marxist Feminism: A Debate* (Toronto: Garamond Press, 1985); Nancy C. M. Hartsock, *Money, Sex, and Power: Towards a Feminist Historical Materialism* (New York: Longman, 1983); Zillah R. Eisenstein, ed., *Capitalist Patriarchy and the Case for Socialist Feminism* (New York: Monthly Review Press, 1978); Zillah R. Eisenstein, *The Radical Future of Liberal Feminism* (New York: Longman, 1981); Cynthia Grant Bowman, "Recovering

Socialism for Feminist Legal Theory in the 21st Century," *Connecticut Law Review* 49, no. 1 (2016): 117–70.

55. Hester Eisenstein, *Feminism Seduced: How Global Power Elites Use Women's Labor and Ideas to Exploit the World* (Boulder, Colo.: Paradigm Publishers, 2009); Nancy Fraser, *Scales of Justice: Reimagining Political Space in a Globalizing World* (New York: Columbia University Press, 2009).

56. E.g., Prabha Kotiswaran, *Dangerous Sex, Invisible Labor: Sex Work and the Law in India* (Princeton, N.J.: Princeton University Press, 2011); Nancy Fraser, *Justice Interruptus: Critical Reflections on the "Postsocialist" Condition* (New York: Routledge, 1997); Rosemary Hennessy, ed., *Materialist Feminism and the Politics of Discourse* (New York: Routledge, 1993); J. K. Gibson-Graham, *The End of Capitalism (As We Knew It): A Feminist Critique of Political Economy* (Minneapolis: University of Minnesota Press, 2006). A huge bibliography of leftist feminist work on the welfare state, work, and the family continues the project in legal studies. For just one example: Lucy Williams, "Poor Women's Work Experiences: Gaps in the 'Work/Family' Discussion," in *Labour Law, Work, and Family: Critical and Comparative Perspectives,* ed. Joanne Conaghan and Kerry Rittich (Oxford: Oxford University Press, 2005): 195–216. For an argument similar to ours about the turn to governance in the pro-gay movement, see Adler, *Gay Priori.*

57. E.g., *Rethinking Marxism: A Journal of Economics, Politics, and Society* (a publication of the Association for Economic and Social Analysis), http://www.rethinkingmarxism.org/; *Class Crits: Toward a Critical Legal Analysis of Economic Inequality,* http://classcrits.wordpress.com/; Institute for Global Law and Policy, Harvard Law School, http://www.harvardiglp.org/. All of these organizations sponsor regular conferences and workshops fostering intellectual law- and policy-reform agendas and activist projects.

58. E.g., J. K. Gibson-Graham, *A Postcapitalist Politics* (Minneapolis: University of Minnesota Press, 2006); Women in Informal Employment: Globalizing and Organizing (WIEGO), http://wiego.org.

59. For organizing strategies adopted by WIEGO in its effort to influence, for instance, the International Labour Organization's Domestic Workers Convention, Thai law on homeworkers' inclusion in social programs, and Ghana's regulation on health care for porters, see "Impact Stories," *WIEGO,* http://wiego.org/wiego/wiego-networks-impact.

CHAPTER 3

Dancing across the Minefield

Feminists Reflect on Generating, Owning, and Critiquing Power

JANET HALLEY

Our hunch is that every feminist with a will to power makes constant judgments about how to assess her options in gaining or relinquishing real-world power, and that feminism is a stronger force for good when it can open up a critical space in which to share the inevitable ambivalences, regrets, and leaps of faith that go with making those calls. In this chapter, we reflect on what is to be gained—and lost—by seeking this critically engaged stance.

When we first encouraged the sustained study of GF in 2006, we heard from some feminists that we simply did not understand how marginal and fragile feminist gains in state and near-state power really were. Feminists were still a *vox clamantis in deserto*. If some feminist ideas and interests had managed to find their way into law, these were crumbs from the table, compromises with patriarchy on patriarchy's terms not worthy of the name "feminist," tiny fragments of the full feminist agenda, which was not merely to ride along on the back of power but to transform it.

These clean-hands stances have some very estimable upsides. Truly being a voice crying in the wilderness presupposes no entanglement in actual power. The flame of one's feminism can burn pure. And feminists have often gained immense space for critical invention by standing resolutely outside—it can be a place of madness, but madness can be prophetic. This is the original meaning of the *vox clamantis in deserto*,[1] and it has been a productive stance for many feminists.[2]

Moreover, admitting one's powerlessness can be descriptively right. Institutional power can benefit from including the loyal opposition, garnering legitimacy for itself and sowing confusion among its critics, without handing over any really meaningful tools of governance. Putting up with this can be a necessary element of an incrementalist or Trojan horse strategy. Denouncing, meanwhile, the puny scope and distorted form of one's gains can be absolutely necessary if one is to keep the flame burning.

There are costs, of course. If you really are taking an outsider stance, you risk being punished for it. You can be hit with shaming campaigns, job denial, death of personal relationships, cross burning on your lawn, and other devastating personal and/or collective losses. The line between prophetess and madwoman is very thin and constantly moving, and it is possible to find oneself too far outside the range of legitimate disagreement to be trusted with any of the levers of power, high or low. These terrible costs—which can include imprisonment and even death, though for most social movements paying these costs is rare—can sometimes be converted into martyrdom, with all its upsides for the movement, but death is always bad for the martyr.

More equivocally, keeping the badness of power and the goodness of the cause in diametrically opposite places in your personal geopolitical map can be really bad for you. You can feel really good about yourself, living in a Manichean universe in which you have a corner on virtue. Your righteousness can run unchecked and become blindly vindictive; you can fall prey to manic grandiosity. You can lose the capacity for internal critique. And you can actually go mad.

Being a voice calling out in the desert and *representing oneself as one* are two different things, moreover—and here the downsides can really begin to accumulate. The conflicting demands of the social movement and the GF role may require feminists to "join up" while *posing* as outsiders. This is a performative task that a critical examination of GF has to detect and understand. It is quite distinct from joining up while *convincing oneself* that one remains an outsider. The former task lies well within the classic labors of an ethic of responsibility; the latter stance is magic realist and, we think, can be dangerous.

Ushering these judgments out of the closet involves *representing* them, and feminists (like participants in any resistant-but-engaged social movement) have developed a rich array of options for doing that. One way of understanding those options comes from Gayatri Chakravorty Spivak's celebrated article "Can the Subaltern Speak?"[3] Drawing on Karl Marx's *The Eighteenth Brumaire,*[4] Spivak addresses the problem—endemic to social movements seeking emancipation—that those movements must be *spoken for.*[5] In Marx's vision of the logic of capital, the proletariat would inevitably become a world movement demanding its own emancipation. The proletariat would be a class not only in itself but for itself.[6] But when the rise of the Second Empire made it clear to Marx that the proletariat had not united, and might never unite, in the struggle for revolution—that instead the French proletariat was just as reactionary as its new leaders—he faced head-on the problem that he, not a proletarian by any means, was speaking for *someone else's* emancipation and was pretty much doomed to continue doing so.

Catharine A. MacKinnon predicted that feminism would solve this problem once and for all, and become the first group forming, speaking, and acting as "a class 'in itself' and a class 'for itself'."[7] "Feminism," she opined, "is the first theory to emerge from those whose interest it affirms."[8] But Spivak used Marx's realization to confront the acute and highly complex failure of feminism to materialize in this morally unproblematic way. Spivak, a key figure in the subaltern studies movement, wrote "Can the Subaltern Speak?" to reflect on the problem that subaltern Indian women had been and still were being multiply erased by voluble and crisscrossing colonial, patriarchal, and class narratives about them. Reflecting explicitly on her position as a highly educated member of the cosmopolitan postcolonial Indian elite, Spivak observed that she could either walk away from their plight or speak for them by speaking about them. She decided on the essay's last page that the only responsible course she could take was to join in the production of discourses *about* them.

This is a problem faced by *every* social movement, even ones guided by individuals and groups sharing the movement's relation to the mode of production, key identity characteristic, or ideological commitment. Disagreements among the constituency about matters large and small, differentials of information and investment in the cause, conflicts of interest among the group, even rising to outright antagonisms—these problems cannot be forced into abeyance merely by securing leadership that shares the group's identity. The problem of vanguardism is endemic.

Following Marx, Spivak argued that those who speak for the subaltern woman *represent* them in two ways: as *proxies* and as *depictors*. *Being a proxy* means representing a constituency in the way a senator represents a state, a lawyer a client, an agent a principal: taking on the role of voicing another, taking on the responsibility for managing another's strategy and tactics, and even deciding on that other's goals. *Depicting* the constituency involves making it visible; giving it a face, a name, a story; constructing its image. Serving as a proxy for and depicting one's constituency are often inconsistent, sometimes conflicting activities; they have different forms of authority and of delegitimation, different temporalities and tools, and different effects on one's self and on the constituency. They can work smoothly together but are more likely to come into conflict. Spivak's essay is a breathtaking account of how proxies for and depictors of the subaltern had, since the very beginning of the colonial encounter, woven the very fabric of the subaltern's impossible existential and expressive situation.

We think that tracking the possibly inconsistent course of representation as proxy on one hand and as depiction on the other is helpful for understanding the various stances feminists have taken to their own will to power. Take, for instance, Spivak's decision, recorded in other writings and interviews, to go public with the idea of "strategic essentialism": the determination by antiessentialist thinkers to articulate "women" or "the subaltern" even as they critique those very categories.[9] Feminists who heed these calls take on the power to speak for other feminists: they take on a proxy role. They claim the authority to speak for the group by virtue of their membership in it.[10] At the same time, they depict the constituency of feminism *as* women, even though their own core feminist critiques call these depictions into question. They are depicting and acting as proxies *in self-aware bad faith,* and they think it is worth it.

From this split role, further divergences quickly emerge. The essentialist depiction, once set in motion in the *langue* of the state, operates within the various logics and politics *of* the state. It really can make a big difference if the judge, for instance, thinks he is dealing with women or recognizing rights to autonomy. No surprise: the lawyer speaks to the court in a language the court already understands; the court takes it up in order to act after its own fashion. But the *depiction* is contested within feminism, even or especially by those who advance it. The simple, placid, and assimilable message of the proxy can be backed by a raging furor within feminism about the decision to advance it. The authority and good faith of the proxy will be called into question; feminists who disagree with the strategy will redouble efforts to undermine the problematic depiction. The movement can move together as a tense coalition or split. Meanwhile, consequences within the state begin to cascade forth, pouring out into the constituency, sometimes delivering the benefits hoped for by the strategic essentialists, sometimes producing new, unfair outcomes that will be called unintended consequences but that may have been entirely predictable. All of this further fuels internal critique.

If calling the depiction "merely strategic" is a way of disavowing these consequences, the strategic feminists will have thrown their own effects into a blind spot; they risk at this point morphing into proxies with no sense of responsibility. But if calling attention to the collaborationist gesture opens a forum in and around feminism to study, describe, and assess those consequences, the representational space can also be a zone of feminist politics and a practice of responsible governorship. This is what Spivak did when she *published* her thinking about the danger and value of strategic essentialism. That space is fraught with danger and possibility, and in the rest of this section we set out some of the various ways in which feminists have avoided and engaged it.

The three snapshots we offer here are by no means the only ones we could showcase. But they draw the outlines of a range of feminist approaches to inclusion and critique, basically from magic-realist denial to near-exit, with costs and benefits all along the way.

Denial Is Not a River in Egypt

One option is to represent women inside real governance institutions while denying that one has any real reins of power in one's hands. The performative demands of governing can require this stance, and sometimes it can be totally accurate. But when it is not required, and not accurate, but sincerely felt, it can be disabling.

Our example of this comes from the UN. The UN is a rigidly hierarchical institution with very limited powers. The secretary general is at the mercy of the Security Council and the General Assembly and feels like a *vox clamantis* all the time; meanwhile, he manages the strict hierarchies ranked below him in ways that remind everyone every day that they are his subordinates. UN players looking up this hierarchy can become so preoccupied by their degraded role inside power that they narrow their constituency to *themselves*. For feminists in the institution, addressing one's own institutional needs can expand to occupy one's reformist horizon.

Joanne Sandler, a self-described feminist bureaucrat in the United Nations, worked within the UN Development Fund for Women (UNIFEM) in the early 2000s while it struggled to create the UN Entity for Gender Equality and the Empowerment of Women (UN Women). UNIFEM had been a subsidiary agency of the United Nations Development Programme, subject to its control, and it was just one of at least four equally subordinate agencies specializing in women's issues at the UN. In part because of Sandler's hard work, the General Assembly combined them all into UN Women in July 2010, raising the rank of the new entity so that it reports directly to the secretary general, has its own budget, and can sign its own checks. UN Women had a budget of $343 million in 2016–17.[11]

Looking forward in 2012, Sandler warned the feminists of UN Women that they would face not *new* challenges but *the same ones* that had plagued them in the days of UNIFEM. According to Sandler, the UN, both before and after the elevation of UN Women, was a patriarchal institution. Being an advocate for women in a patriarchal institution, she argued, is just like being a wife in a patriarchal marriage or even a woman in a battering relationship. UN advocates for gender equality undergo a process parallel to battered women's syndrome (BWS), cycling from denial to guilt to recognition to empowerment, but far too often stalling out at the guilt stage. Sandler predicted that UN Women, like UNIFEM before it, would be to the power structure of the UN what female subordination is to male domination: "It is systemic."[12]

According to Sandler, even though "patriarchy was most effective at limiting UNIFEM's reach and influence by failing to address the level of UNIFEM's leadership," once UN feminists had defeated that strategy, they still faced the "preservationist power of patriarchy." UN Women needed to recognize its ongoing "*institutional inequality*—that is positioning an entire organisation or unit and the people in it at a structural disadvantage because they work on gender equality."[13]

If you work on gender inequality you will suffer it. The proxy relationship that UN feminists bear to subordinated women worldwide disappears into a depiction in which *they* are the powerless ones. This turn makes institutional success within the UN at once impossible *and* the very substance of feminist emancipation. And so, even when they reach the stage of empowerment, their job is their own inclusion: they can become "inside feminist change agent[s]" who can "challenge the institutions of patriarchy and exclusion, whether in the Security Council, the justice system or . . . macroeconomic policymaking."[14] Inclusion is the goal; figuring out how to identify and serve the interests of women while managing global armed conflict, reforming justice institutions, and devising development policy—all of that can wait.

Sandler admits "half jokingly" that, to keep hope alive, she maintained a fantasy of suing her nonfeminist UN colleagues in a sublimely high court of justice for discrimination:

> I long harboured a fantasy of bringing the UN to some type of World Court of Justice for pervasive institutional gender discrimination towards UNIFEM. I would think about the grievances and examples that we would document as evidence in the war room where we built the case. I would see the court room itself, with the plaintiff (UNIFEM) being represented by a multi-national team of brilliant male and female lawyers. I would imagine powerful individuals who had been particularly callous and denigrating about gender equality having to defend their policies and actions. And then I would envision the precedent that it would set and how colleagues who work in gender units, national machineries for women, and other gender "machinery" would stand up in all parts of the world to resist and change their status and impact. This fantasy has rescued me during the low points in the lack of support for gender equality during my dozen years in the UN.[15]

Note the limited scope of Sandler's two remedies: just as her bureaucrats are liberated from BWS through empowerment *within the UN,* her plaintiffs enjoy a vindication that emboldens the "gender 'machinery'" to assert its status and power *in the UN system.* All reference to distributional consequences for actual women in the world drops out of the picture.

Owning Power

The Australian femocrats are a large and diverse cadre of feminists who got installed in state and federal bureaucracy starting in 1972, waxing and waning thereafter in tandem with the fates of the Labour Party,[16] as long as the Left was redistributive in focus. Starting around 2007, femocrat strength depended on feminists' ability to find issues—like gender-based violence—that were not traditionally Left-redistributive and therefore could appeal to increasingly neoliberal centrist and conservative governments.[17] They very early adopted the term "femocrats" to both blazon forth and sardonically devalue their role in government. At the same time, using the term amounted to a public admission that a cadre of feminists had some institutional powers and that sometimes it would be strategically prudent to admit it. Feminists sometimes use the term "entryism" to signal the decision to join the state but only as newcomers, tethered to the threshold.[18] Calling yourself a femocrat admits that you have arrived, that you know it, and that you are prepared to deal with the representational dilemmas that go with being inside. In Marx's and Spivak's terms, calling themselves femocrats enabled these Australian feminists to own the role of proxy with all its problematic relations of delegation and (un)accountability, and the role of depiction with all its theatrical spotlights and scrims.

Femocrats poured out their aspirations, anxieties, strategies, and tactics in interviews with Hester Eisenstein, an American feminist who joined their ranks from 1980 to 1988. Eisenstein published these interviews, embedded in consistently clear-eyed analysis, in the GF must-read book *Inside Agitators: Australian Feminists and the State*.[19] Defining femocrats as feminists working in bureaucracy,[20] Eisenstein exposed the representational double bind in which she and her sisters labored:

As Anne Summers wrote, femocrats were inevitably caught between two *roles*: the mandarin and the missionary. *Mandarin* is the sardonic characterization for bureaucrats: elite, inaccessible, guardians of government secrets. *Missionary* is the bureaucratic term for an uncompromising promoter of a political cause, someone who is discredited by virtue of "having an agenda." If femocrats *acted like* proper mandarins, especially in Canberra, they would *behave as* loyal bureaucrats who won the confidence of their colleagues by *playing by* the bureaucratic rules. They would not leak confidential documents; they would submit gracefully to a policy decision that went against their interests; and so on. In this case, they would lose the trust of the women's movement and be accused of selling out. If, however, they *behaved as* missionaries and fought publicly for the issues they believed in, they would lose their colleagues, trust [*sic*] and become ineffective within the bureaucracy.[21]

Eisenstein here depicts the femocrats' persistent dilemma: how, at any decision point, would a femocrat position herself as a representative of women / women's interests / feminism or, alternatively, as a representative of bureaucratic interests (what proxy role would she adopt); and what garb would she don to convince fellow bureaucrats and/or fellow feminist activists that she was smoothly incorporated in their field of action. How would she depict her loyalties when faced with two audiences demanding conflicting performances? Note how performative Eisenstein's femocrats are: they characterize themselves "sardonic[ally]," they "act like" their roles, "behave as" other roles, and "play by the . . . rules." Eisenstein's endlessly interesting account discloses GFeminists who knew this double bind and its myriad representational capacities in intricate detail but refused to "be caught" in it. Instead, they worked and reworked it until burnout or outright defeat swamped them.

Just one anecdote may suffice.[22] The women's section of a teachers' union pressed Ann Morrow, then a feminist minister of education, to put women's pay disparities on the collective bargaining agenda. It was a classic feminist issue: pay raises tracked seniority; taking time out from work meant losing all one's accrued seniority; and women of childbearing age were suffering severe pay consequences, even for short maternity breaks. When Morrow told the teachers that she had no jurisdiction over a discrimination claim like theirs, they threw down the feminist gauntlet: "You call yourself a feminist, you do it!"[23] Her initial reaction, as she recalled it to Eisenstein, was to "play the same sort of game" with them. She immediately threw responsibility for the issue back on the women teachers, saying she could do nothing until they got their union reps (all men) to bring the issue to the table. She knew it was a "dirty trick"—one she had confronted on the receiving end dozens of times—but she did not disclose that. Instead, she told them it was simple *"Realpolitik."* Meanwhile, she went to her minister and the state's negotiators and insisted that the political cost of ignoring the issue would be too high *for them*: "Morrow felt she could not show the women who had approached her that she was prepared to use her power on their behalf. Thus, although she acted in a way that showed a sense of accountability to the women teachers, she was not free to tell them about it."[24] Her profile as a proxy diverged, diametrically, from her profile as a depictor.

In Morrow's GF sensibility, movement feminists calling her feminist good faith into question was not a moral crisis; it was a move in a game, a flash reveal of the tools at the teachers' disposal. And it moved her to pick up her own distinctively bureaucratic tools—tools she was willing to use even though she knew full well they were "dirty." Morrow slalomed between loyalty to the women teachers and loyalty to the bureaucracy, serving as proxy for both of them at the level of tactics. And she engaged in deep manipulation of an *image* of her proxy role: she selectively disclosed to and withheld from the women teachers elements of her course of action that simultaneously slammed and served them.

Eisenstein's account here and throughout makes it possible to argue that feminist architects of a large takeover of important governmental levers remained loyal to feminist goals and solidarities precisely because they carried an explicit ethos that GFeminists must and do work with unclean hands, all the way up and down the power hierarchies that they inhabit.

The Move to Critique

Many of Eisenstein's accounts of Australian femocrats involve patently double-agent proxies who engage in substantial subterfuge when they depict. Their role perfidy is an open secret. They divide and select among their audiences. They project depictions of themselves and their constituencies with a highly attuned sense of what each audience wants to hear, its tolerance for messages it does not like, and its ability to punish them if they send too little of the former and too much of the latter.

But what if the insider/outsider decides to project critique to the broader feminist community in ways that can be noticed within the legal institutions they are infiltrating? Eisenstein, after all, *published* her accounts of feminist subterfuge, and her femocrat colleagues participated in interviews with her knowing that she was going to make their assessments of their power strategies public.

We think such acts of public critique are absolutely essential now that feminists and feminist ideas are so firmly embedded in legal institutions and legal power.[25] But they can be costly: insider-insiders often feel compelled to attack any feminist who does it, at the very least by depriving her of her insider credentials and her insider job and at the very most by marshaling major institutional resources to discredit her and her ideas, defund her projects, and leave her constituents out in the cold. Why is public critique essential, and what are the costs?

Kate Bedford's gripping articles and book on the World Bank's policy for families, gender, and sexuality in Latin America offer a way of exploring both of these questions.[26] This series of works is based on Bedford's long terms of participant observation and in-depth local interviews about World Bank programming in the Caribbean, Ecuador, and Argentina. She worked closely with, and interviewed, state feminists, nongovernmental organizations, and individuals working within, around, and against the bank. At the time she did this work, the devastating impacts of the World Bank's structural adjustment policies—pushing solely market-centered development plans as hard conditions for development loans—were ricocheting all around the local economies where she worked, while the World Bank itself had moved on to its later, softer, more social approach, combining social planning with market-driven reforms and replacing top-down loan conditionality with local buy-in. Bedford shows in depth how some elements of the World Bank's social policy for families were congenial to her feminism and that of her local feminist allies, and others starkly repugnant to them. Over the course of the three publications, Bedford reflects at considerable length on the reasons for keeping the flame of hope for the World Bank's role alive while engaging in risky critique.

The World Bank's new program involved motivating women to join the paid workforce, motivating men to be better husbands and fathers, and motivating men and women to experience their heterosexual merger to be emotionally, morally, and economically redemptive. All of this would benefit the overall goal of economic development because it would make families more resilient to the shocks of market forces and enable them to replace the shrinking/collapsing public welfare budget with market earnings and mutual dependency. The market and the family as private welfare systems: never let it be said that neoliberal economic policy lacks plans for human intimacy.

Bedford and her feminist allies found much to support in this large shift. It replaced market-side reform that had precipitously and vastly increased women's labor burden without noticing it. Women had been whipsawed by structural adjustment, super-activated to get paid employment at the very moment that public welfare support for their care responsibilities disappeared. New World Bank policy paid more than lip service to the problem of women's roles in paid and unpaid work and the whole gendered and sexual political economy attached to that problem. It actively engaged feminist ideas about social reproduction in liberal political economies. Many ideas of socialist/materialist feminists working on gender and sexuality in liberal political economies were "selectively incorporated," as Kerry Rittich has aptly noted,[27] into the bank's newly social program.

This shift offered once-in-a-lifetime opportunities for leftist feminists like Bedford. She and her allies liked the space it created to work on domestic violence. They found ways of smuggling nonnormative sexual subjects (happily single mothers, sex workers, lesbians), and even contraception as a method of reproductive health, into the funding stream. The simple fact that the relevant economies were churning while the bank was shifting policy meant space for transgression—for what Bedford calls "progressive seizure."[28] Her articles and her book contain gemlike examples of canny, careful, and profound progressive seizures at the local level.

But Bedford also found many elements problematic. She objected to the idea that the poor were responsible for their poverty, that poor Third World men were the demons of the operation and needed serious criminal control and/or therapy, that day care centers were off the agenda and extended-family care provision on it instead, and that law and policy now enforced the idea that heterosexual complementarity was the optimal sexuality. As a leftist she objected to the idea that markets were inevitable and the solution to everything, that public welfare could shrink to almost nothing in favor of private welfare provision through employment and the family, and that affective life could and should be pushed and pulled into shape until it served so-called market imperatives.

Bedford published three times about this complex mesh of engagement with critique: an article in 2008, a book in 2009, and another article in 2013.[29] Longer versions of the articles appear in the book. It is amazing to watch her struggle with the costs and benefits of engagement and critique. There is definitely a before-and-after story here. In 2008 she seems committed to moral purity; in her later publications that stance is replaced by a highly articulate stance of internal critique.

As she brings her 2008 essay on Ecuador to a close, Bedford first sets the bank up as "them" and feminists as "us," and tries to push all responsibility for these policies she rejects onto "them." She breaks this distinction down, acknowledging feminist authorship of many of the bank's policy ideas—only to scare herself and flee back to moral purity.

> Since 1995 the Bank has opened up to other languages, including those that sound far less foreign to feminist policymakers. The distinction between "them" and "us" is far harder to draw when we talk about empowerment as balanced complementary sharing, when we use promises of happy loving couples to get support, when we frame certain men as pathologically violent and irresponsible and seek to include them through domestication. To know how [to answer the question, who speaks these policies, them or us?], then, we must first know what the master's language is, in order that we can know what concessions we are making: how "his" language influences "our" policymaking, and *when "we" are actually generating that language ourselves.* In this sense I suggest that the Bank's current solution to the social reproduction dilemma relies on, and reinforces, common sense languages about sexuality and masculinity that *should not be ours.*[30]

The argument's emotional arc has two stages, which I have emphasized with italics. Bedford first directly faces the possibility that the bank's new household policies are not merely feminist in origin but are being generated by feminists speaking *as* the bank. As feminist ideas assume the mantle of governance and become common sense, they merge into neoliberal ideas that Bedford finds repellent ("the master's language").

This is a crisis for her both in her proxy role and in her representation of feminism—it is way, way too inside—and she suddenly jumps register to what *ought to be*: feminists going forward *should not* be representing, as proxies or as depictors, in this way. Their moral imperative lies *outside*.

Six years later, Bedford published a drastically shortened version of her book chapter on Argentina's Programa de Promoción del Fortalecimiento de la Familia y el Capital Social (Family Strengthening and Social Capital Promotion Program, or PROFAM) and closed it with a very different prescription, taking full responsibility for her unclean hands and insisting that, though actively harmful in many ways, feminists can and should stay involved in the dirty business of World Bank social engineering.

The context for this shift is significant. Bedford's 2008 essay on Ecuador appears in a volume titled *Global Governance: Feminist Perspectives,* which promises to "bring feminist perspectives to bear on the analysis of global governance."[31] The editors encouraged their feminist contributors to take a stance outside governance: it was us analyzing them. But Bedford's 2013 essay appears in a volume titled *Feminist Strategies in International Governance,* where editors Gülay Caglar, Elisabeth Prügl, and Susanne Zwingel explicitly acknowledge so much that is central to the study of GF even in the simple words of their title. Feminists are *in* global governance, they are *strategic* in what they do there (both proxy and depiction are explicitly instrumental), and they have strate*gies* to deploy there. Caglar, Prügl, and Zwingel's volume presents GF as a question not of static domination and subordination, or of monolithic feminist solidarity, but of fragmented and evolving, even potentially conflicting, strategies and tactics.[32]

Bedford's contribution to this later volume first notes that criticizing PROFAM could cause schism between the feminists, the bank, and the church and endanger the "under-the-radar spaces available to those who have smuggled in condoms and sex workers to family strengthening projects."[33] Depicting their constituency boldly and explicitly would reveal the wide gap between it and the constituency envisioned by the bank and the church, and could incite the bank to strip the feminists who did so of their proxy credentials.

Bedford goes on:

My own preference is to take that risk: to advocate for an explicit conversation about who gains, who loses, and what becomes harder to fight for in women's organizing when we endorse this ideal of governing markets and intimacies through sharing balance.[34]

This bold move cracks open the misleading merger of feminist proxy and depiction projects: Bedford is open to learning anew whom she advocates for and how these constituencies can be made visible both among feminists *and* to the bank. She calls for a distributional analysis—for asking who wins, who loses—*before* deciding what feminists *ought to do*. And she acknowledges that some of her feminist allies think that taking stock out in the open is an unaffordable risk. She has thought about it, and disagrees with them.

We think that is a path forward for a robust, renewable GF.

Notes

1. Isa. 40:3; John 1:23.
2. For four very different outsider stances, see, e.g., Mary Daly, "Sin Big (A Feminist's Personal Story)," *New Yorker* 72, no. 2 (February 26 / March 4, 1996): 76–82; Mary Joe Frug, "Re-reading Contracts: A Feminist Analysis of a Contracts Casebook," *American University Law Review* 34 (1985): 1065–140; Valerie Solanas, *S.C.U.M., Society for Cutting Up Men, Manifesto* (New York: Olympia Press, 1968); Judith Butler, *Gender Trouble: Feminism and the Subversion of Identity* (New York: Routledge, Chapman, and Hall, 1990). See also the discussion of radical feminism in the United States before its turn to the state in the Preface, xiii, and in chapter 2, 32–33.
3. Gayatri Chakravorty Spivak, "Can the Subaltern Speak?," in *Marxism and the Interpretation of Culture,* ed. Cary Nelson and Lawrence Grossberg (Urbana: University of Illinois Press, 1988), 271–313.
4. Karl Marx, *The Eighteenth Brumaire of Louis Bonaparte* (New York: International Publishers, 1963).
5. Spivak, "Can the Subaltern Speak?," 272–76.
6. Karl Marx, *The Property of Philosophy* (New York: International Publishers, 1963), 125, 173. For a discussion, see Janet Halley, *Split Decisions: How and Why to Take a Break from Feminism* (Princeton, N.J.: Princeton University Press, 2006), 238–41.
7. Catharine A. MacKinnon, "Feminism, Marxism, Method, and the State: An Agenda for Theory," *Signs* 7, no. 3 (1982): 535n48.
8. Ibid., 543.
9. Gayatri Chakravorty Spivak, "In a Word: Interview," in *Outside in the Teaching Machine* (New York: Routledge, 1993): 1–28; Spivak, "Subaltern Studies: Deconstructing Historiography," in *The Spivak Reader,* ed. Donna Landry and Gerald MacLean (New York: Routledge, 1996), 203–35.

10. For a critique of the "authority of experience" as a basis for proxy/depictor legitimacy, see Joan W. Scott, "The Evidence of Experience," *Critical Inquiry* 17, no. 4 (1991): 773–97.

11. UN Women, "2016–17 Annual Report," 45, http://www2.unwomen.org/-/media/annual-report/attachments/sections/library/un-women-annual-report-2016-2017-en.pdf?vs=2125.

12. Joanne Sandler, "Inside the UN Bureaucratic Machine: What Prospects for UN Women?," in *Strategies of Feminist Bureaucrats: UN Experiences*, ed. Joanne Sandler and Aruna Rao, IDS Working Paper, vol. 2012, no. 397 (July 2012): 15–19.

13. Ibid., 11–14.

14. Ibid., 16–18.

15. Ibid., 19.

16. Hester Eisenstein, *Inside Agitators: Australian Femocrats and the State* (Philadelphia: Temple University Press, 1996).

17. Susan Harris Rimmer and Marian Sawer, "Neoliberalism and Gender Equality Policy in Australia," *Australian Journal of Political Science* 51, no. 4 (2016): 742–58. See chapter 2, 39–44, on the compatibility of a sexual-violence GF agenda with market-based liberal and neoliberal legal and policy thinking.

18. Kate Bedford, "Introduction," in *Developing Partnerships: Gender, Sexuality, and the Reformed World Bank* (Minneapolis: University of Minnesota Press, 2009), xvii.

19. Eisenstein, *Inside Agitators*. The literature on Australian femocrats is large and fascinating: Anna Yeatman, *Bureaucrats, Technocrats, Femocrats: Essays on the Contemporary Australian State* (Sydney: Allen & Unwin, 1990); Louise Chappell, "The 'Femocrat' Strategy: Expanding the Repertoire of Feminist Activists," *Parliamentary Affairs* 55, no. 1 (2002): 85–98; Marian Sawer, "Australia: The Fall of the Femocrat," in *Changing State Feminism*, ed. Joyce Outshoorn and Johanna Kantola (Basingstoke, U.K.: Palgrave Macmillan, 2007), 20–40; Sawer, "Femocrat," in *The Wiley Blackwell Encyclopedia of Gender and Sexuality Studies*, ed. Nancy A. Naples (Maldon, Mass.: John Wiley & Sons, 2016), 1–2. The self-conscious and explicit adoption of a femocrat identity helped to spur significant efforts to assess GF at the national and international levels. See, for example, Dorothy E. McBride and Amy G. Mazur, *The Politics of State Feminism: Innovation in Comparative Research* (Philadelphia: Temple University Press, 2010); Lee Ann Banaszak, *The Women's Movement Inside and Outside the State* (Cambridge: Cambridge University Press, 2010).

20. Eisenstein, *Inside Agitators*, 69.

21. Ibid., 87 (citations omitted).

22. Ibid., 97–99.

23. Ibid., 99.

24. Ibid.

25. See Wendy Brown and Janet Halley, "Introduction," in *Left Legalism / Left Critique,* ed. Brown and Halley (Durham, N.C.: Duke University Press, 2002), 1–37.

26. Kate Bedford, "Governing Intimacy in the World Bank," in *Global Governance: Feminist Perspectives*, ed. Shirin Rai and Georgina Waylen (Basingstoke, U.K.: Palgrave Macmillan, 2008), 84–106; Bedford, *Developing Partnerships: Gender, Sexuality, and the Reformed World Bank* (Minneapolis: University of Minnesota

Press, 2009); Bedford, "Economic Governance and the Regulation of Intimacy in Gender and Development: Lessons from the World Bank's Programming," in *Feminist Strategies in International Governance,* ed. Gülay Caglar, Elisabeth Prügl, and Susanne Zwingel (London: Routledge, 2013), 233–48.

27. Kerry Rittich, "The Future of Law and Development: Second Generation Reforms and the Incorporation of the Social," *Michigan Journal of International Law* 26, no. 1 (2004): 223.

28. Bedford, *Developing Partnerships,* 179.

29. Bedford, "Governing Intimacy"; Bedford, *Developing Partnerships*; Bedford, "Economic Governance."

30. Bedford, "Governing Intimacy," 104–5 (emphases added).

31. Shirin Rai and Georgina Waylen, "Introduction: Feminist Perspectives on Analyzing and Transforming Global Governance," in Rai and Waylen, *Global Governance,* 1–18.

32. Gülay Caglar, Elisabeth Prügl, and Susanne Zwingel, "Introducing Feminist Strategies in International Governance," in Caglar, Prügl, and Zwingel, *Feminist Strategies in International Governance,* 3–4.

33. Bedford, "Economic Governance," 246.

34. Ibid.

PART II

FROM THE TRANSNATIONAL TO THE LOCAL

CHAPTER 4

Governance Feminism in the Postcolony

Reforming India's Rape Laws

PRABHA KOTISWARAN

Part I of this book has powerfully demonstrated the global reach of GF in a range of policy arenas. I examine these developments through a postcolonial lens, specifically in the context of India, and ask whether Indian feminism demonstrates the telltale strategies of Anglo-American GF. A vast literature elaborates on how the Indian women's movement (IWM) and Anglo-American feminism have experienced similar structural shifts, including institutionalization into nongovernmental organizations (NGOs) with funding from the state and foreign funders,[1] the loss of political edge with the emergence of "9-to-5 feminists,"[2] ideological fragmentation in the face of globalization, the emergence of conservative religious forces, generational shifts, and a move away from mass-based political struggles to a more collaborative relationship with the state.[3] If Anglo-American GF arose partly from these shifts, the flowering of Indian GF should come as no surprise.

Postcolonial Governance Feminism in the Making

In recent years, the Indian Parliament has adopted a number of woman-friendly laws, including the Protection of Women from Domestic Violence Act of 2005 (PWDVA); the Sexual Harassment of Women at Workplace (Prevention, Prohibition and Redressal) Act of 2013 (SH Act); and most recently, the Criminal Law (Amendment) Act of 2013 (CLA). Feminists have been key to the passage of these laws.[4]

Through an examination of the 2013 rape law reforms, I ask three central questions, the first two of which are the focus of this chapter: first, can we discern the emergence of Indian GF? Second, what are the implications of the emergence of Indian GF for how we understand transnational feminism? Third, even as Indian feminism finds a foothold within conventional conduits to state power, how does it relate to or reconfigure itself in light of the shift in the state's political functions from government to governance[5] to use both its juridical and discursive powers to govern its political subjects who in turn also self-regulate? By mapping Indian feminists' efforts to amend rape law from 1979 onward and their points of access to the state, I argue that Indian feminism has entered a governance mode in light of three parameters, namely, an increased reliance on criminal law, a deep commitment to a highly gendered reading of sexual violence, and a diluted oppositional stance vis-à-vis state power. I describe the emergence of Indian GF but retain a dispassionate normative stance toward it. Instead, I assess the likely distributive effects of the new rape law with a view to contributing to the self-reflexive ethos of the IWM, including in relation to its increased influence within the corridors of state power.[6]

While it is tempting to read the emergence of Indian GF in terms of the pressing down of highly influential strands of Western carceral feminism on a local context, I argue that Anglo-American GF has had rather limited and contingent influence on Indian feminist thinking despite the former's recent successes in shaping the international law of rape and trafficking. This is because domestic elites, especially legal advocacy elites (feminists included), may borrow transnationally as they interact with feminists from around the world in spaces of transnational modernity[7] but are fairly opportunistic and strategic in doing so. For the most part, the national political and legal landscapes have been far more significant. In fact, as feminist movements around the world gain legitimacy and influence, we can discern "varieties" of GF.

I offer a word of clarification here regarding terminology. Although Halley in chapter 2 uses the term "dominance feminism" to encompass both power feminism and cultural feminism, both forms of dominance feminism do not play out in the Indian context. Hence I focus mostly on "power feminism" and use the term "radical feminism" to connote it. Despite broad structural similarities, Indian GF differs from

Anglo-American GF[8] in at least two respects. The first relates to the use of criminal law. Where in the past decade U.S. radical feminism has been comfortable with carceral projects, Indian GF, even when relying heavily on criminal law, is more skeptical of it, given the extraordinary violence and corruption of the postcolonial state as well as GF's intellectual roots in materialist thought (which views the state as an instrument of class domination). Another significant difference is the presence of a strong political Left in India and an equally vocal materialist, even Marxist feminism that calls into question radical feminist tendencies within Indian GF. These points of convergence and divergence between radical feminism and materialist feminism have political effects, as I demonstrate in relation to the issue of sex work.

Finally, while we define GF to include the instantiation of feminists and feminist ideas into state and state-like power, we are also mindful of how state power extends well beyond the juridical into the discursive or governmental realm. The CLA process, for instance, overhauled rape law but also introduced trafficking offenses. Rape and trafficking in the Indian context have distinct mobilizational profiles, in temporal and substantive terms. Struggles over rape law reform define the very core of the IWM, while trafficking has less domestic resonance. The historical association of trafficking with sex work—an issue riddled by intense feminist polarization both internationally and among Indian feminists—led Indian feminists to largely ignore the problem of trafficking, just as they had historically ignored sex work.[9] The 2013 CLA reform process opened a discussion between feminist and sex workers' groups, and I suggest that a fuller account of GF becomes possible by considering not only how feminists infiltrate state power but also how they form alliances with population groups subject to the state's juridical and governmental powers and whose interests feminists have not prioritized in their law reform agenda. In a companion chapter in *Governance Feminism: Notes from the Field,* I map the struggles in 2013 of feminists and sex workers around rape and sex work / trafficking, respectively, to compare their varied mobilizational bases, their differential perceptions of political opportunities, and their dramatically different dispositions toward state law.[10] I focus on rape in this chapter.

Nirbhaya's Rape and Murder: An Unforeseen Political Opportunity

The incident that triggered the current phase of feminist rape law reform was the brutal gang rape and murder in December 2012 of Jyoti Pandey, a twenty-three-year-old Indian physiotherapy student (the media labeled her Nirbhaya, or "the fearless one"). This event mobilized large-scale protests all over India against state inaction toward violence against women.

On December 16, Nirbhaya and her friend left a South Delhi mall after watching the movie *Life of Pi*. They boarded a private bus (which was operating illegally), and as the bus circled about South Delhi, five men and a juvenile gang-raped and sodomized Nirbhaya and injured her friend before throwing them out of the bus near a fly-over (or bridge), where they lay naked and wounded. The police were eventually called but reportedly spent forty-five minutes arguing about jurisdiction over the case. Nirbhaya spent thirteen days in a precarious medical condition before she died in a Singapore hospital. Large-scale protests led by students demanding state action against Nirbhaya's rape erupted all over India. The federal and Delhi governments fumbled to respond to the growing protests. They used tear gas and water canons against the crowds and imposed a curfew for fear of a so-called law and order situation.

A Delhi fast-track court was set up to try the five accused adults. The juvenile defendant was sent to a reform center for three years. One of the accused men died in Delhi's high-security Tihar jail, perhaps by suicide or murder. The fast-track trial court returned a guilty verdict within eight months on thirteen counts, including murder and rape, and sentenced all four remaining defendants to death. Under Indian law, the death penalty is awarded only in the "rarest of rare" cases for murder and must be confirmed by a higher court. Within six months, the Delhi High Court upheld the sentence. On appeal, the Indian Supreme Court stayed the death penalty against all four convicts, at least two of whom claimed that their right to a fair trial had been compromised given the intense public pressure to execute them by hanging and that they were compelled to retain a state-appointed defender instead of their advocate of choice. In May 2017, the Indian Supreme Court upheld the Delhi High Court's sentence awarding the death penalty.

The public debate in the aftermath of Nirbhaya's rape and murder was shrill with calls for the death penalty and chemical castration. The federal government appointed a three-member committee headed by a former chief justice of the Indian Supreme Court, Justice Jagdish Verma, to suggest law reform. The other committee members were Justice Leila Seth, a retired female judge, and Gopal Subramaniam, a former solicitor general. The Verma Committee solicited feedback from the public through advertisements in major daily newspapers, and received an extraordinary 70,000 submissions. In the report, completed within a month, Justice Verma challenged the government to act immediately.[11] The president of India promulgated the Criminal Law (Amendment) Ordinance of 2013 (Presidential Ordinance), in February 2013. When Parliament reconvened in March, it passed the CLA, which replaced the Presidential Ordinance to amend the rape-related provisions in the Indian Penal Code of 1860, and introduced several new provisions criminalizing violence against women.

The Postcolonial Policy Space: Terms, Actors, and the Language of Reform

For feminists, the dull pain of decades of campaigning in the face of stonewalling by the state was transformed overnight into a renewed possibility for reform. Rape was catapulted into the mainstream of public life, whereas up until 2012, it was almost exclusively a feminist concern.[12] Rape had enjoyed a degree of feminist convergence not known to other issues, and considerable social resonance. Indeed, when the Indian Supreme Court acquitted two police constables who raped Mathura, a fourteen- to sixteen-year-old tribal girl, inside a police station in 1979, protests against the decision had launched the IWM. Nirbhaya's rape was undoubtedly extreme, involving as it did an extraordinarily violent gang of strangers, using techniques of torture such as sodomy with an iron rod. We usually associate these forms of torture only with the police.[13] The brutality of Nirbhaya's attackers and her eventual death meant that the cacophony of conservative voices, which typically pass moral judgment on rape survivors, was minimized, even if not entirely absent. The momentum following her death led to the passage of the CLA, culminating feminist reform efforts over several decades. Although taken by surprise by the level of public support for Nirbhaya, the institutionalization of the IWM had for long rendered Indian feminists insiders to the law reform process. I explain next my conceptual apparatus for understanding feminist influence.

The Indian Women's Movement

Framing political action in terms of a social movement in India has tremendous political appeal harking back to the heady days of large-scale protests in the 1970s and 1980s. The IWM was one such movement. In its postcolonial phase, the IWM aspired for fundamental structural change in place of merely advocating for female interests.[14] It also sought to be "autonomous"—in a political sense—from the prescribed political position of oppressively dogmatic, Left parties,[15] and financially from external, project-based funding as well as foreign funding. I use the term "IWM" to refer to the autonomous phase (and politics) of the movement. Through the 1990s, feminist organizations in the IWM that did not receive external funding dwindled, and their predominant organizational form today is that of the funded NGO. As Nivedita Menon notes, the Seventh National Conference of Autonomous Women's Movements in 2006 was attended almost entirely by funded NGOs,[16] although some bore a historical link to the autonomous IWM.

Other policy actors visible post-Nirbhaya included feminist NGOs, women of left-wing parties, HIV/AIDS NGOs, nonfunded feminist and queer groups, democratic rights groups, feminist women's studies research institutes, university programs,[17] NGOs working with sex workers, membership-based sex workers' associations, state feminists, and single-issue advocacy groups, particularly anti-trafficking NGOs such as Bachpan Bachao Andolan (Save the Childhood Movement) and Shakti Vahini (Powerful Armed Force).[18]

State Feminism

"State feminism" is a term coined by Scandinavian feminists for their own version of femocracy.[19] State feminism specifically refers to the response of postindustrial democracies to demands of second-wave feminism by setting up women's policy agencies to improve women's status.[20] The term "femocrat" in turn, as mentioned by Halley in chapter 3, is an Australian neologism referring to a feminist bureaucrat—a feminist formally appointed to a powerful position in government.[21] Femocracy in a sense is a conceptual precursor to GF.

Australian femocrats identified India and Sweden as the earliest countries to institute state committees, in the early 1970s, to examine gender issues.[22] Indeed, Indian feminists' ascendancy to state power has been facilitated by the state's historical receptivity to gender issues and its institutionalization since the 1970s at two main sites. In 1976, the federal government set up the Women's Welfare and Development Bureau within the Department of Social Welfare, which with several upgrades became the Ministry of Women & Child Development (MWCD) in 2006. Parallel to this, and as a result of UN-related conferences and the IWM's demands, the National Commission for Women (NCW) was set up by the state in 1992 as an autonomous body to mediate between the state and the IWM. However, both the MWCD minister and the chairperson of the NCW are political appointees who are loyal to the ruling party and are neither bureaucrats nor feminists (unlike the femocrats). Hence, I use the term "state feminism" to describe them. Other sites of state feminism include permanent and ad hoc government committees such as the Law Commission of India (LCI) and the Verma Committee, respectively.

The IWM fought hard for the establishment of the NCW as a watchdog body autonomous of the state to monitor the executive's and legislature's initiatives on gender. The NCW technically frames the default policy position on any given "women's" issue and has facilitated the installation and buy-in of feminist ideas in state institutions. In its initial years, the NCW took a strong radical feminist position on issues like sex work, coupled with a cultural nationalist approach to the uniqueness of Indian women's victimhood. Over time, however, the NCW has become a lackluster organization and victim of bureaucratic capture by the MWCD.[23] The government neither consults with nor is accountable to the NCW.[24] The NCW is increasingly preoccupied with representing female interests rather than aiming for structural reform. Instead of being autonomous of the state, the NCW has become autonomous of the IWM.

Theorizing Reform

Upendra Baxi proposes that law reform efforts can be typologized as *regulatory* law reform, namely, changes to statute law or other legal doctrine; *governance* reform or changes in institutional practices; and *social* reform or changes in social attitudes.[25] Regulatory reform invariably leads to some institutional reform, but this is not necessarily the case in India, where the enforcement of laws is poor and failure in day-to-day governance is accompanied by endemic corruption. As an example, the bus in which Nirbhaya was raped, which was used for school trips, was reportedly identified through entries in a police diary recording *hafta* (bribes) paid by the bus owner to the Delhi police to permit its use beyond school hours. Further, regulatory reform is only an initial step in the long struggle for social reform. Thus, even in jurisdictions with relatively sound rape laws, feminists have extensively documented the justice gap caused by high attrition or drop rates in rape complaints. Sticky social norms render the promises of criminal law illusory as reform becomes a "marbled" affair and the rich veins of new law cut across the "plain vanilla" of settled, conventional belief.[26] The chasm between the two is typically mediated by governance reform.[27] Some social movements, meanwhile, want reforms at all three levels, much like the Nirbhaya protests leading to the passage of the CLA, pointing to the highly recursive and interdependent relationship between social reform and regulatory reform.

Specifically in relation to rape, Pratiksha Baxi's ethnography of rape trials in Gujarat illuminates the perverse outcomes of the Indian legal system. Rape trials, according to Baxi, are pornographic in their humiliation of survivors,[28] medicalization "produces" the consent of the survivor to sexual intercourse and reveals the supposed falsity of her complaint,[29] custodial rape is rarely prosecuted,[30] and survivors are routinely pressured by the police, lawyers, and politicians to compromise rape cases even though they are not compoundable.[31] Further, prosecutors insist that survivors withdraw their complaints; some survivors have been murdered for refusing to do so and others have killed themselves. For complaints that make it, courts arbitrarily demarcate between different categories of women depending on their place in what Veena Das calls the system of alliance (i.e., women either circulate within the marital economy or are considered unchaste and fall outside it, becoming available for sexual experimentation).[32] Questions relating to a survivor's sexual virtue appear through capacious medical evidence and assume legal relevance at the sentencing stage.[33] Little surprise, then, that only 5 percent of reported rape cases result in conviction.[34] Not only that, rape trials are used to maintain the heteropatriarchal family by criminalizing socially unaccepted love so that the boundaries between elopement and abduction, love and rape are blurred.[35]

Faced with this justice gap, a few feminists have pursued governance reform, but most have defaulted to demanding additional regulatory reform. Feminists here are formalist—they believe that criminal law can and should be enforced 24/7, and that more criminal law means that the state will enforce it stringently enough to shift social norms and eradicate sexual abuse. Feminists' preference for regulatory reform may well have been due to the lack of a broad, popular base of supporters, although ironically, in 2013 post-Nirbhaya, it was these very public protests that eventually pushed through regulatory reform.

When theorizing the justice gap, Duncan Kennedy's legal realist approach to sexual abuse is helpful. He cautions that criminal laws against the sexual abuse of women will never operate 24/7 and that the legal system will always tolerate a certain level of sexual abuse, namely, the tolerated residuum of abuse, which in turn depends on social decisions about what abuse is and how important it is to prevent it.[36] This affects practices of abuse and social practices of both men and women, whether they themselves are abusers, survivors, or completely unrelated to the abusers and survivors. Kennedy's idea of the tolerated residuum of abuse turns the feminist problematic of the justice gap on its head; questioning the very assumption that the law can eliminate sexual abuse, it tempers unrealistic expectations of regulatory reform. It further points to the vastly varied stakes of different groups of men and women in the laws against sexual abuse, thus problematizing feminists' explanation for the justice gap, namely, that the law furthers the "interests of men."[37] It is through this legal realist lens that I assess Indian GF and the distributive effects of feminist-inspired rule changes.

From Rape to Sexual Assault to Sexual Violence: The Long Feminist Struggle for Rape Law Reform and the Rise of Indian Governance Feminism

The CLA follows a trajectory of rape law reform that is familiar to the Anglo-American legal world. At the highest level of generality, this process, often undertaken with substantial feminist input, expands the conduct element of the offense of rape to include nonpenile penetration and specifies gender neutrality as to the survivor and sometimes the defendant. Many jurisdictions have also changed consent standards. Whereas earlier, the prosecution would have to prove both force and nonconsent, typically through the survivor's resistance, today the prosecution often need prove only her lack of consent, irrespective of whether the defendant used force or not. Earlier, where a defendant's unreasonable yet honest belief in the survivor's consent exonerated him, now such a belief must be reasonable. Additional reforms include expanding the situations where the survivor's nonconsent is presumed, with or without the possibility of rebuttal, fixing an age of consent for statutory rape, and abrogating the common law immunity for marital rape. In addition, rape shield laws prevent or highly circumscribe adducing evidence as to the survivor's sexual history with the defendant or others. The 2013 amendments to Indian rape law mirror these trends, particularly by widening the *actus reus* of rape, defining consent, expanding the scenarios where lack of consent is presumed, and instituting rape shield provisions.

The CLA is the culmination of almost thirty-five years of feminist efforts to force the Indian state to reform rape law. Beginning in 1979, feminists' long road to the CLA was punctuated by several rounds of negotiations with the state and by repeated cycles of outcome failure[38] leaving the IWM beleaguered. With the Nirbhaya incident, the state's apathy came to an end, but its response was influenced by a heightened public demand for retributive justice. Feminists felt cornered and had to choose between their commitment to gender equality and their resistance to state power.[39] While this perception of beleaguered feminists has resonance, it does not present the full picture.

I argue that, between 1979 and 2013, the relationship between Indian feminist groups and the state (and criminal law reform) underwent a substantial transformation. Not only were feminists slowly yet surely clarifying their own legal understanding of rape; their ideas were also beginning to find a foothold within the state through the LCI and the NCW. Post-Nirbhaya, the Verma Committee, the most open point of reception for feminists, effectively channeled their ideas into the CLA. Although feminists ultimately lost out on crucial issues including marital rape, greater accountability for rape by the armed forces through the principle of command responsibility, the repeal of special laws granting exemplary powers to the military such as the Armed Forces (Special Powers) Act of 1958, and the age of consent, their successes were not insubstantial and could be traced back to their powerfully articulated theory of sexual violence. I track these successes in terms of three parameters of GF: Indian feminist groups' resort to criminal law for addressing gender inequalities; their conceptualization of gender inequality, particularly violence against women; and their mode of engaging with the state. I argue that there exists a distinctively Indian GF, which differs significantly from Anglo-American GF, on the issue of rape.

Reliance on Criminal Law

Compared with feminist movements elsewhere, a crucial point of departure for Indian anti-rape struggles is the high levels of sexual violence inflicted by the state itself. Indeed, the Mathura rape case, which inaugurated the autonomous phase of the IWM in the 1970s, arose from the Supreme Court's acquittal of two policemen who had raped a tribal teenager. The arc of Indian feminist advocacy against rape thus extends from its opposition to custodial sexual violence inflicted by the police in the 1970s and 1980s to sexual violence perpetrated by the armed forces in conflict-ridden parts of the country today. Resorting to the state for criminal law reform has thus always been a fraught affair for fear of its misuse. The IWM has also been acutely aware of the symbolic promises of law reform given the chronic under-enforcement of law by a weak postcolonial state. However, as I will show, the zone of opposition to criminal law has shriveled within Indian feminism over the past three decades. Feminists' resolute opposition to the death penalty for rape post-2013 is a far cry from their deep suspicion of all aspects of criminal law at the start of the IWM.

Gendered Understanding of Violence

Indian feminists' increased reliance on criminal law between 1983 and 2013 is inextricably linked to their reconceptualization of rape during this period. The three major feminist approaches to rape can be outlined as follows:

1. Rape as violence (the Canadian model)
2. Rape as uniquely gendered violence
3. "Rape as violence where violence precisely *is* sex" (the radical feminist model)[40]

Indian feminists, according to Menon, adopted the second approach.[41] They had always privileged the special, sexual, and gendered violence of rape. Although the second and third approaches appear distinct on paper, they are ideologically highly compatible, and possibilities for slippage between them are ever present.

Consider the third approach: radical feminists understand almost all heterosexual sex as coercive because it is only "if force were defined to include inequalities of power, meaning social hierarchies, and consent were replaced with a welcomeness standard, [that] the law of rape would begin to approximate the reality of forced and unwanted sex."[42] Legally speaking, then, a defendant must be prosecuted on the basis of the complainant's testimony as to the social hierarchy between her and her assailant and the unwanted nature of the sex rather than whether it was consented to or not. Some philosophers of criminal law would further argue that penetrative sex by a man with a woman would prima facie be a moral wrong where it was unjustified even if it was consented to.[43] To be justified, such sex must confer value, respect, and humanity on the woman. A crucial basis for this feminist approach is the uniquely gendered violence of rape (in other words, the second approach).

Conversely, feminists pursuing the second approach attribute sexual violence to pervasive gender hierarchies. This appreciation for social coercion led Indian feminists to name all rapes as acts of power. Fairly early on in the anti-rape struggles, a member of Parliament demanded that the law presume the lack of consent in all cases of "power rape"; the LCI even recommended this. Indeed, "power rape" or rape under conditions of economic domination was a crucial contribution of the IWM, although the 1983 amendment (which I return to below) recognized a more limited category of power rape, namely, rape in state custody or custodial rape.[44] As I discuss later, these political formulations had legal implications in 2013, when the presumption of the lack of consent was extended well beyond custodial situations to everyday situations of dominance. Thus, we see how Indian feminists' demands came close to those of radical feminists. Indeed, over the past three decades, Indian feminists have (perhaps unconsciously) switched back and forth between the second and third approaches. This gendered understanding of rape, as I will show, became highly contested and challenged by lesbian, gay, bisexual, and transgender (LGBT) advocates, children's rights advocates, and, in 2013, by Marxist feminists.

Shifting Modes of Engagement with the State

In addition to feminists' increased reliance on criminal law and their uniquely gendered perspective on violence against women, I also track feminism's changing relationship with the state. According to Ritu Menon and Kalpana Kannabiran, the 1990s were significant in this respect:

> The 1990s marked something of an unusual departure for the Indian women's movement as far as campaigning on issues was concerned. For one, terms and strategies like "advocacy" and "lobbying" began to be used much more commonly than before; parliamentarians and pressure groups were sought out to hear representations and field questions in Parliament; women's groups engaged in discussions and organized campaigns with national and state commissions on women on several issues, ranging from sex work to child abuse and the impact of globalization on women; and any number of "gender sensitisation" trainings were carried out with the judiciary, the police, bureaucrats. . . . Underlying these efforts and activities was the implicit- and sometimes explicit-acknowledgment that a purposive interaction with institutional machinery and systems was critical in influencing positive outcomes for women; specifically for incorporating a gender perspective into the policy and planning process. In one sense, this "mainstreaming" of women's issues marked an important break from the protest activism of the late 1970s and 1980s, when street demonstrations, demands for legal reform, and more direct confrontations with the state were much more in evidence.[45]

The mainstreaming of women's issues by the postcolonial state to further economic development also rendered feminism a professional option for many women. As Srila Roy notes:

> The professionalization of feminism has enabled women, with little or no political commitments, to practice feminism as a profession rather than as politics. Compulsions to obtain and retain funding have not only limited the autonomy of women's groups but also obstructed any fresh thinking on what constitutes feminism itself: "it is as if we know what 'feminism' is, and only need to apply it unproblematically to specific instances" (Menon, 2004: 220). The original political thrust of the women's movement has been "blunted" by this corporatization and careerism; from the militant feminists of the 1980s, we have now become

(as a veteran of the women's movement told Menon) "nine-to-five feminists."[46]

As I will show, feminist struggles to reform rape law starkly reflected this trend. To rewind and further elucidate my core arguments on the rise of Indian GF, I offer some historical background on rape law in the sections that follow.

Rape in the Indian Penal Code: A Brief Introduction

Since Thomas Macaulay's Indian Penal Code (IPC) was introduced in 1862, its rape provisions have been substantially amended only twice, once in 1983 and again in 2013. In the thirty years between 1983 and 2013, the IWM was highly engaged in rape law reform. I list the major points of intervention chronologically in Figure 1 and deal primarily with substantive criminal law rather than procedural and evidentiary laws.

The key IPC provision on rape is Section 375, which defines the crime; Section 376 prescribes the punishment.[47] Before 1983, rape was defined as sexual intercourse by a man with a woman under the following five circumstances: when it was against her will, when it was without her consent, when consent was obtained under fear of death and harm, when it involved impersonation of her husband, or when the victim was less than sixteen years old (with or without her consent). Sexual intercourse by a man with his wife (the wife not being less than fifteen years old) was not rape.

Related "sexual" offenses, which were considered alongside rape, included Sections 354, 509, and 377.[48] Section 354 deals with assault or criminal force on a woman with intent to outrage her modesty. Section 509 criminalizes any word, gesture, or exhibition of an object with the intention of insulting the modesty of a woman. Section 377 provides for conviction of any person who "voluntarily has carnal intercourse against the order of nature with any man, woman, or animal." It is typically used to harass (and sometimes prosecute) those engaging in same-sex intercourse. In 2009, the Delhi High Court "read down" Section 377 as unconstitutional; the Indian Supreme Court in 2013 overruled the Delhi High Court decision to uphold its

1979	Mathura judgment from the Supreme Court
1980	84th Report of the Law Commission of India
1983	Amendment to the Indian Penal Code, 1860
1993	NCW Draft Amendments to Sexual Assault Law
1999	Sakshi petition to the Supreme Court
2000	Report of the 172nd Law Commission of India
2002	AIDWA Bill
2010	The Criminal Law (Amendment) Bill ("Sexual Assault Bill")
2010	The Criminal Law Amendment Bill, by feminists ("Sexual Violence Bill")
2012	The Criminal Law Amendment Bill
2013	Report of the Committee on Amendments to Criminal Law (Verma Committee Report)
2013	The Criminal Law (Amendment) Ordinance
2013	The Criminal Law (Amendment) Act

FIGURE 1. A Summary of Proposals for Rape Law Reform.

constitutionality.[49] Any change to the rape provisions had implications for these related sexual offenses. To illustrate, if Section 377 were repealed, rape would have to become gender neutral if there were to be any provisions to address the rape of men and children.

From Suspicion to a Faltering Faith in Criminal Law: Rape Law through the 1980s and 1990s

Indian feminists' struggles on rape law started post-Mathura. The Supreme Court reasoned that Mathura's seeming lack of resistance meant that she had consented to sexual intercourse. Four law academics wrote an open letter against the decision, which launched spontaneous countrywide protests by women's groups,[50] effectively inaugurating the autonomous phase of the IWM. In response, the government convened the LCI to suggest rape law reforms.

Feminists inserted themselves in the reform process early on. In 1980, the LCI met with eight women's groups that proposed ambitious changes for gender matching (e.g., the rape survivor's mandatory examination by a female police officer)[51] and for female social workers' involvement in rape investigations alongside the police and in the trial. The LCI rejected all these demands on the grounds of impracticability, but also out of fear of a "trial by the public" with the trial being instrumentalized to wage caste and class warfare.[52]

In 1983, the Indian Parliament amended the rape law. Incorporating several of the LCI's recommendations, the amendment expanded the grounds for finding a lack of consent to include survivors who were of unsound mind, intoxicated, or drugged. Consent was not defined. Although the LCI recommended inserting a rebuttable presumption of lack of consent in all instances where a woman so claimed,[53] and Parliament member Geeta Mukherjee tabled an amendment to presume nonconsent in all cases of "power rape,"[54] the 1983 amendment allowed this presumption only for custodial rape,[55] rape of a pregnant woman, and gang rape. Under the newly introduced Section 114A of the Indian Evidence Act of 1872 (IEA), once sexual intercourse by a man in a position of authority was proved, and the rape survivor stated that she did not consent, her lack of consent was presumed.[56]

Minimum punishments of between seven years and life were introduced for rape along with increased penalties of between ten years and life for custodial rape, gang rape, rape of a pregnant woman, and rape of a child under the age of twelve. Courts could impose lesser penalties if they adduced "special and adequate" reasons. There was no marital rape immunity when the parties were living separately under a separation decree or customarily, but the punishment was lower than for stranger rape. Similarly, marital rape of a wife between the ages of twelve and sixteen (sixteen being the age of consent) resulted in only a two-year prison term. In a legal paternalist move, meanwhile, even consensual sexual intercourse between a man in a position of authority and a woman in his custody was criminalized. Provisions such as Section 155(4) of the IEA, permitting the defendant to adduce evidence as to the immoral character of the survivor, and Section 146, dealing with witness cross-examination and often used to discredit the rape survivor, were left untouched.

After Prime Minister Indira Gandhi's State of Emergency, feminists (and leftist scholars and activists more generally) were deeply suspicious of state power.[57] Lotika Sarkar, a feminist legal academic who, with colleagues, penned the Open Letter to the Supreme Court in the Mathura case, was once asked why they had not demanded a blanket presumption of lack of consent in all instances of rape rather than in custodial situations only. Memories of the emergency of 1977 still fresh in her mind, she responded: "Do you want to hand over such power to the government, just after we have come out of the Emergency? Don't you realise that such power could be used to stifle all political dissent?"[58] Human rights groups reminded feminists that a blanket presumption of lack of consent might be used "by managements against trade union militants, by rural vested interests against revolutionary activists, by caste Hindu chauvinists against dalits."[59] In 1981, feminists' intense suspicion of state power meant that they were wary even of (now commonsensical feminist) procedural protections like in-camera rape trial proceedings recommended by the 84th Report of the LCI for the benefit of both parties. Feminists, although resistant to the glamorization of rape by the press, passed a resolution about in-camera rape trials, stating:

> We feel this is a direct attack on the ability of women's organizations to organize on the issue of violence against women. The danger extends further, because, on the pretext of protecting women, the Bill is in fact a blatant attempt to impose press censorship, which assumes significance in the context of increasing atrocities and repression of people's movements. We therefore resolve we will defy this provision of the Bill . . . specially by unitedly protecting our alternative media.[60]

After the 1983 amendments, feminists vowed to take great care with future demands lest the state use them to curb civil liberties.[61] Feminists also cast a critical eye on their apparent successes, especially in a 1994 report showing that conviction figures for rape after 1983 were lower than before 1983.[62] Criminalizing custodial rape had little effect on the ground;[63] its increased punishment yielded fewer convictions.[64] Feminists were thus consistently attuned to the unintended consequences of criminal law.

In 1993, the newly established NCW worked with eleven feminist activists to propose Draft Amendments to Sexual Assault Law, this being *the* feminist statement on sexual violence in the post-1983 reform phase.[65] The 1993 draft understood rape as "a unique form of violence because of its sexual character."[66] The proposal recommended replacing rape with two subcategories of sexual assault—sexual assault involving penetration (penile and nonpenile) and nonconsensual touching, gesturing, or exhibiting any part of the body for a sexual purpose.

The draft proposed a second category of aggravated sexual assault based on several new grounds such as the age, disability, or pregnancy of the survivor; the defendant's powerful position in relation to the survivor; gang rape; where the assault resulted in grievous bodily harm; or where rape occurred over a protracted period of time. The draft also eliminated the marital rape immunity and—amid considerable disagreement within the group, especially as to the increased criminalization of adolescent sex—proposed eighteen as the age for consent.[67] Feminists also disagreed over treating the rape of a pregnant survivor as aggravated sexual assault, with some objecting that this reinforced patriarchal perceptions of women as wombs. Notwithstanding disagreement, they retained these proposals. With the expanded definition of sexual assault, they also recommended deleting Sections 377, 354, and 509.

In 1999, Sakshi, a feminist legal advocacy NGO established in 1993, filed a petition in the Indian Supreme Court seeking clarification of the term "sexual intercourse" under the IPC to address growing levels of child sexual abuse. On the Supreme Court's direction, the LCI submitted its 172nd Report. The LCI recommended replacing "rape" with "sexual assault" that was gender neutral as to the defendant and the survivor. Penetration was expanded to include nonpenile penetration. The commission failed to define consent or delete the marital rape immunity. It pegged the age of consent at sixteen and retained judicial discretion on minimum sentences. The LCI additionally proposed the offenses of aggravated sexual assault and unlawful sexual touching and the repeal of Section 377. The LCI consulted with only three feminist civil society groups, although there were many feminist voices in the debate.[68]

Although viewed as a paradigm shift from the reformatory strategy of the 84th Report of the LCI,[69] the proposed gender-neutral offense of sexual assault was fiercely opposed by feminists out of fear of its misuse to file countercomplaints against women.[70] A gender-neutral offense meant to address same-sex rape was meaningless as long as Section 377 remained on the books (even though the LCI recommended its repeal), with no legal protections for the LGBT community. Moreover, could not transgender persons, most at risk of rape, simply be treated as women under a gender-specific rape law?[71] With the proposed deletion of Section 377, feminists called for a gender-neutral offense and indeed a separate law against child sexual abuse.

Here, feminists recollected that only antiterror laws reversed the evidentiary burden in favor of the prosecution; democratic concerns had to figure in their calculus.[72] Similarly, although feminists unanimously opposed the marital rape immunity, some wondered privately if the husband's incarceration would not adversely affect a financially dependent wife and disincentivize her reporting of marital rape. Where women often wanted only to chastise their husbands rather than remove them from their lives,[73] perhaps a civil law solution was more effective? Also, given the inherent violence of compulsory marriage, criminalizing marital rape rather than treating it as grounds for divorce would leave "the impunity of the citadel" of marriage intact.[74]

From Sexual Assault to Sexual Violence and the Rise of Certitude in Criminal Law

Despite feminist efforts in the 1990s to reform rape laws, there was limited momentum for legal change. In 2002, an amendment to the IEA of 1872 deleted Section 155(4) (which allowed a person accused of rape to adduce evidence of the survivor's "generally immoral character") and further provided in Section 146 that a survivor could not be cross-examined on her "general immoral character." In 2010, when the government proposed fast-track courts for rape, several women's organizations wrote an open letter to the Law Ministry inviting a consultation on the 172nd LCI Report. They made some predictable demands,[75] but, significantly departing from the 1990s when they understood rape as sexual assault,[76] they now demanded new laws on sexual violence. In response, in March 2010 the Home Ministry proposed the Criminal Law (Amendment) Bill of 2010, a fairly minimalist document[77] that feminists dismissed as a "greatly diluted version" of the LCI's proposals.[78] By May 2010, signatories to the open letter drafted their own Criminal Law (Amendment) Bill of 2010.[79]

The bill, like the 1993 draft, was the IWM's aspirational statement on sexual violence. To a legislative draftswoman, however, its broad formulation of offenses fell far short of the civil liberties principles that limit criminalization by requiring precision, clarity, and fair labeling. Certain offenses were broad enough to be constitutionally suspect. Significantly, with the expansive understanding of rape as sexual violence, Indian feminists' attachment to a gendered script of sexual subordination intensified even as their suspicion of state power and of criminal law trailed off.

Specifically, the bill proposed a new IPC chapter on "sexual violence" in place of the existing chapter on "offences against the body."
The statement of objects and reasons states:

> Sexual crimes form a continuum. Sexual violence includes but is not
> limited to sexual acts which involve penetration by the penis . . . In
> recognition of the structural and graded nature of sexual violence this
> Bill grades offences based on concepts of harm, injury, humiliation and
> degradation, using well-established categories of sexual assault, aggra-
> vated sexual assault, and sexual offences.[80]

The continuum of sexual violence included situations where women
were assaulted, stripped, disrobed, paraded naked, subject to sexually
humiliating words or actions, subject to any sexual contact with or exposure of male sex organs, sexually touched, sexually harassed, and
where their sexual and reproductive organs were mutilated. Highlighting the sex-based nature of these crimes, feminists segregated them as
special, different, and possibly more harmful than other bodily offenses. They effectively proposed a new bill on sexual violence, which
I call the Sexual Violence Bill.[81]

Thus between 1993 and 2010, Indian feminist discourse on rape
shifted from viewing it as sexual assault to it being part of a continuum of sexual violence. Feminist opposition to gender neutrality best
exemplifies this and was integral to the IWM's core identity.[82] Given
the exceptionally high rate of violence against women, or India's "rape
culture," feminists considered gender neutrality to be a Western idea[83]
that was premature and unsuitable for domestic realities and would
lead to false complaints against women.[84] This pragmatic argument,
however, soon morphed into a radical feminist normative argument
that women never rape. To quote Flavia Agnes:

> As far as women's situation is concerned, throughout the two decades
> of struggle, not a single case of a reversal of gender roles, in the realm
> of sexual offence, had ever surfaced in the Indian context nor at any
> time formed part of the discourse. In this entire history, no one has
> ever advanced the plea of sexual violation by women. On the contrary,
> the core concern has been sexual violations by men not only of women,
> but children—both male and female and other men. The social sanction
> awarded to aggressive male sexuality, expressed through violent,

penetrative sex, both within and outside marriage, in the closeted se-
crecy of bedrooms and in the public domains of civilian spaces; and the
violations by the state in custodial situations—these has [*sic*] been the
central focus of the debate. And yet, paradoxically . . . women have now
been posed as offenders . . . which is far removed from the ground reality of their social existence.[85]

In the face of gender neutrality, the IWM ultimately was a *women's*
movement. But by now feminists were painfully aware that rape law
was a critical site for addressing violence against the LGBT community and children; this was, after all, one rationale for the LCI's recommendations. Feminists regrouped to consider this by involving LGBT
and children's rights groups to deliberate the Sexual Violence Bill.

Feminists had three options here. The first, simplest option was to
make the offense of rape gender neutral as to the survivor but not to
the defendant. The second was to create separate offenses within the
same statute against the rape of women, children, and LGBT persons.
The third was to create entirely separate legislations for these groups.
The Sexual Violence Bill adopted the second strategy to propose three
distinct offenses:

1. Sexual violence by a man on a woman
2. Sexual assault by a man on a person other than a woman
3. Sexual assault by a person on a child

This formulation shows that Indian feminists subscribed to a deeply
gendered radical feminist view of violence against women. In their calculus, only biological males could commit sexual violence against
adults; biological females could not. Females could, however, abuse
male and female children; children here occupied the social role of
the woman. Feminists were unwilling to imagine women's sexual
aggression toward adults, even when they occupied a dominant religious, caste, or class background vis-à-vis less powerful biological
males. The bill did not propose to prosecute such women, for rape or
other offenses.[86]

Once again, the violence suffered by females was considered graver
than that of nonfemales. Female sexual harm was "sexual violence";
sexual harm of men, transgender persons, and children was merely
"sexual assault."[87] This hierarchy of harms necessitated a separate

offense of sexual assault of a person *other than a woman,* which includes men and transgender persons. Thus, feminists remained strongly committed to the male–female dyad to theorize patriarchal sexual violence and cordoned off antifemale sexual violence from gender-based violence. Feminists struggled to address the experiences of transgender persons—they acknowledged that a complainant's gender identity should be based on his or her declaration, not a medical examination; yet a transgender person declaring a female identity could complain only of sexual assault against a person "other than a woman."

Feminists also successfully campaigned for and drafted a new law on sexual violence against children, namely, the Protection of Children from Sexual Offences Act of 2012.[88] LGBT survivors of rape, however, continued to pose a serious challenge to the feminist demand of a gender-specific rape offense. Certain LGBT groups, such as People for Rights of Indian Sexual Minorities, opposed gender neutrality because lesbians and effeminate men could be prosecuted for rape.[89] Moreover, as long as Section 377 criminalized consensual sex between same-sex couples, gender-neutral rape seemed both redundant and premature. Other LGBT groups, such as Aanchal and the Humsafar Trust, however, opted out of the feminist fold to strategize independently for a gender-neutral rape law.[90]

The Sexual Violence Bill also boldly reconceptualized consent as the woman's unequivocal voluntary agreement, listing numerous situations where the lack of consent was presumed. These covered not only custodial situations involving the police but also situations of collective violence or intimate violence, or where the perpetrator was in a position of social, political, or economic *dominance.* "Economic/social dominance" was defined as "situations of religious, ethnic, linguistic, caste and class dominance, including (but not limited to) both formal and informal employment situations such as landlord-agricultural labourer, contractor-labourer, employer-domestic worker."[91] The overlapping effects of social status and labor relationships on women exemplify an intersectional analysis. However, this broad construction of coercion risks recasting even consensual sexual contact with a man from a dominant background as sexual violence, thereby undermining women's sexual agency. Practically, the similarity between the paternalism of feminists, on the one hand, and that of caste councils and families who use rape law to prevent intercaste marriage, on the other, is notable.

Feminists also expanded aggravated sexual assault to address rape by armed forces, rape during communal and caste violence, and the rape of disabled women.[92] They drew on the international criminal law concept of command responsibility to impose obligations on public servants, viewing rape as torture when committed in custody or during occupation or conflict.[93]

Even as the Indian feminist narrative of rape articulated exclusively in terms of the sexual subordination of women by men became entrenched, rape was viewed less as forced sexual intercourse than as sexual intercourse without consent and under coercion. Feminist expectations of criminal law grew even as political and legal struggles that previously threatened to destabilize feminist consensus on rape remained unresolved.

The Criminal Law (Amendment) Bill of 2012

No official response to the Sexual Violence Bill was forthcoming until the government introduced the Criminal Law (Amendment) Bill of 2012, on December 4, 2012. The 2012 bill redesignated rape as gender-neutral sexual assault and, as in 2010, expanded sexual assault to include nonpenile penetration, increased the age of consent to eighteen, and retained the marital rape immunity.[94] Aggravated sexual assault covered a defendant who was a relative or in a position of trust and authority or social, political, or economic dominance, or where the survivor was disabled, grievously hurt, or subject to persistent sexual assault. Feminists had suggested these grounds in 1993, and they were incorporated in the government's 2010 bill. The 2012 bill introduced only one new offense (on acid attacks), increased punishments under Sections 354 and 509, and strengthened existing rape shield provisions but definitely did *not* address sexual violence as feminists desired.[95]

Feminism in Power: The Criminal Law Reforms of 2013

The extensive back-and-forth between the government and feminists on rape, which had unfolded over almost thirty years, was soon to shift pace. Twelve days after the government introduced the Criminal Law

(Amendment) Bill of 2012, Nirbhaya was raped and murdered. The government almost immediately appointed the Verma Committee to look into law reform.

The Verma Committee as a Site of State Feminism

The Verma Committee shifted the tone of the public debate, saturated until then with calls for the death penalty and chemical castration. Its report instead held the state responsible for failing to prevent women's abuse. It addressed head-on the rape inflicted by state personnel and family members, including husbands, by removing legal immunities these acts enjoyed. The committee labeled caste councils, which informally outlawed intercaste romance and marriage, as illegal. It proposed a long list of new offenses criminalizing disrobing, voyeurism, trafficking, employing a trafficked person, seduction by a person in authority, sexual assault, stalking, gang rape, and rape resulting in death or a persistent vegetative state. Recollect that the Criminal Law (Amendment) Bill of 2012, introduced pre-Nirbhaya, proposed only one new offense, that against acid attacks. The newly proposed offenses were broadly defined and had steep punishments compared with previous penalties for similar offenses. For example, sexual assault, meant to cover nonconsensual, nonpenetrative forms of sexual contact, was punishable by five years' imprisonment or a fine or both. Thus, fondling a woman on the bus could attract up to five years' imprisonment. The committee also proposed criminalizing the police's refusal to record a first information report (FIR) regarding a sexual offense.[96] The committee further proposed command responsibility, increased the punishments for existing offenses, and introduced life imprisonment without parole for repeat offenders.

The Verma Committee thus proposed criminalizing the full range of acts that feminists designated as sexual violence. The report exemplifies Indian feminists' attachment to the script of gender subordination and the unique nature of gendered harm needing the heavy-handed response of criminal law. The committee benefited from its interactions with the ninety-two feminist NGOs and individuals who, not content with writing to the committee, met committee members in January 2013. They even took credit for dissuading the committee from recommending the death penalty for aggravated rape. Feminists as repeat players could obtain access to state bodies. Not surprisingly, they enthusiastically welcomed the committee's report as signaling a "paradigm shift" in thinking on violence against women.

However, Indian feminists were not alone in influencing the committee. The committee thanked at least one American radical feminist—Diane Rosenfeld—for her contributions. Single-issue NGOs such as the Bachpan Bachao Andolan, or BBA (roughly translated into Save the Childhood Movement), focusing on missing children and child trafficking, also engaged extensively with the committee. Committee members themselves were acquainted with feminist lawyers. Justice Verma had delivered the Vishaka judgment on sexual harassment[97] initiated by Naina Kapur from Sakshi, and Justice Leila Seth was a member of the 172nd LCI.[98] The third committee member, Gopal Subramaniam, as solicitor-general, had represented the government of India in an appeal against the Mumbai High Court's decision upholding the bar dancers' right to livelihood and in a public interest litigation (PIL) brought by BBA on child trafficking in circuses. His arguments in both cases suggest some familiarity with feminist legal arguments, particularly of Catharine A. MacKinnon, with little appreciation for the range of Anglo-American and Indian feminist thinking on law.

The influence of radical feminists and anti-trafficking groups (such as the BBA) is best reflected in the second-longest chapter in the committee's report, which deals with trafficking. The report claims that missing children are trafficked into sex work, later justified as voluntary prostitution. Their trafficking sets the climate for "a rape culture."[99] Radical feminists routinely make these arguments—prostitution for them is paradigmatic of sexual violence against women, rape being only one manifestation. They also often conflate sex work with trafficking for sex work.[100] In order to eliminate trafficking in this logic, sex work has to be eradicated. This constellation of radical feminist ideas currently travels around the world as a form of anti-trafficking discourse. Thus, although trafficking has historically been a low priority issue for the IWM, anti-trafficking NGOs such as the BBA (not a feminist organization) have uncritically internalized these arguments, which, when presented to the Verma Committee, made their way into the report. Little surprise, then, that the committee, when proposing a new offense of trafficking, did not distinguish between trafficking and voluntary sex work.[101]

Consider other vignettes of feminist reasoning in the Verma Committee Report. It offers familiar radical feminist tropes of victimhood, harm, the special harm of rape to one's dignity, and the collapsing of different harms into each other requiring a zero-tolerance approach to milder harassment to prevent the serious harm of sexual assault.[102] Thus, publicly molesting women and girls could eventually cause psychological problems and even lead to suicide.[103] From the conflation of sexual harms it is only a short step to the policing of any sexual activity. Thus, we learn that "aggravated sexual assault must include all stages of affront to human dignity which is the quintessence of human rights, beginning with *any act with a sexual overtone*."[104] The surest way to eliminate sexual subordination is to avoid sexual activity altogether. Also, although the committee understood rape as an exercise of patriarchal power, in calling for the deconstruction of the societal shame and stigma of rape, it reiterated the social understanding of rape as a personal horror. Women and girls are innocent, fragile victims in this script.

In the aftermath of the Nirbhaya incident, the postcolonial state had to be seen as responsive to violence against women to ensure its legitimacy. The Verma Committee as a productive site of state feminism did precisely this when it channeled feminist ideas of many stripes (mostly Indian materialist feminism but also slivers of Anglo-American radical feminism and some gender-speak from nonfeminists) into a hyperstructuralist feminist argument for law reform and increased criminalization.

The Criminal Law (Amendment) Act of 2013

The president promulgated the Criminal Law (Amendment) Ordinance of 2013, in February 2013.[105] The ordinance did not reflect the spirit of the Verma Committee Report and was decried by feminists as ensuring that "the impunity of every citadel" was intact, including of the family, marriage, public servants, the army, and the police.[106] When Parliament reconvened, amid considerable debate on the age of consent, it passed the Criminal Law (Amendment) Act of 2013 (CLA), replacing the presidential ordinance.

The CLA offered mixed results for feminists, who lost out on key issues. The age of consent was increased from sixteen to eighteen.[107] Marital rape immunity was not only retained but expanded to "sexual acts," not just sexual intercourse. Despite assurances that the age threshold for criminalizing marital rape would be increased, there was no change. Only marital rape of a wife under the age of fifteen is punishable.

However, feminists also had reason to celebrate. Section 375 retains the gender specificity of rape—only a man can commit rape and only against a woman. Rape now covers penile and nonpenile penetration. The CLA defines consent as "an unequivocal voluntary agreement where the woman by words, gestures or any form of verbal or non-verbal communication, communicates willingness to participate in the specific sexual act." A substantial portion of this definition appeared in the Sexual Violence Bill and the Verma Committee Report before being modified for the CLA. Explanation 2 to Section 375 clarifies that the lack of physical resistance shall not be construed as consent. This was again formulated in the Sexual Violence Bill.

To cut back on judicial leniency in rape sentencing,[108] Section 376(1) prescribes a minimum sentence of seven years with no room for judicial discretion, and a maximum of life. The grounds under which aggravated rape under Section 376(2) can be charged have been doubled, from seven to fourteen. Many of these additional grounds were first proposed by feminists in 1993 and listed in the Sexual Violence Bill. They are based on the status of the defendant (being a member of the armed forces, relative, guardian, or teacher or person in a position of trust or authority, or in a position of control or dominance), the status of the survivor (pregnant woman, less than 16 years of age, incapable of giving consent, or suffering from mental or physical disability), the context of the rape (communal or sectarian violence), or the harm caused to the survivor (grievous bodily harm, repeated rape). Section 114A of the IEA of 1872 expanded the rebuttable presumption of lack of consent beyond custodial rape situations to cover all cases of aggravated rape. Gang rape, earlier grounds for aggravated rape, is now a separate offense punishable by a minimum sentence of twenty years. The CLA imposes a minimum sentence of twenty years, and up to life or the death penalty, for rape resulting in death or a persistent vegetative state. The punishment for repeatedly committing aggravated rape is life imprisonment or the death penalty. The Verma Committee had proposed that all these offenses receive stringent punishments but not the death penalty.

The CLA also expands a preexisting offense criminalizing consensual intercourse in a custodial situation by a public servant to now include any person in a position of authority or in a fiduciary relationship. The term "person in a position of authority" is not defined and could result in a legal paternalist denunciation of women's sexual choices. A significant provision aimed at governance reform penalizes the police's failure to register an FIR. The CLA also incorporated the Verma Committee's recommendations (in turn influenced by feminists' theory of sexual violence) by including separate offenses against stalking, committing an acid attack, voyeurism,[109] disrobing, trafficking, and sexual harassment. Many of the new offenses are non-bailable, and repeat offenders are subject to increased penalties.[110] The CLA also strengthens rape shield provisions. There is no better evidence of feminist influence on Indian rape law than the contrast between the government's 2012 bill pre-Nirbhaya and the Verma-inspired CLA.

Criminal Law's Expanse, Feminism's Discontents

As my discussion of the various feminist proposals so far makes clear, the expansion of the anti-rape platform to one of sexual violence (as exemplified by the Sexual Violence Bill) envisioned a correspondingly enlarged role for criminal law. Whether or not the CLA has its desired effects, on the face of it, the universe of criminal law has expanded. Feminists' main criticism of the CLA in fact remains its under-criminalization of marital rape and rape by the armed forces. Whereas in the late 1970s and early 1980s feminists were suspicious even of in-camera rape trials, today, feminists are unanimously opposed to criminal law only where it prescribes the death penalty for rapists.[111]

The intrafeminist disagreement over the exclusivity of rape as a form of male–female violence was not resolved in 2013. Feminists were faced with the LGBT question once again. This time around, feminists were content with gender neutrality as to the survivor but not as to the perpetrator.[112] However, their fierce opposition to gender-neutral rape in the 2013 ordinance caused the government to revert to a gender-specific definition in the CLA. Reeling from this missed opportunity, Aarti Mundkur and Arvind Narrain, advocates for the LGBT community, wrote in a widely read op-ed:

Looking at the tenor of the debates leading up to the Bill becoming a law, one would be forgiven if one got the impression that the struggle was mainly between a misogynistic and patriarchal viewpoint which found full play in Parliament and the voices of women who sought to make the case for the right to live with dignity, free from the oppression of sexual violence. However there remains a third viewpoint which, unfortunately, has found no voice in any mainstream discussion on the issue of sexual violence. This viewpoint emerges most strongly from the lived experiences of members of the transgender community.[113]

Although directed at lawmakers, the op-ed's tone is one of betrayal and indirectly blames feminists for refusing to acknowledge rapes within the LGBT community. As Mundkur and Narrain observe:

The resistance to broaden the category of victim to that of any person stems from a viewpoint that the word "person" would dilute the identity of women as traditional victims of sexual violence. Recognising the heroic struggle of Mathura and Bhanwari Devi against sexual violence, ought not to mean that we disregard the struggles of persons such as Kokila.[114]

In effect, Indian feminism successfully managed contestations to its rape narrative, thereby consolidating a narrative of sexual subordination that is remarkably close to Anglo-American radical feminism. In the process, it was unable to seriously engage with male and transgender sexual violence.[115]

An equally serious but less examined (and largely academic rather than policy-oriented) challenge has come from Marxists. Indian feminists are no political or intellectual strangers to materialism. While in the United States, feminist frustration with the Marxist treatment of gender produced a decisive break in the form of radical feminism or feminism "unmodified," in the Indian context, materialist feminism has for long remained a decisive marker for feminist identity. Indian feminists broke away from dogmatic leftist political parties to escape their own trivialization as "bourgeois feminists" but never took a clean conceptual break from the critique of capitalism. Indian feminism's roots in materialism help explain its ambivalence toward state power, existing alongside a deep attachment to a highly gendered analysis of women's subordination. An intersectionality analysis often helps some materialist feminists bridge political commitments to gender and class, but this has not precluded challenges from other materialists, be they Marxists or socialists. Hence, when feminists in the 1970s proposed that the law presume the lack of consent in all instances of rape, human rights groups (an important part of the progressive Left) chided them as to potential misuse of the law.[116] Nandita Haksar, a feminist human rights lawyer, offered a socialist theory of rape wherein rape by the police in rural areas was considered "a weapon of class domination."[117] In contrast to feminists' interest in "working out legal definitions of rape and description of individual cases," socialist feminists were keen to mobilize against violence by linking it to other struggles and engaging in "a programme of defensive resistance."[118] Law was *not* their preferred venue for political struggle. A materialist critique of Indian feminists' engagement with rape law has emerged only sporadically since the 1970s.

Nirbhaya's rape and murder offered Indian leftists a renewed opportunity to relate neoliberalism to violence against women and assess the IWM's strategy on rape law reform.[119] Some made a causal economic claim, reflected in a lengthy newspaper quotation included in the Verma Committee Report, that the lack of jobs outside casual work, the lack of recreational spaces, and a crisis of sexuality produced a mass of young, prospectless, and violent men.[120] Thus, between 1991 (when structural adjustment policies came into effect) and 2011, India's rapid economic growth and prosperity explained a reduction in serious crimes and in arrests of men for murders and rioting. However, this also exacerbated existing economic inequalities, resulting in increased sexual violence against women. Arrests for rape, molestation, and sexual harassment thus doubled during this twenty-year period.[121] The cultural variant of this causal argument proposed that the anomie of urban India drove violence against women.[122] The political variant blamed a Janus-faced Indian democracy, which permitted mass mobilization against rape but whose ruling class simultaneously cultivated a culture of violence and political patronage in India's slums to produce goons and bullies who raped.[123]

Materialist feminists also causally linked neoliberal economic policies to increased crimes against women. Maya John, a historian, offered a Marxist theory of rape,[124] initiating an online dialogue with Kavita Krishnan, a leading Indian feminist voice in the 2013 protests. John's thesis is that every class has its own women's question. Whereas in the 1970s and 1980s, rape in India, particularly in rural areas, could be characterized as "power" rape and explained by the overlapping structures of patriarchy, caste, religion, and feudal class status, Nirbhaya's rape in the heart of urban India was perpetrated by powerless migrant men.[125] According to John, Indian feminists' persistent explanation of urban rape in terms of patriarchy (portrayed as a coherent system) and ahistorical gender inequalities downplayed class inequalities. She argues that the "brutality of city-life is breeding potential rapists and victims in significant proportions."[126] Working-class men "returning from long, arduous hours of work; heavily underpaid; and hence, malnourished and poorly dressed" are not able to attract upper-class women.[127] Meanwhile, capitalism bombards working-class men with images of sex. Upper-class women incessantly indulge in hyper-femme behavior.[128] All this builds up the sexual desire of working-class men, who have no option but to "steal sex" from both upper-class women and vulnerable working-class women. Rape by the perpetrator becomes an individuated, nonpolitical, sexist reaction serving a sexual purpose, not a class-conscious, collective, political reaction.

John recognizes the inconsistencies of bourgeois legality, including its failure to criminalize date rape and marital rape and its individuated understanding of rape, which, while anchoring notions of bodily autonomy, also entrenches those of community and family honor. She also condemns the death penalty for rape as a patriarchal demand. She endorses as "noble" Indian feminists' efforts in enlarging the scope of rape to include "bad" sex—sex with the woman's nominal consent and free of physical coercion but without her *complete* consent. She is dissatisfied both with liberal feminists who would *not* view bad sex as rape and with radical feminists, who in her view understand all sex, whether bad or not, as rape, thus ignoring the possibility of pleasurable sex once women are liberated. John is concerned that Indian feminists view legal demands as final rather than intermediate steps toward "larger anti-systemic struggles."[129] After all, no matter how expansive bourgeois law becomes, true consent is possible only when the material basis of male–female relationships is transformed.

John's harshest critique is reserved for Indian feminists' lack of a class analysis and their management of commitments to gender and class equality through dual systems theory[130] and a theory of intersectionality[131] with overlapping systems of oppression.[132] She is critical of feminists' failure to account for the differential, sometimes contrasting stakes that women and men in varied class positions develop vis-à-vis each other.[133] Feminists' primary preoccupation with gender inequalities means they fail to recognize that the rape of upper-class women by lower-class men is highly unlikely unless they are situationally vulnerable (for example, stranded alone on a highway), or that upper-class women, through their hyperfemme behavior, consolidate their class status by attracting sexual partners from their class while causing lower-class men to inflict rape on them and working-class women. Notably, John does not consider the role women in privileged class or caste or religious positions play in inciting "their" men to sexually violate women from oppressed classes.

John's Marxist theory of rape exemplifies familiar Marxist arguments that feminists (including the author) find problematic—her treatment of stranger rape as paradigmatic; her hydraulic view of working-class male sexuality as natural, uncontrollable, and in need of satisfaction through any orifice; her commodification of female sexuality, which is capable of being "stolen"; her attribution of false consciousness to hyperfemme women, and her aspiration for a socialist utopia where adequate leisure will ensure romantic, fulfilling, and pleasurable sex. Moreover, there is little empirical basis to causally link neoliberalism and sexual violence, as most rapes in India do not involve strangers.[134] Only 2 percent involved strangers in 2012,[135] and 43 percent of rapists are older men, not young men from the slums. Moreover, Sudhir Krishnaswamy and Shishir Bail analyze National Crime Records Bureau data to show that particular regions rather than cities tend to be hotspots for rape.[136] Krishnan also dismisses the idea that a *lumpen proletariat* produced by neoliberalism is prone to criminal behavior, highlighting instead its potential for positive political change.

As skeptical as Indian feminists are of causal Marxist theories of sexual violence, they can hardly deny the role of class in producing women's vulnerability to violence. Indeed, if Nirbhaya's family had a chauffeur-driven car like many upper-class Indian families, she and her companion would not have resorted to a private bus after having been refused by as many as fifty autos[137] as they left Saket Mall. The neoliberal backdrop for Nirbhaya's rape and murder and the resultant protests were unmistakable, ranging from the rise of big media and their ratings-driven sensationalist "carpet-bombing" or campaign journalist coverage[138] of issues (which feminists argue reduced complex political messages to headline-grabbing sound bites) to the massive restructuring of urban spaces and the growing disparity in wealth over the past two decades. John's challenge to Indian feminists' lack of a materialist theory of sexual violence is therefore pertinent.[139]

In particular, John's thesis is valuable for refusing to prioritize an ahistorical idea of patriarchy. Even when highlighting how class inequalities generate sexual violence, she does not imagine that class simply converges to further entrench gender inequality. Instead, she maps out the differentiated stakes that both women and men from different classes have in both patriarchy and capitalism. This helps us acknowledge that an apparently gender-friendly rule change could end up promoting the interests of certain women while adversely affecting not only men but other women, thereby fundamentally problematizing feminism's brief to accurately represent anything as coherent as "women's interests." John's exposition of the graded and long-term nature of law reform also remains less susceptible to a tunneled vision focused on specific rule changes that is unable to anticipate the full range of unintended consequences. She thus poses the crucial question of what a materialist feminist agenda for law reform, if any, looks like. Would it prioritize social reform or some combination of social reform and/or governance reform and relegate regulatory reform to the background?

Alibis to Collaboration: Feminists and Rape Law Reform

As we have seen, feminists embraced criminal law and tightened their script of sexual subordination in advocating for rape law reform. The third dimension of GF is borne out in the IWM's increasingly collaborative engagement with the state. This holds true for rape as well and is facilitated in turn by the IWM's prioritization of law reform, the emergence and consolidation of state feminism, and the increasingly influential role played by lawyers at the forefront of feminist struggles.

Law and the Indian Women's Movement

The law has played a central role in the struggles of the IWM.[140] Feminist engagement with regulatory reform in the 1980s generated several successes when laws against rape, dowry deaths,[141] sati,[142] sex selection of fetuses, and sexist media representations were passed.[143] When these legal reforms did not translate into justice for women but rather produced perverse interpretations in the hands of state institutions, feminists revisited their faith in the law. Upendra Baxi proposes a useful typology of Indian advocates to include nihilists, evangelists, moderates, and eclectics. Nihilists trash the law and have little faith in its ability to deliver justice. Evangelists passionately but also blindly appeal to the law as a site of reform. Moderates have tempered expectations of the law's potential for justice. Finally, eclectics harbor unpredictable dispositions toward the law.

Analyzed through Baxi's lens, Indian feminists have been moderates. They stopped short of articulating demands only in legal terms.[144] This caused considerable concern within IWM ranks, as feminists introspected whether their increased reliance on the state and on criminal sanctions indicated their own lack of power or theoretical firmness in addressing structural issues relating to patriarchy and gender discrimination.[145] One feminist human rights lawyer opined that Indian feminists had fallen into the trap of the liberal human rights model[146] and that continual recourse to the law was no substitute for building a social movement; a socialist feminist similarly called for mass-based militant politics.[147] To be sure, no part of the IWM was deluded as to the law's emancipatory potential; women's groups saw "legal reform as a broad strategy to achieve legitimacy and social recognition, and some short-term legal redress."[148] A combination of a generational gap in feminists' expectations of the law[149] and the harsh realities of the weak enforcement of much-anticipated new laws led the pendulum to swing within the IWM from a high reliance on the law to a more critical and nuanced approach to its strengths and limitations.

By 2004, Menon was doubtful whether the law was able to deliver even short-term legal redress, leading her to conclude that "while the law may not have failed us, we may have outgrown the law."[150] Some feminists even characterized the law's place in feminist praxis as melancholic.[151] The law, however, remains a significant and indeed fecund

site for feminist intervention, particularly by feminist lawyers, producing a paradoxical situation wherein the "law has become simultaneously the most used and criticized sphere for thinking about justice for
women."[152] As Sunder Rajan observes, "It is, ironically, the conspicu-
ous success of the women's movement in the field of legal reform that
led to the doubts about its efficacy as strategy."[153]

Feminist Lawyers

Feminist lawyers' increased prominence explains law's paradoxical
place in the IWM fueling a shift in the IWM's equation with the
law—from a moderate to an evangelical one. Already in 1997 Sakshi's
use of PIL (a domestic legal innovation with generous standing requirements[154]) led to the institution of the 172nd LCI and its proposal
of gender-neutral sexual assault. But feminist activists resisted "the
hectic pace of legal activism spurred by big NGOs that negate the history of struggles of oppressed groups and their present needs and realities."[155] They criticized Sakshi for proposing a gender-neutral sexual
assault law considering state violence against sexual minorities. As
litigation and consultative processes overshadowed popular mobilization by the IWM, the democratic deficit of these legalistic and consultative strategies became apparent.[156]

Feminist lawyers have had continued success in achieving regulatory
reform and, although their achievements have not been critically examined, recent legal developments on gender justice can be traced back to
key feminist legal figures. Sakshi's PIL in the Vishaka case (on sexual
harassment) ultimately resulted in the SH Act of 2013, while proposals
against domestic violence by feminist lawyer Indira Jaising resulted in
the PWDVA of 2005.[157] Feminist lawyer Vrinda Grover was part of a
working group constituted by the National Commission for Protection
of Child Rights to draft a law against child sexual exploitation; the Protection of Children from Sexual Offences Act was passed in 2012.
Grover and Karuna Nandy also assisted with drafting the CLA. Other
groups, such as the Majlis Legal Centre, founded by feminist lawyer
Flavia Agnes, have not only lobbied for law reform but are extensively
engaged in providing legal services in collaboration with the state, placing them in conflict with other more activist feminist groups.[158]

The paradoxical status of the law in the IWM notwithstanding,
feminists have extensively collaborated with the state at many sites of

state feminism with the goal of regulatory reform, assisted in no small measure by the increasingly evangelical role played by feminist law-yers. In fact, since India pioneered state feminism, the IWM has always had room for collaboration through consultation with the state; this was accompanied by protest on the streets. The shift within the IWM from protest to collaboration therefore refers to the changing mix of protest in relation to collaboration, namely, less protest and more collaboration. I next turn to an examination of how the issue of rape traveled in institutions of state feminism.

Rape and State Feminism

Through the 1990s, feminists found several venues of state feminism to collaborate with the state, including the LCI, expert state bodies such as the NCW, state commissions for women established at the pro-vincial level, the National Human Rights Commission, and a whole host of UN agencies, such as UN Women. Feminists used multiple venues in the case of rape as well. In earlier sections of this chapter, I elaborated on feminists' collaboration with the LCI as far back as 1980, the NCW in 1993, and the LCI once again in 2000. As the NCW started to appropriate genderspeak to offer little more than pure protection-ism and to legitimize state violence,[159] however, Indian feminists se-cured other venues of influence.[160] They engaged with the Home Min-istry by presenting their Sexual Violence Bill in 2010. By 2013, there was a feminist on the National Advisory Council, an elite coterie of academics that advised the Congress Party leader, who exerted de facto control over the government. In this position she had access to drafts of the CLA, which she shared with other feminists. Feminists further engaged with the Verma Committee in 2013. Ironically, post-CLA feminist claims that the state "betrayed" them reflect feminists' proximity to state power and the relatively direct access that Indian feminists have had to governmental bodies.

Winners and Losers: A Distributional Analysis of the Criminal Law (Amendment) Act

I have charted so far the emergence of Indian GF on the issue of rape and its consequent influence on the CLA. Not surprisingly, feminists welcomed the CLA as a step forward for Indian women.[161] Without judging the effects of Indian GF as necessarily negative, I offer in the spirit of collective reflection (a process feminists have already initiated)[162] an early and hopefully dispassionate evaluation of the likely consequences of the sections on rape in the CLA. I start by assessing the likely benefits of governance reform before considering specific rule changes through a legal realist lens.

Prioritizing Governance Reform

As already noted, regulatory reform is hardly adequate for securing justice; it must be supplemented by governance reform and social change. Feminist efforts to bridge the justice gap have resulted in an increased number of punitive provisions in the CLA but also significant new governance initiatives relating to free medical treatment, compensation for survivors of sexual abuse, and legal measures to require the police to take complaints of rape seriously. In addition, there are several gender-matching provisions in amendments to the Criminal Procedure Code of 1973, on the assumption that appointing female investigators and judges in rape cases will protect the survivor's interests.[163]

The CLA mandates that all hospitals provide free medical treatment to survivors of rape and acid attacks and penalizes the failure to do so.[164] The CLA also requires payment of a "just and reasonable" fine to an acid attack survivor to meet medical expenses that could otherwise leave her heavily indebted. The CLA thus offers systemic reform, which is likely to benefit the survivors of sexual abuse. Women are already seeking compensation, which they consider as the state's recognition of their injury.[165]

Section 166A of the CLA penalizes a police officer with imprisonment between six months and two years and a fine for failing to record a complaint alleging a sexual offense. Rape has always been a cognizable offense,[166] but Section 166A dramatically alters the police's incentive for recording rape. Section 166A, however, does not specify whether it is limited to complaints by survivors, and thus implicates a difficult debate within the IWM. In the face of complainants' reluctance to pursue a criminal law path, since 2013, third parties such as NGOs have filed complaints with the police, who then pressure the survivor to cooperate. Feminists object that this undermines the complainant's agency and transfers women's rights to their employers, family members, community, and neighbors, and thence to "an all-powerful, all-encompassing state."[167]

Yet feminists themselves may disregard the survivor's autonomy. In a recent case, when approached by a rape survivor, prominent feminist Madhu Kishwar[168] videotaped her verbal complaint, reportedly asking her leading questions throughout. The recording was distributed to the media and the NCW.[169] The police used Section 166A to make the recording the basis for an FIR against the accused, who, unable to bear the public humiliation, committed suicide. Section 166A's conferral of power on third parties (feminists included) that are committed to protecting the "rights" of women at *any* expense has already had serious unintended consequences.

Assessing Regulatory Reform through the Lens of Legal Realism

I now analyze the likely distributive effects of the black-letter rules pertaining to rape. For this analytical exercise, I temporarily set aside the vexed problem of the justice gap and specifically deploy a legal realist lens. A legal realist makes two primary assumptions. The first assumption is that in any given scenario, there are far more legal rules at play than typically meets the eye. Therefore, as much as we may think of wage labor contracts merely in terms of contract law, Morris Cohen, an American legal realist, argued that contract law can be operationalized only because the state chooses to exercise its sovereign powers in favor of one party over another. For him, contract law was a subsidiary branch of public law.[170] Similarly, Robert Hale theorized the relationship between labor law and property law.[171] These insights go against many orthodoxies of modern law, including an assumed fundamental divide between public law and private law. Applying this analysis to rape, then, feminists need to consider not only criminal law but also background legal rules (e.g., family law rules) that determine the bargaining powers of offenders and survivors of sexual abuse.

Duncan Kennedy elaborates on a second assumption that legal realists make:

> We do not assume that the legal system as a whole *deliberately decrees* one thing or another . . . Rather, we conceptualize the network

(of private rights and public regulations) as providing background rules that constitute the actors, by granting them all kinds of powers under all kinds of limitations, and then regulating interactions between actors by banning and permitting, encouraging and discouraging particular tactics of particular actors in particular circumstances.[172]

In other words, the inability of the legal system to address sexual violence cannot be explained away simply by the material and ideological stranglehold of patriarchy, capitalism, or capitalist patriarchy over it. Instead, men and women are viewed as having varied sets of bargaining endowments that they exercise against each other, leading to fluid even if predictable outcomes.[173] This does not mean that my legal realist assessment of rules is postfeminist; it simply approaches the CLA with a fluid understanding of how its rearrangement of legal entitlements affects the bargaining power of men and women vis-à-vis each other. As outlined by Halley in the Conclusion to this volume, this involves setting out the actors involved, not merely identifying the central legal rules but also unearthing background legal rules and then identifying the "surplus" (as she calls it) rather than offering an account solely of the injury (discrimination, inequality, violence) and the law's response to it.

Thinking of Rape Relationally

To enable a legal realist analysis of the CLA, I propose thinking about rape in relational terms. Rape has for long been understood as unwanted sexual intercourse violently inflicted by a stranger in response to which the state steps in to protect societal interests by prosecuting and convicting the offender. In the past few decades, with sustained feminist advocacy, rape law in common law jurisdictions has begun to seek to protect women's sexual autonomy rather than patriarchal interests in their chastity. Alongside these transformations, criminal law also increasingly adopts a contextual approach to rape by taking into account some aspect of the status of the offender or the survivor or both and/or the relationship between them.[174] The CLA follows this trend by naming certain forms of relational rape as aggravated rape (e.g., where the defendant is a relative, guardian, or teacher). Approaching rape relationally exposes a larger set of background legal rules, thereby enabling a more precise distributive analysis of rule changes.

A relational approach to rape is also necessary in light of recent crime statistics. In almost 86 percent of registered rape cases, the offender was known to the survivor.[175] Custodial rape cases (in police or judicial custody or in a hospital), meanwhile, accounted for only 197 out of 36,735 cases.[176] A study conducted by the national newspaper *Hindu* of rape cases that came before six Delhi district courts in the CLA's first year of operation confirms these trends. Of the 583 cases studied,[177] 41 percent involved consensual sex where family members registered rape cases to protest women's choices of sexual partners. In 23 percent of the cases, the couple engaged in consensual sexual intercourse on the basis of a failed promise to marry. Two-thirds of the rape cases thus dealt with consensual sex. Of the remaining percentage of cases involving nonconsensual intercourse, almost twice as many cases implicated a defendant known to the survivor than did not. Only 21 of the 583 cases involved stranger rape.

Based on these profiles of prosecutions for rape, my distributive analysis of the CLA focuses on two main categories of sexual interactions—(1) nonconsensual sex including (a) between strangers or between parties known to each other but not in a prior legal relationship or (b) between parties in a preexisting legal relationship (e.g., marriage or employment); and (2) consensual sex including (a) where third parties object to such consensual sex or (b) where consent is given by one party contingent on the satisfaction of a certain condition by the other. I discuss each in turn, reserving nonconsensual sex between parties in a preexisting legal relationship until the end.

Nonconsensual Sex between Strangers/Parties Known to Each Other but Not in a Prior Legal Relationship

Before 2013, rape was defined as penile, penetrative sex by a man upon a woman against her will or without her consent or where consent was given but was fundamentally vitiated (due to threat of harm, impersonation, intoxication, unsoundness of mind, or where the woman was less than sixteen years of age). Consent was not defined. Offenders could thus equate silence, submission, the lack of protest, or the lack of resistance with consent and thereby secure acquittals.[178] Pre-CLA, although the Punjab and Haryana High Court had clearly stated that mere submission to sex could not be treated as consent for which a voluntary and conscious acceptance of what was proposed was needed,[179] in practice, courts continued to look to physical indicators of force and resistance to prove lack of consent. Courts sometimes drew on the global definition of consent under Section 90 of the IPC, which refers to consent obtained under fear of injury or misconception of fact.[180]

Rape under the CLA can be examined under the following headings.

Actus Reus

Under the CLA, rape is nonconsensual penile, nonpenile, and nonpenetrative sex that is perpetrated by a man against a woman or that he causes another person to perpetrate, not just against the woman but also between the woman and a third party.[181]

Lack of Consent

The CLA expands the grounds of nonconsent listed under Section 375, a key aspect being the increase in the age of consent to eighteen. The CLA defines consent as "an unequivocal voluntary agreement when the woman by words, gestures, or any form of verbal or non-verbal communication, communicates willingness to participate in the specific sexual act."[182]

Judicial pronouncements on the meaning and scope of consent are awaited. Yet the task is a daunting one. How do we, for instance, understand the term "voluntary"? Does it mean the lack of visible physical coercion as understood in the liberal tradition? Or should one look to MacKinnon, who claims that "force and desire are not mutually exclusive under male supremacy. So long as dominance is eroticized, they never will be."[183] In other words, burdened by the false consciousness fostered by patriarchal sex, there is little difference between coercion and consent; even if a woman agrees to sex voluntarily, her consent may not be meaningful.[184] Indian feminists' idea of power rape assumes the presence of such intangible social coercion under circumstances of extreme power imbalance. Then there are legal realists who claim that all parties negotiating sex operate under varying degrees of coercion, as they are endowed differentially by immediately relevant as well as background legal rules.

Even assuming that we could legally fix the meaning of consent, how is it to be communicated? Drawing on Halley's analysis of the affirmative consent requirement under California law, it is not clear whether consent under the CLA can be signified through engagement in the sexual act or if a separate word, gesture, or communication is essential.[185] Moreover, sexual interactions extend over a time period and involve numerous sexual microacts. Does unequivocal consent have to be communicated for every microsexual act?

Mens Rea

What is the mens rea for the crime of rape?[186] The defendant may desire sex specifically without the survivor's consent, or may be aware that the survivor does not consent and be indifferent to that fact (i.e., reckless), or may be oblivious to whether she consents or not (e.g., negligent). The CLA does not specify the required mens rea for rape. However, commentators differ on whether a defendant with an honest (but mistaken) belief as to consent is guilty of rape.[187]

Burden of Proof

To prosecute rape under Section 375, the state's lawyers need to prove, beyond a reasonable doubt, the fact of sexual intercourse and the absence of an unequivocal, voluntary agreement communicated by the complainant in relation to a specific sexual act. Here they can rely solely on the survivor's testimony. Indian courts have consistently held that "conviction can be founded on the testimony of the prosecutrix alone unless there are compelling reasons for seeking corroboration."[188] For this, her testimony has to inspire confidence and be reliable. The defense would then have to introduce evidence to show that the incident did not occur or that the survivor consented, thereby generating doubt as to the prosecution's case. Because of rape shield laws,[189] however, the defense cannot go into the survivor's sexual history for whether she is habituated to sex, is of loose moral character, or is of easy virtue; into her clothing; or into her past association or acquaintance with the accused. The defense can realistically go only into the details of her movement on the day of the incident, her state of mind then, her disposition toward the accused, and her conversations with the accused and others after the incident.

Furthermore, Section 376 of the CLA lists several forms of aggravated rape, whereas per Section 114A of the IEA of 1872, if the woman were to claim lack of consent, this shall be presumed for evidentiary purposes. This presumption is, however, rebuttable, and it is up to the defense to adduce evidence of consent.

Consider the use of the CLA against stranger rape. With the CLA's new definition of consent, it would be easier to prosecute men for having sex with women not only where women resisted, fought back, and screamed but also where they began to resist but gave up, did not even begin to protest due to disadvantageous circumstances, did not want the sex but felt socially pressured to agree as a result of their upbringing, or were worried that resisting would result in adverse consequences for themselves and their families. The prosecution is assisted here by precedent not requiring corroboration of the survivor's testimony and tough rape shield laws.

Further, with the expansion of power rape from purely custodial contexts to everyday situations of power imbalance, and the attendant reversal of the burden of proof, it would be easier for the prosecution to convict several categories of rapists who are acquainted with the survivor. These include abuse by an uncle or father-in-law of a young relative, by a medical professional caring for a pregnant patient, by a teacher or PhD supervisor of a female student, by an employer of a domestic worker, by an upper-caste head of village of a female *dalit* farmworker, by a garment factory owner of a female worker, and by a Hindu nationalist of a female Muslim neighbor during communal riots. In other words, the CLA could potentially reduce the tolerated residuum of abuse to enhance women's sexual autonomy.

Consensual Sex between Partners

While the affirmative consent standard built into the CLA will target much forced sex, it will also have repercussions for consensual sex. Consider a woman who desired sex itself during a sexual encounter but was ambivalent about the man or the circumstances, a woman who desired sex with the man but was ambivalent as to the specific acts, a woman who desired sex including all the specific sexual acts but did not communicate her consent to every single act, or a woman who communicated consent by simply engaging in sex rather than by offering verbal or other affirmation of consent. The CLA's definition of consent also begs the question of whether a woman (or a man) can ever possess complete capacity, freedom, and information to agree unequivocally to sex. The CLA, moreover, assumes full rationality and single-mindedness, whereas a woman could be mistaken, confused, or conflicted about her state of mind; could change her mind; could forget her previous state of mind; or could be of two minds at the same time.[190] In all these instances, the affirmative consent standard could recast consensual sex as rape.

Further, feminists have long noted how Indian rape law "is intrinsically connected with notions of honour, sexuality and marriage."[191] This is manifest especially in parental and social control over the sexual relationships of young adults. Marriage is the compulsory institutional form within which sexual relationships are permitted. To the extent that marriage is considered a social relationship between not just two individuals but their extended families and communities, the decision to have sex assumes expansive social significance. Where young adults transgress the mandate of the marital form and/or sexually liaise with a person of the wrong social status, parents and families mobilize various forms of law, including criminal law, to target their alliances.

Parents who disapprove of their daughter's sexual alliances can file a complaint of kidnapping, abduction, or rape, or obtain a writ of habeas corpus against her male partner for private detention and bring her back to the patriarchal household.[192] Recollect that rape is a cognizable offense and that the *survivor's* complaint is not essential to initiate criminal proceedings; a complaint by a third party suffices. Where pre-CLA the age of consent was sixteen, Section 375 increases it to eighteen years old. Hence, for a considerably higher number of adolescent couples who engage in sex across caste, class, or religious lines, or even within these boundaries but against their families' wills, the male could face prosecution for rape launched by the female's family.[193] Parents can also mobilize a provision on aggravated rape against teenage sex. Clause (i) of Section 376(2), added in 2013, lists intercourse with a female under sixteen years of age as aggravated rape; pre-CLA, rape of a female between twelve and sixteen would have simply been rape.

Parents of an adult woman can pursue a charge for aggravated rape under clause (k) of Section 376(2), also added in 2013, pertaining to rape by a man in a position of control or dominance. The terms "control" and "dominance" are not defined; the Sexual Violence Bill of 2010, drafted by feminists, defines them as covering "situations of religious, ethnic, linguistic, caste and class dominance, including (but not limited to) both formal and informal employment situations such as landlord-agricultural labourer, contractor-labourer, employer-domestic worker." Clause (k) is therefore ripe for an interpretation that consensual sex between two adults from different religious, caste, or class communities is aggravated rape.

Misuse of these provisions is further enabled by Section 114A of the IEA, which introduces a rebuttable presumption of lack of consent for aggravated rape. A woman under family pressure could claim lack of consent, thereby shifting the burden of proof to the defendant to prove consent. By pointing to the potential abuse of Sections 375 and 376, I am not suggesting that women lie about rape but that increasing the age of consent under Section 375 and inserting new categories of aggravated rape for girls between twelve and sixteen years old and for women subject to power rape, offers families additional opportunities for pressuring their daughters into pressing rape charges. Unless the offender is under the age of eighteen (and therefore a juvenile and not subject to criminal proceedings), he could be arrested for rape. Recollect that aggravated rape is punishable with minimum mandatory imprisonment for ten years to life (for the duration of natural life).

Consensual Sex Contingent on an Unfulfilled Condition

In India, given the continuing stigma of premarital sex, women who have sex with men because they were promised marriage but who were later spurned have prosecuted their partners for rape. Some high courts have convicted these men on the basis of Section 90 of the IPC, under which consent given under misconception of fact is not consent. Yet other high courts and more recently the Indian Supreme Court have ruled that a mere breach of promise to marry will not result in a conviction for rape.[194] Instead, the offender's motives have to be examined. A man would be guilty of rape only if his intention all along was to have sex without marrying, not if marriage failed to materialize for unavoidable circumstances. These decisions were, however, rendered pre-CLA.

Could a breach of promise to marry plus sexual contact be considered rape under the CLA? Very simply put, yes. The new definition of consent, requiring an unequivocal, voluntary agreement communicated for specific sexual acts, places a premium on female sexual autonomy. Consider the evolving jurisprudence around conditional consent in England and Wales,[195] where Section 74 of the Sexual Offences Act of 2003 has an affirmative consent standard similar to that of the CLA. English appellate courts have interpreted Section 74 quite broadly to find that there was no consent in a series of recent cases: a Muslim wife consented to sex with her husband on the condition that he not ejaculate inside her but he did so;[196] a woman consented to sex with Julian Assange on the condition that he use a condom but he did not;[197] and an adolescent girl filed a complaint of sexual assault against a transgender person on the basis that she consented to sexual activity with a male, not a female.[198]

These decisions to uphold women's sexual autonomy are far from uncontroversial. Criminal law scholars have long debated whether "consensual" sex based on a mistaken fact amounts to rape.[199] The disagreement is particularly stark when upholding women's sexual autonomy risks marginalizing vulnerable sexual minorities such as transgender persons.[200] An alternative seems to be to prosecute defendants for a less serious offense like obtaining sex by false pretenses, previously available under the Sexual Offences Act of 1956.

The CLA's affirmative consent standard could thus be used to prosecute men who falsely promise marriage, for rape. Media crime correspondents also point to this possibility in cases of a fallout in live-in relationships and a refusal to fulfill the promise of marriage.[201] In fact, one can imagine any number of cases where consent to sex was given on the woman's knowledge of certain facts about the defendant, which she may later find to be inadequate, misleading, or false for purposes of informed consent. Criminalizing these as rape will undoubtedly bring redress to some women but will dramatically rearrange patterns of sexual bargains between consenting adults outside of marriage. Feminists will need to assess whether in the long run it will enhance women's sexual choices, a precious goal for feminists, historically speaking.

Nonconsensual Sex between Parties in an Existing Legal Relationship

If 86 percent of Indian rapists are known to their survivors, a significant proportion of rape must occur in relationships formed at two institutional sites—the workplace and the family. Within months of the

CLA coming into force, rape in both contexts was debated extensively, and the significance of background legal rules—employment law and sexual harassment law in the case of rape at work, and family law and domestic violence law in the case of marital rape—became apparent.

Employment Relationship

Pre-CLA, guidelines issued by the Indian Supreme Court in the Vishaka case required sexual harassment committees to be set up in all workplaces as a stopgap arrangement until Parliament legislated on the issue. In the absence of a specific offense of sexual harassment, a survivor could file charges under Sections 354, 509 (outraging modesty), or 294 (dealing with obscenity) of the IPC. The SH Act was passed in 2013. It builds on the Vishaka guidelines and creates a civil law framework for addressing sexual harassment. It also mandates the employer to assist the complainant in filing a criminal case and to initiate such a complaint where the facts suggest a crime.

So how has the CLA addressed rape at the workplace? In 2013, the CLA introduced a new criminal offense of sexual harassment. Section 354A criminalized "unwelcome physical contact and showing pornography against a woman's will," "a demand or request for sexual favours" (punishable with rigorous imprisonment for three years or a fine), and "making sexually coloured remarks" (punishable with rigorous imprisonment for one year and/or a fine). This definition substantially mirrors that of sexual harassment under the SH Act and the Vishaka guidelines. However, Section 354A is poorly drafted; it criminalizes "making sexually coloured remarks" with *no indication* of whether this has to be against the woman's will, potentially criminalizing consensual sexual banter. The term "sexual" lacks definition, ripe for use by vigilantes to freeze sexual speech.[202]

Further, consider the combined effect of Section 354A and the SH Act. An employer in receipt of a complaint of sexual harassment (now a crime) is obligated under the SH Act to initiate a criminal case. The employer may consider using Section 294, 509, 354, or 354A. Charges under Sections 509 and 354 are subject to Section 166A, requiring the police to file a complaint at risk of penalty. In turn the police will solicit the survivor's cooperation; she now *must* pursue a criminal law remedy when sexually harassed. As feminists point out in private, a survivor cannot then opt out of the criminal process, as withdrawing a complaint filed by her employer would not only compromise adjudication of her complaint but also expose her to prosecution for filing a false complaint under Section 14 of the SH Act. If charges are filed under Sections 294 and 354A (which are not subject to Section 166A), however, she may be able to pursue action under the SH Act alone.

Although women can avail of civil and criminal remedies against sexual harassment, the burdens of supporting criminal prosecution are immense. This was evident in one of the first test cases under the CLA of the alleged rape by digital penetration and sexual harassment by Tarun Tejpal, an editor of *Tehelka,* an Indian newspaper, of his junior journalist colleague in a hotel elevator in Goa. The survivor initially filed a complaint with her employer instead of with the police for fear of adverse publicity, but the newspaper had no internal sexual harassment complaints committee. Her correspondence was leaked to the media, forming the basis of an FIR filed by the Goa police against Tejpal for aggravated rape as he was in a position of authority vis-à-vis her. Pre-CLA, nonpenile penetration was not rape, nor was sexual harassment a separate offense. So the complainant's employer could have processed the complaint internally. Post-CLA, however, the criminal justice system took over and the complainant had little say in the matter. She cooperated with the police but only when Tejpal cast aspersions on her and his family intimidated her. This was amid considerable personal hardship (she resigned from her job soon after the incident became public) and without meaningful witness protection. The case illustrates the limitations of the criminal law process when compared with civil redressal.[203]

Another case relates to the alleged sexual harassment of a law intern by a former Supreme Court judge. Her law school had no complaints committee, and she was unwilling to file a criminal complaint with the police, nor did she cooperate with them when an NGO activated Section 166A to make the police file an FIR. As influential public figures defended the judge, however, she publicized her complaint through Indira Jaising, a feminist lawyer. Amid mounting pressure, the former judge resigned. This demonstrates the ability of feminists, the media, and opportunistic NGOs to mobilize legal and extralegal strategies to hold powerful men accountable even if complainants are not entirely on board. It will take a strong complainant to resist their pressure.[204]

The intern, however, skillfully chose to shame the judge rather than cooperate with the police. Her ambivalence toward the law and its limits is worth recollecting: "Despite the heated public debates, despite a vast army of feminist vigilantes, despite new criminal laws and sexual harassment laws, I have not found closure. The lack of such an alternative led to my facing a crippling sense of intellectual and moral helplessness."[205] If nothing else, feminists could give pause to their evangelical pursuit of regulatory reform and ask if and how reform can address the needs of women we claim to speak for.

Marital Rape

A key drawback of the CLA was its refusal to remove the husband's immunity for marital rape. Pre-CLA, under Section 375, sexual intercourse by a man with his wife above fifteen years old was *not* rape. If he raped her when she was between twelve and fifteen years old, he was liable for up to two years' imprisonment, a fine, or both. If he raped her when they were living separately under a separation decree or according to custom or usage, he faced up to two years in prison and a fine. Outside these scenarios, husbands could rape their wives without facing prosecution. The CLA expanded this immunity. Under Section 375, the husband's immunity now extends to sexual intercourse *and sexual acts.*

There is effectively no immunity for marital rape when the couple is separated, as Section 376B states that a husband rapes when he has unwanted sexual intercourse with his wife when they are separated "under a decree of separation or *otherwise."* His punishment has also increased from two years to a period between two and seven years.

The marital rape immunity has been challenged in court—in the Kerala High Court by a practicing lawyer and in the Delhi High Court and Supreme Court by two NGOs, neither of which is explicitly feminist,[206] on the basis that the immunity violates the equality clause of the Indian Constitution. Although initially dismissed,[207] the Supreme Court in October 2017 held that sexual intercourse with a girl under eighteen years of age is rape regardless of whether she is married or not. In July 2017, the Delhi High Court decided to hear writ petitions challenging the constitutionality of the marital rape immunity. Meanwhile, some feminist lawyers claim that India suffers from a marital rape crisis of tragic proportions.[208] Human rights groups cite a survey conducted by the United Nations Population Fund in which a third of all Indian men admitted to a forced sexual act with their wives, while the Rice Institute found that fewer than 1 percent of marital rapes were reported.[209]

Feminists, meanwhile, are *not* pursuing the marital rape campaign single-mindedly. Instead, Madhu Mehra, of Partners for Law in Development, a legal resource group for women, claims that the marital rape campaign privileges and exceptionalizes nonconsensual penetrative sex as the ultimate violation that women face (over, say, life-threatening domestic violence), thereby inviting protectionist measures from the state. Feminists, according to her, need to challenge normative sexuality and have community engagements on a "broader sexuality agenda."[210] Meanwhile, wives could pursue other legal remedies: sue for divorce, press charges for cruelty under Section 498A of the IPC,[211] or pursue civil remedies under the PWDVA of 2005.

A legal realist "tail" accompanies this normative feminist rethink. Feminists have put on the table the full range of criminal and civil remedies to ask how women might use them to negotiate their autonomy (sexual and otherwise). Thus, asks one lawyer, if marital rape were a crime, how would an acquittal for marital rape impact a civil lawsuit for divorce?[212] Another noted that a wife may charge rape for leverage in a property dispute; the Section 166A mandate to file a rape charge means that the police may do this more routinely in family disputes.[213]

A word on background conditions—recollect that the Indian female workforce participation rate is relatively low at 28 percent.[214] This accompanied by a high rate of marriage and the lack of remuneration for wives' domestic labor means that many wives (and their children) are economically dependent on their husbands and fathers for basic needs. Add to this a cultural context where wives are viewed as domestic and sexual laborers, not equal parties in a companionate marital relationship. Further, almost a third of married women suffer from physical abuse, 14 percent from emotional abuse, and 10 percent from severe domestic violence.[215]

Possible legal venues for wives against marital rape and sexual abuse include filing criminal charges relating to outraging modesty (Sections 509, 354), sexual harassment (Section 354A), obscenity (Section 294), unnatural sex (Section 377),[216] and cruelty (Section 498A). However, the extension of the marital rape immunity to sexual acts (in addition to sexual intercourse) under Section 375 of the CLA is a likely obstacle.[217]

They could also use the PWDVA, a civil law with an expansive definition of domestic violence and a full range of remedies (including residence, protection, maintenance, and compensation orders) adjudicated
by magistrates' courts. Alternatively, a wife could file for divorce in the
family court on the grounds of cruelty. An analysis of cases under the
PWDVA and relating to divorce on grounds of cruelty reveals that this
ground is rarely used to address marital rape.[218] Moreover, women also
struggle to access the legal system. The chronic lack of institutional
capacity already incentivizes counseling and settlement in the preliti-
gation phase whether in respect to Section 498A, domestic violence, or
divorce.[219]

To fully appreciate the CLA's distributional effects on wives, I propose differentiating them into three categories:[220] (1) wives who are
subject to marital rape but are *not* close to the point of exit or divorce,
(2) wives who are subject to marital rape and are close to the point of
exit, and (3) wives who are close to the point of exit but are *not* sexually
abused.

Wives Who Are Subject to Marital Rape but Are Not Close to Exit

The first category of wives is subject to a continuum of forced sex from
unwanted sexual intercourse to unpalatable sexual acts accompanied
by physical, emotional, or social harassment. In light of prevalent economic background conditions, the wife may simply assume such unwanted sex to be part of the marriage "deal" and, in response, adopt a
range of under-the-radar strategies from feigning illness to holding
back on her household commitments. She may next resort to family,
friends, and other elders to counsel her husband. If this fails, she may
consider legal options, but resorting to state law (or airing family disputes or problems publicly) could invite the husband's retaliation and
a demand for divorce. Moreover, she may still want her husband in her
life rather than behind bars. For her, even a complaint to the police
may readjust marital bargaining power in her favor. In the decade following the PWDVA's passage, the public awareness it has generated
means that husbands now inflict stealth levels of violence sufficient to
assert their control over their wives without being visible enough to
warrant a visit from the local policeman.[221] The wife in this category
may use the PWDVA but is unlikely to pursue criminal action. The
expanded marital rape immunity, in any case, does not shift her bargaining endowments very much.

Wives Who Are Subject to Marital Rape and Are Close to Exit

These wives are subject to marital rape and/or extreme physical violence. A husband's sodomization of one such wife with a torch after which she bled for sixty days led her to challenge the constitutionality of the marital rape immunity. These wives, having long endured escalating sexual violence, are closer to the point of exit and therefore more determined to pursue legal action than wives in the first category.[222] They may initially be reluctant to use criminal law because of both the husband's expanded immunity under Section 375 and the need for protracted engagement with the corrupt and inefficient Indian police. This leaves them with the PWDVA and family law. Pursuing both criminal law (for offenses other than rape, such as cruelty and unnatural sex) and civil law options means that their outcomes become interdependent. Initially, irrespective of whether criminal charges result in conviction or acquittal, merely filing such a charge improves a wife's bargaining power in the civil system. An acquittal for sexual abuse will, however, undermine her divorce case on the basis of cruelty; a conviction will have the opposite effect. A success in the civil arena, on the other hand, may or may not assist with conviction; a failure in the civil realm will negatively affect the criminal outcome. A complainant may of course choose not to pursue both options. Yet for some wives, a civil remedy will simply not suffice. One survivor of marital rape refused to legally divorce her husband so that he could not remarry and abuse another woman, insisting that he be punished.[223]

Wives Who Are Close to Exit but Are Not Sexually Abused

Questioning the need for criminalizing marital rape, some feminists point to Section 498A of the IPC as it deals with cruelty against a wife inflicted by her husband or relatives. Section 498A, passed in 1984 after years of campaigning by the IWM against dowry deaths, has ironically developed a reputation for opportunistic use by wives. After all, nothing shames a family more than when a husband and his parents are arrested and spend a night in jail, that too upon the mere verbal allegation of the wife. According to Srimati Basu, a feminist ethnographer of family courts, women commonly file criminal and civil cases simultaneously. The threat of jail time, loss of employment, and social embarrassment provides them leverage for a better divorce settlement, alimony, and custody settlements.[224] This led the Indian

Supreme Court in 2005 to label Section 498A a tool of "legal terrorism" used mercilessly by "disgruntled wives." In July 2017, the Indian Supreme Court issued guidelines to ensure that Section 498A was used appropriately. The removal of the marital rape immunity in 2013 may have added another bargaining tool (rendered especially powerful by the definition of consent) for this category of wives against their husbands.

The use of Section 498A by wives, their families, and feminists in NGOs has fostered an Indian men's rights movement (MRM). The MRM calls for "due process in criminal charges, gender neutrality in custody and maintenance with attention to class and economic resources, protection from violence, and funds for economic development of needy men."[225] Basu in her study of the MRM acknowledges that feminists may refrain from publicly critiquing women's misuse of Section 498A,[226] as they deem this leverage to be crucial for financial settlement in divorce cases. Yet "they cannot, in good conscience, ignore the problems some people face from thin yet long-lasting criminal charges and the danger of losing modest lifelong savings in defending them."[227] Ultimately, she suggests that feminists need to support men's civil rights to regain credibility.

The CLA has undoubtedly shifted women's bargaining endowments vis-à-vis those of men in the context of rape. Had the CLA removed the husband's immunity for marital rape, it would have had mixed consequences. For wives not close to the point of exit but who have been raped, it would have likely had only a symbolic effect. For wives in divorce proceedings but not subject to marital rape, it would have enhanced their bargaining power to negotiate better outcomes. Wives who were raped and close to the point of exit would have benefited the most, although even for them, the benefits are not obvious given the complex interrelationship between criminal and civil remedies.

In conclusion, despite my analysis of the unpredictable effects of regulatory reform, I remain unconvinced that there is any justification (legal or otherwise) for the exceptionalist treatment of wives under rape law. Although the Indian government argued against criminalizing marital rape on the basis that marriage in India is considered a sacrament, feminists have exposed the vast levels of legitimated sexual abuse within marriage. We must also acknowledge the complex bargains struck between men and women, whether sexually abused or not, before, during, and at the termination of a marriage. Reconsideration by some feminists of the criminalization of marital rape is therefore welcome.

The Criminal Law (Amendment) Act Reconsidered

I have so far offered a legal realist analysis of the CLA's rape provisions. Having argued for a relational approach to rape, I highlighted the significance of background legal rules in determining women's bargaining power. Additionally, I make no a priori assumptions on the likely outcomes of the CLA's enforcement and instead point to the various scenarios in which women and/or men win and/or lose under the new law.

The CLA's attempts at governance and regulatory reforms, the introduction of the new definition of consent under Section 375, and an expansion of the remit of power rape under Section 376 could potentially reduce the tolerated residuum of abuse of highly vulnerable women. Moreover, the symbolic effects of criminal law are immense and will likely lead to the readjustment of expectations on the part of both perpetrators and survivors of abuse. Indeed, in the months after the CLA's passage, there was visibly more reporting of rape in the media. Crime statistics already indicated a steady increase in reports of crimes against women between 2010 and 2012, with roughly 15,000 additional cases reported every year since 2010. However, in 2013 this number increased dramatically by 50,000 cases to reach a total of 309,546.[228] In 2014, the total number of cases increased to 337,922, registering a higher rate of increase than between 2010 and 2012. Figures for rape more specifically show an increase of 9.2 percent in 2011 over 2010, 3.0 percent in 2012 over 2011, 35.2 percent in 2013 over 2012, and 9 percent in 2014 over 2013. The political groundswell that Nirbhaya's rape and murder generated in a vast cross-section of the Indian population had implications for the willingness of survivors to report rape.

At the same time, the CLA's high threshold of affirmative consent, the increase in the age of consent, the widening of the ambit of power rape, and the reversals of burden of proof in favor of survivors supplemented by precedent on not requiring corroboration of a survivor's testimony have the potential for recasting a lot of consensual sex as rape. The potential for misuse of these apparently beneficial provisions in the hands of families who disagree with women's sexual choices is immense. Conversely, an affirmative consent standard, which is meant to protect women's sexual autonomy, can also undermine their zones of sexual freedom by penalizing the breach of promise to marry as rape, for this reflects the premium placed on marriage in Indian society, thus reinscribing the hegemony of the heteropatriarchal institution of marriage. Meanwhile, the criminalization of sexual harassment under the CLA is not necessarily beneficial for female employees, as evident in the Tejpal case. The wide-ranging definition of sexual harassment as a way of desexualizing the workplace in order to counter sexual subordination not only is unrealistic but brings with it erotic costs for both men and women.

Similarly, while there is no reason whatsoever for rape law to distinguish between married and unmarried women, the criminalization of marital rape, had it been achieved in 2013, would have had disparate effects on different segments of married women. At best, it would have had symbolic value for wives who are raped but unwilling to exit their marriage, and it would have been undoubtedly crucial for wives who were sexually abused and close to exiting the marriage. For wives who were not abused but were exiting marriage, criminalizing marital rape may have added to their negotiating tool kit with long-term adverse effects for men subject to the criminal justice system. Thus, several provisions of the CLA, if enforced properly, can root out the worst male sexual abusers, which is beneficial to society as a whole, but not without running the risk of undermining the erotic lives, choices, and sexual agency of both women and men.

Any benefits for women and their improved bargaining power, however, need to be assessed against the costs of the highly carceral CLA. After all, the CLA increases penalties for existing and new offenses and introduces minimum mandatory sentencing without judicial discretion. The CLA, we are also told by sentencing experts, gets sentencing completely wrong.[229] Mrinal Satish predicts that the CLA will result in higher acquittal rates; and where cases result in convictions, "there will be a tendency to award the same sentence which will continue to build cynicism towards [the] sentencing process, the criminal justice process and the entire legal process."[230] Worse, and embarrassingly for feminists, after decades of isolating the use of the death penalty to "the rarest of the rare" cases on constitutional grounds, the CLA introduces it for violent rape.

In *Shakti Mills,* the first case to result in a conviction under Section 376E of the CLA, the Mumbai trial court sentenced to death three defendants for the gang rape of two women under almost identical circumstances. Trials for both cases were conducted simultaneously with conviction in one case leading to an additional charge and subsequent conviction in the second case. It was presided by a zealous female judge and argued by a prosecutor who is an antiterror expert; both liberally invoked patriarchal notions of rape,[231] much to feminist discomfort.[232] Feminists staunchly opposed this sentence as a mockery of Section 376E,[233] especially because the defendants were 18, 20, and 27, two were Muslim, and the third was from a lower caste. The defendants could have been sentenced to life imprisonment, after all. Feminists need to be prepared for the possibility that enhanced penalties under the CLA may deter police from arresting and prosecutors from pressing charges. Judges will be predisposed to acquitting the defendant because, in their minds, the punishment is not commensurate with the offending behavior.[234] The special public prosecutor in the Nirbhaya case expressed this very concern, that post-CLA, a higher number of offenses may be recorded but tougher penalties would result in fewer convictions.[235]

There are many other missed opportunities and drafting errors in the CLA for feminists to keep on their radar screen for future reform. The CLA retains the gender specificity of all provisions (except trafficking and acid attacks) even where men are subject to similar forms of violence. Significantly, the gender-specific definition of rape means that women who cause another person to engage in unwanted sexual activity, especially in the context of communal, caste, or sectarian violence, will escape punishment. John refers to women's role in such violence through the 1990s.[236] Conversely, male, transgender, and intersex survivors of rape are not covered by Section 375. Moreover, several acts are consolidated under the *actus reus* of rape under Section 375, which would typically warrant separate offenses with different punishments with some not qualifying as rape. There is no gradation in these acts. Elsewhere, they are distributed across four offense headings under the Sexual Offences Act of 2003 (Sections 1–4). There are other drafting errors in the CLA, which will require a careful interpretation by courts. For instance, one exception to Section 375 is where penetration is for a medical procedure or intervention. Such penetration is presumably consensual, but the exception is not worded in these terms and could potentially exempt a nonconsensual medical penetration from liability for rape. Further, the trafficking offense omits listing forced labor as a form of exploitation, departing from the Article 3 definition of trafficking under the UN Protocol to Prevent, Suppress and Punish Trafficking in Persons, Especially Women and Children, supplementing the UN Convention against Transnational Organised Crime 2000. Although forced labor is a labor law offense, the CLA missed an opportunity to send a message denouncing the forced labor of millions of male and female workers in several labor sectors. That Indian feminists had no response to this omission is revealing of the IWM's priorities. Sex workers' groups were so preoccupied with resisting the conflation of sex work with trafficking that they overlooked this omission.

Conclusion

From my study of Indian feminist strategizing on rape law reform over the past thirty-five years, I argue that their ideas have found more than a foothold in institutions of state power. No matter how tentative feminists remain about their influence on the state, as Indian GF comes into its own, feminists can hardly deny that they have far more opportunities for being heard and taken seriously now than ever before. Feminist ideas circulate in the veins of the CLA, and entire provisions can be traced back to feminist documents. Indeed, they took credit for the CLA.[237] Few feminists expressed concerns about increased criminalization as a way to protect women's safety and security.[238] An early assessment of the CLA suggests a trail of unintended consequences but also some limited scope for a reduction in the tolerated residuum of abuse. How should Indian GF manage this bittersweet moment of success? The challenges, as I see them, are numerous.

The Nirbhaya incident has revealed a generational rift within the Indian feminist community as younger feminists not only seem more skeptical of the law's promises than veteran feminists but also feel threatened to go against prevalent feminist "common sense."[239] Young feminists have nevertheless questioned feminists' faith in the CLA and its "harsh punitive regime,"[240] and the latter's fetishizing of sexual violence over the "violence of the state, caste oppression, displacement, poverty, [and] hunger."[241] Indian GF has been defensive; feminists argued against the urge: "To keep on talking about these cases till everyone is convinced there are serious problems with the law, that feminists lost their head in 2013, and that behind every high profile case there is a grand conspiracy against the accused. Please let's stop."[242] Notably, it was legal expertise that was mobilized to counter detractors. Vrinda Grover argued that characterizing the CLA as "draconian" was misplaced and misconceived.[243] The impulse to admonish critique is worrisome for the future of Indian feminism. We might instead take a cue from young activists who call on us to stage an abeyance from law or engage in unruly politics[244] or immerse ourselves in microexperiments[245] in governance reform.[246] If the seductions of law reform are too great to let go, we might at the very least introspect and unpack the entire gamut of the CLA's likely impact in regulating sexual abuse.

Looking outward, meanwhile, the landscape for feminist reform in India has fundamentally changed. Far from being the lone proponents of women's rights, feminists find themselves in a crowded field today, amid state feminists, single-issue NGOs, and fragile configurations of population groups like sex workers, all laying claim to the feminist mantle. Genderspeak has, after all, become a common political language resorted to by both progressive and conservative actors. If we are keen to hold on to the critical impulses of the IWM, something more than "pure" genderspeak is necessary. Taking up Maya John's challenge of articulating a materialist feminist theory of rape might be in order. In my mind, such a theory would have to resist the seductions of liberal, radical, and Marxist feminism and intersectionality analysis. We might consider untethering ourselves from an exclusively gendered script of sexual violence, recognizing the radical fluidity of gender identities, acknowledging that women in privileged positions can also perpetuate violence, taking into account the interests of men (at least some of the time), heeding men's call for new forms of political debate about sexual violence,[247] and articulating new forms of feminism such as choice feminism.[248]

We may even recollect the formative moments of our own vocabulary of sexual violence. Kavita Panjabi in a thought-provoking article draws on two short stories to map an alternate political imaginary around rape. In the first story, by Mahasweta Devi, Draupadi, the tribal Naxalite protagonist who is gang-raped by army men, approaches the commanding officer who directed her rape with her naked, bleeding body to mock his masculinity with a loud laugh, making him fear her.

Emblematic of the fraught relationship between Marxism and Indian feminism, Panjabi's second story is "Black Horse Square" by Ambai. Here, Rosa, a raped trade union activist, resists feminists' privileging of her rape as sexual violence over the violent torture of her male comrades at the hands of the state. She resists the sexualization of rape, which she insists heightens its use as a weapon. Could we then ever hope to mine the very dissonance deep in the heart of Indian GF, which resists rape by the state and its armed forces in far-flung parts of the country even while keeping faith in the state's benevolence in ordinary times closer to home? In the din of reporting by the "master of all moral indignation," namely, the media, such ruminations may not be enough and may even be pointless.[249]

Or we might invest all our efforts in consciousness raising, which has so far been the lasting legacy of Nirbhaya's rape and murder.[250] When a play inspired by Jyoti Pandey called *Nirbhaya* toured London, an Action Aid postcard with a raised arm and the V sign summoned each viewer to condemn violence against women. Outside the theater, playgoers and survivors of violence pinned their handwritten postcards to a large display board for public viewing. What better sign of GF could there be? I wondered to myself. The play itself recounted the happenings of the night of December 16, 2012, and four women then enacted scenes of child sexual abuse, gang rape, and dowry-related burning. As the play unfolded, it was revealed that they were not actors but survivors of violence—strangers who in the wake of the Nirbhaya incident had stumbled upon each other on Facebook and decided to reveal their painful, repressed memories publicly. Testimonial theater became the vehicle of consciousness raising to realize anew the feminist slogan of the personal as political. As we traverse the long path toward Nirbhaya's spirit of fearlessness and her desire to fight back, Meena Kandaswamy, a *dalit* poet, reminds us: "We are not the walking dead; every day comes alive because of us. We even own the nights. Patriarchal pride dies between our thighs."[251] It is this possibility that we should mine.

Notes

I am very grateful to my coauthors for their sustained engagement and excellent feedback on my chapter. In addition, I thank Duncan Kennedy and Upendra Baxi

134   *Prabha Kotiswaran*

for their extensive and thoughtful comments. My sincere gratitude to Trideep Pais, a Delhi-based criminal defense lawyer who offered invaluable insights on several aspects of Indian criminal law and procedure. My thanks also to Pratiksha Baxi and Peer Zumbansen for their valuable feedback. I also thank the participants at a Jindal Global Law School faculty seminar, particularly Ashley Tellis, Saptarshi Mandal, Amit Bindal, Prashant Iyengar, Dipika Jain, and Kimberly Rhoten. Mrinal Satish and Aparna Chandra at the National Law University, Delhi, offered valuable insights on key arguments. I also thank the participants at a workshop at the Centre for South Asian Studies (University of Toronto), particularly Ritu Birla; participants at the Governance Feminism Workshop held at Harvard Law School; and participants at the Seminar Series at the Centre for the Study of Law and Governance, Jawaharlal Nehru University, and at the Centre for Women's Development Studies, New Delhi, for their feedback.

1. Rajeswari Sunder Rajan, *The Scandal of the State: Women, Law, and Citizenship in Postcolonial India* (Durham, N.C.: Duke University Press, 2003); Nivedita Menon, *Recovering Subversion: Feminist Politics beyond the Law* (Urbana: University of Illinois Press, 2004); Srila Roy, "Melancholic Politics and the Politics of Melancholia: The Indian Women's Movement," *Feminist Theory* 10, no. 3 (2009): 341–57.

2. Menon, *Recovering Subversion*.

3. Kalpana Kannabiran and Ritu Menon, *From Mathura to Manorama: Resisting Violence against Women in India* (New Delhi: Women Unlimited, 2007).

4. Flavia Agnes and Audrey D'Mello, "Protection of Women from Domestic Violence," *Economic & Political Weekly* 50, no. 4 (2015): 76–84.

5. Peer C. Zumbansen, "Law after the Welfare State: Formalism, Functionalism, and the Ironic Turn of Reflexive Law," *American Journal of Comparative Law* 58, no. 3 (2008): 769–805.

6. See the four reports on various themes published by Partners for Law in Development in 2015, available at http://pldindia.org/pld-updates/trainings-sexual-harassment-rajasthan/.

7. Sally Engle Merry, *Human Rights and Gender Violence: Translating International Law into Local Justice* (Chicago: University of Chicago Press, 2006).

8. I use this instead of "Western feminism." The common law background of the United States, Canada, the United Kingdom, and India also enables a better comparison between legal regimes.

9. Prabha Kotiswaran, ed., *Sex Work* (New Delhi: Women Unlimited, 2011), xxix.

10. Prabha Kotiswaran, "Governance Feminism's Others: Sex Workers and India's Rape Law Reforms," in *Governance Feminism: Notes from the Field,* ed. Janet Halley, Prabha Kotiswaran, Rachel Rebouché, and Hila Shamir (Minneapolis: University of Minnesota Press, forthcoming).

11. *Report of the Committee on Amendments to Criminal Law*, January 23, 2013, http://apneaap.org/wp-content/uploads/2012/10/Justice-Verma-Committee-Report.pdf.

12. Protesters ranged from "funded NGOs to radical feminists; from students of Jawaharlal Nehru University to students from numerous private institutions like management institutes, engineering colleges, coaching centres and schools; from committed activists to people who merely wanted to be captured on camera and

wanted to check out the 'pretty' girls assembled at the protest venues; from Bhagat Singh Kranti Sena, to Shiv Sena activists; from misogynist 'babas' (godmen), to funded 'anti'-corruption crusaders; etc." Maya John, "Class Societies and Sexual Violence: Towards a Marxist Understanding of Rape," *Radical Notes,* May 8, 2013, https://radicalnotes.org/2013/05/08/class-societies-and-sexual-violence-towards -a-marxist-understanding-of-rape/.

13. The juvenile reportedly spent eight years in government remand homes where employees had sexually abused him.

14. Nandita Gandhi and Nandita Shah, *The Issues at Stake: Theory and Practice in the Contemporary Women's Movement in India* (New Delhi: Kali for Women, 1992), 16.

15. Gandhi and Shah, *Issues at Stake,* 285.

16. Nivedita Menon, *Seeing Like a Feminist* (New Delhi: Zubaan, 2012), 219.

17. Ibid.

18. Several such organizations have emerged in the wake of increased international funding for anti-trafficking work. Laura Agustín calls this phenomenon the rescue industry. Laura María Agustín, *Sex at the Margins: Migration, Labour Markets, and the Rescue Industry* (London: Zed Books, 2007).

19. Anna Yeatman, *Bureaucrats, Technocrats, Femocrats: Essays on the Contemporary Australian State* (Sydney: Allen and Unwin, 1990), 64–65, citing Drude Dahlerup from Showstack Sassoon, "Introduction," in *Women and the State: The Shifting Boundaries of Public and Private* (London: Unwin Hyman, 1987), 28.

20. Joyce Outshoorn and Johanna Kantola, eds., *Changing State Feminism* (New York: Palgrave Macmillan, 2007), 1.

21. Ibid.

22. Hester Eisenstein, *Inside Agitators: Australian Femocrats and the State* (Philadelphia: Temple University Press, 1996), 21.

23. Sadhna Arya, "The National Commission for Women: A Study in Performance" (New Delhi: Centre for Women's Development Studies, 2010), 21, 22, 25.

24. Ibid., 30, 41.

25. Conversation with Professor Upendra Baxi, July 2014.

26. Victoria Nourse, "The 'Normal' Success and Failures of Feminism and the Criminal Law," *Chicago-Kent Law Review* 75, no. 3 (2000): 951–78.

27. I refer to social reform sought through regulatory changes. Social reform can certainly occur without changes in state law.

28. Pratiksha Baxi, *Public Secrets of Law: Rape Trials in India* (New Delhi: Oxford University Press, 2014), xli.

29. Ibid., xl.

30. Ibid., 7.

31. Ibid., 182. Noncompoundable offenses cannot be subject to compromise by parties.

32. Veena Das, "Sexual Violence, Discursive Formations and the State," *Economic & Political Weekly* 31, nos. 35/37 (1996): 2411–18.

33. Mrinal Satish, "Chastity, Virginity, Marriageability, and Rape Sentencing," *Law and Other Things* (blog), January 4, 2013, http://lawandotherthings.blogspot .com/2013/01/chastity-virginity-marriageability-and.html.

34. Kannabiran and Menon, *From Mathura to Manorama,* 27.

35. Baxi, *Public Secrets,* 190, 346.

36. Duncan Kennedy, *Sexy Dressing, Etc.* (Cambridge, Mass.: Harvard University Press, 1993).

37. Ibid., 150.

38. See Arjun Appadurai's work on failure, in particular his MN Srinivas Lecture: "The Ecology of Failure: Reflections on Democracy, Participation, and Development" (King's College, London, March 27, 2014), https://www.youtube.com/watch?v=H8vnNFDRwPU.

39. Debolina Dutta and Oishik Sircar, "India's Winter of Discontent: Some Feminist Dilemmas in the Wake of a Rape," *Feminist Studies* 39, no. 1 (Spring 2013): 293–306. One feminist dilemma the authors discuss is the potential use of censorship laws to ban a rapper's song titled "I am a rapist."

40. Menon, *Recovering Subversion,* 110.

41. Ibid. But see Lotika Sarkar, "Rape: A Human Rights versus a Patriarchal Interpretation," *Indian Journal of Gender Studies* 1, no. 1 (1994): 70–71, where she criticizes an understanding of rape as a sexual offense rather than as an act of violence.

42. Catharine A. MacKinnon, *Women's Lives, Men's Laws* (Cambridge, Mass.: Harvard University Press, 2005), 247.

43. Jonathan Herring and Michelle Madden Dempsey, "Rethinking the Criminal Law's Response to Sexual Penetration: On Theory and Context," in *Rethinking Rape Law: International and Comparative Perspectives,* ed. Clare McGlynn and Vanessa E. Munro (Abingdon, U.K.: Routledge, 2010), 30–43.

44. Baxi calls the conceptualization of custodial rape the most unique feminist contribution to exposing the sexual politics of the state. Baxi, *Public Secrets,* 7.

45. Kannabiran and Menon, *From Mathura to Manorama,* 80.

46. Roy, "Melancholic Politics and the Politics of Melancholia," 343.

47. The Indian Penal Code, No. 45 of 1860, India Code §§ 375–76, http://indiacode.nic.in.

48. Ibid., 354, 509, 377.

49. Akila R.S., "Section 377: The Way Forward," *The Hindu,* May 19, 2016, http://www.thehindu.com/features/magazine/section-377-the-way-forward/article5740242.ece.

50. Vina Mazumdar, "Political Ideology of the Women's Movement's Engagement with Law," in *Engendering Law: Essays in Honor of Lotika Sarkar,* ed. Amita Dhanda and Archana Parashar (Lucknow, India: Eastern Book Company, 1999), 339–74, 351. See also Baxi, *Public Secrets,* 54nn41–42.

51. Law Commission of India, *Eighty-Fourth Report on Rape and Allied Offences: Some Questions of Substantive Law, Procedure and Evidence,* 1980, 15, http://lawcommissionofindia.nic.in/51-100/report84.pdf.

52. Notably, the commission justified trial in camera for the benefit of the survivor and the defendant given the stigma of a rape allegation. Ibid., 29.

53. Ibid., 35.

54. It read: "Where a woman is raped under economic domination or influence or control or authority, which includes domination by landlords, officials, management personnel, contractors, employers and moneylenders, either by himself or by persons hired by him, each of the persons shall be deemed to have committed power

rape." Lok Sabha debates, December 1, 1983, cited in Baxi, *Public Secrets,* 34. The amendment did not pass. Opposing it, P. Venkatasubbaiah argued that it would encourage false complaints by "unscrupulous women."

55. This covers rape by a police officer, public servant, or manager or staff member of a jail, remand home or other custodial institution, or hospital.

56. Indian Evidence Act, No. 1 of 1872, India Code § 114A, http://indiacode .nic.in.

57. The emergency years were when then prime minister Indira Gandhi unilaterally imposed a national emergency across the country for twenty-one months between 1975 and 1977. She ruled by decree. Elections were suspended, civil liberties of citizens (particularly those of her political opponents) severely curtailed, the press censored, and large-scale forced sterilization of the population undertaken.

58. Mazumdar, "Political Ideology of the Women's Movement's Engagement with Law," 353.

59. Vibhuti Patel, "'Law on Rape' Reviewing Rape: Proposed Changes in the Law by Lawyers Collective," *Economic & Political Weekly* 15, no. 1 (1980): 2138. *Dalits* are "outside" the caste system and considered untouchables.

60. Nandita Haksar, "Human Rights Lawyering: A Feminist Perspective," in Dhanda and Parashar, *Engendering Law,* 75.

61. Ibid., 76.

62. Laxmi Murthy, "Criminal Law Amendment, 2000 (CLA)," Partners for Law in Development, 2006, 2, http://pldindia.org/wp-content/uploads/2013/04/Comments -by-Laxmi-Murthy-to-Criminal-Law-Amendment-Bill-2000.pdf.

63. People's Union for Democratic Rights (PUDR), *Custodial Rape: A Report on the Aftermath,* (Delhi: Secretary, PUDR, 1994), 24.

64. Menon, *Recovering Subversion,* 123.

65. Ibid., 111.

66. Ibid., 113. Menon concludes this from the proposal's emphasis on the "sexual purpose" of touch, gestures, or sounds/words making these actionable under the law.

67. Ibid., 126–28. The benefits of prosecuting child sexual abuse outweighed the cost of criminalizing consensual adolescent sex. Citing inconsistencies between civil law and criminal law whereby marriage under the age of eighteen was illegal, but rape against one's teenage wife over the age of fifteen was not, feminists argued for a higher age of consent.

68. Apart from Sakshi and the NCW, the LCI consulted with the All-India Democratic Women's Association (AIDWA) and Interventions for Support, Healing, and Awareness. All three NGOs participated in drafting the 1993 proposal.

69. Rukmini Sen, "Law Commission Reports on Rape," *Economic & Political Weekly* 45, nos. 44/45 (2010): 86.

70. Menon, *Recovering Subversion,* 137.

71. Partners for Law in Development, "Background to Discussions by Women's Groups on Sexual Assault Amendments (2001–2010)," March 29, 2010, 15, http://feministlawarchives.pldindia.org/wp-content/uploads/background-to -discussions-by-womens-groups-to-sexual-assault-amendments.pdf.

72. Murthy, "Criminal Law Amendment."

73. Ibid., 4.

74. See Nivedita Menon, "The Impunity of Every Citadel Is Intact—The Taming of the Verma Committee Report, and Some Troubling Thoughts," *Kafila* (blog), February 3, 2013, http://www.outlookindia.com/article.aspx?283779.

75. These were to expand rape to include nonpenile penetration, eliminate the marital rape immunity, and enact a separate law on child sexual abuse.

76. The open letter noted: "We need to develop a gradation of sexual assault which squarely names sexual harassment, molestation, stalking, parading, stripping as sexual violence [not amounting to rape]. Once again, we must remind you that the way victims experience these forms of assault must inform the way the law is named i.e., as sexual violence. We need to codify other forms of sexual violence." Open letter of women's organizations to Dr. M. Veerappa Moily, "Amend Laws on Sexual Violence in India," January 2010.

77. It renamed rape as sexual assault, expanded the *actus reus* to include nonpenile penetration, retained the gender specificity of rape for adults, proposed a gender-neutral offense of sexual assault and sexual abuse for minors, and increased the punishment for rape including through minimum mandatory punishment. However, the bill did not address sexual violence, raised the age of consent to eighteen, and retained the marital rape immunity for adult wives. Aggravated sexual assault was expanded to cover defendants who were relatives or in positions of authority vis-à-vis the survivor or were in a position of "economic or social or political dominance." This expansion reflects suggestions feminists made in 1993.

78. Sen, "Law Commission Reports on Rape," 87. Kirti Singh, who drafted the 2002 AIDWA Bill, criticized the Sexual Assault Bill; see T. K. Rajalakshmi, " 'Bill Not Comprehensive': An Interview with Kirti Singh (advocate, Supreme Court)," *The Hindu,* June 19, 2010, http://www.frontline.in/static/html/fl2713/stories/20100702 271311400.htm.

79. Madhu Mehra, Mary John, and Farah Naqvi to Shri D. K. Sikri, "Criminal Law Amendment Bill, 2010: Response of Women's Groups," http://feministlawar chives.pldindia.org/wp-content/uploads/CLA-WOMENS-GROUPS-AND-OTHERS -NOTE-ON-SEXUAL-VIOLENCE.pdf.

80. Ibid., 5.

81. There was internal disagreement on terminology. See Kalpana Kannabiran, "Rethinking the Law on Sexual Assault," *The Hindu,* June 22, 2010, http://www.the hindu.com/todays-paper/tp-opinion/rethinking-the-law-on-sexual-assault/article 480312.ece.

82. To quote: "In this dismal scenario, the proposed changes that make the rape laws gender-neutral will in our understanding *completely undermine any and all gains* already made by the women's movement . . . In the present society, we oppose gender neutrality not only where rape is concerned but also in any legislation pertaining to maintenance, domestic violence or sexual harassment at the workplace." Partners for Law in Development, "Background to Discussions by Women's Groups," 12 (emphasis added).

83. Naina Kapur, who headed Sakshi, is a Canadian-born Indian lawyer.

84. The objection to gender neutrality is not limited to rape. When the Criminal Law (Amendment) Bill, 2012, proposed a gender-neutral offense against acid attacks, the Women's Rights' unit of the Lawyers Collective objected because in India men carried out acid attacks against women; prosecutors could resort to the IPC's

provision on grievous bodily harm to deal with acid attacks against gay men and transgender persons. By this logic, a new offense on acid attacks was unnecessary. The organization's HIV unit, meanwhile, insisted on gender neutrality because gender-neutral laws such as the Immoral Traffic Prevention Act of 1986 did not undermine women's interests but gender-specific laws did not benefit transgender and transsexual persons.

85. Flavia Agnes, "Law, Ideology and Female Sexuality: Gender Neutrality in Rape Law," *Economic & Political Weekly* 37, no. 9 (2002): 846–47.

86. See, for example, UK Sexual Offences Act, Section 4, 2003 (causing another to engage in a sexual activity without consent), can be used against women.

87. Substantively, the offenses overlap greatly but also differ significantly. The offense of sexual violence against women includes sexual touching, exposing male sexual organs, and sexual harassment; these are excluded from the offense of sexual assault on persons "other than women." Similarly, aggravated sexual assault on a person "other than a woman" excludes situations applicable to women such as sexual assault by a person in a position of trust, authority, or social or economic dominance.

88. Vrinda Grover, "Submissions to Justice Verma Committee on Law, Policing, and Related Matters to Ensure Justice and Curb Impunity for Sexual Violence against Women," January 5, 2013, http://feministsindia.com/women-and-law/justice -verma-submissions/vrinda-grover/. Prior to the enactment of the Protection of Children from Sexual Offences Act of 2012, initiatives were undertaken by different groups and drafts submitted to the Ministry of Women and Child Development. One such initiative was by the National Commission for Protection of Child Rights, which constituted a working group on "Protection of Children from Sexual Offences Bill." This working group was chaired by retired justice A. P. Shah and comprised of Advocate Maharukh Adenwala, Adocate Aparna Bhat, Advocate Yug Choudhary, Dipa Dixit, Anuroopa Giliyal, Advocate Vrinda Grover, Advocate Arundhati Katju, Professor Babu Mathew, Advocate Mayank Misra, Professor K. N. Chandrashekaran Pillai, Advocate Siddharth Sharma, and Shanta Sinha. Of particular interest in the Act is Section 30. It requires any culpable state of mind to be presumed; the prosecution only has to prove the *actus reus*. Such absolute liability offenses are highly unusual even if meant to maximize prosecutions. Section 29 requires that for penetrative and nonpenetrative sexual assault, whether aggravated or not, once the person is prosecuted for committing, abetting, or attempting to commit it, he or she shall be presumed to have committed, abetted, or attempted the act. In other words, defendants are presumed guilty until proved innocent.

89. Partners for Law in Development, "Background to Discussions by Women's Groups," 4.

90. Ibid., 9, 13.

91. Mehra, John, and Naqvi to Sikri, "Criminal Law Amendment Bill, 2010," p. 9.

92. Kannabiran, "Rethinking the Law on Sexual Assault."

93. Ibid.

94. The marital rape immunity did not apply where the wife was less than sixteen years old.

95. In July 2012, after the bill was circulated, 92 feminist organizations and 546 individuals protested its provisions through a petition to the chairperson of the ruling party.

96. Filling out the FIR is essential for the police to launch an investigation leading to charge sheeting and trial.

97. Vishaka and others v. State of Rajasthan and others (1997) 6 SCC 241.

98. I thank Mrinal Satish for this point.

99. Verma Committee, "Amendments to Criminal Law," 200.

100. The committee likely accepted claims made by the BBA, which the committee specifically thanks.

101. Indian sex workers protested; I track this issue in "Governance Feminism's Others: Sex Workers and India's Rape Law Reforms," in Halley et al., *Governance Feminism: Notes from the Field.*

102. Verma Committee, "Amendments to Criminal Law," 18.

103. Ibid., 143.

104. Ibid., 18 (emphasis added).

105. Like previous proposals, the ordinance replaced rape with gender-neutral sexual assault, covered nonpenile penetration and sexual touching, raised the age of consent to eighteen, and retained the marital rape immunity. Key differences from previous drafts included its incorporation of several new offenses and increased penalties from the Verma Committee report besides proposing the death penalty for aggravated sexual assault (resulting in death or a persistent vegetative state, and for repeat offenders).

106. Menon, "The Impunity of Every Citadel Is Intact."

107. The Hindu nationalist party in power since May 2014 wanted the age of consent to be eighteen; the then–ruling party Congress, sixteen. A one-time probation for young men engaged in consensual sex with a person younger than eighteen years old was considered but not accepted.

108. Mrinal Satish in Partners for Law in Development, *Critical Reflections: Criminalisation and Sexuality,* 2015, 11, http://pldindia.org/wp-content/uploads/2015/11/3-Criminalization-and-sexuality.pdf.

109. Leading up to the CLA, politicians proposed punishing false complaints as women may use the offenses of stalking and voyeurism to harass politicians prior to the general elections or male employers who refused to employ them.

110. Non-bailable offenses are where the defendant is not entitled to be released on bail automatically. The court has the discretion to grant or refuse bail.

111. See Indira Jaising, "Speech as on 19 Jan to Justice Verma Committee by Indira Jaising," http://www.lawyerscollective.org/updates/speech-as-on-19-jan-to-justice-verma-committee-by-indira-jaising-indira-jaising. She uses the concept of institutional bias to advocate against gender discrimination but seamlessly transitions to demanding criminal law reform. See also Pratiksha Baxi, "Rape, Retribution, State: On Whose Bodies?," *Economic & Political Weekly* 35, no. 14 (2000): 1199. Baxi argues that the desire for imposing capital punishment reflects a patriarchal mindset as it aims to deter men from inflicting pathological sex/violence against women while legitimizing "normal" levels of violence against women.

112. See, for instance, "Lawyers Collective, Submissions to the Justice Verma Committee: Recommendations for Amendments to the IPC and Allied Laws," 6, http://pldindia.org/wp-content/uploads/2013/03/Submissions-by-Lawyers-Collective.pdf.

113. Aarti Mundkur and Arvind Narrain, "Betraying the Third Way," *The Hindu*, June 13, 2016, http://www.thehindu.com/opinion/op-ed/betraying-the -third-way/article4630899.ece.

114. Ibid. On the rape of a transgender person in 2004, see Outright Action International (formerly known as the International Gay & Lesbian Human Rights Commission), "India: Rape and Police Abuse of Hijra in Bangalore; Call for Action by SANGAMA," June 24, 2004, https://www.outrightinternational.org/content/india -rape-and-police-abuse-hijra-bangalore-call-action-sangama.

115. Baxi, *Public Secrets*, 46.

116. These human rights / civil liberties groups were not well funded and worked in a repressive political climate; they are a far cry from contemporary Western human rights groups, which are often well resourced and transnationally mobile. In the postemergency years, feminists shared common political ground with human rights organizations against state violence. Kannabiran and Menon, *From Mathura to Manorama*, 125.

117. Haksar, "Human Rights Lawyering," 80.

118. Ibid.

119. For links between neoliberalism, human rights discourse, and "carceral" feminism, see Elizabeth Bernstein, "The Sexual Politics of the 'New Abolitionism,'" *Differences* 18, no. 3 (2007): 128–51; Linda Singer, *Erotic Welfare: Sexual Theory and Politics in the Age of Epidemic*, ed. Judith Butler and Maureen Mac-Grogan (London: Routledge, 1993); Merry, *Human Rights and Gender Violence*, 230; see also Vasuki Nesiah, "Uncomfortable Alliances: Women, Peace, and Security in Sri Lanka," in *South Asian Feminisms*, ed. Ania Loomba and Ritty Lukose (Durham, N.C.: Duke University Press, 2012), 139–61.

120. Verma Committee, "Amendments to Criminal Law," 218.

121. Ibid., 219.

122. Ashis Nandy, "An Anomic, Anarchic, Free-Floating Violence . . . Is Looking for Targets," interview by Aditya Srivastava, April 20, 2013, http://www .governancenow.com/views/interview/anomic-anarchic-free-floating-violence -looking-targets.

123. Prachee Sinha, "Run with Gender, Hunt with Class," *Kafila* (blog), January 2, 2013, https://kafila.online/2013/01/02/run-with-gender-hunt-with-class-guest-post -by-prachee-sinha/.

124. John, "Class Societies and Sexual Violence"; for Krishnan's response, see Kavita Krishnan, "Capitalism, Sexual Violence, and Sexism," *Kafila* (blog), May 23, 2013, https://kafila.online/2013/05/23/capitalism-sexual-violence-and-sexism-kavita-krish nan/; Nitya Rao, "Rights, Recognition, and Rape," *Economic & Political Weekly* 48, no. 7 (2013): 19. Rao confirms that growing indebtedness, illegal work, and drug and alcohol abuse in North Delhi have intensified the struggle to assert male identities.

125. See Arundhati Roy, interview by BBC, December 22, 2012, http://www .youtube.com/watch?v=4uQobrC002M; she attributes the high visibility and mobilizational appeal of the Nirbhaya incident to the rape and murder of a middle-class woman by lower-class men from the "criminal poor."

126. John, "Class Societies and Sexual Violence," 3.

127. Ibid., 14.

128. Hyperfemme behavior includes, according to John, Bollywood actresses' raunch culture; women working as bar dancers, wedding performers, flight attendants, and secretaries; slut walks; fashionable flash mobs; and support for legalizing prostitution. Patriarchal femininity includes aspiring for a zero dress size; wearing body-hugging clothes, see-through tops, miniskirts, and high heels; painting nails; getting piercings; securing implants; and reclaiming disempowering terms like "slut/whore/bitch/cunt." Ibid.

129. Ibid., 10.

130. According to John, in dual systems theory, "upper class women, who are oppressors and exploiters as part of the dominant economic class, can still be oppressed due to the prevalence of patriarchy. According to the same theory, working-class women are oppressed and exploited not just by the dominant economic class but also by patriarchy. In other words, the dual systems theory projects patriarchy as a comprehensive *system* that co-exists along with capitalism." Ibid.

131. Kimberlé Crenshaw, "Demarginalizing the Intersection of Race and Sex: A Black Feminist Critique of Antidiscrimination Doctrine, Feminist Theory, and Antiracist Politics," *University of Chicago Legal Forum* 1989, no. 1 (1989): 139–67. Crenshaw theorized Black women's experiences through the metaphor of the traffic intersection, hence her theory of intersectionality. She notes that Black women often "experience double discrimination—the combined effects of practices which discriminate on the basis of race, and on the basis of sex. And sometimes, they experience discrimination as Black women—not the sum of race and sex discrimination, but as Black women" (149). John ("Class Societies and Sexual Violence") refers to the Indian adaptation of this theory to map the convergence of multiple identities including class, gender, caste, race, sexuality, and nationality.

132. To illustrate, upper-caste men commonly disrobe a *dalit* woman and parade her naked through the village to punish caste transgressions. Acknowledging that a lower-caste woman bears this brunt of a convergence of patriarchy and the caste system, feminists called for the new offense of disrobing in the CLA.

133. John, "Class Societies and Sexual Violence," 17. She gives the example here of the mistress–maid relationship.

134. Of the 24,923 rapes reported across India in 2012, 24,470 were committed by persons known to the complainants. Vasundhara Sirnate, "Good Laws, Bad Implementation," *The Hindu,* February 1, 2014, http://www.thehindu.com/opinion /lead/good-laws-bad-implementation/article5639799.ece. In 2014, this figure was 32,187 out of the 37,413 reported rapes. National Crime Records Bureau, "Crime in India," 2014, 86, http://www.ncrb.gov.in/. The disproportionate coverage of stranger rapes can be attributed to media bias. See Divya Arya, "Reporting Sexual Violence in India: What Has Changed since the Delhi Gang Rape?," *Economic & Political Weekly* 50, no. 44 (2015): 57–66.

135. Ibid., 59.

136. Sudhir Krishnaswamy, Shishir Bail, and Rohan Kothari, "Urban-Rural Incidence of Rape in India: Myths and Social Science Evidence" (working paper, Law, Governance and Development Initiative, Azim Premji University, Bangalore, 2013). Of the 24,923 cases of rape registered in 2012, only 3,035 took place in major cities. See "India's Pro-rapist Lobby," *The Hindu,* June 12, 2016, http://www.thehindu .com/opinion/editorial/indias-prorapist-lobby/article5901936.ece.

137. Autos are three-wheeled vehicles that operate as taxis.

138. Arya, "Reporting Sexual Violence in India," 61.

139. For an attempt to theorize sexuality and neoliberalism, see Stephen Legg and Srila Roy, "Neoliberalism, Postcolonialism, and Hetero-Sovereignties," special issue, *Interventions: International Journal of Postcolonial Studies,* ed. Stephen Legg and Srila Roy, 15, no. 4 (2013): 461–73.

140. Mary E. John, ed., *Women's Studies in India: A Reader* (Gurgaon, India: Penguin Books, 2008), 263.

141. Ibid., 264.

142. Menon, *Recovering Subversion,* 5.

143. Menon, *Seeing Like a Feminist,* 195.

144. Haksar, "Human Rights Lawyering," 80.

145. M. P. Singh, "Gender, Law, and Sexual Assault," *Economic & Political Weekly* 32, no. 11 (1997): 543–50.

146. John, *Women's Studies in India,* 279.

147. Menon, *Recovering Subversion,* 6.

148. Ibid., 206.

149. Sunder Rajan, *The Scandal of the State,* 31. Older feminists viewed legislation as a tool for social reconstruction; younger feminists were more skeptical. See Mazumdar, "Political Ideology of the Women's Movement's Engagement with Law," 350, 372. See also Menon, *Recovering Subversion,* 7.

150. Menon, *Recovering Subversion,* 232.

151. Baxi, *Public Secrets,* 43.

152. John, *Women's Studies in India,* 266.

153. Sunder Rajan, *The Scandal of the State,* 32.

154. "Standing," deriving from the term *locus standi,* means the right or ability to bring an action or to appear in a court.

155. Partners for Law in Development, "Background to Discussions by Women's Groups," 13.

156. Menon, *Recovering Subversion,* 136–37; Partners for Law in Development, "Background to Discussions by Women's Groups," 11.

157. Kannabiran and Menon, *From Mathura to Manorama,* 67.

158. Madhusree Dutta, "Why I Am Not Celebrating 25 Years of Majlis," March 25, 2016, http://www.eyeartcollective.com/why-i-am-not-celebrating-25-years-of -majlis/.

159. Kannabiran and Menon, *From Mathura to Manorama,* 200, 201n57.

160. They recently demanded a comprehensive review of the NCW's performance and a transparent, democratic, and nonpartisan selection process for members.

161. Madhu Mehra, "Taking Stock of the New Anti Rape Law," *Kafila* (blog), May 5, 2013, https://kafila.online/2013/05/05/taking-stock-of-the-new-anti-rape-law-madhu-mehra/amp/.

162. See the four reports on various themes published in 2015 by Partners for Law in Development, available at pldindia.org/resources/.

163. See amendments to the Criminal Procedure Code, No. 2 of 1974, India Code §§ 26, 154, 161, http://indiacode.nic.in.

164. Sections 357C of the Criminal Procedure Code of 1973, and 166B of the Indian Penal Code.

165. Partners for Law in Development, *Critical Reflections: Feminist Praxis and Dialogue*, 2015, 16, http://pldindia.org/wp-content/uploads/2015/11/4-Feminist-Praxis-and-dialogue.pdf.

166. A cognizable offense means that a survivor's complaint is not necessary for the police to file an FIR against the accused.

167. Anusha Rizvi and Manisha Sethi, "Confronting Certainties," *HardNews*, March 9, 2014, http://www.hardnewsmedia.com/2014/03/6247.

168. Kishwar, who was earlier part of the IWM, now supports the Hindu nationalist party. Some feminists denounced her speaking on the complainant's behalf and going to social media without a fair investigation. Nivedita Menon, "Feminist Reflections on the Tragic Suicide of Khurshid Anwar," *Kafila* (blog), February 17, 2014, https://kafila.online/2014/02/17/feminist-reflections-on-the-tragic-suicide-of-khurshid-anwar/amp/. However, Menon's attribution of the video's leakage to the "impatience of youth" was criticized as downplaying the seriousness of the incident.

169. Rizvi and Sethi, "Confronting Certainties."

170. Morris Cohen, "The Basis of Contract," *Harvard Law Review* 46, no. 4 (1933): 553.

171. Robert Hale, "Bargaining, Duress, and Economic Liberty," *Columbia Law Review* 43, no. 5 (1943): 603.

172. Duncan Kennedy, "Legal Economics of U.S. Low Income Housing Markets in Light of 'Informality' Analysis," *Journal of Law in Society* 4 (2002): 80 (emphasis added).

173. See Kennedy, *Sexy Dressing, Etc.*, 83–125.

174. To illustrate, although the key provisions of the Sexual Offences Act, 2003 (rape, assault by penetration, sexual assault, and causing another to engage in sexual activity), seem to implicate strangers, other provisions distinguish between survivors on the basis of their capacity to consent (children and young adult, person with mental disorder), or on the relationship between the abuser and the abused (involving abuse of position of trust, sex with family members, sex with care worker, sex with adult relative).

175. National Crime Records Bureau, "Crime in India," 86.

176. Ibid.

177. Rukmini S., "The Many Shades of Rape Cases in Delhi," *The Hindu*, July 29, 2014, http://www.thehindu.com/data/the-many-shades-of-rape-cases-in-delhi/article6261042.ece.

178. See Halley's discussion of the difference between assent and consent. Janet Halley, "The Move to Affirmative Consent," *Signs* 42, no. 1 (2015): 257–79.

179. Rao Harnarain Singh v. State of Punjab (1958) Cri LJ 563.

180. Section 90 of the IPC reads, "A consent is not such a consent as intended by any section of this Code, if the consent is given by a person under fear of injury, or under a misconception of fact, and if the person doing the act knows, or has reason to believe, that the consent was given in consequence of such fear or misconception."

181. *Actus reus* refers to the physical conduct element of a crime.

182. Explanation 2 to Section 375 of the CLA.

183. Catharine A. MacKinnon, *Toward a Feminist Theory of the State* (Cambridge, Mass.: Harvard University Press, 1989), 177.

184. Ibid., 178.
185. Halley, "The Move to Affirmative Consent," 4.
186. "Mens rea" refers to the state of mind of the accused.
187. Ratanlal Ranchhoddas, *Ratanlal and Dhirajlal's Indian Penal Code (Act XLV of 1860),* 31st ed. (Nagpur, India: Wadhwa and Company, 2006), 1923–24. See also M. V. Sankaran, "Mens Rea in Rape: An Analysis of Reg. v. Morgan and Sections 375 and 79 of the Indian Penal Code," *Journal of the Indian Law Institute* 20, no. 3 (1978): 438–62.
188. State of Himachal v. Asha Ram (2005) 13 SCC 766; State of Himachal Pradesh v. Raghubir Singh (1993) 2 SCC 622. See also State of Maharashtra v. Chandraprakash Kewalchand Jain (1990) AIR 658. These decisions were confirmed by the Supreme Court in Narender Kumar v. State (NCT of Delhi), (2012) 7 SCC 171. The Supreme Court in 1983 went so far as to say that Indian women rarely lie about rape irrespective of whether they are from rural areas or urban areas and their station in life. Bharwada Bhoginbhai Hirjibhai v. State of Gujarat (1983) 3 SCC 217. "Where evidence of the prosecutrix is found suffering from serious infirmities and is inconsistent with other material, and the prosecutrix makes deliberate improvements on material point with a view to rule out consent on her part and there is no injury on her person even though her version may be otherwise, no reliance can be placed upon her evidence (Vide: Suresh N. Bhusare & Ors. v. State of Maharashtra (1999) 1 SCC 220)." Narender Kumar v. State (NCT of Delhi), (2012) 7 SCC 171.
189. The CLA also amends Sections 53 and 146 of the IEA so that when consent is at issue, evidence as to the survivor's previous sexual experience with *any person* (including the offender) cannot be admitted.
190. Halley, "The Move to Affirmative Consent," 6.
191. Partners for Law in Development, *Critical Reflections: Marriage, Sexuality, and the Law,* 2015, 3, http://pldindia.org/wp-content/uploads/2015/11/1-Marriage-sexuality-and-the-law.pdf.
192. Perveez Mody, *The Intimate State: Love-Marriage and the Law in India* (New Delhi: Routledge, 2008); Pratiksha Baxi, "Habeas Corpus: Juridical Narratives of Sexual Governance" (working paper, Centre for the Study of Law and Governance, Jawaharlal Nehru University, New Delhi, 2009).
193. Baxi, "Habeas Corpus," 7. Baxi notes that where the female refuses to bring a charge of rape against her lover, she can be jailed for abetting her own rape, kidnapping, and abduction.
194. Dilip Kumar v. State of Bihar 2005 Supreme Court Cases (Cri) 253.
195. Indian courts regularly draw on English law.
196. R. (F) v. Director of Public Prosecutions (2013) 2 Cr. App. R. 21.
197. Julian Assange v. Swedish Prosecution Authority (2011) EWHC 2849.
198. R v. McNally (2013) EWCA Crim 1051.
199. For example, Jonathan Herring, "Mistaken Sex," *Criminal Law Review* (2005): 511–24. Herring argues that if B makes a mistake about a matter relating to the sexual conduct of A, including about A's state of mind (or marital status, wealth, sexual prowess, love for her), which had she known the truth about, she would not have agreed to sex and he knew / ought to have known this, then there is no consent.
200. Alex Sharpe, "Expanding Liability for Sexual Fraud through the Concept of 'Active Deception': A Flawed Approach," *Journal of Criminal Law* 80, no. 1

(2016): 28–44. See also Aeyal Gross, "Rape by Deception and the Policing of Gender and Nationality Borders," *Tulane Journal of Law & Sexuality* 24 (2015): 1–33.

201. Arya, "Reporting Sexual Violence in India," 59.

202. See Ratna Kapur, "Sexual Escapades and the Law," in John, *Women's Studies in India,* 287. Kapur discusses the Vishaka judgment and subsequent cases and criticizes the vast breadth and scope of the definition of sexual harassment and its "erosion of the possibility of sexual freedom" (ibid.).

203. Troubled by the Tejpal case, feminists in the Anwar suicide case expressed the need to seek out civil redressal mechanisms before going to the police. Menon, "Feminist Reflections on the Tragic Suicide of Khurshid Anwar." See also Ayesha Kidwai in Partners for Law in Development, *Critical Reflections: Feminist Praxis and Dialogue,* 14.

204. The intern requested the media to respect her autonomy, fully reiterating her ability to pursue appropriate proceedings at appropriate times. "Statement of Stella James," November 12, 2013, https://jilsblognujs.wordpress.com/2013/11/12 /statement-of-stella-james/.

205. Stella James, "Through My Looking Glass," *Journal of Indian Law and Society* (blog), November 6, 2013, https://jilsblognujs.wordpress.com/2013/11/06/through -my-looking-glass/.

206. The Kerala High Court dismissed the petition in October 2015; the Delhi High Court petition was filed by RIT Foundation, an NGO, and dismissed in July 2015, "Delhi HC Junks PIL Seeking Criminalization of Marital Rape," *Hindustan Times,* July 12, 2015, http://www.hindustantimes.com/delhi-news/delhi-hc -junks-pil-seeking-criminalisation-of-marital-rape/story-I9anJUC475iaPSn 4fOhz6L.html. The Supreme Court petition was filed by the NGO Independent Thought.

207. Dominique Mosbergen, "India's Marital Rape Crisis Reaches 'Tragic Proportions,'" *Huffington Post India,* November 24, 2015, http://www.huffingtonpost .com/entry/india-marital-rape_us_564d8c21e4b00b7997f9469e.

208. Ibid.

209. Priya Nanda, Abhishek Gautam, Ravi Verma, Aarushi Khanna, Nizamuddin Khan, Dhanashri Brahme, Shobhana Boyle, and Sanjay Kumar, *Masculinity, Intimate Partner Violence and Son Preference in India: A Study* (New Delhi: International Center for Research on Women, 2014); Aashish Gupta, "Reporting and Incidence of Violence against Women in India," September 25, 2014, http://riceinstitute .org/research/reporting-and-incidence-of-violence-against-women-in-india/.

210. Partners for Law in Development, *Critical Reflections: Marriage, Sexuality, and the Law,* 3. This includes a broader assessment of the offense of adultery; the remedy of the restitution of conjugal rights; how considerations of chastity affect maintenance payments; and the law's treatment of withholding sex (one high court called this cruelty) and of extramarital sex.

211. Section 498A of the IPC was specifically passed to prevent the harassment of wives by their husbands or relatives for dowry.

212. Partners for Law in Development, *Critical Reflections: Marriage, Sexuality and the Law,* 19.

213. Partners for Law in Development, *Critical Reflections: Criminalization and Sexuality,* 21.

214. Sonali Das, Sonali Jain-Chandra, Kalpana Kochhar, and Naresh Kumar, "Women Workers in India: Why So Few among So Many?" (working paper, International Monetary Fund, Washington, D.C., 2015), https://www.imf.org/external/pubs/ft/wp/2015/wp1555.pdf.

215. Agnes and D'Mello, "Protection of Women from Domestic Violence," 80.

216. Wives use Section 377, the anti-sodomy provision against marital rape. Partners for Law in Development, *Critical Reflections: Marriage, Sexuality and the Law,* 18.

217. Trideep Pais, a Delhi trial court lawyer, confirms that husbands do invoke this expanded immunity; the police oblige them some of the time.

218. Saptarshi Mandal, "The Impossibility of Marital Rape: Contestations around Marriage, Sex, Violence, and the Law in Contemporary India," *Australian Feminist Studies* 29, no. 81 (2014): 255–72.

219. Agnes and D'Mello, "Protection of Women from Domestic Violence," 80.

220. A fourth category covers wives who are not abused and not considering divorce. Wives in the first and second categories are not mutually exclusive; violence against a wife in the first category could escalate to the point of her wanting a divorce.

221. Roy in Partners for Law in Development, *Critical Reflections: Criminalization and Sexuality,* 6.

222. Given the social premium on being married, in the Indian context, I assume that violence would be a strong reason for wives to consider exit.

223. Parul Agarwal, "India Marital Rape Victims' Lonely Battle for Justice," *BBC News,* May 26, 2015, http://www.bbc.com/news/world-asia-india-32810834.

224. Srimati Basu, "Gathering Steam: Organising Strategies of the Indian Men's Rights Movement," *Economic & Political Weekly* 50, no. 44 (2015): 69.

225. Ibid., 68.

226. Ibid., 69.

227. Ibid., 74.

228. National Crime Records Bureau, "Crime in India," 83.

229. Mrinal Satish in Partners for Law in Development, *Critical Reflections: Criminalization and Sexuality,* 13.

230. Ibid.

231. "Nikam's Arguments in Rape Case Come under Fire," *The Hindu,* April 6, 2014, http://www.thehindu.com/news/cities/mumbai/nikams-arguments-in-rape-case-come-under-fire/article5877384.ece. According to Nikam, "Rape was an attack not only on a woman's body but also on her mind, chastity, prestige and self-honour which cannot be healed unless the victim dies."

232. Flavia Agnes, "Why I Oppose Death for Rapists," *Mumbai Mirror,* April 5, 2014, http://www.mumbaimirror.com/mumbai/cover-story/Opinion-Why-I-oppose-death-for-rapists/articleshow/33250078.cms. The NCW welcomed the verdict. "Opinions Divided on Shakti Mills Verdict," *The Hindu,* April 5, 2014, http://www.thehindu.com/news/cities/mumbai/opinions-divided-on-shakti-mills-verdict/article5872943.ece.

233. Agnes, "Why I Oppose Death for Rapists."

234. Mrinal Satish argues that the introduction of stringent penalties leads to their infrequent use by courts. Satish in Partners for Law in Development, *Critical Reflections: Criminalization and Sexuality,* 11.

235. Anuradha Raman, "Define, Refine, Redefine: Are the New Laws against Sexual Harassment and Rape 'Draconian'? The Tejpal Debate," *Outlook India*, March 3, 2014, http://www.outlookindia.com/article.aspx?289597.

236. Mary E. John, "Rethinking Violence," *Economic & Political Weekly* 50, no. 44 (2015): 36.

237. Mehra, "Taking Stock of the New Anti Rape Law."

238. See Ratna Kapur, "Gender Justice, Interrupted," *The Hindu*, March 29, 2013, http://www.thehindu.com/opinion/lead/Gender-justice-interrupted/article 12404830.ece.

239. See also comments by Farah Naqri and Ayesha Kidwai in Partners for Law in Development, *Critical Reflections: Feminist Praxis and Dialogue*, 8, 13.

240. The charge sheet in the Shakti Mills case was 600 pages; in the Tejpal case, it was 2,846 pages.

241. Rizvi and Sethi, "Confronting Certainties."

242. Rebecca John, "Correcting Inconsistencies—A Response to Anusha Rizvi and Manisha Sethi," *Kafila* (blog), March 12, 2014, https://kafila.online/2014/03/12/correcting-inconsistencies-a-response-to-anusha-rizvi-and-manisha-sethi/.

243. Vrinda Grover, "Look before You Creep," *Outlook India*, March 3, 2014, http://www.outlookindia.com/magazine/story/look-before-you-creep/289599.

244. Akshay Khanna points to recent antisexist campaigns in Delhi that have redefined protest politics and are irreverent of mainstream institutions. Akshay Khanna in Partners for Law in Development, *Critical Reflections: Criminalization and Sexuality*, 4.

245. Feminists point to the sexual harassment committees they set up at Jawaharlal Nehru University. Uma Chakravarti in Partners for Law in Development, *Critical Reflections: Feminist Praxis and Dialogue*, 18.

246. Pratiksha Baxi argues that any attempt at law reform must be grounded in law's practice; it is therefore essential for both legal academics and the feminist movement to adopt an empirical, sociolegal approach to rape law reform. Baxi, *Public Secrets*, 341, 345.

247. Rahul Roy in Partners for Law in Development, *Critical Reflections: Criminalization and Sexuality*, 5.

248. Tejaswini Madabhushi, Maranatha Grace T. Wahlang, and Gitanjali Joshua, "Locating 'Hyderabad for Feminism' in the Present Struggle against Violence," *Economic & Political Weekly* 50, no. 44 (2015): 43.

249. Rahul Roy in Partners for Law in Development, *Critical Reflections: Criminalization and Sexuality*, 5.

250. See Madabhushi, Wahlang, and Joshua, "Locating 'Hyderabad for Feminism,'" for a description of their use of Facebook in Hyderabad following the Nirbhaya protests.

251. Meena Kandaswamy, "How Do We Break the Indian Penile Code? This Cultural Sanction of Rape Must Stop, the State Has to Speak," *Outlook India*, January 14, 2014, http://www.outlookindia.com/magazine/story/how-do-we-break-the-indian-penile-code/283463.

CHAPTER 5

Anti-trafficking in Israel

Neo-abolitionist Feminists, Markets,
Borders, and the State

HILA SHAMIR

This chapter explores the impact of a group of Israeli feminists—in particular, neo-abolitionist feminists, a branch within dominance feminism that focuses on the abolition of prostitution—in the context of anti-trafficking legislation and policy in Israel in the early 2000s. From an ignored issue in the late 1990s, human trafficking, particularly trafficking into the sex industry, became a prominent and dynamic policy area because of the unflagging efforts of governance feminists. The network of feminists in the United States, which was an important force in shaping the Trafficking Victims Protection Act (TVPA) and the U.S. State Department Trafficking in Persons (TIP) report agenda, worked in conjunction with Israeli feminist organizations and other nongovernmental organizations (NGOs) to introduce new legislation and institutions that led to a significant change in the Israeli sex industry: the almost complete elimination of migrant sex workers from the industry and the eradication of cross-border trafficking into the country. Consequently, by 2011, Israel was upgraded from its shameful Tier 3 placement in the U.S. 2001 TIP Report, indicating noncompliance with the TVPA's minimum standards, to the highest-ranking Tier 1 status, indicating full compliance.

Neo-abolitionist feminist reform efforts constitute a spectrum of interventions, and not all of these were fully successful. The fruitful collaboration of neo-abolitionist feminists and the Israeli state had two main outcomes. First, their efforts led to the creation of an extensive and relatively generous "post-exploitation" rehabilitation package for designated victims of trafficking. When optimally applied, the package of services ensures delayed deportation and provides victims with temporary work and stay visas, accommodation at a designated victims' shelter, medical and psychological care, legal aid, and some job training. However, the overall effect of this package of services is questionable. It should be noted that out of the thousands of women estimated to be trafficked into Israel, only a few hundred were identified and even fewer stayed in the victims' shelter.[1] Given the limited reach of these measures, it can be assumed that a second type of outcome was probably more effective in combatting trafficking. This was a wide-scale deportation and repatriation of migrant sex workers and victims of trafficking out of Israel and the prevention of further cross-border trafficking into the local sex industry. Deterrence of trafficking activity was effectuated through frequent brothel raids targeting non-Israelis, increased prosecution of traffickers, and harsher penalties for traffickers. Immigration restrictions and tighter border control prevented migrant sex workers and victims of trafficking from entering Israel. Israeli neo-abolitionist feminists took advantage of the momentum of these developments and, in 2008, shifted focus to the issue of prostitution, grounded on the premise that all prostitution is trafficking, and began lobbying for the adoption of a Swedish-model "end-demand" bill that criminalizes johns.

This chapter explores the work of neo-abolitionist (dominance) feminists in Israel in the area of anti-trafficking. It traces their politics, strategies, failures, and successes, and assesses their power and its limits. It shows that Israeli dominance feminists' collaboration with the state—as "femocrats"[2] and through new governance modes of civil society engagement with the state—was extremely effective in curtailing trafficking into the sex industry by strengthening the state's sovereigntist aspects, namely, its police and sovereign borders.

The chapter proceeds in four sections. The first section introduces the legal concept of trafficking in persons and describes the emergence of cross-border trafficking into the Israeli sex industry in the 1990s, and the immigration regime that served as its backdrop. The second section details the modes of operation and institutional settings utilized by dominance feminists to alter the state's response to this phenomenon. The third section looks at the two central achievements of feminist anti-trafficking activism: the establishment of a "rescue and rehabilitation" infrastructure alongside the effective tightening of the state borders and intensified police raids on brothels. In the fourth section, a distributive analysis assesses the costs and benefits of dominance feminists' anti-trafficking achievements and explores some consequences to the discursive economy around migration, labor, and borders in Israel. This section discusses the interaction between GF and sovereigntist state power, on the one hand, and labor market exploitation, on the other. The chapter analyzes the Israeli case contextually, both in the sense of its unique local circumstances and also in terms of the general insights it offers as to how neo-abolitionist feminists succeed at intervening, participating, and, in some cases, dominating certain policy and legislatives spheres.

Human Trafficking and Trafficking into the Israeli Sex Industry

Human Trafficking

The past decade witnessed growing interest in human trafficking as a legal category in international and national law. The two central expressions of international willingness to address trafficking are the United Nations' Protocol to Prevent, Suppress, and Punish Trafficking in Persons, Especially Women and Children, of 2000 (Trafficking Protocol)[3] and the U.S. TVPA of 2000.[4] The Trafficking Protocol is the most significant international anti-trafficking instrument to date, while the impact of the TVPA has (quite intentionally) stretched far beyond U.S. borders to shape foreign anti-trafficking policies.[5] Since coming into force, their combined operation has transformed how the world contends with human trafficking.

The crime of trafficking in these two instruments has taken on a new meaning. While in the twentieth century trafficking was legally understood to mean the movement of women and girls across borders for the purpose of prostitution,[6] definitions in the protocol and the TVPA are much more encompassing and include the experiences of men and women in forced labor, servitude, slavery or slavery-like practices, and organ removal, within or beyond the borders of their countries of origin. Under article 3 of the protocol, trafficking comprises three components: (1) a particular *action*—"the recruitment, transportation, transfer, harbouring or receipt of persons"; (2) certain *means* for car-rying out the action—"the threat or use of force or other forms of co-ercion, of abduction, of fraud, of deception, of the abuse of power or of a position of vulnerability or of the giving or receiving of payments or benefits to achieve the consent of a person having control over an-other person"; and (3) the end *purpose* of exploitation.[7] The protocol defines exploitation sweepingly to include, at a minimum, "the ex-ploitation of the prostitution of others or other forms of sexual ex-ploitation, forced labour or services, slavery or practices similar to slavery, servitude or the removal of organs."[8] This broad definition is considered one of the protocol's most significant achievements in that it is gender neutral and extends beyond sex trafficking to include vari-ous types of labor market exploitation, even within the borders of the victim's own country.[9] The TVPA's definition of trafficking is similarly broad, though it includes a separate definition of sex trafficking, which eliminates the coercion requirement, defining sex trafficking as "the recruitment, harboring, transportation, provision, or obtaining of a person for the purpose of a commercial sex act."[10] However, the TVPA limits its operational terms only to "severe forms of trafficking in per-son," which reintroduces the coercion element. Severe forms of sex trafficking are defined as "sex trafficking in which a commercial sex act is induced by force, fraud, or coercion,"[11] as well as "the recruitment, harboring, transportation, provision, or obtaining of a person for labor or services, through the use of force, fraud, or coercion for the purpose of subjection to involuntary servitude, peonage, debt bond-age, or slavery."[12]

After ratifying the Trafficking Protocol and in compliance with TVPA minimum standards, many countries passed anti-trafficking legislation and developed anti-trafficking policies. The result has been the rapid development of a remarkably uniform anti-trafficking frame-work across the globe.[13] In fact, according to the United Nations Office on Drugs and Crime, by 2009 as many as 125 countries had enacted specific anti-trafficking legislation.[14] The emerging framework, which incorporates elements of the Trafficking Protocol and the TVPA into national anti-trafficking laws, consists of laws that adopt what has become known as the "three P's" paradigm—prevention, prosecution, and protection. Under this framework, anti-trafficking measures concentrate mostly on the criminalization of trafficking, as well as on creating programs to assist, rehabilitate, and eventually repatriate trafficked persons. A main point of criticism about the responses to trafficking is that the implementation of these international and national legal instruments has focused on sex trafficking (the trafficking of women and girls into the sex industry for the purpose of prostitution) while tending to ignore labor trafficking (the trafficking of persons for the purpose of labor exploitation into other labor sectors).[15] As the following sections detail, Israel followed this general trend both in legislation and in implementation.

Trafficking in Israel

In Israel, trafficking has so far been recognized and addressed only in relation to migrants: documented and undocumented migrants as well as asylum seekers. The developments in Israel's immigration regime therefore serve as an important backdrop to the rise in human trafficking.

Israel's immigration regime is structured to accommodate the migration and settlement of Jews in Israel. It therefore gives primacy to ethnonational criteria in allocating full membership in the polity.[16] At the center of this migration regime is the Law of Return—1950, which grants citizenship to all Jews on the basis of Israel's designation as the homeland of the Jewish people.[17] The idea of Israel as the land of the Jews has been the political cornerstone and moral justification of the Israeli state since its establishment in 1948. The original aspiration was to have an economy that sustains itself solely by relying on the immigration and settlement of Jews from around the globe, with no need for non-Jewish immigration.[18] However, this idea quickly proved unattainable. From its early days the Israeli labor market relied on the labor of noncitizens: since 1967, Palestinian day laborers entering from the Occupied Palestinian Territories (OPT); later, migrant guest workers from various countries; and, more recently, asylum seekers primarily from Africa.

Israel opened its markets to labor migration (other than day laborers) in 1993, following the first Palestinian uprising in the OPT (the First Intifadah) and the signing of the Oslo Accords, when Palestinians were no longer permitted to enter Israel for work purposes. The "sealing off" of the OPT created a shortage in certain labor-intensive sectors of the Israeli labor market and took jobs and income away from

Palestinians in the OPT.[19] As a solution to this labor shortage, the Israeli government initiated a guest worker visa program in the fields of construction, agriculture, and in-home care.

Workers come to Israel from a wide array of countries, and predominantly from China, Romania, and Bulgaria (to work in construction); from the Philippines, India, Sri Lanka, Nepal, and Romania (to work as in-home care workers); and from Thailand (to work in agriculture).[20] As is often the case, once the Israeli economy opened up to migrant labor, demand for cheap labor steadily increased and the formal routes of migration that had opened up were accompanied by "shadow" paths of migration for undocumented workers who entered labor sectors other than the ones designated by the state as experiencing labor shortage. Undocumented workers worked in various off-the-book jobs such as sex workers, nannies and domestic workers in private homes, dishwashers, cleaners or cooks in restaurants, and support staff in hotels. Such workers became undocumented through either overstaying their tourist visas, violating their work visas, or being smuggled or trafficked into the country across the Egyptian border. Because of their precarious and temporary status, the new documented and undocumented workers quickly became some of the most vulnerable workers in the Israeli labor force, and some—mostly sex workers, agriculture workers, and some in-home care workers—experienced exploitation that led to their recognition as victims of trafficking.[21]

Israel's response to undocumented migration was clear and stark: the creation of an immigration police unit devoted to detaining and deporting undocumented labor migrants,[22] the deeper criminalization of "infiltration" into Israel and of trafficking in persons, and a slow and gradual development of workers' rights protections for migrant workers as well as human rights protections for victims of trafficking.[23]

The rise of sex trafficking is related to another new migration pattern into Israel. During the early 1990s, with the end of the Cold War, Israel was experiencing a significant wave of migration of (mostly) Jews from the Former Soviet Union (FSU).[24] During this wave of migration, approximately one million migrants became, through the Law of Return, instant new Israeli citizens.[25] In Israel, and throughout the West, the collapse of the Soviet Union opened up new routes of trade and migration.[26] An increase in trade and migration to the West for

work and other purposes was triggered by the struggling FSU economies, which were undergoing the painful process of economic restructuring. This increase was compounded by the belief held by many in
the FSU that they would find gainful employment as unskilled laborers upon migration to the wealthy West.

Informal shadow markets, fed by cross-border trade in goods and
labor, emerged, joining the established formal markets and routes of
trade and migration. This included a new market in undocumented
migration for the purpose of sex work and trafficking into the sex industry. It is estimated that between 1995 and 2005, thousands of
women entered Israel illegally—some of them trafficked and others
smuggled from the former Soviet republics of Moldova, Russia, and
Ukraine—to work in the local sex industry.[27] The concurrent legal immigration of FSU Jews to Israel facilitated a transnational association
between Eastern European and Israeli actors. The result was the development of a sophisticated apparatus for smuggling persons and human
trafficking for the purpose of prostitution, which expanded during this
period to the point of completely dominating the Israeli sex industry.

Trafficked women and non-Jewish migrant sex workers arriving in
Israel in the early 1990s either entered the country as tourists and
overstayed their visas or used falsified documentation to enter as Jewish immigrants. As the state authorities became aware of the phenomenon, young women arriving from the FSU became automatically
"suspect," and border control was tightened. In response, the migration routes were changed, and women were smuggled or trafficked into
Israel through a third country, mainly across the Egyptian border on
the outskirts of the Sinai Desert. Border crossing through the Sinai
Desert usually entailed long journeys by foot in the scorching desert
sun and was often accompanied by rape and violence.[28]

NGO reports from the early 2000s described horrifying working
conditions for many of these women in Israel. According to these reports, women were bought and sold, and transferred from one brothel
to another; their travel documents were confiscated; and they incurred
huge debts, received little or no pay, and had no control over the number of clients they were made to service. They were imprisoned in
brothels or apartments and frequently subjected to rape, violence, and
threats to their own lives and those of their families, by traffickers,
pimps, and clients.[29] Having entered Israel illegally, the women were

considered "illegal stayers." Thus, when the women were arrested by the police, usually in raids on brothels, they were promptly deported from the country. Interviews with victims of trafficking suggested that most of them came to Israel knowing that they would engage in sex work, and that at least some of them were satisfied with their working conditions, wanted to stay in Israel for a longer period of time, and even if deported hoped to be able to return.[30]

Hardly any research has been done on the scope or nature of prostitution engaged in by Israeli sex workers, and thus there is no definitive documentation of what Israeli sex workers did in the years between 1995 and 2006 or how the trafficking of women and the migration of sex workers influenced the sex market. Yet it was clear at the time that an overwhelmingly high percentage of all sex work in Israel was performed by migrant sex workers from the FSU, some of whom were the victims of trafficking.[31]

With the increase of trafficking into the sex industry and sex worker migration into Israel, dominance feminists became engaged in a campaign to abolish sex trafficking and prostitution. This is a tale of remarkable success. Because of their intense activities, there was a marked improvement in the treatment of identified victims of sex trafficking, and moreover, there is general agreement among the Israeli police, relevant government ministries, and all involved NGOs that transnational sex trafficking into Israel has been by and large curtailed.[32] The Israeli sex sector now comprises mostly Israeli workers, although some are relative newcomers from the FSU who entered the country legally under the Law of Return, 1950, and are therefore citizens.[33] How was this achieved?

Neo-abolitionist Feminist Anti-trafficking Efforts in the 2000s

Feminists have proved to be powerful actors in the regulation of sex work and trafficking in human beings for the purpose of prostitution. At the international level, this has manifested in the intense involvement of feminist NGOs in the drafting and ratification of the UN Office on Drugs and Crime 2000 Trafficking Protocol;[34] this is also the case at the national level in the United States[35] and in many other national contexts. Here I map out and assess the activism of Israeli neo-abolitionist feminists in civil society—as well as civil service—toward the regulation of trafficking in persons for the purpose of prostitution.

Israeli feminists took no part in the formulation of the original Israel Penal Code provisions relating to prostitution. The provisions, in their original form, were inherited from the British during their mandate rule in prestate Palestine between 1923 and 1948 and represent the achievements of early twentieth-century British abolitionists. The Penal Code criminalizes pimping, holding or renting out a site for prostitution, and living off the profits of a prostitute. In line with the abolitionist tradition, the act of prostitution itself is not criminalized, assuming that the prostitute is a victim of circumstances and therefore should not be criminalized. Yet despite the Penal Code's abolitionist orientation, prostitution in Israel is widely tolerated.[36] The main vehicle of this tolerance is the Attorney General directive 2.2, "Enforcement Policy in Offences related to Prostitution,"[37] which instructs police not to investigate "regular" prostitution unless there is suspicion of aggravating circumstances. According to the directive, aggravating circumstances include trafficking, underage prostitution, drugs, involvement of known criminal actors, and nuisance to neighbors.[38] Other institutional forums that contribute to a general tolerance of sex work—to both the benefit and detriment of individual sex workers—are the labor courts, which have recognized sex workers' employment rights;[39] the tax authorities, which regularly collect taxes from sex workers and pimps;[40] and the national social security authorities, which similarly view sex work as any other source of income, deny welfare benefits to sex workers who generate income from sex work, and require restitution of any benefits paid to a prostitute prior to the discovery of her income's source.[41]

Until the 1980s, the public policy discourse on prostitution in Israel had traditionally been dominated by two main approaches, neither of which was directly infused with feminist commitments: a conservative approach that viewed prostitution as a moral problem and tended toward its criminalization, and a liberal approach that perceived prostitution as a matter of individual choice that should generally not be subject to regulation. Proponents of the conservative stream spearheaded the 1962 amendment of the Israeli Penal Code, criminalizing renting out or holding an apartment used for prostitution, even if the owner or holder of the property is the sex worker herself.[42] This conservative stance was reinforced in an Israel Supreme Court decision from 1965 that held that the apparent contradiction between the Penal Code's noncriminalization of prostitutes themselves and the amendment's criminalization of prostitutes working from their own apartments can be reconciled given the public policy disfavoring prostitution and seeking its abolition.[43]

The liberal thread of the prostitution debate found expression in the Israeli parliament, the Knesset, when some legislators proposed excluding sex workers who work from their own apartments from the scope of the 1962 amendment, a position that was ultimately rejected in the Knesset.[44] A liberal stance was also evident in the 1977 final report of a specially appointed state commission into the subject of prostitution, which called for the establishment of zones of legalized prostitution, where prostitutes would be able to work safely and not be criminalized. Since feminism was only just emerging in Israeli civil society at that time, the commission did not hear testimony from feminist organizations. Its recommendations, which were not adopted, were based mostly on pragmatic considerations mixed with some generally liberal, and mildly liberal, feminist arguments.[45]

Traces of the pragmatic liberal position to prostitution persist in the "pockets" of tolerance for prostitution described above. However, since the renewal of the debate over the legitimacy of prostitution in the context of human trafficking, prostitution has been subsumed into the discussion of sex trafficking. From the outset, the latter discourse has been dominated in Israel by a dominance feminist neo-abolitionist position originating in the United States.[46] Leora Bilsky has noted that American legal feminist theory and ideas were transplanted into Israel in the 1970s with the return of female academics from studies in the United States, who then began to adapt American feminist theory to the local context and teach it at Israeli universities.[47] With regard to prostitution, Israeli feminists generally adopted the stance of American dominance feminism, namely, that all forms of prostitution are a manifestation of male domination and should, therefore, be abolished.

As early as 1997, Amnesty International, in collaboration with Israeli feminists and NGOs, began working to raise public awareness of the trafficking of women into the sex industry in Israel but struggled.[48] Their voices began to be heard only in 2000, following the enactment of the TVPA in the United States, a statute to which American neo-abolitionist feminists contributed significantly.[49] To ensure compliance with its minimum standards for eliminating trafficking, the TVPA imposes a set of financial sanctions on noncomplying countries. The TVPA stipulates that a country assessed as noncomplying and given a Tier 3 ranking risks losing nonhumanitarian, non-trade-related foreign assistance from the United States. This includes military and security aid. In the 2001 TIP report, Israel was ranked a Tier 3 country. Fearing the economic consequences of this status, the Israeli government began to take the phenomenon of trafficking more seriously, and its efforts quickly bore fruit: in the 2002 report, Israel was upgraded to Tier 2 and, in 2011, to Tier 1.[50]

The change in approach to trafficking in Israel, from a neglected issue to a high priority on the public agenda, was not necessarily the product of a deep commitment to protecting the dignity of trafficking victims or honoring UN conventions ratified and signed by the Israeli government. Rather, this was the heavy transnational imprint of U.S. law on the Israeli state, effected through its threat to withhold financial assistance.[51] However, the *form* of the Israeli response to the need to eliminate trafficking can be seen as the result of the work of Israeli neo-abolitionist feminists. While the main elements of national anti-trafficking responses were surprisingly similar around the globe,[52] there was still significant room for variations in a particular national context in relation to many elements of the dominant anti-trafficking regime. Elements such as the extent of criminalization, the distribution of enforcement across various labor sectors, the response along the borders, the shelters' format, and the rehabilitation and assistance package available to trafficking victims could all appear in myriad local variations. In Israel neo-abolitionist feminists had significant, and at times determinative, influence in the design of these and various other elements of the anti-trafficking regime.

The first Israeli response to trafficking in persons came in 2001, the same year Israel received a Tier 3 ranking in the TIP report, in the form of an amendment to the Penal Code criminalizing trafficking for the purpose of prostitution. This amendment was hastily passed to appease U.S. and international pressure and, therefore, without soliciting much input from Israeli civil society. In 2006, after a lengthy drafting process that was slowed down by two rounds of elections and governmental transitions, the Israeli Knesset passed the Prohibition of Trafficking in Persons Law. The bill had been drafted jointly by the parliamentary Subcommittee on Trafficking in Women and the parliamentary Constitution, Law and Justice Committee, but this time with extensive involvement of feminist organizations in the drafting process. Unlike the 2000 amendment to the Penal Code, which criminalized only trafficking into the sex industry, the 2006 law broadened the definition of trafficking to include exploitation in other labor sectors under the rubric of forced labor and slavery as well as organ removal.[53] This definition of trafficking complies with its conception in the 2000 UN Trafficking Protocol, and the enactment of the law paved the way for Israel to ratify the protocol.

One development stemming from the Israeli government's efforts to be "upgraded" in tier ranking was the establishment of the parliamentary Inquiry Commission on Trafficking in Women in 2000, which later became the Subcommittee on Trafficking in Women ("the trafficking subcommittee"). The inquiry commission was initiated by feminist Knesset member Zehava Galon, a member of the left-wing Meretz Party; she first chaired the commission and then chaired the subcommittee until 2009, at which point another feminist Knesset member, Orit Zuaretz, a member first of Kadima and then of Hatenua, both centrist parties, served as its chair until 2012.[54] A special relationship evolved between the subcommittee and Israeli feminist organizations. Originally invited as experts to report on their experiences in the field, feminists soon became prominent participants and permanent invitees at subcommittee meetings,[55] with a network of feminist and anti-trafficking NGOs[56] serving as primary sources of information on trafficking in Israel. By gathering data on the lives of trafficking victims, generating statistics, estimating numbers, and collecting testimony, these organizations pressured politicians and high-ranking police and ministerial officials into taking action, advised them on the type of action they should take, and assisted them in executing the action they eventually opted for.[57] The feminist organizations became more than mere suppliers of information and also participated in formulating the subcommittee's agenda and drafting proposed bills.

The feminist organizations that worked with the subcommittee followed strong neo-abolitionist intuitions, influenced by a form of

American dominance feminism.[58] The composition of the anti-trafficking coalition of organizations varied over the years.[59] One leading member of the coalition until about 2007 was the Hotline for Migrant Workers,[60] which is not a feminist organization per se and whose feminist politics are therefore not easily categorized. The organization deals with a wide range of issues, relating mostly to the detention and imprisonment of undocumented migrant workers, and included on its staff are feminist lawyers and activists. The Hotline had weaker neo-abolitionist commitments than the feminist organizations that participated regularly in subcommittee meetings. Thus, when cross-border trafficking into the sex industry decreased and designated victims were transferred to shelters and no longer detained in prisons, the Hotline's focus shifted predominantly to the detention of labor-trafficking victims, refugees, and asylum seekers. It did not follow in the footsteps of other feminist NGOs, which, at that stage, redirected their efforts to the abolition of all prostitution, a campaign that will be discussed below.

Another leading organization in the anti-trafficking coalition has been the Isha L'Isha ("Woman to Woman") feminist center, located in the northern city of Haifa. As the dominant anti-trafficking and anti-prostitution NGO in Israel,[61] Isha L'Isha is engaged in a wide range of causes, including women in security and peace processes (seeking to maximize the impact of UN Security Council Decision 1325), women's reproductive rights, and prostitution and sex trafficking. The organization takes a clear neo-abolitionist stand on sex work, strongly opposing its legalization, and holds sex trafficking and prostitution to be one and the same.

Until 2013, sex workers' organizations were not included among the NGOs active on the Knesset trafficking subcommittee, for the simple reason that no such organization existed in Israel until 2012. In that year, the Association for the Regulation of Sex Work was founded, a sex workers' association that is lobbying for the legalization of sex work in Israel. With the exception of this new association, the NGOs that work with the subcommittee seem to be in relative agreement with the mostly neo-abolitionist views and demands they present to the subcommittee.[62]

In this framework of direct and unmediated interaction between civil society organizations and the state, Israeli feminists have anchored their governance mode of operation and engaged in the regulation of sex work and human trafficking. In fact, when the subcommittee did not reconvene following the 2013 national elections, the participating organizations petitioned the newly appointed chair of the Knesset Committee on the Status of Women and requested the renewal of the subcommittee's meetings. In their petition, they argued:

> In its eleven years of operation, the subcommittee was a model of collaboration between NGOs and the *Knesset* and contributed significantly to anti-trafficking efforts. Since the previous *Knesset* completed its term nine months ago, the subcommittee has not met, and this has had harsh on-the-ground consequences, including a lack of enforcement, a lack of coordination and protection, and, most importantly, the critical lack of an open door to the Israeli parliament for the silenced voices of women victims of trafficking and, more generally, in prostitution.[63]

As a result of this appeal, the subcommittee was reconvened with a new chairperson. However, for the first time, the appointed chair was not a feminist Knesset member but, instead, a former high-ranking male police officer, Knesset member David Tsur from the centrist Hatenua Party.[64]

Israeli dominance feminists have worked to raise awareness of the trafficking phenomenon in civil society, the Knesset, and state bureaucracies; to strengthen and enforce its criminalization; and to promote a victim-centered approach to trafficking. In pursuing these goals, they have sought to bolster institutional and public exposure to the plight of sex-trafficking victims and pushed for an increase in the rate of arrest, prosecution, and conviction of traffickers and for more severe sentencing. Simultaneously, they have worked to ensure that trafficking victims are treated as victims and not as perpetrators and to guarantee their protection and rehabilitation as well as their right to bring tort claims against their traffickers for damages.

In addition to these efforts, dominance feminists have pursued other avenues for bringing about change. They have submitted shadow reports to the U.S. TIP office and used media campaigns and outreach to journalists to bring attention to the subject. They have worked to raise awareness and disseminate information within state bureaucracies, particularly the police,[65] as well as turning to the Israeli judicial system to advance various related causes.

While many aspects of the dominance feminist anti-trafficking activism were generally agreed on by all coalition members, some aspects were highly controversial and led to rifts among members. One such instance was the coalition's original decision to focus on trafficking in women for the purpose of prostitution rather than on prostitution as an issue per se. Tehila Sagy, a participant in the coalition's early deliberations, reported that Amnesty International, a prominent member of the coalition at the time and one of the first NGOs to document trafficking in Israel, made clear in these meetings that its mandate was to focus solely on trafficking and not to address prostitution. The Amnesty representative explained that the international office had not authorized the Israeli branch to participate in a coalition that seeks to abolish prostitution. As a result, a dominance feminist organization, Machon Toda'a ("Consciousness Center"),[66] left the coalition, declaring that it could not be a member of a coalition that distinguishes between prostitution and trafficking and thereby legitimates prostitution as a valid choice.[67] Sagy suggested that, in this context, the Israeli organizations had caved in to the Amnesty International position, when in fact, much like Machon Toda'a, their position contradicted that of Amnesty International. She based this assessment on the prohibitionist stance the same organizations had taken in relation to pornography.[68] It is likely that these organizations understood the alliance to be a strategic opportunity to direct attention to prostitution by way of the issue of trafficking. And indeed, once cross-border sex work and trafficking had declined, they seized the opportunity to shift the focus to prostitution in general and push for "end-demand" legislation.

Another issue on which dominance feminists were split was the question of what legal claim should be brought on behalf of sex workers seeking wages and compensation for exploitation from pimps and traffickers. In a number of cases, feminist lawyers filed claims for trafficking victims in the labor courts and succeeded in securing them full recognition of their rights as workers, such as minimum wage, annual leave pay, and dismissal compensation.[69] Indeed, since the 1990s, even before the issue of trafficking had gained prominence, the Israeli labor courts have recognized the existence of an employment relationship between pimps and sex workers.[70] More recently, in the 2009 *Kuchik* case, where the plaintiff was identified as a victim of trafficking, the labor court ruled that in cases of extreme coercion, no employment relationship exists between the parties. Nonetheless, relying on a purposive interpretation of the relevant protective employment laws, the court granted the plaintiff her employment rights in full. However, neo-abolitionist feminists have predominantly come to the understanding that claiming workers' rights serves to legitimate prostitution and is therefore harmful to the end cause of abolition. Following intense criticism of this strategy since *Kuchik* in feminist circles, feminist lawyers and NGOs have refrained from turning to the labor courts on behalf of sex workers.[71] Tort actions have become neo-abolitionist feminists' preferred route in seeking compensation for trafficking victims, as the focus is on the plaintiff as a victim of harm and not as an agent claiming rights as a party (presumably consenting) to an employment contract.[72]

The involvement of NGOs in legislative processes and policymaking is not unique to the context of trafficking in persons and, in fact, characterizes the recent trend toward "new governance."[73] In the Israeli context, new avenues for these organizations to influence policy and legislation have opened up since rights discourse and the concept of dignity became more central in Israeli jurisprudence with the 1992 passage of the Basic Law: Freedom of Occupation and the Basic Law: Human Dignity and Liberty (which, combined, are considered Israel's still-partial bill of rights) and since NGOs gained direct access to parliamentary processes. It is also clear that civil society organizations do not and will not always succeed in these political struggles, and it remains questionable and context-dependent as to how much power they actually wield in practice.

In the context of the anti-trafficking campaigns, the power of the trafficking subcommittee itself can be questioned. First, structurally, the powers of parliamentary committees in Israel are more constrained than those of American congressional committees. In the United States, working with congressional committees is essentially the only way to promote legislation inside Congress. In Israel, in contrast, parliamentary committees serve as important sources of information on the matter they address but lack any particular legislative authority.

Second, while the trafficking subcommittee has successfully proposed and passed several important laws, amendments, regulations, and procedures in the years since its establishment, many of its proposals have thus far failed to pass, including what is perhaps the most desired goal of neo-abolitionist feminists working with and serving on the subcommittee: a proposal to adopt the Swedish end-demand model of partial abolition, which provides for the criminalization of clients.[74] Another neo-abolitionist feminist campaign that did not meet with success was the push to revise the Attorney General directive on prostitution-related prosecutions, which is amended and updated every several years. Despite repeated neo-abolitionist feminist appeals to the Attorney General to make substantive amendments to the directive, so far only the rhetoric has been modified. For example, the 2006 version of the directive noted that it in no way "detracts from the goal of reducing the scope of prostitution." The 2012, and later the 2014 version reflects a stronger abolitionist orientation, referring to an aspiration to "abolish prostitution altogether as a phenomenon that in and of itself causes injury to women's dignity." But despite these rhetorical modifications, the directive's operative sections have not been amended. Since 2012 the directive declares that "the solution to the problem of men and women who engage in prostitution (that is not illegal per se) exceeds the scope of responsibility of law enforcement entities and requires a public discussion and an interdisciplinary engagement of all relevant actors, including those who specialize in rehabilitation."[75] Accordingly, the directive still instructs police to refrain from investigating prostitution absent aggravating circumstances.

Third, even when subcommittee proposals have been enacted into legislation, implementation by the executive or judiciary branch has, at times, been only partial. One example is the 2005 Restriction on Use of a Place for Purposes of Preventing Commission of Offenses Law,[76] which defines pimping, trafficking into the sex industry, and owning or renting a place for the purpose of prostitution as offenses. This law, which was proposed by the subcommittee, authorizes the police to seek a court order to shut down brothels. Police reports to the subcommittee stated that, although the law had been successfully used to close (at least temporarily) some brothels,[77] there are a number of significant hurdles to its effective implementation. In 2012, for example, the police reported that only three court orders had been issued in the Tel Aviv area. This, they asserted, was due to courts' reluctance to issue such orders given the Attorney General directive.[78]

Finally, the successful outcomes of certain campaigns were not long lasting and eventually were reversed. One example is the anti-trafficking police unit, whose creation neo-abolitionist feminists pushed for through the subcommittee. Although such a unit was eventually established in 2009, its mandate was not devoted exclusively to trafficking into the sex industry, and it was disbanded in 2011. In response, the subcommittee chairperson at the time, Knesset member Orit Zuaretz, along with two NGOs, petitioned the Israel Supreme Court, claiming that the police had violated its agreement with her as subcommittee chair.[79] The petition was eventually withdrawn.

Yet alongside frustrating losses, dominance feminists have won some noteworthy anti-trafficking battles. To those I turn next.

Dominance Feminists' Successes: Softer on Trafficking Victims, Harder on Traffickers

The 2000 amendment to the Israel Penal Code criminalizing trafficking itself was largely in response to pressure from the U.S. TIP office.[80] However, many of the developments that followed in its wake, as well as the actual contents of the anti-trafficking measures, can be seen as a direct result of successful dominance feminist lobbying and activism. While the ultimate goal of Israeli neo-abolitionist feminists is the abolition of prostitution, their dual short-term goal was ensuring that the state goes "softer" on victims of trafficking, on the one hand, and "harder" on traffickers, on the other.

Softer on Victims of Trafficking

Until 2004, undocumented women who were found by law enforcement authorities in brothels were treated no differently than any other undocumented migrant: they were detained and then promptly deported.[81] Dominance feminists working through the parliamentary trafficking subcommittee and the courts pushed for their treatment as victims of severe human rights violations and for the establishment of special victims' shelters. In raising the issue in the subcommittee, as well as in representing trafficking victims in court and through amicus briefs, dominance feminist activists successfully argued for a right to out-of-prison accommodation and police protection for trafficking victims who agree to serve as prosecution witnesses.[82] They argued that rather than being detained or deported, these women should be rescued and rehabilitated.[83] Indeed, several court decisions from 2000 held that trafficking victims serving as prosecution witnesses should not be detained while waiting to testify and that the police should ensure that their basic needs are met. Following these rulings, the police gradually began accommodating these witnesses in hostels rather than detaining them in prisons. Yet the alternative to police detention did not provide a full rehabilitation package or police protection, and, moreover, the women were promptly deported after giving testimony.

In 2004, owing to the combined force of U.S. pressure and the neo-abolitionist feminist lobby in the trafficking subcommittee,[84] the Israeli government commissioned the operation of a victims' shelter for women (Ma'agan) and, in 2009, a victims' shelter for men (Atlas). Atlas was established to accommodate male victims of trafficking in various labor sectors. Both shelters are open to identified victims of trafficking, and each can house up to thirty-five men or women (and the women's children) at a time.[85] The shelters provide residents with accommodation, meals, clothing, medicine, and hygiene products, as well as social, medical, and psychological aid, translation services, employment training opportunities, spending money,[86] and, in the women's shelter, child care. The shelters operate in an open format, meaning that residents can come and go as they please, although in the women's shelter, residents who are not employed outside the shelter must request special permission to leave the shelter before 3:00 p.m.[87] No parallel requirement applies to the residents of the men's shelter.[88] At first, the women's shelter was open only to victims willing to testify against their traffickers. Feminists criticized this practice in the trafficking subcommittee, arguing that the state had a moral obligation to rehabilitate trafficking victims and that all identified victims should be allowed to stay at the shelter.[89] As a result of this criticism, since 2006, the shelter offers accommodation to all designated victims of trafficking regardless of whether they are witnesses in the prosecution of their traffickers.[90]

In 2004, the minister of interior set procedures for granting trafficking victims temporary visas to stay and work in Israel, in response to numerous petitions submitted by neo-abolitionist feminists to the Ministry and at subcommittee meetings on the matter. At first, the visas were conditioned on cooperation with law enforcement authorities.

But in 2006, again due to U.S. pressure and the work of dominance feminist activists, this requirement was dropped. Identified trafficking victims were now granted yearlong permits to stay for a "rehabilitation period," which, in rare circumstances, can be extended. While there are no criteria defining what such rare circumstances may be, researchers Daphna Hacker and Orna Cohen give two examples of approved applications: one was approved to facilitate the completion of a women's vocational course, and another to help a woman finance her mother's health care costs.[91]

Finally, due to Israeli NGO lobbying in the Knesset, legislation proposed by the trafficking subcommittee was passed in 2006, making trafficking victims eligible for free legal counsel from the Israeli Public Defender Office.[92] Public defense attorneys now represent victims in a variety of types of litigation, including claims brought against the state, police, and traffickers.

The package of rights and services extended to victims of trafficking is evidence of the impressive achievements of dominance feminists in this context. While all of this likely would not have happened without strong U.S. pressure and Israel's low TIP ranking, the direction, the particular contents of the means chosen, and the prioritization of certain measures over others are the direct result of neo-abolitionist feminist efforts. This arrangement is significantly more generous than the current treatment of any other undocumented workers, smuggled persons, asylum seekers, or "run of the mill" exploited workers in Israel. Once perceived as undocumented workers threatening the Jewish character of Israel as well as its sovereignty, trafficked persons are now viewed and treated as victims of human rights violations for which the state is willing to take responsibility and grant unprecedented privileges, chief among which is eligibility for temporary stay visas and work permits. Certainly, there is no lack of implementation problems, including failures in identifying trafficking victims, bureaucratic and procedural hurdles to receiving assistance and visas, and instances of involuntary repatriation of victims. Yet the very existence of this anti-trafficking regime is an impressive achievement in its extension of a new array of rights and services to severely exploited persons.

Despite this impressive set of developments, this assistance was eventually extended to a very small group of trafficked persons. A mere 657 women were identified as victims of trafficking between 2001 and 2012,[93] and only 367 were referred to the trafficking victims' shelters between 2004 and 2013.[94] Accordingly, it can be assumed that the more effective set of policies that led to the eventual eradication of cross-border sex trafficking was the second group of policies, which I turn to next.

Tougher on Traffickers

The criminalization of trafficking occurred primarily because of pressure from the U.S. State Department and was not the direct action of Israeli dominance feminists. Yet Israeli feminists embraced, strengthened, translated, and gave local meaning to this international pressure in Israeli law and within the Israeli penal system. Their goal became a carceral feminist[95] one: ensuring strong punishment and deterrence of trafficking. Thus, dominance feminists lobbied for more police brothel raids, more rescuing of victims, and more prosecutions and convictions of traffickers, as well as more severe sentences for traffickers, including the payment of damages to victims. Below, I outline a partial list of the main neo-abolitionist feminist achievements in this campaign.

Through their work with the trafficking subcommittee, neo-abolitionist feminists raised awareness about the smuggling of women through the Sinai Desert and pushed for tighter border control.[96] Feminist lawyers in the Attorney General's Office argued for judges to lower the standard of proof for the consideration requirement in the Penal Code's trafficking provision—the requirement to prove that women were bought or sold that was an element of the crime of trafficking—to circumstantial evidence alone.[97] They also successfully argued before the courts to include peripheral actors, such as a brothel's employees (cashiers, for example) and owners of real estate on which brothels are run (who fell under existing prostitution-related criminal provisions) in the definition of trafficking.[98]

The lobbying efforts of dominance feminists in the subcommittee, in collaboration with feminist parliament members and bureaucrats, also led to changes in police enforcement priorities, an increase in the rate of brothel raids, and the prosecution of sex traffickers.[99] They also succeeded in securing compensation for trafficking victims through torts claims[100] and the establishment of a state-run fund to compensate victims, funded by fines and monies confiscated from traffickers.[101] Furthermore, the rise in public awareness of the lax punishment of traffickers led to a steady harshening of sentences.[102]

Each of these achievements, which represent only some of the neo-abolitionist feminists' victories, was preceded by a long history of strategic decisions, compromises, partial successes, and, at times, even some disappointment at the eventual outcome. Although much of this activism yielded a far from perfect result from a neo-abolitionist feminist perspective, it nonetheless transformed Israel's sex sector. Cross-border trafficking into the sex industry in Israel was halted for the most part,[103] an outstanding achievement for the relevant Israeli governmental ministries, law enforcement agencies, and the American TVPA,[104] as well as for the Israeli dominance feminists involved, and remarkable in relation to other countries across the world. The specific impact of GF is evident in the stark contrast between how Israel has contended with sex trafficking and its far less impressive record on non-sex-work-related trafficking offenses. Despite that the 2006 Prohibition of Trafficking in Persons Law defines trafficking broadly to include exploitation in other labor sectors,[105] there has been barely any prosecution of non-sex-work-related trafficking offenses.[106] Moreover, although victims of labor trafficking do enjoy the same rights and access to shelter extended to victims of trafficking into the sex industry,[107] the state makes little effort to identify labor trafficking victims or to enforce anti-trafficking measures in any of these sectors.[108]

The Combined Effect

As a result of these two sets of policies—softer on victims, harder on traffickers—since around 2006, there has been broad agreement among both the authorities[109] and civil society organizations and activists that the trafficking of non-Israeli women into the Israeli sex industry has been successfully combated.[110] As previously explained, this has been the direct result of U.S. pressure, Israeli neo-abolitionist feminists' efforts, and the general approach of the Israeli government, law enforcement authorities, and society at large as to the need to contend with non-Jewish undocumented migrants in the sex industry.

The effectiveness of Israel's anti-trafficking campaign can be attributed to the combination of a strict immigration policy, a strong police and prosecutorial crackdown on brothels employing undocumented workers, and the extension of some services and rights to some victims of sex trafficking, all operating on the background of the broad tolerance of prostitution in Israel.[111] This latter background condition, which I argue below has been key to the success of the Israeli anti-trafficking campaign, is seen as deeply problematic by neo-abolitionist feminists, and despite their efforts they did not succeed in changing it. How did this combination of policies operate on the ground?

Crucial to the efforts to curb trafficking into the Israeli sex industry were strict border control strategies. Beginning in the early 2000s, it became nearly impossible for non-Jewish, single young women from Eastern Europe (the typical profile of sex trafficking victims) to enter Israel by either air or sea.[112] The only option open to traffickers was to smuggle women in by foot, usually through the Sinai Desert. To stop human trafficking as well as gun and drug trafficking across this border—and, most notably, to contend with the thousands of African asylum seekers[113] who had entered Israel through the Sinai Desert since 2007—Israel constructed a border fence, making any smuggling or trafficking on that route nearly impossible.[114] Clearly, the border fence was *not* built because of neo-abolitionist feminist efforts; in fact, construction work on the barrier began only in 2009, when trafficking into the sex industry had already declined dramatically. But it is interesting to note that dominance feminists made the first steps toward the notion of such a fence: years earlier, in response to dominance feminist demands, military officers had appeared on numerous occasions before the trafficking subcommittee, promising to build such a fence.[115]

Strict border control was accompanied by the reality of de facto toleration of the existence of the Israeli sex sector. Prior to the police response to sex trafficking, there were low levels of enforcement in relation to Israeli sex workers. In fact, at the first stages, in the early 2000s, frequent raids targeted brothels that employed non-Israeli sex workers, while Israeli sex workers were mostly unaffected by the newfound police attention to the sex industry.[116] As explained, the Penal Code embodies a partial abolitionist approach to prostitution, in that it criminalizes anyone who profits from prostitution except the sex worker and the client.[117] Yet because of the Attorney General directive,[118] the prohibition on prostitution-related offenses was not enforced in most cases. As a result, Israel's sex industry operated mostly aboveground and was tolerated and recognized by various state entities.[119] The anti-trafficking strategy of law enforcement agencies was, therefore, not the permanent closure of brothels (which would have most likely pushed them underground). Instead, police regularly monitored and raided brothels, focusing mostly on underage girls and non-Israelis working there. In these raids, police checked identification documents and little else; only in the case of non-Israelis and minors did they take further action.

In line with the victim-centered approach to trafficking, undocumented women found in brothels through police raids were generally identified as victims of trafficking. There is no single procedure for identifying victims of trafficking into the sex industry, and identification is at the police officer's discretion. In all cases of identification of trafficking victims, the police need only preliminary proof that the individual is a victim to send her to the victims' shelter. Dominance feminists objected to the police's exclusive discretion in identifying victims of trafficking into the sex industry.[120] To inform the police of the realities of sex trafficking, they conducted workshops and lectures on the subject;[121] in addition, on an informal level, police officers involved in identifying victims of trafficking worked closely with feminist groups and other NGOs throughout the identification process.[122]

The identification process in relation to victims of non-sex-work-related trafficking is more elaborate. In 2008, an interministerial committee was formed for the purpose of designing an identification procedure for victims of labor trafficking, and several months later it issued its "Procedure for the Identification of Victims of Slavery, Forced Labor and Labor Exploitation."[123] The procedure issued lists of indicators of trafficking that the interviewer should look for. It includes a list of visible indicators (such as depression, signs of violence, signs of illness, etc.) and of indicators the interviewer should inquire about in the interview (such as violation of labor rights, worker isolation, economic sanctions employed by the employers, etc.). This elaborate process can be explained by the assumption that determining whether trafficking for the purpose of labor exploitation occurred is a more complicated task than determining trafficking for the purpose of prostitution.[124] This is possibly due to the prevalence of the neo-abolitionist position on prostitution, according to which a woman's mere involvement in prostitution automatically makes her vulnerable to (or a victim of) trafficking, whereas the same assumption does not apply in relation to workers in other labor sectors.[125]

Once a woman was identified as a victim of trafficking into the sex sector, she was sent to the victims' shelter and encouraged to testify against her traffickers. If she decided not to testify, she was allowed a yearlong "reflection period," after which she was repatriated to her country of origin. Only several hundred such identifications occurred in the past decade.[126] Non-Israeli women who were found by police at brothels in raids or in other circumstances and for various reasons were not identified as trafficking victims were detained and deported. No information is available on the precise number of women who were deported as a result of increased enforcement. Given the estimate of thousands of migrant sex workers and victims of trafficking in Israel in the early 2000s,[127] however, the number of deportations must have been quite high.

As a result of such anti-trafficking efforts, the Israeli sex industry transformed dramatically in the decade between the mid-1990s and the mid-2000s. The majority of sex workers were, yet again, Israeli citizens, and the worst forms of exploitation in this sector were eliminated.[128]

Israeli neo-abolitionist feminists view this as only a partial realization of their ultimate goal.[129] Although cross-border trafficking into the sex industry was all but stopped, the complete abolition of prostitution is still far in the distance. With the subsiding of the trafficking and migration of women into the sex industry, neo-abolitionist feminists shifted focus to the abolition of prostitution but continued to refer to their efforts as directed against trafficking, under the understanding that all prostitution is trafficking.[130] This dominance feminist position can explain the step taken by Israeli feminists in their engagement with the state around prostitution: a drive to promote an "end-demand" bill—criminalizing johns—that has been drafted by NGOs working with the trafficking subcommittee. This development can also explain why the trafficking subcommittee reconvened in 2013 under the title the Subcommittee on Trafficking in Women and Prostitution.[131] This change in title signaled the subcommittee's new interest in Israeli sex workers. Although the definition of trafficking in Israeli law does not subsume all prostitution under trafficking, adding the term "prostitution" to the subcommittee's name sought to ensure that the two issues would be viewed and treated as one and the same phenom-enon. Yet as the subcommittee's expanded title indicates, Israeli anti-trafficking activism continues to be directed mainly at exploitation within the sex industry, while trafficking into other industries is mostly ignored.

In response to the subcommittee's proposed end-demand bill, Is-raeli sex workers began to organize for the first time.[132] In 2013, a group of sex workers founded the Association for the Regulation of Sex Work; earlier attempts to organize had failed.[133] The sex workers' representa-tives began writing op-eds, giving interviews to the press, and attend-ing the trafficking subcommittee meetings in an attempt to present their perspective against the end-demand bill.[134] Thus, sex workers are utilizing GF for the first time in Israel. It remains to be seen whether their own voices will actually be heard in a political arena filled with feminist organizations claiming to speak on their behalf.

Cost–Benefit Analysis and Unintended Consequences: Nationalism, Borders, and Markets

The following distributive analysis details the intended and unintended consequences of the anti-trafficking campaign in Israel, examining the costs and benefits generated for a diverse group of stakeholders. A wide distributive analysis would include a myriad of stakeholders: lo-cal and migrant sex workers, victims of trafficking, severely exploited migrant labor in non-sex-work-related sectors, women who stopped working as sex workers because of the changing legal regime, men who buy sex services ("clients") and men who do not buy these ser-vices, the women who live with men who buy sex services and those who live with men who do not, and the ripple effect of women enter-ing or exiting the sex industry on other labor markets. Various ques-tions that are often left unexplored by dominance feminists are sig-nificant in such an analysis: this analysis not only brings to the forefront the well-being of different groups of men and women, but also focuses on the effect of regulation on the structure of markets and wider ideo-logical categories (nationality, exploitation) and policy trends (e.g., neoliberalism and restrictive immigration regimes)—all of which are crucial to understanding the distributive consequences of any given policy.

In what follows, I engage in a somewhat narrower distributive analysis. Rather than examining the entire range of stakeholders noted above, I focus on women who were trafficked into the sex industry and other sex workers, groups that are traditionally the central concern of neo-abolitionist feminist policymakers engaged in the regulation of commercial sex. Exploring the effects of this campaign on the discursive economy, I also mention the impact of these policies on victims of trafficking outside the sex industry and other migrant workers, while pointing to unintended ideological ramifications of reinforcing nationalism, borders, and a particular understanding of free markets. Thus, the distributional analysis here will not take into account all relevant stakeholders.

Using a cost–benefit analysis can be problematic in the explosive context of sex work because it attempts to identify benefits in situations that many see as inherently harmful and costs in a context that is possibly redemptive. Accordingly, Israeli dominance feminists might argue that even if, for example, migrants' sex work leads to some limited benefits for the women involved, these should be disregarded as illegitimate or negligible or strategically harmful even to mention as benefits. I disagree. I maintain that looking at the distributive effects for a wider range of stakeholders and in a broader scope of human contexts does not legitimate any benefit produced by women's work when it is exploitative. On the contrary, this approach allows the wide range of incentives (including those for the women themselves) to come to the surface. Far from undermining feminist goals, it is crucial to revitalizing (and, to an extent, interrupting) the current trajectories of GF. As a methodology, such an analysis can provide a fresh, pragmatic vision of the regulation of trafficking and sex work; it can induce dominance feminists to break away from the narrow conception of law as capable of either prohibition or permission (a view dictated by the current commitments of many strands of GF) and enable a more realist perception of choice, agency, and consent.

Benefits

The benefits of the Israeli anti-trafficking campaign perhaps seem relatively self-evident. First and foremost, the most extreme form of exploitation in the Israeli sex industry was mostly eliminated. Non-Israeli women who worked in severely exploitative conditions, who were subjected to threats, violence, and rape, and who had little or no control over their working conditions and wages were "rescued"[135] or deported and, in any event, extracted from the Israeli sex industry. It can be reasonably assumed that the prosecution of violent traffickers and removal of the most vulnerable workers from the sex industry improved the bargaining position, and consequently the working conditions and wages, for the remaining sex workers.

Second, the vulnerability of sex workers to exploitation became a national concern in Israel. As a result, since 2008, the Israeli government has funded programs to assist sex workers who want to exit the industry. Public as well as private funding led to the initiation of various projects aimed at providing services to sex workers, mostly to assist them in "breaking the cycle of prostitution" and for "rehabilitation."[136] Resources are still grossly insufficient to provide aid to all the relevant women or to meet their needs in full. But the mere existence of such programs can be seen as a benefit generated by the dominance feminist anti-trafficking campaign.

A third benefit was the provision of the package of services to identified victims of trafficking into the sex industry. This feature of the anti-trafficking regime was a stark deviation from Israel's otherwise highly exclusionary immigration regime and treatment of undocumented workers, smuggled persons, asylum seekers, and other exploited workers.

Finally, due to American and Israeli civil society pressure, the scope of the rights and services developed for victims of trafficking into the sex industry was steadily expanded and extended to victims of trafficking into other labor sectors. Thus, dominance feminist anti-trafficking work ultimately assisted migrant workers in non-sex-work-related sectors, primarily exploited agriculture and caregiving migrant workers, as well as African asylum seekers who endure torture and exploitation in crossing the Sinai Desert to enter Israel. The majority of current residents at the trafficking victims' shelters are from these groups of victims.[137]

This list of benefits, while perhaps short in length, in fact represents an immense and possibly internationally unparalleled transformation in a country's treatment of undocumented sex workers, most resulting from and all heavily influenced by the work of neo-abolitionist feminists.

Costs

The successes of Israeli neo-abolitionist feminists came at a cost. There were costs to migrant sex workers and victims of trafficking into the sex industry in Israel and for other exploited workers as well. There was also a discursive cost, in the strengthening of policies that the very same feminists might have objected to in other circumstances: a shift toward neoliberal justifications, a further restriction of Israel's immigration policy regarding non-Jews, and the legitimizing and bolstering of Israel's border-building capabilities as a strong security state.

Certainly, Israeli neo-abolitionist feminists would identify none of these costs as something of their own doing and would likely assert that they had achieved as much as was possible in a hostile environment.[138] They may be right. I assume the costs I note here to be an unintended outcome of their efforts; and some might argue that even if they were predictable, these costs were quite simply "worth it" as they are outweighed by the benefits. The critical account that I offer below does not tally up the costs and benefits, however. Rather, it seeks to create a space to discuss strategy, compromises, power, and ambivalence. Furthermore, some of these costs may be shared by other feminist anti-trafficking campaigns in other national contexts, and the applicability of the lessons in the Israeli case may transcend their local context.

The first cost was borne by women who were returned to their countries of origin, whether identified as victims of trafficking (repatriated) or not (deported). We know practically nothing of what happened upon return to the many women who were repatriated or deported.[139] However, we do know why they left their countries of origin and what they likely experienced while in Israel. Most, if not all, of the women came to Israel for economic reasons: following the economic upheaval of the transition from communism to capitalism, economic opportunities were limited in their home countries and they sought better economic futures for themselves and their families.[140] Many incurred great debts to cover the costs of their journey to Israel, which were often used as leverage against them and continued to balloon while the women were working in brothels. Furthermore, many of the women came to Israel knowing that they would work in the sex sector;[141] some had already been working as sex workers back home. Many, but not all, experienced harsh working conditions, violence, and severe exploitation while in Israel. Others had a better work experience and hoped to remain in Israel for a longer period of time.[142]

The limited research that does exist on repatriation processes across the world suggests that, in general, many repatriated trafficking victims face a harsh economic reality and possibly stigma and marginalization upon their return home, which could lead them to migrate or be trafficked again.[143] Some are reintegrated into their communities with the assistance of local NGOs, but even in such cases, the women are not always guaranteed a better economic future, debt forgiveness, or positive social reintegration. Of course, it is impossible to know whether they would have been worse off had they stayed in Israel than what they experience in their countries of origin or with subsequent migratory attempts. But it is still important to understand that deportation and repatriation are not easy processes and that "returning home" is not necessarily a happy ending for many of these women who sought to escape the realities they were forced to return to.

While human rights projects tend to be suspicious of large deportation schemes,[144] this end result was not thoroughly problematized within the Israeli anti-trafficking campaign. Neo-abolitionist feminists successfully worked to prevent the arrest and deportation of victims of trafficking; rescuing them from traffickers, rehabilitating them, and extending their stay in Israel for several years was the goal. But the strict exclusionary logic of Israel's immigration regime—allowing the naturalization of non-Jews only in relatively rare circumstances[145]—was not, and probably could not have been, challenged by neo-abolitionist feminists. As discussed above, granting trafficking victims temporary stay and work visas regardless of their collaboration with prosecution was already a remarkable achievement given Israel's immigration policy.[146] Accordingly, neo-abolitionist feminists attempted to delay deportation of those identified as victims and to make their reintegration smoother through the support of NGOs in their countries of origin and by filing civil suits on their behalf for damages. Yet even those identified as victims were eventually repatriated, and the many women who were picked up in raids and not identified as victims were simply deported from Israel. The result was the mass deportation and repatriation of thousands of women, with possibly some grave personal consequences that went almost entirely unnoticed and unrecognized.

The second cost of the Israeli dominance feminist anti-trafficking campaign arises from the approach to rehabilitation that structures the daily lives of trafficking victims in the victims' shelter. While the shelter provides women with housing and other important services, this is carried out in an acutely paternalistic framework. As Hacker and Cohen suggest, the Israeli victims' shelters in general lack a coherent definition of rehabilitation, especially in relation to male victims of trafficking and women who were trafficked into non-sex-work-related sectors. With respect to victims of trafficking for the purpose of prostitution, various assumptions seem to guide the rehabilitation process,[147] namely, that they are victims of trauma who require socialization to engage in a productive life and intimate relationships, and that high levels of supervision and control are necessary for the process to be effective. The rehabilitation process was developed in line with the experiences of therapists with the rehabilitation of soldiers suffering from posttraumatic stress disorder (PTSD) and of battered women. As a result, the women's daily routine is constructed on "clear boundaries, law and behavioral norms, as well as moral criteria and the demand that these will be scrupulously observed alongside an accepting and inviting atmosphere that nurtures, contains, involves, and cares for the residents."[148] This routine begins with a set wake-up time, followed by group discussion, and, later on, maintenance work at the shelter, including cleaning and meal preparation. The shelter is considered an open shelter, and the women can come and go as they please; but women who do not work outside the shelter cannot leave the premises before 3:00 p.m. without special permission, and all women need to be back at the shelter by midnight. In sum, life in the women's shelter is heavily supervised and is structured around a long list of strict rules. Hacker and Cohen posit that these limitations seem to be driven by gendered perceptions and "entail a degree of paternalism, oppression and lack of confidence in the women's abilities."[149]

In contrast, the men's shelter places relatively minimal restrictions on its residents. They do not have a parallel daily routine and are not subject to close behavioral supervision. Furthermore, they can come and go as they please during the day, though they are also required to return by midnight. Finally, the shelter's main function with respect to its residents is to find them fair employment. No such goal appears in the programs of the women's shelter.

An additional difference between the two shelters relates to how the men's and women's economic needs are addressed. Presumptions regarding women's needs and desires have oriented the rehabilitation in the shelter toward psychological counseling and away from economic self-sufficiency. Providing women with work habits and a vocation is an important goal at the women's shelter but not so much for its economic purpose as for its socializing effect. Yet studies of such shelters suggest that many victims (of both labor trafficking and trafficking into the sex industry) are in fact principally interested in finding employment with decent working conditions.[150] This is particularly true of sex and labor trafficking victims who voluntarily migrated to find work but whose undocumented status made them vulnerable to exploitation.[151] In contrast, at the men's shelter, the main rehabilitative goal is to find men employment with good working conditions rather than to offer psychological counseling.[152] As a result, men usually stay in the shelter for a short period of time, from several days to no more than several weeks, whereas women usually spend longer periods of time at their shelter, ranging from months to years.[153]

The differences in daily structure and rehabilitative approach at the two shelters could be to the detriment of both the male and female victims and appear to be rooted in a neo-abolitionist conception of the harms of prostitution and traditional gender role assumptions about both men and women. The neo-abolitionist tradition with which Israeli GF is infused conceives of prostitution as violence against women and a harm in and of itself, and thus the women's shelter is structured to address PTSD rather than economic exploitation. Because prostitution is seen as inherently different from any other form of labor, the women at the shelter are treated primarily as in need of psychological assistance and socialization into "normal" life. Men (and some women) who were exploited in other labor sectors are perceived, first and foremost, as economic actors, and the assistance provided to them is, therefore, primarily economic. However, since the shelters were originally developed for women trafficked into the sex industry, they have no clear conception of the mental or physical needs of people trafficked into other labor sectors—male or female. This clear distinction between sex work and other work means that the women's economic needs are largely untreated at the shelter, while the men's emotional needs are similarly mostly ignored.

A third cost of the dominance feminist anti-trafficking campaign is borne by Israeli sex workers, who are now more exposed to police harassment. Prior to the implementation of anti-trafficking policies and due to the tolerance for prostitution by the authorities in Israel, the sex industry and sex workers were by and large not subjected to police investigations absent aggravating circumstances. As a result, a certain relationship of trust developed between the police and sex workers, with the latter not hesitating to turn to the police for assistance when they were the victims of violence, and doing so with relatively little fear of negative repercussions or arrest.[154] But the implementation of the anti-trafficking regime led to frequent police raids on brothels and a higher level of enforcement of existing anti-prostitution legislation, which ended up targeting not only traffickers and pimps but also Israeli sex workers. As is often the case across the world, in Israel, police attention to prostitution was accompanied by harassment and violence toward sex workers, a deepening distrust between sex workers and the law enforcement authorities, and, as a result, a weakened bargaining position of sex workers in their interaction with clients and others.[155]

Discursive Economy Analysis

Thus far I have focused on the costs entailed for those who are at the center of feminist anti-trafficking efforts—the female victims of trafficking into sex industry and sex workers—and benefits and costs to other victims of trafficking. Yet, as alluded to earlier, the anti-trafficking regime had ripple effects on Israeli immigration policy and wider labor market issues. The remaining four consequences of the dominance feminist anti-trafficking campaign that I discuss relate to the discursive economy effects of the anti-trafficking campaign in relation to Israel's labor, immigration, and security policies.

The first consequence relates to victims of trafficking into non-sex-work labor sectors and to labor market exploitation as a wider phenomenon. Israel's guest work regime is structured so that documented agriculture and construction workers (mostly men) become vulnerable to trafficking.[156] Yet their exploitation goes largely unnoticed by the Israeli authorities, with very little enforcement of labor laws, hardly any labor inspectors, and no repercussions for abusive employers in this context. The trafficking subcommittee is a subcommittee of the Committee on the Status of Women and focuses only on women's issues; it therefore has never inquired into other forms of trafficking. Thus, while Israel was elevated to Tier 1 status in the 2012 TIP report, it was doing almost nothing to stop labor trafficking into non-sex-work-related labor sectors.

In fact, the anti-trafficking campaign in Israel can be seen as exemplifying the logic of what Bernard Harcourt calls the Neoliberal Penality:

> A form of rationality in which the penal sphere is pushed outside political economy and serves the function of a boundary: the penal sanction is marked off from the dominant logic of classical economics as the only space where order is legitimately enforced by the State. On this view, the bulk of human interaction—which consists of economic exchange—is viewed as voluntary, compensated, orderly, and tending toward the common good; the penal sphere is the outer bound, where the Government can legitimately interfere, there and there alone.[157]

The criminalization of trafficking does just this. By focusing attention on the horrors of trafficking into the sex industry and on that alone, the vulnerability of other workers—whether non-Jewish migrant workers or other unskilled workers—is camouflaged and normalized.[158]

Moreover, the broad engagement with trafficking into the sex industry creates the impression that the Israeli government is deeply committed to eradicating severe forms of labor exploitation. Yet the fact that only a small proportion of trafficked persons are actually identified as trafficking victims[159] combined with the sweeping persistence of extreme exploitation in labor markets in Israel implies an end result of little more than an (unjustifiably) clear conscience.

The second consequence, deriving from the predominant victim-centered human rights approach in the Israeli anti-trafficking regime and common to the globally prevailing anti-trafficking paradigm, is the sublimation of the strong economic aspect of this exploitation. The Israeli anti-trafficking paradigm, much like the global one, assumes that a worker's vulnerability is caused merely by her individual relationship with a criminal wrongdoer and disregards the structural elements—related to migration, employment and labor law, and economic opportunities—that constrain workers' migratory status and bargaining position.[160] This anti-trafficking framework assists individual victims by prohibiting trafficking and extending certain rights and services to trafficked persons once they have been rescued. Its objective is to extricate individuals from the harmful work environment and ensure ex-post aid, while victims play a relatively passive role in the process of their rescue, rehabilitation, and repatriation. It does not equip women with the tools to improve their situation as sex workers and continue working in Israel. The only way open to them is out: out of the sex sector and out of the country.

A third consequence relates to Israel's ethnonationalist immigration regime. Israel's anti-trafficking policies correspond well with its wider immigration policy that welcomes all Jews while mostly excluding all non-Jews and with its policy regarding the relatively new phenomenon of undocumented migration.[161] As previously described, in the mid-1990s Israel began allowing guest workers into the Israeli labor market, in certain labor sectors.[162] The formal paths of "legal" entry also created a thriving market of "illegal" or undocumented workers, many of whom became undocumented by violating their strict visa requirements that, until 2010, bound them to a single employer,[163] thus severely limiting their labor market mobility and opportunities to improve their working conditions and pay.

Focusing attention on undocumented migration solely in the sex sector and offering a service package that culminates in the deportation of trafficking victims was relatively unthreatening to the Ministry of Interior and police authorities. As described, dominance feminists managed to crack this regime slightly with their successful lobbying for temporary work and stay visas for victims of trafficking, a right that no other group of undocumented migrants has been accorded. Yet these visas were only temporary and granted to only a small number of identified sex-trafficking victims. Indeed, of the thousands of estimated victims of sex trafficking, by 2013 a mere 657 women had been identified as victims and a mere 191 had received temporary visas.[164] The vast majority of exploited migrant workers had been promptly deported.

Finally, there is the boost anti-trafficking gave to border closure and control. This consequence relates to the institutional on-the-ground response to sex trafficking that was manifested in the mechanism of border control. An outcome of dominance feminists' anti-trafficking campaign was the effective use of border control to prevent the entry of trafficking victims and migrant sex workers and, admittedly less directly related, the eventual construction of the barrier to prevent any unauthorized crossing along the Egyptian border. These measures are perhaps unique to Israel. U.S. "wall" talk notwithstanding, few countries have such deeply embedded exclusionary practices like constructing a border barrier and preventing the entry of neighboring communities into its territory as Israel does, in the context of trafficking as well as its ongoing occupation of the Palestinian Territories.[165] Although the barrier along the border with Egypt was ultimately constructed to deal not with sex trafficking but with the entrance of African asylum seekers and economic migrants, protocols from trafficking subcommittee meetings reveal that the seeds of the idea were planted at the strong urging of dominance feminist anti-trafficking activists. Given this, it is not surprising that Israel is perhaps one of the only countries that has managed to seal its borders and stop trafficking and migration into the sex industry. Anti-trafficking arguments produced a relatively easy consensus across the political spectrum as to the necessity for the higher level of national security and border control that Israel eventually employed.

Conclusion

This chapter presents the story of the near eradication of trafficking into the sex industry in Israel and the crucial role neo-abolitionist feminists played in this process. It maps out the immense success of Israeli neo-abolitionist feminists and the benefits that their activism and work led to, as well as the costs and unintended consequences of this activism. It focuses particularly on tracing and explaining neo-abolitionist feminist successes, but the same discussion can perhaps explain why these feminists failed when they did. Roughly put, it appears that they succeeded when their agenda coincided with the nationalist/sovereigntist neoliberal agenda and failed where they attempted to more deeply challenge exclusive sovereign authority and neoliberal market ideology. In this context, two of their main failures are most prominent: their lobbying for the legislation of an end-demand bill and their push for an amendment of the Attorney General directive on prosecution of prostitution-related offenses.

As described, the Attorney General directive instructs police to investigate prostitution only in aggravating circumstances. Although its rhetoric shifted toward a neo-abolitionist approach over the years, as of this writing no parallel amendment of its operative articles has occurred. A possible explanation for this is the government's aversion to intervening in markets that do not glaringly entail coercion, that do not involve "perfect" victims, and, perhaps more importantly, do not include undocumented work. The existing reluctance to intervene in markets with Israeli workers that do not necessarily include extreme coercion can explain the failure to adopt an end-demand bill criminalizing sex workers' clients (but not sex workers themselves).

Yet the failures in these two campaigns may be only temporary setbacks. The current Israeli neo-abolitionist feminist strategy on both fronts is to adapt the narrative about Israeli sex workers to neoliberal penality rationality. They attempt to characterize all sex workers as victims of trafficking, that is, as persons who, due to a personal history of sexual exploitation and patriarchal harms, cannot be conceived as freely choosing subjects. Accordingly, sex workers who claim otherwise—such as the representatives of the new sex workers' association—must be dismissed as suffering from false consciousness. Furthermore, Israeli neo-abolitionist feminists portray the sex sector as inherently violent, outside "normal" market interaction, and, thus, a zone in which governmental intervention can be justified without destabilizing other forms of market exchange, however unjust.

The Israeli case is perhaps an acute example of the consequences of an effective anti-trafficking campaign—with good and bad outcomes—and its connection to the tightening of borders, reinforcement of exclusive immigration regimes, and legitimation of other forms of market exploitation. It is acute because dominance feminist anti-trafficking efforts in Israel are situated in a particularly restrictive ethnonational migration regime in a strong security state.

Yet perhaps the Israeli situation is less anomalous than it at first appears. Some scholars have already suggested that, during the Trafficking Protocol negotiations, the participating feminist NGOs' preoccupation with prostitution diverted their lobbying efforts away from other labor- and migration-related issues and allowed the member states' security interest in curbing illegal migration to determine most of the protocol's contents.[166] Furthermore, specific case studies of the operation of anti-trafficking policies in different national contexts have shown similar patterns and effects: the unintended consequences for other forms of labor trafficking, the paternalistic approach to victims of sex trafficking, the harms of repatriation for trafficking victims, and the use of the concept of trafficking to further other political agendas such as strict immigration regimes and enhanced border control.[167] Thus, these outcomes may not be unique to Israel, and the insights from the Israeli experience can serve other feminists in their anti-trafficking efforts.

Notes

1. Maria Rabinowitz, *Survey of the Actions Taken by Israel to Combat Human Trafficking: Dealing with Trafficking in Women* (Jerusalem: Knesset Research and Information Center, 2013), 41–42, 60 (in Hebrew); Daphna Hacker and Orna Cohen, *Research Report: The Shelters in Israel for Survivors of Human Trafficking*, submitted to the U.S. Department of State, 2012, 62, http://hotline.org.il/wp-content/uploads/202508941-The-Shelters-in-Israel-for-Survivors-of-Human-Trafficking.pdf (detailing numbers for 2004–2010). See the discussion of the exact numbers below in the text surrounding notes 93–94.

2. Hester Eisenstein, *Inside Agitators: Australian Femocrats and the State* (Philadelphia: Temple University Press, 1996), xii (defining femocrats as "feminist women who became bureaucrats in a quest of social change. Femocrats were senior public servants who owed their positions to pressure from the organized women's movement"). See discussion of the term and its relevance to GF in chapter 3 of this book.

3. United Nations, "Protocol to Prevent, Suppress, and Punish Trafficking in Persons, Especially Women and Children, Supplementing the United Nations Convention against Transnational Organized Crime," opened for signature on December 12, 2000, S. Treaty Doc. No. 108-16, 2237 U.N.T.S. 319 (entered into force December 25, 2003) (hereafter cited as Trafficking Protocol).

4. Trafficking Victims Protection Act of 2000, Pub. L. No. 106-386, div. A, 114 Stat. 1466 (codified as amended in scattered sections of 18 U.S.C. & 22 U.S.C.), amended by Trafficking Victims Protection Reauthorization Act of 2003, Pub. L. No. 108-193, 117 Stat. 2875 (codified at 18 U.S.C. § 1595 & 22 U.S.C. § 7109(a) [2006]), Trafficking Victims Protection Reauthorization Act of 2005, Pub. L. No. 109-164, 119 Stat. 3558 (2006) (codified in scattered sections of 18 U.S.C., 22 U.S.C. & 42 U.S.C.), and William Wilberforce Trafficking Victims Protection Reauthorization Act of 2008, Pub. L. No. 110-457, 122 Stat. 5044 (codified in scattered sections of 8 U.S.C., 18 U.S.C. & 22 U.S.C.) (hereafter cited as TVPA).

5. Janie Chuang, "The United States as Global Sheriff: Using Unilateral Sanctions to Combat Human Trafficking," *Michigan Journal of International Law* 27, no. 2 (2006): 439.

6. International Agreement for the Suppression of the White Slave Traffic, May 18, 1904, 35 Stat. 1979, 1 L.N.T.S. 83. Later international instruments dealing with trafficking include the following: International Convention for the Suppression of the White Slave Traffic, May 4, 1910, 98 U.N.T.S. 101; International Convention for

the Suppression of the Traffic in Women and Children, September 30, 1921, 53 U.N.T.S. 39; International Convention for the Suppression of the Traffic in Women of Full Age, October 11, 1933, 150 L.N.T.S. 431; Convention for the Suppression of the Traffic in Persons and of the Exploitation of the Prostitution of Others, December 2, 1949, opened for signature on March 21, 1950, 96 U.N.T.S. 271.

7. Trafficking Protocol, art. 3(a); see also Anne T. Gallagher, *The International Law of Human Trafficking* (Cambridge: Cambridge University Press, 2010), 29–42 (discussing the three elements of the definition).

8. Trafficking Protocol, art. 3(a).

9. Anne T. Gallagher, "Human Rights and Human Trafficking: Quagmire or Firm Ground? A Response to James Hathaway," *Virginia Journal of International Law* 49, no. 4 (2009): 789.

10. TVPA, § 103(9).

11. Ibid., § 103(8)(A).

12. Ibid., § 103(8)(B).

13. Gallagher, "Human Rights and Human Trafficking," 791. ("This framework is truly remarkable—not just in the speed of its development, but also in its uniformity and relatively high level of consistency with international standards.") Rhacel Salazar Parreñas, "Trafficked? Filipino Hostesses in Tokyo's Nightlife Industry," *Yale Journal of Law and Feminism* 18, no. 1 (2006): 169–77.

14. United Nations Office on Drugs and Crime, *Global Report on Trafficking in Persons* (Vienna: UNODC, 2009), 22 (reporting that out of the 155 countries surveyed in the report, 63 percent had passed laws addressing trafficking in persons while 17 percent had passed laws covering only certain elements of trafficking).

15. E.g., Grace Chang and Kathleen Kim, "Reconceptualizing Approaches to Human Trafficking: New Directions and Perspectives from the Field(s)," *Stanford Journal of Civil Rights and Civil Liberties* 3, no. 2 (2007): 320–21; Janie A. Chuang, "Rescuing Trafficking from Ideological Capture: Prostitution Reform and Anti-trafficking Law and Policy," *University of Pennsylvania Law Review* 158, no. 6 (2010): 1657.

16. Gershon Shafir and Yoav Peled, "Citizenship and Stratification in an Ethnic Democracy," *Ethnic and Racial Studies* 21, no. 3 (1998): 408–27.

17. Law of Return, 5710-1950, SH No. 51, p. 159 (Isr.); Ruth Gavison, *The Law of Return at Sixty Years: History, Ideology, and Justification* (Jerusalem: Metzilah Center, 2010).

18. This vision of a wholly Jewish economy excluded the Palestinian citizens of Israel, who were viewed as outsiders to the Israeli body politic and economy and were governed by military rule until 1967. Yoav Peled, "Ethnic Democracy and the Legal Construction of Citizenship: Arab Citizens of the Jewish State," *American Political Science Review* 86, no. 2 (1992): 432–43.

19. Leila Farsakh, "Palestinian Labor Flows to the Israeli Economy: A Finished Story?," *Journal of Palestine Studies* 32, no. 1 (2002): 13–25.

20. See Rebeca Raijman and Nonna Kushnirovich, *Labor Migrant Recruitment Practices in Israel* (Emek Hefer, Israel: Ruppin Academic Center, 2012), 10–11, http://lib.ruppin.ac.il/multimedia_library/pdf/38849.pdf; Gilad Nathan, *The OECD Expert Group on Migration (Sopemi) Report: Immigration in Israel 2011–2012* (Jerusalem:

Knesset Research and Information Center, 2012), 9–13, http://www.knesset.gov.il
/mmm/data/pdf/me03131.pdf. At the end of 2013 there were 71,352 documented
migrant workers in Israel and approximately 15,366 undocumented migrant workers. Their primary sectors of employment (combined): 6,742 in construction, 22,447
in agriculture, and 52,477 in care work. Population and Immigration Authority,
Data on Foreigners in Israel: 2013 (Jerusalem: Population and Immigration Authority, 2014), 5 (in Hebrew), https://www.gov.il/BlobFolder/generalpage/foreign
_workers_stats/he/%D7%A1%D7%99%D7%9B%D7%95%D7%9D%202013.pdf.

21. Hila Shamir, "A Labor Paradigm for Human Trafficking," *University of California Law Review* 60, no. 1 (2012): 120–26.

22. Adriana Kemp, "Reforming Policies on Foreign Workers in Israel," *OECD Social, Employment, and Migration Working Papers* No. 103 (2010): 15; Amiram Gil
and Yossi Dahan, "Between Neo-Liberalism and Ethno-Nationalism: Theory, Policy,
and Law Regarding Deportation of Migrant Workers in Israel," *Mishpat U-Mimshal*
10 (2007): 370 (in Hebrew).

23. Hila Shamir and Guy Mundlak, "Spheres of Migration: Political, Economic,
and Universal Imperatives in Israel's Migration Regime," *Middle East Law and Governance* 5 (2013): 122–34.

24. Law of Return, 5710-1950, SH No. 51, p. 159 (Isr.); Yinon Cohen, "From Haven to Heaven: Changes in Immigration Patterns to Israel," *Israeli Sociology* 4, no. 1
(2002): 46, 48 (in Hebrew). Cohen notes that between 20 and 40 percent of migrants
were not Jewish.

25. Law of Return, 5710-1950, SH No. 51, p. 159 (Isr.); Sammy Smooha, "The Mass
Immigrations to Israel: A Comparison of the Failure of the Mizrahi Immigrants of
the 1950s with the Success of the Russian Immigrants of the 1990s," *Journal of Israeli History* 27, no. 1 (2008): 12–17.

26. Trade between the East and the West occurred during the Cold War period
despite (American-led) sanctions, but it was limited, disrupted, and distorted. See
Jari Eloranta and Jari Ojala, eds., *East–West Trade and the Cold War* (Jyväskylä, Fin-
land: University of Jyväskylä, 2005).

27. The Israeli police estimated that during this period, three thousand women
were trafficked every year into the Israeli sex industry. Ministry of Public Security,
*Report of the Inter-Ministerial Team on the Actions to Be Taken in Response to Chang-
ing Patterns in Human Trafficking for the Purpose of Prostitution and Related Crimes*
(Jerusalem: Ministry of Public Security, 2010), 3 (in Hebrew), https://jyx.jyu.fi
/dspace/bitstream/handle/123456789/13424/9513921786.pdf;sequence=1. Donna
Hughes offered the highest estimation of "more than 10,000" women trafficked an-
nually. Donna M. Hughes, "The 'Natasha' Trade: The Transnational Shadow Market
of Trafficking in Women," *Journal of International Affairs* 53, no. 2 (2000): 632.

28. The restrictive immigration policies in the West and lack of a legal basis for
realizing migration intentions mean that, for many men and women, the only route
to accomplishing their migratory plan is through traffickers. Thus, some suggest, an
important background rule that enables and enhances trafficking is the migratory
restriction policies adopted by "developed" countries. See, e.g., Saskia Sassen, "Is
This the Way to Go?—Handling Immigration in a Global Era," *Stanford Agora* 4
(2003): 2. "I want to argue the direction we are taking in our immigration policies

towards greater police . . . is promoting illegal trafficking and weakening our rule of law and thereby our democracies." Ibid.

29. Nomi Levenkron and Yossi Dahan, *Women as Commodities: Trafficking in Women in Israel 2003* (Tel Aviv: Hotline for Migrant Workers / Isha L'Isha—Haifa Feminist Center / Haifa: Adva Center, 2003), 26–30, http://hotline.org.il/en/publi cation/women-as-commodities-trafficking-in-women-in-israel-2003/; Nomi Levenkron et al., *National NGOs' Report to the Annual UN Commission on Human Rights: Evaluation of National Authorities' Activities and Actual Facts on the Trafficking in Persons for the Purpose of Prostitution in Israel* (Tel Aviv: Awareness Center / Hotline for Migrant Workers, 2003), 6–7, 21–22.

30. Levenkron and Dahan, *Women as Commodities*, 19, 35; Daphna Hacker, "Strategic Compliance in the Shadow of Transnational Anti-Trafficking Law," *Harvard Human Rights Journal* 28, no. 1 (2015): 11, 12, 20–21, 32.

31. Menahem Amir, an expert on organized crime in Israel, estimated in 1997 that 70 percent of the women engaging in prostitution in Tel Aviv were from the former Soviet republics. See Martina Vandenberg, *Trafficking of Women into Israel and Forced Prostitution: Report of the Israel Women's Network* (Jerusalem: Israel Women's Network, 1997) (in Hebrew).

32. Ministry of Public Security, *Report of the Inter-Ministerial Team*, 3.

33. Hannah Safran and Rita Chaikin, "Between Trafficking in Women and Prostitution: The Evolution of a Social Struggle," in *Blood Money: Prostitution, Trafficking in Women and Pornography in Israel*, ed. Esther Herzog and Erella Shadmi (Haifa, Israel: Pardes Publishing House, 2013), 237–38 (in Hebrew).

34. Trafficking Protocol; see Anne Gallagher, "Human Rights and the New UN Protocols on Trafficking and Migrant Smuggling: A Preliminary Analysis," *Human Rights Quarterly* 23, no. 4 (2001): 1001–3; Melissa Ditmore and Marjan Wijers, "The Negotiations on the UN Protocol on Trafficking in Persons," *Nemesis* 4 (2003): 79–88; Chuang, "Rescuing Trafficking from Ideological Capture," 1675–76, 1705.

35. Chuang, "Rescuing Trafficking from Ideological Capture," 1677–80.

36. Tehila Sagy, "It Takes a Whole Village to Create a Prostitute: The Struggle of Human Rights Organizations in Women Trafficking and Its Contribution to Regulation of Prostitution in Israel," in *Studies in Law, Gender, and Feminism*, ed. Daphne Barak-Erez et al. (Srigim, Israel: Nevo Publications, 2007), 585–86, 613–14 (in Hebrew).

37. Enforcement Policy in Offences related to Prostitution, 2.2 Att'y Gene. Directive (2014) (Isr.) (hereafter cited as 2.2 Att'y Gene. Directive).

38. Ibid., art. 6–8.

39. ANLC 247/07 Anonymous–Kuchik (September 24, 2009) (Isr. Labor Court).

40. Parliamentary Inquiry Commission on Trafficking in Women, "Ministry of Finance—Income Tax and VAT," in *Parliamentary Inquiry Commission on Trafficking in Women: Final Report* (Jerusalem: Knesset, 2005), chap. 7 (in Hebrew); Israel Tax Authority, "Suspects Arrested for Operating Brothels and for Tax Evasion for Income Arising from Them," press release, *Israel Tax Authority*, August 22, 2012 (in Hebrew), http://taxes.gov.il/about/spokesmanannouncements/pages/ann_220812.aspx.

41. Nomi Levenkron, "What Is a Law Student Doing in a Brothel?," *Hamishpat* 17, no. 1 (2013): 190, 198 (in Hebrew); Minutes of Meeting No. 6 of the Subcommittee on Trafficking in Women, 18th Knesset (December 2, 2009) (in Hebrew); Gilad

Nathan, *Authorities Assistance to Victims of Human Trafficking in Welfare and Health* (Jerusalem: Knesset Research and Information Center, 2009) (in Hebrew).

42. As mentioned earlier, sex workers are perceived as victims rather than perpetrators under Israeli law. Yet this 1962 amendment to the penal code criminalized "holding property that is used for prostitution" and thereby ensured that when sex workers own or rent the apartment they work from, they become "holders" of the property and, therefore, subject to criminal prosecution. Penal Code Amendment Law (Prostitution Offenses) 5723-1962 SH No. 370, p. 78 (Isr.).

43. 94/65 Turgeman v. Attorney General 19(3) PD 57 [1965] (Isr.).

44. Minutes of Meeting No. 52 of the Constitution, Law, and Justice Committee, 5th Knesset (April 2, 1962) (in Hebrew).

45. Ministry of Justice, *Report of the Committee for Examining the Problems of Prostitution Headed by Judge Hadassa Ben-Itto* (Jerusalem: Ministry of Justice, 1977) (in Hebrew).

46. Yael Simonds-Yoaz, "'We Are All One Big Coalition': On the Consensus and Absolute Truths in the Israeli Legal Discourse on Prostitution and Trafficking in Women" (LL.M. thesis, Tel Aviv University, 2009), 125 (in Hebrew).

47. Leora Bilsky, "Cultural Imports: The Case of Feminism in Israel," *Iyunei Mishpat* 25 (2001): 524 (in Hebrew). For a different take on the genealogy of Israeli feminism, as stemming from a socialist-collectivist ideology, see Frances Raday, "Feminist Legal Theory, Legislation, and Litigation in Israel: A Retrospective," in *Studies in Law, Gender, and Feminism*, ed. Daphne Barak-Erez et al. (Srigim, Israel: Nevo Publications, 2007), 41–43 (in Hebrew). I agree with Bilsky's approach, at least in respect to developments in Israeli feminism since the 1970s. In support of this reading, see also Marcia Freedman, "Theorizing Israeli Feminism: 1970–2000," in *Jewish Feminism in Israel: Some Contemporary Perspectives,* ed. Kaplana Misra and Melanie Rich (Lebanon, N.H.: Brandeis University Press, 2003), 1–16.

48. Vandenberg, *Trafficking of Women into Israel;* Amnesty International, *Israel: Human Rights Abuses of Women Trafficked from Countries of the Former Soviet Union into Israel's Sex Industry* (London: Amnesty International, 2000), https://www.amnesty.org/en/documents/mde15/017/2000/en/.

49. Chuang, "Rescuing Trafficking from Ideological Capture," 1677–80.

50. U.S. Department of State, *Trafficking in Persons Report* (Washington, D.C.: Government Printing Office, 2012), 194–95.

51. Safran and Chaikin, "Between Trafficking in Women and Prostitution," 241; Hacker and Cohen, *Research Report,* 30–31.

52. Gallagher, "Human Rights and Human Trafficking," 791.

53. Prohibition of Trafficking in Persons (Legislative Amendments) Law, 5766-2006, SH No. 2067, p. 2 (Isr.); Penal Code 5737-1977, SH No. 2067, p. 2, 377A (Isr.).

54. The inquiry commission was appointed in 2000. It submitted an interim report in 2002, completed its work in 2004, and submitted its final report in 2005. Between 2005 and 2007, it operated as a parliamentary subcommittee of the State Control Committee, and in 2007 it became a subcommittee of the Committee on the Status of Women. It should be noted that in addition to the parliamentary committees, the government also set up a forum to address human trafficking. In 2006, the government established the Inter-ministerial Committee to Formulate Policy

on the Issue of Human Trafficking, headed by the Justice Department. Advocate Rachel Gershuni and, later on, Dr. Merav Shmueli from the Justice Department were appointed the inter-ministerial coordinators for the committee and were key figures in anti-trafficking efforts. In 2006, the government also appointed a permanent Chiefs of Staff Committee—made up of the chiefs of staffs of key governmental ministries—to design Israel's anti-trafficking policy. The Chiefs of Staff Committee approved two national programs: a National Program to Combat Human Trafficking for the Purpose of Prostitution and a National Program to Combat Human Trafficking for the Purpose of Slavery and Forced Labor. Both national programs were approved by the government in 2007. See Rabinowitz, *Survey of the Actions Taken by Israel to Combat Human Trafficking*, 5–6.

55. Safran and Chaikin describe "daily and constant contact" between the organizations and the committee chair. Safran and Chaikin, "Between Trafficking in Women and Prostitution," 240.

56. Ibid. An anti-trafficking coalition of feminist and other organizations operated between 1997 and 2004. In 2004, internal disagreements (discussed in detail later on) led to the dismantling of the coalition, although the organizations continued to work in close collaboration.

57. Nomi Levenkron, "The Goat, the Clinic, and Trafficking in Women," *Ma'asey Mishpat: Tel Aviv University Journal of Law and Social Change* 1 (January 2008): 81–82 (in Hebrew).

58. See Simonds-Yoaz, "We Are All One Big Coalition," 71–72.

59. The original list of organizations included the Association of Rape Crisis Centers in Israel; battered womens' shelters in Herzliya and Haifa; Amnesty International; Israel Women's Network; Hotline for Migrant Workers; "We are Equal," The Movement for New Masculinity; Workers' Hotline; Center for Jewish Pluralism; Mizrahi Democratic Rainbow; Association for Civil Rights in Israel; Isha L'Isha; and the Lesbian Feminist Community. See Sagy, "It Takes a Whole Village to Create a Prostitute," 596. Yet, as noted, the composition of the coalition changed over the years.

60. In 2014, the organization changed its name to the Hotline for Refugees and Migrants. The name change reflects not only the organization's shift in focus but also the changing reality of trafficking and migration in Israel. See Hotline for Refugees and Migrants, http://hotline.org.il/.

61. For information about the Isha L'Isha organization, see http://www.isha.org .il/eng/.

62. Simonds-Yoaz, "We Are All One Big Coalition," 78.

63. Petition from Rita Chaikin, project director of the Isha L'Isha Organization, and officials from fourteen other organizations to Knesset member Dr. Aliza Lavie, chairperson, Committee on the Status of Women (May 19, 2013) (in Hebrew) (hereafter cited as Petition from Chaikin to Reconvene the Subcommittee).

64. In an interview, Tsur expressed a distinctly nonfeminist stance on regulating prostitution. According to Tsur, the problem with regulating prostitution is that prostitution itself is not criminalized in Israel. In response to the question of whether prostitution is still a matter of concern, he replied, "Certainly. Start from the fact that prostitution is not defined as a crime in Israeli law. So someone who

actually trafficks or runs a brothel could be incriminated only for the offense of running an establishment illegally." Mazal Mualem, "How Israel Stopped the Sale of Women," interview by *Al Monitor,* September 11, 2013, http://www.al-monitor .com/pulse/originals/2013/09/israel-women-trafficking-sinai-egypt.html#.

65. Safran and Chaikin, "Between Trafficking in Women and Prostitution," 245. Safran and Chaikin describe the close and productive relationship Isha L'Isha developed with the police and specifically mention informative workshops Isha L'Isha representatives coordinated and taught at the police academy and their value. See also U.S. Department of State, *Trafficking in Persons Report,* 195; Shelly Levi, *Educational and Informational Activities to Raise Awareness of Trafficking in Women* (Jerusalem: Knesset Research and Information Center, 2007), 10 (in Hebrew).

66. For information about the Todaa Center, see http://www.macom.org.il/todaa -home.asp.

67. Sagy, "It Takes a Whole Village to Create a Prostitute," 596–97.

68. Ibid., 597. There was significant overlap between the organizations in the Anti-Trafficking Coalition and the organizations that were members of the Coalition of Feminist and Social Organizations against Pornography, which operated at the same time.

69. See ANLC 247/07 Anonymous–Kuchik (September 24, 2009) (Isr. Labor Court).

70. See, e.g., NLCH 180-3/56 Ben-Ami Mechon Classa v. Glitzcensky 31 PD 389 [1998] (Isr. Labor Court). In the *Ben-Ami* case, Chief Judge Adler, writing for the court, explained, "Even a woman who engages in the profession of prostitution deserves the minimum legal protections provided by law, since even a woman who is exploited and is employed as a prostitute is a human being. This ruling does not encourage this profession, nor does it make it legal . . . We are not discussing the contractual relationship between the parties or the legality of the contract; we are merely dealing with providing minimal protections set in the relevant employment rules" (393).

71. See Safran and Chaikin, "Between Trafficking in Women and Prostitution," 245.

72. See Shulamit Almog, "Prostitution and Labor Law," *Labor Society and Law* 12 (2010): 306 (in Hebrew); Nomi Levenkron, "'Money of Their Own': Civil Claims by Victims of Trafficking against Their Traffickers: And Yet They Move," in *Empowerment by Law,* ed. Mimi Eisenstadt and Guy Mundlak (Srigim, Israel: Nevo Publications, 2008), 492–93 (in Hebrew); Tsachi Keren-Paz, *Sex Trafficking: A Private Law Response* (New York: Routledge, 2013).

73. Orly Lobel, "The Renew Deal: The Fall of Regulation and the Rise of Governance in Contemporary Legal Thought," *Minnesota Law Review* 89, no. 2 (2004): 344–45; Gráinne de Búrca and Joanne Scott, "Introduction: New Governance, Law, and Constitutionalism," in *Law and New Governance in the EU and the US,* ed. Gráinne de Búrca and Joanne Scott (Oxford: Hart Publishing, 2006), 2.

74. Knesset members proposed several bills, beginning in 2008. Notable ones are: Prohibition of Consumption of Prostitution Services and Community Treatment (Legislative Amendments) (Bill No. 1) (2013) (Isr.); Prohibition of Consumption of Prostitution and Provision of Assistance to Prostitution Survivors (Bill) (2017) (Isr.); National Fight Against Prostitution Consumption and Provision of Assistance to Prostitution Survivors (Bill) (2017) (Isr.).

75. 2.2 Att'y Gene. Directive, art. 2.

76. Restriction on Use of a Place for Purposes of Preventing Commission of Offenses Law, 5765-2005, SH No. 1998, p. 426 (Isr.).

77. See, e.g., Minutes of Meeting No. 3 of the Subcommittee on Trafficking in Women, 17th Knesset (November 14, 2006), 13–14 (in Hebrew). The police reported that from January to October 2006, more than thirty court orders to shut down brothels were issued under the new law, with twenty-two shut down in Beer Sheba and eight in Tel Aviv (ibid.). See also Minutes of Meeting No. 4 of the Subcommittee on Trafficking in Women, 18th Knesset (November 11, 2009), 11 (in Hebrew) (the police reported that over sixty court orders were issued between 2007 and 2008, most of them in Tel Aviv). Minutes of Meeting No. 14 of the Subcommittee on Trafficking in Women, 18th Knesset (April 28, 2010), 15 (in Hebrew). The police reported that in 2009, seventy-two court orders were issued.

78. Minutes of Meeting No. 2 of the Subcommittee on Trafficking in Women and Prostitution, 19th Knesset (July 8, 2013), 7 (in Hebrew).

79. HCJ 5465/11 Member of Knesset Zuaretz v. Minister of Public Security (July 20, 2011) (Isr.).

80. U.S. neo-abolitionist feminists were instrumental in shaping American anti-trafficking policies. See Chuang, "Rescuing Trafficking from Ideological Capture," 1677–80; Elizabeth Bernstein, "Militarized Humanitarianism Meets Carceral Feminism: The Politics of Sex, Rights, and Freedom in Contemporary Anti-Trafficking Campaigns," in "Feminists Theorize International Political Economy," ed. Shirin M. Rai and Kate Bedford, special issue, *Signs* 36, no. 1 (2010): 46–47.

81. Hacker and Cohen reported that between 2000 and 2004, "approximately 1000 women were located in brothels and deported from Israel." Hacker and Cohen, *Research Report,* 60.

82. MApp (TA) 91548/00 State of Israel v. Veriubkin (2000) (not published) (Isr.). This was just the first step in the process of extending rights to victims of trafficking. In 2006, the rights granted to victims of trafficking were expanded to include those who did *not* cooperate with the prosecution as well. See note 91 and accompanying text.

83. Hacker and Cohen, *Research Report,* 60.

84. See Minutes of Meeting No. 24 of the Parliamentary Inquiry Commission on Trafficking in Women, 15th Knesset (February 13, 2002), 5–13 (in Hebrew); Minutes of Meeting No. 25 of the Parliamentary Inquiry Commission on Trafficking in Women, 15th Knesset (March 4, 2002), 17, 24 (in Hebrew); Minutes of Meeting No. 31 of the Parliamentary Inquiry Commission on Trafficking in Women, 15th Knesset (June 26, 2002), 5 (in Hebrew).

85. See Hacker and Cohen, *Research Report,* 12, 36–37, 54–55.

86. Ibid., 99. Weekly allowance for shelter residents is about $38.

87. Ibid., 57.

88. Ibid., 110. The women are required to return by midnight on weekdays and by 5:00 a.m. on Fridays and are permitted to leave the shelter between 10:00 a.m. and midnight on Saturdays.

89. Minutes of Meeting No. 18 of the Parliamentary Inquiry Commission on Trafficking in Women, 16th Knesset (July 6, 2004), 16, 21 (in Hebrew).

90. Minutes of Meeting No. 2 of the Subcommittee on Trafficking in Women, 17th Knesset (October 25, 2006), 12, 16 (in Hebrew).

91. Ibid., 11, 21; Hacker and Cohen, *Research Report,* 80–83. For more information on the visa granting process, see Tal Raviv and Nomi Levenkron, *Permits for Victims of Human Trafficking in Israel: The Reality and the Ideal* (Tel Aviv: Hotline for Migrant Workers, 2006) (in Hebrew). For information on the number of visas granted, see Rabinowitz, *Survey of the Actions Taken by Israel to Combat Human Trafficking,* 56.

92. Prohibition of Trafficking in Persons (Legislative Amendments) Law, 5766-2006, SH No. 2067, p. 2 (Isr.); Penal Code 5737-1977, SH No. 2067, p. 2, 377A (Isr.); Levenkron, "'Money of Their Own,'" 471.

93. Rabinowitz, *Survey of the Actions Taken by Israel to Combat Human Trafficking,* 41–42.

94. Ibid., 60. Out of these, 293 were victims of sex trafficking and the remaining 74 were victims of labor trafficking and slavery. For data on shelter referrals between 2004 and 2010, see Hacker and Cohen, *Research Report,* 62.

95. Elizabeth Bernstein, "The Sexual Politics of the 'New Abolitionism,'" *Differences: Journal of Feminist Cultural Studies* 18, no. 3 (2007): 128–51. See also the discussion in chapter 2 of this book.

96. See Minutes of Meeting No. 4 of the Subcommittee on Trafficking in Women, 17th Knesset (November 20, 2006) (in Hebrew).

97. CrimA 1609/03 Borisov v. State of Israel 58(1) PD 55 [2003] (Isr.).

98. VCR 3234/06 State of Israel v. Brechman (May 1, 2006) (Isr.); Nomi Levenkron, *"Another Delivery from Tashkent": Profile of the Israeli Trafficker,* ed. Tomer Kerman, trans. Susann Codish and Ed Codish (Tel Aviv: Hotline for Migrant Workers, 2007), 36, http://lastradainternational.org/lsidocs/481%20Another_Delivery_From_Tashkent-English.pdf.

99. For reports on the increase in raids, see Minutes of Meeting No. 3 of Subcommittee on Trafficking in Women, 17th Knesset (November 14, 2006) (in Hebrew); Minutes of Meeting No. 12 of the Subcommittee on Trafficking in Women, 17th Knesset (November 12, 2007) (in Hebrew); Minutes of Meeting No. 4 of the Subcommittee on Trafficking in Women, 18th Knesset (November 11, 2009) (in Hebrew); Minutes of Meeting No. 21 of the Subcommittee on Trafficking in Women, 17th Knesset (October 29, 2008) (in Hebrew).

100. See Almog, "Prostitution and Labor Law," 306; Levenkron, "Money of Their Own," 492–93; Keren-Paz, *Sex Trafficking.*

101. Penal Code 5737-1977, SH No. 6759, 558, 377E(D) (Isr.); Penal Regulations (Governance of the Fund for the Management of Property Forfeited and Fines Collected in Human Trafficking and Slavery Offenses), 2009, KT 6759, 558, 558 (Isr.).

102. Yonatan Erlich, *Sentencing in Trafficking in Women Cases in 2005—Quantitative Analysis* (Jerusalem: Knesset Research and Information Center, 2006) (in Hebrew); Rabinowitz, *Survey of the Actions Taken by Israel to Combat Human Trafficking,* 51–52.

103. Rabinowitz, *Survey of the Actions Taken by Israel to Combat Human Trafficking,* 14–16.

104. Hacker, "Is the Trafficking Victims Protection Act a Transnational Success?"

105. Prohibition of Trafficking in Persons (Legislative Amendments) Law, 5766-2006, SH No. 2067, p. 2 (Isr.); Penal Code 5737-1977, SH No. 2067, p. 2, 377A (Isr.).

106. At the time of this writing, there have been only two convictions for slavery-related offenses and forced labor: CrimC (Jer.) 1346-11-10 State of Israel v. Julani (February 29, 2012) (Isr.), http://www.ynet.co.il/articles/0,7340,L-4196622,00.html; CrimC (Jer.) 6749-08-11 State of Israel v. D. A. (September 10, 2013) (Isr.).

107. For a fascinating description and analysis of the differences in how rehabilitation is conceived in the men's shelter and women's shelter and the distinction between labor trafficking and sex trafficking, see Hacker and Cohen, *Research Report,* 108–11, 113–16.

108. Rabinowitz, *Survey of the Actions Taken by Israel to Combat Human Trafficking,* 46–47. See also U.S. Department of State, *Trafficking in Persons Report,* 194–95, asserting that Israel's "efforts to address labor violations of foreign workers that could lead to trafficking vulnerability continued to lag."

109. 2.2 Att'y Gene. Directive, art. 5; Mualem, "How Israel Stopped the Sale of Women."

110. Safran and Chaikin, "Between Trafficking in Women and Prostitution," 237; Petition from Chaikin to Reconvene the Subcommittee; Levenkron, "What Is a Law Student Doing in a Brothel?," 186. Feminist organizations claim some Israeli women have been trafficked into the Israeli sex industry and that some pimps are, in fact, traffickers. The police claim that this is not the case. See U.S. Department of State, *Trafficking in Persons Report,* 195; Ministry of Public Security, *Report of the Inter-Ministerial Team,* 11.

111. See notes 36–41 and accompanying text. For a more detailed discussion, see Hila Shamir, "Feminist Approaches to the Regulation of Sex Work: A Sympathetic Reading of the Gap between the Law on the Books and the Law in Action," in *The Governance of Regulation: Law and Policy,* ed. Yishai Blank, Roy Kreitner, and David Levi-Faur (Tel Aviv: Buchmann Faculty of Law, Tel Aviv University, 2016), 121 (in Hebrew); Gadi Taub, "Trafficking and Prostitution: The Israeli Experience," *Neo,* 2013 (in Swedish), http://traffickingroundtable.org/wp-content/uploads/2013/07/Taub-on-the-Israeli-experience.pdf.

112. Taub, "Trafficking and Prostitution"; Minutes of Meeting No. 3 of the Parliamentary Inquiry Commission on Trafficking in Women, 15th Knesset (March 3, 2001), 7 (in Hebrew); Minutes of Meeting No. 8 of the Parliamentary Inquiry Commission on Trafficking in Women, 16th Knesset (November 10, 2003), 5-6 (in Hebrew); Levenkron and Dahan, *Women as Commodities,* 22.

113. Most African asylum seekers are designated as "infiltrators" in Israeli law. See Prevention of Infiltration (Offenses and Jurisdiction) (Amendment No. 3 and Temporary Order) Law 5772-2012, SH No. 2332, p. 119 (Isr.); Shamir and Mundlak, "Spheres of Migration," 112–72.

114. The border barrier between Israel and Egypt in the Sinai Desert was completed in December 2012. It is 5 meters high and 240 kilometers long. Amos Harel, "Without the High Court of Justice and B'Tselem: This Is the Way to Build a Wall," *Haaretz,* November 11, 2011 (in Hebrew), http://www.haaretz.co.il/magazine/1.1563614. The barrier is highly effective at closing off the border. In the first three months of 2013, there were only thirty-six entrants, as opposed to the thousands entering

monthly in 2003. See Amihai Attali, "Trespassing: A Visit to the Border with Egypt," *NRG Ma'ariv,* March 23, 2013 (in Hebrew), http://www.nrg.co.il/online/1/ART2 /454/636.html.

115. Shuki Sade, "The Wall of Money: Who Profits from Building the Billion Shekel Wall along the Egyptian Border?," *The Marker,* November 12, 2011 (in Hebrew), http://www.themarker.com/markerweek/1.1562931; Minutes of Joint Meeting No. 4 of the Committee for the Struggle against Drugs and the Subcommittee on Trafficking in Women, 17th Knesset (November 20, 2006), 22–23 (in Hebrew); Minutes of Meeting No. 12 of the Subcommittee on Trafficking in Women, 17th Knesset (November 12, 2007) (in Hebrew).

116. Levenkron, "What Is a Law Student Doing in a Brothel?," 186–87. Later on, as Levenkron describes, when there were hardly any non-Israeli sex workers left, police began harassing Israeli sex workers as well.

117. Penal Code 5737-1977, SH No. 1746, pp. 226, 199–203 (Isr.).

118. 2.2 Att'y Gene. Directive.

119. See notes 36–41 and accompanying text. For a more detailed discussion, see Shamir, "Feminist Approaches to the Regulation of Sex Work."

120. Hacker and Cohen, *Research Report,* 71 (citing Knesset member Zehava Galon, who argued that the determination should be entrusted to mental health specialists and not the police).

121. Safran and Chaikin, "Between Trafficking in Women and Prostitution," 242, 245; Rabinowitz, *Survey of the Actions Taken by Israel to Combat Human Trafficking,* 67.

122. See the comments of Advocate Uri Sade from the NGO Hotline for Migrant Workers: "Human rights organizations carry out most of the identification of victims of trafficking in the custody facilities prior to the deportation of women." Minutes of Meeting No. 1 of the Subcommittee on Trafficking in Women, 17th Knesset (July 19, 2006), 23 (in Hebrew).

123. See Ministry of Social Affairs and Social Services, *Conclusions of the Inter-Ministerial Governmental Committee for the Formulation of an Identification Procedure* (Jerusalem: Ministry of Social Affairs and Social Services, 2008); Rabinowitz, *Survey of the Actions Taken by Israel to Combat Human Trafficking,* 7.

124. See the comment of Rachel Gershuni: "The main problem is that it is more difficult to identify victims of trafficking for the purpose of labor exploitation than victims of trafficking for the purpose of prostitution." Minutes of Joint Meeting of the Committee for Examining Foreign Workers' Problems and the Subcommittee on Trafficking in Women, 17th Knesset (December 26, 2007), 17 (in Hebrew). See also the comments of Advocate Adi Vilinger from the NGO Hotline for Migrant Workers: "One of the most problematic issues in trafficking for the purpose of labor exploitation is detection and identification. And it is not necessarily because the authorities do not work properly. It is because of the nature of the offense which is characterized primarily by isolation and by people who do not know how to speak English and Hebrew." Minutes of Meeting No. 7 of the Committee for Examining Foreign Workers' Problems, 18th Knesset (July 6, 2009), 14 (in Hebrew).

125. Hacker and Cohen, *Research Report,* 60.

126. Rabinowitz, *Survey of the Actions Taken by Israel to Combat Human Trafficking,* 41–42.

127. See note 27 for further details on the estimated number of women who were trafficked between 2001 and 2006.

128. See Rabinowitz, *Survey of the Actions Taken by Israel to Combat Human Trafficking*, 4.

129. Safran and Chaikin, "Between Trafficking in Women and Prostitution," 254–55.

130. "Since the dissolution of the previous *Knesset* nine months ago, the sub-committee has not been convened and this has had immediate consequences . . . on the silenced voices of women victims of trafficking and women in prostitution in general." Petition from Chaikin to Reconvene the Subcommittee.

131. Until the 19th Knesset, the subcommittee was called the Subcommittee on Trafficking in Women. During the 19th Knesset, its name was changed to the Sub-committee on Trafficking in Women and Prostitution. See Minutes of Meeting No. 14 of the Committee on the Status of Women, 19th Knesset (May 28, 2013) (in Hebrew). See the comments of Knesset member Yifat Kariv in this meeting. Before becoming a Knesset member, Kariv had founded and operated a program to assist youth in prostitution. In the fourteenth meeting of the Committee on the Status of Women, Kariv stated, "I think there is a need to expand the subcommittee's scope to include not only the phenomenon of trafficking in women but also prostitution . . . Finally, distinguished chairwoman, I ask you to take this subcommittee and ex-pand it to the issue of prostitution and trafficking in women. Let's decide that in the next decade we will abolish this phenomenon and transform women's status as owners of their bodies and souls." Ibid.

132. A similar dynamic emerged in Sweden, where enactment of end-demand legislation led to the establishment of a sex workers movement. See Nomi Levenk-ron, "Could the Master's Tools Dismantle the Master's House? Sweden's Criminal-ization of Clients as a Case Study on the Potential of Legislation to Transform the Sex Industry" (LL.M. thesis, Tel Aviv University, 2011), 101 (in Hebrew).

133. No research or data are available on sex workers' attempts to organize in Israel. However, I was involved in one such failed attempt. In 2010, a group of sex workers approached the Human Rights Clinic at Tel Aviv University seeking as-sistance to form such an association. The initiative failed because of the Israel As-sociations Registry requirement for the provision of the full names, addresses, and Israeli Identity Numbers of seven of the founding members to register the associa-tion. Some of the founders were reluctant to make this information public, and, consequently, the association was never registered or formalized.

134. Chair of the Israeli Association for the Regulation of Sex Work, "A Profes-sion Like Any Other Profession," *The Seventh Eye*, July 4, 2013 (in Hebrew), http://www.the7eye.org.il/70218; Avishag Sivan-Glanz, "Even Prostitutes Have a Right to Their Bodies," *NRG Ma'ariv*, June 25, 2012 (in Hebrew), http://www.nrg.co.il/online/1/ART2/380/628.html; Chair of the Israeli Association for the Regulation of Sex Work, "The Association for the Regulation of Sex Work," interview by Neri Livne, *Haaretz*, July 18, 2013 (in Hebrew), http://www.haaretz.co.il/magazine/.premium-1.2075326; Minutes of Meeting No. 2 of the Subcommittee on Traffick-ing in Women and Prostitution, 19th Knesset (July 8, 2013) (in Hebrew). Four of the participants in this meeting were representatives from the sex workers' association.

135. The term "rescue," which is often used in anti-trafficking campaigns, is highly problematic because it tends to camouflage the harms brought about by such processes to the "rescued" women. See Aziza Ahmed and Meena Seshu, "'We Have the Right Not to Be "Rescued" . . .': When Anti-Trafficking Programmes Undermine the Health and Well-Being of Sex Workers," *Anti-Trafficking Review*, no. 1 (June 2012): 149–68.

136. The main organizations are Saleet, Feminine Horizon, the Levinsky Health Clinic, and the Mobile Clinic in Haifa. Another interesting civil society initiative is the Turning the Tables program, which offers former sex workers courses in fashion design and assistance in finding alternative employment in fashion. See http://www.israelgives.org/amuta/580549905.

137. Hacker and Cohen, *Research Report,* 12, 84–90.

138. See, for example, the statement issued by two main Isha L'Isha activists, which summarizes their activities as follows: "The success of anti-trafficking efforts suggests that real change can be made in the lives of individual women, but that it is difficult to change society as a whole. The widespread misuse of women's bodies and the prevalence of violence against women did not change and the situation of many women in society is still grim." Safran and Chaikin, "Between Trafficking in Women and Prostitution," 254–55.

139. A new program for safe repatriation that aims to assist victims of trafficking in reintegrating into their countries of origin assisted only two victims. See Rabinowitz, *Survey of the Actions Taken by Israel to Combat Human Trafficking,* 64.

140. Laura Agustin, "Leaving Home for Sex: Cosmopolitanism or Sex Trafficking or Both?," *The Naked Anthropologist* (blog), September 25, 2011, http://www.laura agustin.com/leaving-home-for-sex; Levenkron, "Money of Their Own," 462; Safran and Chaikin, "Between Trafficking in Women and Prostitution," 246–48, 251.

141. Levenkron and Dahan, *Women as Commodities,* 19–21.

142. The Bangladesh Thematic Group on Trafficking, *Revisiting the Human Trafficking Paradigm: The Bangladesh Experience; Part 1: Trafficking of Adults* (Geneva: International Organization for Migration, 2004), 37–47, http://publica tions.iom.int/system/files/pdf/revisiting_trafficking_bangladesh.pdf; Levenkron and Dahan, *Women as Commodities,* 35.

143. Marie Segrave, "Order at the Border: The Repatriation of Victims of Trafficking," *Women's Studies International Forum* 32, no. 4 (2009): 256–59; Dina Francesca Haynes, "Used, Abused, Arrested, and Deported: Extending Immigration Benefits to Protect Victims of Trafficking and to Secure the Prosecution of Traffickers," *Human Rights Quarterly* 26, no. 2 (2004): 262–63; Kuniko Takamatsu and Susu Thatun, *Some Reflections on the Repatriation of Trafficked Persons: The Case of Myanmar and Thailand; Uprooting People for Their Own Good? Human Displacement, Resettlement, and Trafficking in the Greater Mekong Sub-Region,* ed. Dang Nguyen Anh and Supang Chantavanich (Hanoi, Vietnam: Social Science Publishing House, 2004).

144. For Israeli examples, see the campaign against the deportation of children of migrant workers and the NGO campaign against the deportation of African migrant workers / asylum seekers. Shamir and Mundlak, "Spheres of Migration," 152–53; Dana Weiler-Polak, "Hundreds Protest in Tel Aviv against the Deportation of

Asylum-Seekers from South Sudan," *Haaretz*, March 17, 2012 (in Hebrew), http://www.haaretz.co.il/news/education/1.1665829.

145. The 1950 Law of Return was amended in 1970 to permit the immigration of certain family members of Jews (children, grandchildren, spouses, and spouses of the children and grandchildren of Jews), even if they themselves are not Jewish (section 4A). Gavison, *Law of Return at Sixty Years.*

146. Shamir and Mundlak, "Spheres of Migration," 113–16, 134.

147. Hacker and Cohen, *Research Report,* 103–8.

148. Ibid., 108.

149. Ibid.

150. Ibid., 87–89, 93–98.

151. Mike Dottridge, introduction to *Collateral Damage: The Impact of Anti-Trafficking Measures on Human Rights Around the World,* ed. Mike Dottridge (Bangkok, Thailand: Global Alliance against Traffic in Women, 2007), 12 (stating that most people who are trafficked left home to make a living elsewhere and are, in fact, economic migrants).

152. Hacker and Cohen, *Research Report,* 113–14.

153. Ibid., 166.

154. Shamir, "Feminist Approaches to the Regulation of Sex Work."

155. For a discussion of the situation in Israel, see Levenkron, "What Is a Law Student Doing in a Brothel?," 187–92. See also Chair of the Israeli Association for the Regulation of Sex Work, "The Association for the Regulation of Sex Work." For a comparative look at other national contexts, see Anna-Louise Crago, *Arrest the Violence: Human Rights Abuses against Sex Workers in Central and Eastern Europe and Central Asia,* ed. Acacia Shields (Edinburgh: Sex Workers' Rights Advocacy Network, 2009), http://www.opensocietyfoundations.org/sites/default/files/arrest-violence-20091217.pdf.

156. Shamir, "Labor Paradigm for Human Trafficking," 120–26.

157. Bernard E. Harcourt, *The Illusion of Free Markets: Punishment and the Myth of Natural Order* (Cambridge, Mass.: Harvard University Press, 2011); Bernard E. Harcourt, "Neoliberal Penality: A Brief Genealogy," *Theoretical Criminology* 14, no. 1 (2010): 4; see also Chantal Thomas, "Disciplining Globalization: International Law, Illegal Trade, and the Case of Narcotics," *Michigan Journal of International Law* 24, no. 2 (Winter 2003): 563–68.

158. See also David Kennedy's critique of human rights advocacy, which he claims legitimates "everyday" evils by highlighting extreme evils, thereby "excus[ing]" and "justify[ing] too much." David Kennedy, *The Dark Sides of Virtue: Reassessing International Humanitarianism* (Princeton, N.J.: Princeton University Press, 2004), 25.

159. Rabinowitz, *Survey of the Actions Taken by Israel to Combat Human Trafficking,* 41–42.

160. Shamir, "Labor Paradigm for Human Trafficking," 122–25.

161. See, e.g., Marina Solodkin, Minutes of Meeting No. 12 of the Subcommittee on Trafficking in Women, 16th Knesset (December 5, 2005), 11 (in Hebrew).

162. See notes 19–21 and accompanying text.

163. Gilad Nathan, *Status, Recruitment, and Employment of Foreign Workers* (Jerusalem: Knesset Research and Information Center, 2006), 2–4 (in Hebrew). The

arrangement was declared unconstitutional by the Supreme Court. See HCJ 4542/02 Kav LaOved Worker's Hotline v. Government of Israel 61(1) PD 346 [2006] (Isr.).

164. Rabinowitz, *Survey of the Actions Taken by Israel to Combat Human Trafficking*, 41, 56. Ninety-four women received B1 visas after agreeing to testify against their traffickers, ten received B2 visas, and eighty-seven received yearlong rehabilitation visas.

165. For the devastating damage caused by the separation barrier to Palestinian communities, see B'Tselem, *Arrested Development: The Long-Term Impact of the Separation Barrier* (Jerusalem: B'Tselem, 2012), http://www.btselem.org/download/201210_arrested_development_eng.pdf.

166. "The end result confirmed the harsh truth that these negotiations had never really been about human rights. Any victories on our side were both hard won and incomplete." Gallagher, "Human Rights and Human Trafficking," 790–91; see also Janet Halley, Prabha Kotiswaran, Hila Shamir, and Chantal Thomas, "From the International to the Local in Feminist Legal Responses to Rape, Prostitution / Sex Work, and Sex Trafficking: Four Studies in Contemporary Governance Feminism," *Harvard Journal of Law and Gender* 29, no. 2 (2006): 335, 389–91.

167. Dottridge, introduction to *Collateral Damage*, 14–20.

CHAPTER 6

When Rights Return

Feminist Advocacy for Women's
Reproductive Rights and against
Sex-Selective Abortion

RACHEL REBOUCHÉ

"Reproductive rights are human rights" has become a mantra in international human rights advocacy. Supporting this mantra are the concerted efforts of feminist activists working through United Nations bodies for abortion law liberalization at national and international levels.[1] The academics and advocates who promoted women's rights in international law argued that sexual and reproductive rights emanate from treaties and declarations that protect rights to autonomy, equality, and health.[2] Feminists have made the case for reading abortion rights into national constitutions and international human rights declarations, and, in a few cases, have written abortion rights into constitutional and international documents. As a result of their efforts, a large, globally important feminist institution for reproductive rights now exists. Although the issue of abortion remains controversial, international human rights law has become a hospitable place for abortion advocacy. Women's rights advocates have not won all they wanted, but in the area of reproductive rights and abortion law, they have had surprising success given the deep opposition to abortion rights in some places.

Reproductive rights campaigns borrow heavily from liberal feminist ideas about women's agency and freedom to control their bodies, which have been formative to North American abortion rights.[3] Specifically, U.S. activism has shaped the international movement for reproductive rights by insisting that, at least before viability, abortion for any reason must be legal.[4] At the same time reproductive rights gained momentum at the level of international human rights law, U.S. feminists were losing battles in courts and in statehouses over domestic, constitutional rights to abortion. U.S. reproductive rights organizations have looked to human rights not only to thwart proposals to confer rights on fetuses, but also to give feminists a forum for rights-based claims that might support abortion advocacy nationally.[5]

The well-known issue of abortion to deselect the sex, often female, of a potential child has undermined the liberal feminist campaign for broad legal permission for abortion. Prenatal selection of male fetuses has been a hotly debated topic for more than four decades. Liberal feminist ideas were the first to influence UN agencies that denounced sex selection as discrimination and pursued solutions that were not abortion bans. Liberal feminists spoke out against practices in other countries that appeared to perpetuate the legal or cultural inferiority of women or to treat women as second-class citizens. Those practices ran counter to the equality rights that bolstered so many of their arguments. But a long-standing dilemma has been how to reconcile campaigns for women's equality with the rejection of any law that attempts to restrict abortion based on the reason for termination.

The desire to avoid restrictions on abortion conflicted with dominance feminist thinking on sex selection and other so-called harmful cultural practices. At the same time that abortion rights were incorporated into international human rights law, dominance feminism was leaving its imprint on the field by demonizing certain customs, including son preference. When the practice represents male-preferring values, dominance feminism does not necessarily share liberal feminism's discomfort with banning abortion. Dominance feminist approaches emphasized the coercion of and violence against women in all sex-selective abortions. And such an approach frames sex selection as a form of subjugation that results in the trafficking of women, societal militancy, and violence.[6] These claims pervade so many different literatures that they have become common sense, even though they are almost impossible to prove.

Liberal feminist responses can appear complicit with discriminatory practices; thus, many abortion rights advocates incorporate aspects of the violence narrative by arguing that sex-selective abortion is the product of coercion and distinguishable from abortions that women freely choose.[7] As the first section of this chapter demonstrates, dominance feminism has left a mark on international human rights law but has had limited sway in advocacy for abortion rights and against sex-selective abortion bans in the United States. It is at best an uneasy truce.

This chapter discusses the well-known example of sex-selective abortion as a means to examine a fundamental disagreement between the liberal feminist commitment to rights and the dominance feminist impulse to prohibit sexist or subordinating practices. What is an old conversation has new life in the United States. The feminists who support abortion rights in the United States have seen their arguments, made at the international level, turned against them in domestic legislation that bans sex-selective abortion in the name of women's rights.[8] The transit of feminist ideas as international human rights principles has produced a complex reality for U.S.-based feminists, in which their own claims of rights and narratives of violence can come back to haunt them at home. These advocates may not have wanted reason-based prohibitions on abortion, but their interventions in sex selection abroad can support arguments for criminal bans and have given anti-abortion advocates in the United States persuasive tools. And U.S. Supreme Court cases decided after *Roe v. Wade*[9]—particularly *Gonzales v. Carhart*[10]—opened the door for anti-abortion strategies that co-opt international feminist arguments against sex-selective abortion.

This chapter first examines the international campaign for reproductive rights that entrenched a liberal feminist understanding of abortion rights. It considers how that activism translated into a compromise on sex-selective abortion in international human rights law—rejecting abortion bans (although not in every country) while at the same time disapproving of the practice as discrimination and promoting cultural change through public education campaigns. The chapter then demonstrates how, at the same time, international human rights documents incorporated dominance feminist approaches to sex selection, or sex selection defined as violence against women, and how that rhetoric has supported anti-abortion strategies in the United States. The chapter's final section analyzes why responses of the U.S. reproductive rights movement have been unpersuasive in debates about sex-selective abortion. The chapter concludes by considering the challenges of enforcing a sex-selective abortion ban in the United States and the tensions between feminist arguments and two perspectives—one related to disability rights and the other rooted in postcolonial critique.

Abortion, Sex Selection, and Women's Rights

Current international human rights law condemns prenatal sex selection. The 180 signatories of the 1994 International Convention on Population and Development (ICPD) Programme of Action pledged to "eliminate all forms of discrimination against [girls] . . . which result in . . . prenatal sex selection."[11] What "sex selection" means varies, and UN documents often list various practices together. Preferring the gender of a child can happen prenatally, with abortion or through assisted reproductive technology, or postbirth through the neglect of girls and the infanticide of female newborns.

There has been a long-standing campaign against these practices, and specifically against sex selection, with interest ebbing and flowing over the last forty years. Much of this attention has corresponded to the introduction of prenatal, sex-determination technologies (such as ultrasound) or the release of demographic studies that revealed skewed sex ratios at birth in various countries.[12] Until recently, sex selection was described consistently in the United States as an international issue and not a domestic problem.

Following the lead of feminists concerned about securing abortion rights, interagency bodies have been careful about how they refer to sex-selective abortion. For example, the World Health Organization (WHO), in collaboration with the United Nations Population Fund (UNFPA), UN Women, UNICEF, and the Office of the High Commission on Human Rights, called for two actions to curb sex selection but did not mention abortion. The 2011 Interagency Statement urged for laws "to be enacted and enforced to deal with the abuse of sex selection technologies" and for policies that "enhance household perceptions of the value of daughters."[13] A human rights campaign to liberalize abortion law shaped this approach, in no small part because the feminist leaders who gained power within the UNFPA and other agencies had connections to U.S. reproductive rights activism.[14]

This section first explains the increasing feminist influence on population issues in the 1980s and the international campaign for abortion rights that took hold in the 1990s. It sets out a brief history of activism that both supports and conflicts with feminist opposition to sex selection. It demonstrates how liberal feminism helped define campaigns that relied on international human rights law as a means to secure stronger reproductive rights in national contexts.[15] This section concludes by describing the ways in which international human rights law characterizes sex-selective abortion as both gender discrimination and violence against women.

From Population Control to Reproductive Rights

The issue of abortion first attracted international attention as a method of population control when studies of population growth in the 1950s and 1960s began to forecast an explosion of births that would lead to a scarcity of resources.[16] Governments, with significant leadership by the United States, funded and supported an emergent population control movement that sought to reduce global poverty and to suppress the spread of communism.[17] Population control efforts culminated in the creation of the UNFPA in 1969.[18] The U.S. government was pivotal in establishing and funding the UNFPA and in encouraging other countries to support the agency as it became a subsidiary organ of the UN.[19]

Early international conferences on population and development dealt with women's reproductive health in terms of controlling the world's birthrate. The 1974 Third World Population Conference agenda, for example, referred to women's rights to reproductive decision making briefly and without elaboration. The 1984 International Conference on Population focused on family planning measures as a way to alleviate poverty and to relieve pressures on environmental resources by reducing family size. Women's rights, as conceptualized by feminists, were all but absent in the original framework for population control.

In addressing the indifference to the women's rights claims, feminists approached population politics not just as protesters or outsiders but with a will to power—to manage the UNFPA and to advance an agenda for women's reproductive rights. In the late 1960s and 1970s, women's rights advocates condemned national policies that encouraged involuntary or forced sterilization, abortion, and use of contraceptives.[20]

They made classic liberal arguments: the state should not coerce women's reproductive decisions or control women's fertility, whether to use birth control, be sterilized, or carry a pregnancy to term. And these feminist claims explicitly included abortion. Liberal feminist writings have theorized and justified a woman's right to abortion as synonymous with rights to autonomy and equality and as fundamental to ensuring women's equal standing with men.[21]

A right to reproductive autonomy, as inextricably linked to women's equality, aligned with family planning goals of the population control movement.[22] While feminists wanted to enable women to control the timing and occurrence of pregnancy so that women could pursue personal and professional development, those advocating population control wanted lower birthrates without resorting to the coercive tools states had used to control population growth.[23] The agendas of liberal feminism and population control coalesced in policies that did not force women to terminate pregnancies or use contraceptives but that permitted and may have encouraged women to elect abortion.

The changing leadership of international population groups began to reflect feminist understandings of abortion rights and increasingly adopted the language of reproductive rights. By the late 1980s, the UNFPA, the International Planned Parenthood Foundation, and the Ford Foundation all had leaders with feminist-aligned politics.[24] Non-profit groups titled themselves reproductive rights organizations and quickly became part of what Dorothy Hodgson described as a "women's rights industry" that "creates careers, channels funds, inspires commitments, gives credibility to new actors, creates and disrupts social networks, and legitimizes intellectual and political frameworks."[25] Women's rights advocates changed the conversation about birthrates to one about women's equality, reproductive choice, and wellness.

In the 1990s, reproductive rights advocates who had worked in U.S.-based nongovernmental organizations (NGOs) began to focus on human rights advocacy.[26] Human rights frameworks conferred legitimacy and intelligibility on claims for reproductive choice and health, and the liberal feminist commitment to legal rights made sense in the burgeoning field of human rights law. The 1994 ICPD was a pivotal step toward "reproductive rights as human rights" and laid the groundwork for abortion rights advocacy to come.[27] The resulting ICPD Programme of Action framed rights to reproductive health care and decision making as central to women's empowerment and full equality with men. It was one of the first global conferences on population that had a high level of NGO involvement, with the result that civil society and government representatives worked closely together to draft consensus principles.[28] Women's rights groups, of which U.S. feminists were a significant constituency, made up a large part of that NGO presence.[29]

However, as women's rights advocates became leaders in UN and intergovernmental agencies concentrating on reproductive health, the particular issue of abortion remained controversial and difficult to discuss. Although the ICPD Programme of Action stressed the importance of safe, effective, and affordable health services in jurisdictions where abortion was legal, it did not mention a right to abortion.[30] The advocates in feminist nonprofits at once celebrated the ICPD's treatment of abortion and mourned it as a concession to the Vatican representatives, who opposed all language on fertility control; to representatives from Islamic states, who opposed the individual nature of an abortion right, divorced from family decision making; and to members of Latin American governments that adopted a generally pro-natalist position extolling women as mothers.[31] The 1995 Beijing Declaration and Platform for Action of the Fourth World Conference on Women (Beijing Platform) drew on the wording and general intent of the ICPD but urged states to protect women's health by repealing or revising laws that punished women for terminating pregnancies.[32] This too fell short of full-throated support for an abortion right, but it was a significant feminist achievement nevertheless.

Some state representatives at meetings following the ICPD grew less resistant to abortion rights as U.S. politicians and government officials became increasingly attached to anti-abortion strategies. With the election of President George W. Bush, supporting liberal abortion rights signaled opposition to U.S. foreign policy. The Bush administration replaced the Clinton femocrats of the 1990s with anti-abortion officials who engaged with ICPD implementation processes only to disrupt them. Marge Berer, the first chair of the Gender Advisory Panel at the WHO Department of Reproductive Health and Research, later recalled that Latin American countries softened their stance on abortion to protest U.S. Department of State efforts to block implementation of the ICPD Programme of Action. The U.S. government, moreover, angered state representatives by withdrawing the funding of the U.S. Agency for International Development (USAID) from foreign agencies and nonprofits that provided abortion services or information about abortion (the popularly named "gag rule") and by requiring clinics to sign anti-abortion pledges before receiving USAID funds.[33] The U.S. government's opposition to the non-abortion provisions of the ICPD, such as sex education for adolescents, also encouraged country representatives to revisit their positions on abortion. Berer writes: "Outrage and dismay at [U.S. actions] in many cases motivated a renewed effort to campaign for safe, legal abortion."[34]

The global effects of anti-abortion politics in the United States and an antipathy to U.S. exceptionalism created a sense of political urgency. There were now international fora (gatherings on the implementation of the ICPD, for instance) in which to contest conservative abortion politics and to shape international pro-abortion activism. Reproductive rights advocates worked with international organizations to strengthen human rights arguments for the reform of national abortion laws. For example, feminists engaged with the process of writing country reports for the Convention on the Elimination of All Forms of Discrimination against Women (CEDAW) Committee and lobbied the CEDAW Committee to issue General Recommendation 24, which interpreted the CEDAW's right to health as a state duty to prevent women from having unsafe abortions and to stop punishing women who terminated pregnancies.[35] As General Recommendation 24 demonstrates, human rights law became a tool to encourage states to reform penal codes or criminal laws governing the termination of pregnancy.[36]

As a result of this activism, several contemporary human rights standards describe abortion liberalization as part of a state's responsibility to protect women's lives and health. The 2013 Montevideo Consensus on Population and Development "urge[s] States to consider amending their laws, regulations, strategies and public policies relating to the voluntary termination of pregnancy in order to protect the lives and health of women and adolescent girls, to improve their quality of life, and to reduce the number of abortions."[37] This statement departs from the compromise on abortion rights in the ICPD Programme of Action. Instead of restating the ICPD's language—rights to abortion services *when legal*—Montevideo calls on all states to consider abortion rights as crucial to women's quality of life and health. Likewise, in 2014, the UNFPA and the WHO held an expert meeting in anticipation of the twentieth anniversary of the ICPD. A background paper on access to safe abortion, prepared for the meeting, stressed the international consensus on the need to decriminalize abortion and enable women to seek safe termination services.[38]

Advocates for reproductive rights have not won all they wanted at the level of international human rights law. But "reproductive rights as human rights" have assisted feminists in wielding power within UN machinery and negotiating the text of international documents; the mantra presently leaves a mark on a range of conversations.[39] And it is now common to talk about abortion rights as part of women's rights to privacy, liberty, physical integrity, nondiscrimination, and health.[40] These human rights justifications support reproductive rights movements as vehicles for the broader diffusion of global social justice,[41] and those justifications reach national courts, which have relied on human rights rhetoric to uphold permissive laws or to strike down abortion restrictions.[42]

U.S. advocates have been closely connected to international work on behalf of reproductive rights, and U.S. abortion law has been at once a model and an antimodel.[43] On the one hand, supreme or constitutional courts across the world have cited U.S. abortion rights as emblematic of progressive abortion law reform—that is, legal permission for terminations without restriction as to reason or for reasons broadly defined and interpreted.[44] It is foundational to the U.S. model of abortion advocacy that the purpose of law reform is to remove as many legal restrictions on abortion, in terms of timing and grounds, as possible.

On the other hand, a human rights approach has been attractive to the U.S. reproductive rights movement, which was losing ground to anti-abortion activists and confronting the shortcomings of a rights narrative rooted in constitutional privacy. The constitutional right to abortion, as adopted by U.S. courts, does not encompass positive duties and has not kept pace with concepts of substantive equality.[45] The U.S. Supreme Court, for instance, held that the government could omit termination services from public health insurance programs, gutting access to abortion funding for low-income women.[46] U.S. reproductive rights groups have reckoned with the reality that an unfunded right to abortion is valuable only to those who can afford it. Some groups took on the mantle of reproductive justice, as opposed to reproductive rights, in renaming their organizations and reconfiguring their policy agendas.[47] This put them in alliance with movements focused on vulnerable populations of women, including women in the global South, and advocating for a range of reproductive health services, including but not exclusively abortion.[48]

Reproductive justice, however, is still firmly rooted in human rights as the "better version" of U.S. privacy rights. But there is a hidden trap even here. Arguing for abortion as a woman's human *right* essentially seeks legal permission for terminations, and that permission will have limits.[49] And rights advocacy shelters a corresponding blind spot—*why* women seek abortions. Because the question of *why* women terminate pregnancies is at the center of the debate around sex-selective abortion, this blind spot is a feminist vulnerability.

Feminist Campaigns against Sex Selection

Son preference, from the start, galvanized feminist movements against the practice of sex-selective abortion, but with different visions for how to address the issue.[50] This section maps two feminist approaches. The first is the antidiscrimination approach, largely reflected in the work of the UNFPA and of reproductive rights advocates, and informed by liberal feminist understandings of abortion rights. This approach seeks to root out gender inequality by eliminating discriminatory laws and by challenging gender stereotypes prevalent in societal attitudes, which are solutions that notably avoid banning sex-based abortion. The second approach treats sex selection as violence, casting son preference both as private violence against (and experienced by) women and public violence that permeates society when men outnumber women. The demonization of so-called harmful cultural practices accentuated in this second narrative helps cast sex selection as gender violence.

Liberal feminist interventions explain son preference as a consequence of legal and cultural discrimination. UN Women defines sex-selective abortion as a "form[] of discrimination against women [that is] symptomatic of the devalued status of women in society."[51] That is, when people act on preferences for boys, sex selection perpetuates gender discrimination. In resisting reason-based abortion bans, liberal feminists needed other arguments if they were to denounce son preference.

International human rights bodies and reproductive rights advocates call for law reform and cultural change that puts women and girls on equal footing with men and boys—the elimination of laws and practices that treat women differently than men or perpetuate a subordinate status for women.[52] The previously mentioned Interagency Statement of the Office of the High Commission on Human Rights, the WHO, UNFPA, UNICEF, and UN Women, for example, advocated for policies that encourage "attitudes supportive of greater equality."[53] The statement's recommendations included amending marriage and inheritance laws, increasing education for women, providing women equal pay and access to paid employment, eradicating dowry practices, and offering financial incentives for parents with daughters, such as housing and pension payments or college and school scholarships for girls.[54] To address sexist cultural beliefs and practices, proposed solutions are typically community education and political awareness campaigns.[55]

Coupled with educational campaigns, interagency materials take the liberal feminist position that restricting access to certain reproductive technologies or to safe abortion threatens the human rights of women. In accord with a broader reproductive rights agenda, UNFPA documents try to dissuade countries from restricting abortion based on the reason for termination (nonmedical fetal characteristics, for instance) or overly limiting access to ultrasound or other prenatal screening technology.[56] The rationale is squarely grounded in liberal feminist support for choice and autonomy rights, which "demand that each individual woman be permitted to make choices regarding the continuation of her pregnancy using whatever criteria she wishes."[57] A nondiscrimination approach accommodates liberal feminism's rejection of laws that prescribe the reasons for abortion.[58] This rejection incorporates a slippery slope argument that is common in U.S. abortion debates: one reason-based abortion ban could open the door to any number of other restrictions. And that is not a hollow fear. As described in more detail below, anti-abortion movements seek incremental restrictions en route to far broader ones, and liberal feminists believe they cannot concede any ground to abortion foes who pursue this strategy.[59]

The liberal feminist commitment to gender equality, however, created a well-known paradox. Abortion helps liberate women from motherhood, which can be empowering, but son preference is the epitome of valuing men over women and undermines equality between the sexes.[60] A solution at the international level was to cabin off sex-selective abortion as the consequence of coercion, not of choice. This solution is seen in UNFPA materials, such as a staff directive that instructs employees "to emphasize the powerlessness of women requesting sex selection."[61]

Dominance feminism took that argument one step further and framed sex selection as a universally abhorrent and abusive practice—a form of violence against women—that law should prohibit or criminalize. This strand of feminist advocacy, viewing prenatal sex selection as a form of violence, also became a part of international human rights campaigns to address violence against women and end certain cultural practices. The Beijing Platform, for example, encouraged states to "enact and enforce legislation against the perpetrators of practices and acts of violence against women, such as female genital mutilation, female infanticide, prenatal sex selection and dowry-related violence,"[62] and provided that "acts of violence against women also include forced sterilization and forced abortion, coercive/forced use of contraceptives, female infanticide and prenatal sex selection."[63] Shortly after Beijing, the United Nations Department of Public Information equated sex-selective abortion with infanticide or the neglect of the basic needs of daughters: "Some females fall prey to violence before they are born, when expectant parents abort their unborn daughters, hoping for sons instead."[64]

These declarations left an enduring mark on international conversations about sex selection. UN Women recently listed "prenatal sex selection" with types of violence that are "harmful cultural or traditional practices," a category that includes "female genital mutilation, female infanticide, child marriage, forced marriage, dowry-related violence, acid attacks, honor crimes, and abuse of widows."[65] Explanations of sex selection as violence and a harmful cultural practice start from the premise that women experience unavoidable pressures to select sons because they are subject to pervasive patriarchal coercion.[66] This is a depiction of the pregnant woman as a victim and not as a decision maker.[67] Catharine A. MacKinnon argued that abortion to select for fetal sex should not be permitted because "the decision [to abort because of sex] is not a free one, even absent governmental intervention, where a male life is valued and a female life is not."[68]

Dominance feminist claims that all sex-based abortions are coercive collided with liberal feminist arguments for unencumbered abortion rights and put liberal abortion-rights feminists on the defensive. Demographic evidence of son preference, particularly in India and China but also in South Korea, the Philippines, and other countries, made strategies to reduce societal sexism, like community education campaigns, seem inadequate. Liberal feminist incrementalism against violence made some feminists vulnerable to accusations of complicity: public eduational campaigns failed to respond directly to practices that harmed women and might not distinguish women's interests from those of their communities. April Cherry argued that, although "abortion gives women control over whether or when to have children, sex-selective abortion gives men (husbands and families) greater influence over women's reproduction and the sexual composition of future generations."[69] She added that "feminists need to go out on a limb and define sex selection as a human rights abuse . . . Whether it is sex-selective abortion, female genital mutilation, or domestic violence, it is a form of patriarchal oppression."[70]

Dominance feminists argued that their liberal feminist counterparts minimized the harm of son preference because of their opposition to reason-based abortion restrictions. To take an early example, political philosopher Mary Anne Warren argued that women's autonomy rights included a right to sex-selective abortion in her 1985 book *Gendercide*. She chose the term "gendercide" because it was gender neutral—that is, pregnant women might choose to abort male fetuses, too. For some of her contemporaries, "gendercide" was the watered-down version of the harm of sex selection. For example, Christine Overall argued that "using 'gendercide' rather than 'gynecide' or 'femicide' blurs this fact in the same way that a term like 'spouse abuse' hides the fact that it is almost always wives and other female partners (not husbands and male partners) who are beaten in instances of so-called domestic violence."[71] She continued:

> It may in fact be kinder on an individual basis to avoid producing daughters who will suffer grievous injury through nutritional deprivation, genital mutilation, sexual abuse, exploitive labour, and dangerous procreation. But choosing sons for that reason is still a way of saying yes, however obscurely or reluctantly, to patriarchal power and the

oppression of women. It is the expression of a failure to oppose the system.[72]

What made this split in feminism possible? It helps to recall that, in general, dominance feminism is less attached to abortion rights than liberal feminism is. Earlier dominance feminist writings were skeptical of campaigns to legalize abortion and argued that abortion was another means to assist in men's sexual exploitation of women.[73] Abortion permission dealt with unwanted pregnancy; as such, it provided cover for the nonconsensual sex that produced some pregnancies. Moreover, the ability to reject parenthood and child rearing does not upend the patriarchal system that devalues pregnancy and exploits women's caregiving. Instead, law reform strategies should concentrate on eradicating practices, even abortion for the "wrong" reason, that reinscribed sexism and reinforced violence against women. Dominance feminism was ready to see abortion as pervasively coercive against women.

However, that critique did not translate into U.S.- or UN-based reproductive rights activism. As abortion rights came increasingly under attack in U.S. legislatures and courts, liberal feminism continued to shape advocacy. Instead of questioning whether abortion is, in fact, inherently coercive, U.S. advocates and academics debated which right (equality, privacy, or autonomy) best secured constitutional protection for the termination of pregnancy.[74] Robin West lamented that the reproductive rights movement has seldom questioned its liberal feminist underpinnings and that dominance feminist critiques are all but absent in the United States. West wrote:

[Abortion] shifts the focus away from addressing the social and sexual imbalances that result in unwanted pregnancies to the unwanted pregnancy itself, and strongly suggests that the appropriate social and individual response to unwanted sex is to protect the decision to end the pregnancy. This has the effect of minimizing the social costs of sexual inequality for the strong and the weak both, rather than ending the sexual inequality itself. *Roe*, then, legitimates both unwanted sex and the hierarchies of power that generate it . . . These arguments, I think, were never answered satisfactorily by feminist supporters of *Roe v. Wade*.[75]

Dominance feminist claims have successfully shaped the population movement and permeate conversations about global sex demographics. In these fields, sex-selective abortion is not only an act of violence against individual women but also a practice that purportedly results in violence on a large scale if men outnumber women. In the early 1990s, MacKinnon argued that "aborting female fetuses may further erode women's power as women make up less and less of the population."[76] Over two decades later, Mara Hvistendahl coined the phrase "rampant demographic masculinization" to describe the process in which a society with too many men becomes militaristic, aggressive, and violent.[77] With a surplus of sex-starved men, sex trafficking, bride buying, and forced marriages are the predicted results: "In China and India, [men] visit brothels staffed by prostitutes forced into sex work... [because] the supply of women dried up."[78] Some state actors have found these arguments compelling. The *Trafficking in Persons Report 2013*, for example, critiqued China's sex ratios: "The [Chinese] government did not address the effects its birth limitation policy had in creating a gender imbalance and fueling trafficking, particularly through bride trafficking and forced marriage."[79] Similarly, in a statement to European states, a 2011 Council of Europe Resolution described the societal consequences in stark terms:

> The Assembly wishes to warn Council of Europe member states against the social consequences of prenatal sex selection, namely population imbalances which are likely to create difficulties for men to find spouses, lead to serious human rights violations such as forced prostitution, trafficking for the purposes of marriage or sexual exploitation, and contribute to a rise in criminality and social unrest.[80]

The nondiscrimination approach of liberal feminism does not stand up well against the rhetoric of imminent mass societal consequences.[81] The language can be extreme. Sex selection has been compared to the Holocaust in "eliminating" prenatally more "girls" than "the number of Jews killed in the Holocaust by the Nazis."[82] Christophe Guilmoto has labeled it "the sex selection epidemic" that costs "more lives than HIV/AIDS."[83] Equating violence against women (here, son preference) to global atrocities provides a justification for dominance feminist solutions—such terrible acts must be illegal and deserve strong reactions from states.[84] The 2011 Council of Europe Resolution calls on states to "introduce legislation with a view to prohibiting sex selection in the context of assisted reproduction technologies and legal abortion, except when it is justified to avoid a serious hereditary disease."[85] The council supports this statement with the violence narrative: "The social and family pressure placed on women not to pursue their pregnancy because of the sex of the embryo/foetus is to be considered as a form of psychological violence and that the practice of forced abortions is to be criminalised."[86] In several countries, bans on sex determination are expressions of feminist concerns about the practice, not necessarily of anti-abortion politics.[87] In India, for example, it was feminist mobilization that drove the prohibition of prenatal sex determination.[88]

In keeping with dominance feminist claims, this would suggest that *all* sex-selective abortions—no matter the place, the woman, or the context—are the result and the cause of gender violence. It is, as Maneesha Deckha described it, a "steady and overwhelming discourse of tragedy and victimization."[89] Those deploying sexual violence arguments try to avoid sounding like cultural imperialists.[90] But that project is not immune from criticism, particularly from activists working within a postcolonial frame or rejecting feminists' reliance on criminal law. In this book, similar critiques of dominance feminist strategies are detailed in Prabha Kotiswaran's treatment of criminal reforms to Indian rape law (chapter 4) and Hila Shamir's assessment of the consequences of Israeli anti-trafficking laws (chapter 5). As explained in the next section, dominance feminism arguments can support conservative projects that make it hard for liberal feminists to defend sex-selective abortion in the United States.

Sex-Selective Abortion in the United States

For its own criminalization project, the U.S. anti-abortion movement has relied on dominance feminist tropes about violence and liberal feminist arguments about sex discrimination. That movement has found a robust site for activism in state-level legislative campaigns against sex-selective abortion.[91] The problem of sex-selective abortion as "gendercide" now appears in a range of antichoice, conservative forums, from bills that ban sex-selective abortion, modeled on legislative guides published by Americans United for Life, to articles published in *Christianity Today* and the *National Catholic Register*.[92]

This campaign has garnered attention in news media and gained traction in state legislatures. Until 2012, only two states in the United States prohibited terminations of pregnancy on the basis of fetal sex and only one of those laws was in effect before viability.[93] Since then, and at the time of writing, twenty-five state legislatures have considered bills on sex selection, with nine states passing laws, two of which have been enjoined by courts.[94] In 2009, the U.S. Congress considered but did not pass the Susan B. Anthony and Frederick Douglass Prenatal Nondiscrimination Act (PRENDA); in subsequent years, PRENDA has been reintroduced in Congress and garnered bipartisan support.[95] The focus in this section is on PRENDA because it serves as the most comprehensive example of how anti-abortion legislators have co-opted feminist arguments made in international human rights documents and meetings.

Under PRENDA, any person who knowingly performs or facilitates "an abortion undertaken for purposes of eliminating an unborn child of an undesired sex . . . or race" may be fined, sentenced to up to five years in prison, and enjoined from further medical practice, and may face civil action by the patient, by the father of the fetus, and by the parents of the patient.[96] PRENDA does not punish women for terminating pregnancies; instead, it frames sex selection as the manifestation of violence and discrimination against women, holding women blameless. It describes sex selection "as an act of sex-based or gender-based violence, predicated on sex discrimination [and] one of the most evident manifestations of sex or gender discrimination in any society."[97] According to PRENDA, sex-selective abortions are "often the product of violence and coercion,"[98] exacerbating the vulnerability women face in pregnancy.[99] These are, as the last part demonstrates, not novel arguments; this language could have been lifted from the UN Interagency Statement on sex selection.[100] And they are arguments rooted in human rights. PRENDA cites the UN Commission on the Status of Women[101] and quotes from the work of Amartya Sen, who famously estimated that 100 million women are missing because of neglect of girls and preference for boys (although he did not directly address sex-selective abortion).[102]

PRENDA also refers to societal violence that will erupt if men outnumber women:

Experts worldwide document that a significant sex-ratio imbalance in which males numerically predominate can be a cause of increased violence and militancy within a society. Likewise, an unnatural sex-ratio imbalance gives rise to the commoditization of humans in the form of human trafficking, and a consequent increase in kidnapping and other violent crime.[103]

PRENDA describes the United States as out of step with international condemnation of sex selection by failing to pass a law criminalizing it.[104] In this vein, PRENDA denounces sex selection as "ha[ving] no place in a civilized society" and describes it as "barbaric" three times.[105] PRENDA cites recent studies on sex ratios at birth, which suggest that son preference exists in the United States, particularly in immigrant communities "tracing their origins to countries where sex-selective abortion is prevalent."[106] The bill compares sex selection in the United States with practices in China and India, and it predicts that the United States will become a "safe haven" for people seeking to evade their home countries' prohibitions of sex determination.[107] PRENDA's characterization of other countries and immigrant communities as barbaric resonates with some feminists' denouncement of "harmful cultural and traditional practices" in the global South.[108]

Given the international trajectories of feminist activism around sex selection, one might wonder whether dominance feminists would support a sex-selective abortion ban in the United States. However, no feminist organization wrote in support of PRENDA at the hearing for the bill. There is hardly any current U.S. feminist perspective—dominance or otherwise—that is vocal and mainstream in its support for banning sex-selective abortion. Liberal feminism occupies the field, as seen in the U.S. reproductive rights movement's commitment to abortion without restriction. Feminist NGOs have dismissed PRENDA as a thinly veiled anti-abortion strategy.[109] Beyond this dismissal, reproductive rights advocates make two arguments against sex-selective abortion bans: the U.S. Constitution does not permit restrictions based on the reason for an abortion, and sex selection occurs too infrequently to result in the negative consequences PRENDA forecasts. Both arguments do not address—they actually sidestep—the women-protective underpinnings that both dominance and liberal feminist ideas have helped advance.

Feminist Responses: Constitutional and Practical Arguments

Reproductive rights advocates argue that a reason-based ban applied before viability, such as PRENDA, places an undue burden on women's abortion choice and is therefore prohibited by the U.S. Supreme Court's 1992 decision in *Planned Parenthood of Southeastern Pennsylvania v. Casey*.[110] In *Casey*, the court held that states could restrict abortion before viability to protect women's health and the integrity of potential life so long as the regulation did not create an "undue burden" on a woman's choice to terminate a pregnancy.[111] As noted, the commitment to keeping reason-based bans off the books has been a defining concern of the U.S. reproductive rights movement.[112] Yet resorting to constitutional protections has left the U.S. reproductive rights movement with legal strategies that are subject to the decisions of courts, which can be hostile to abortion and willing to read *Casey* narrowly.

Contemporary sex-selective abortion bans highlight the limitations of constitutional arguments, and U.S. Supreme Court case law undermines the certainty with which reproductive rights advocates contest the constitutionality of bans. The 2007 U.S. Supreme Court case *Gonzales v. Carhart* endorsed several state interests that justify restricting abortion rights throughout a woman's pregnancy. In *Gonzales,* the court upheld a federal law that barred physicians from using a specific abortion procedure (intact dilation and evacuation, or intact D&E) performed sometimes, though infrequently, before viability.[113] PRENDA's drafters had in mind the state interests supported by *Gonzales* when they wrote the bill—those of protecting women, protecting the medical profession, and protecting the "unborn." And it has not been difficult to flip feminists' protection of women and "missing girls" into the anti-abortion arguments of PRENDA. Nondiscrimination and violence critiques of sex selection closely parallel these three state interests that the Supreme Court has identified as justifying a ban of certain abortion procedures throughout pregnancy.

First, the *Gonzales* majority held that banning intact D&E protected women from regret they would feel once they learned what the procedure entailed. In an infamous passage, Justice Kennedy wrote, "while we find no reliable data to measure the phenomenon, it seems unexceptionable to conclude that some women come to regret their choice to abort the infant life they once created and sustained."[114]

PRENDA tracks Justice Kennedy's language, claiming that women who abort because of fetal sex suffer "shame, guilt, and sadness over their inability to 'save' the daughters they have aborted."[115] These women, according to PRENDA, "are at increased risk for psychological and physical morbidity, documented by their descriptions of depression, anxiety, chronic pain, physical abuse."[116] PRENDA seeks to protect women from this regret by shielding them from the coercion to abort female fetuses.[117] Aspects of PRENDA's language as well as Justice Kennedy's position resonate with arguments offered by dominance feminists—law should prohibit sex-selective abortion because the practice of son preference dehumanizes and demeans women.[118]

Second, in *Gonzales,* the Supreme Court described the state's legitimate interest in protecting the integrity of the medical profession.[119] The court suggested that "abortion doctors" might not objectively apply a health exception to a ban on intact D&E because they would profit from performing the procedure.[120] PRENDA makes a similar claim: health professionals cannot resist the expanding population of patients looking for prenatal sex determination services.[121] PRENDA refers to a new prenatal technology (a prenatal screen described below) that will intensify the pressures on physicians to offer patients information on fetal sex.[122] Both liberal and dominance feminists have described ultrasound for sex determination in countries such as India in similar terms—it is inexpensive, widespread, and profitable, and physicians cannot resist the market for it. One reason this argument may make sense to PRENDA supporters and to the public generally is because it has been repeated for decades in feminist discussions about how to curb other countries' sex-selection problem.

Third, *Gonzales* refers to states' interests in protecting the integrity of potential life, describing intact D&E's treatment of fetal tissue as "brutal and inhumane."[123] PRENDA's invocation of sex selection as "uncivilized," "barbaric," and "abhorrent" expresses similar condemnation.[124] This language again tracks dominance feminist–inspired international standards that list sex selection with "harmful cultural or traditional practices," such as acid attacks and honor crimes. PRENDA also speaks to preserving the integrity of "unborn life" by controlling prenatal genetic engineering and thwarting the eugenic policies that could emerge if patients can pick and eliminate fetal characteristics in the womb.[125] Feminist calls to save the world's "missing girls" lost to son preference imagine a population of unborn children who would have shaped the world in gendered (and presumably positive) ways.

A state interest in protecting potential life also includes stunting the purported negative social effects of an imbalanced birth ratio of boys to girls.[126] Like PRENDA, early writings on sex selection predicted that "cumulative male surplus will thus produce a society with some of the rougher features of a frontier town," resulting in "the diminution of the number of agents of moral education and the increase in the number of criminals."[127] Connections between the rise of trafficking and sex selection, even as a hypothetical phenomenon, give credence to predictions of "rampant demographic masculinization," though without acknowledging the gender stereotypes that attach to it.[128] The dominance feminist arguments that commodification of and violence against women will proliferate if men outnumber women rest on stereotypes about women's moral superiority, docility, and peacefulness.[129]

Although liberal feminists have argued that previability bans are unconstitutional, PRENDA follows the road map set out in *Gonzales* and therefore could potentially withstand a constitutional challenge. This is not to say that feminists should or could give up on constitutional protection; a slippery slope toward reason-based bans feels treacherous. There is a real concern that if states can prohibit abortion because of fetal sex, states could set other grounds for permission.[130] And undoubtedly the anti-abortion movement has gained momentum in advancing reason-based bans. In 2016, thirteen bills banning sex selection were introduced; in the first half of 2017, ten bills were introduced.[131] As this legislation and the hundreds of other anti-abortion bills debated every year in state legislatures demonstrate, reproductive rights advocates face continual and considerable opposition. But the synergies between domestic, conservative, anti-abortion positions and international, dominance feminist arguments give legislation like PRENDA bite, making it difficult to dismiss it as a mere anti-abortion ploy.

Constitutional rights may or may not protect feminists' interest in previable, unencumbered abortion. An alternative taken by the mainstream reproductive rights movement is to question whether and to what extent sex selection happens in the United States. But the U.S. reproductive rights movement may also be losing that argument by losing the battle of public opinion; if the public believes that son preference exists anywhere, arguments that sex selection is rare could prove unpersuasive.

In tandem with constitutional arguments, U.S. liberal feminists argue that sex-selective abortion bans try to eradicate a practice that does not exist or is too infrequent to be worth the costs of suppressing it.[132] The testimonies of women's rights groups in hearings on PRENDA are emblematic. The Center for Reproductive Rights (CRR), the National Asian Pacific American Women's Forum, and NARAL Pro-Choice America stated in testimony against PRENDA that sex-selective abortion does not happen often enough to constitute a real problem.[133] This is the established position of U.S.-based organizations that oppose bans but have not historically challenged sex-selective abortion legislation in courts, although this may be changing.[134] During the *Casey* litigation, then CRR litigator Lynn Paltrow was asked why CRR did not litigate Pennsylvania's prohibition of sex-selective abortion—the oldest sex selection law in the country. She replied that the provision was a "red herring."[135] Similarly, in a lawsuit over a 2014 North Dakota anti-abortion law (described in the next section), CRR dropped a challenge to bans on abortion for fetal sex or for other prenatal characteristics, explaining that the provisions would not affect the patient population.[136]

The anti-abortion movement, on the other hand, has focused on making moral and ethical claims, sounding in women's rights, which are designed to galvanize public antipathy for abortion. In 2012, sting operations sent impostors undercover to Planned Parenthood clinics posing as pregnant women seeking abortions of female fetuses.[137] The videos were then posted online, one of which showed a staff member explaining at what point in pregnancy a patient can learn the sex of the fetus and wishing the patient, "Good luck, and I hope you get your boy."[138] Nothing that the Planned Parenthood employee said was counter to law; the state in which the video was recorded had not banned sex-selective abortion. The clip, however, damaged Planned Parenthood's public image, even if this was one person out of thousands.[139]

Debates about the occurrence of sex selection are hard to resolve, in part because research on birth ratios is inconclusive and in part because the practice can be difficult to detect and thus to measure. Undermining arguments that sex selection is virtually nonexistent, demographic and ethnographic studies raise the possibility that sex selection may occur more frequently in some U.S. communities than in others.[140] These studies are not, for the most part, the work of anti-abortion advocates. For instance, demographic research published in peer-reviewed journals offers evidence that there are higher numbers of male births than female births in some Chinese, South Korean, Filipino, and Indian families.[141] In addition, an ethnography published in *Social Science and Medicine* concluded that certain ethnic groups felt pressure to have sons. Researchers from the University of California, San Francisco, interviewed sixty-five Indian immigrants in the United States who had sex-selective terminations between September 2004 and December 2009.[142] The women reported varying levels of coercion from their communities and their family members; some participants experienced violence resulting from carrying or giving birth to daughters. Of the women interviewed, 40 percent had already terminated prior pregnancies with female fetuses and 89 percent of the women pregnant with female fetuses planned to pursue abortions.[143] Participants reported that a facilitator of coercion was the law: they and their family members believed sex-selective abortions were easily available in the United States.

The response of abortion supporters has been to challenge studies' methodology and conclusions or to call for additional data.[144] For example, Sneha Barot argues that demographic research does not establish the cause of disparate sex ratios, which could be prepregnancy techniques involving fertility treatments and not necessarily abortion.[145] Likewise, a 2014 report published by the International Human Rights Clinic at the University of Chicago Law School concluded there was no evidence of son preference in the first births, as compared with the third births, of both foreign-born parents and parents identifying with Indian, Chinese, or Korean ancestry.[146] Both responses are efforts to change the conversation from one about the ethics of sex determination to a battle of birth ratios—to suggest that sex selection is a manufactured problem, at least in the United States.[147]

This contradicts, however, the international feminist activism that paints son preference as a universally abhorrent "harmful cultural or traditional practice." The frequency of son preference, particularly when the practice is framed as violent or barbaric or uncivilized, would be irrelevant for those with moral opposition to it.[148] Frequency, however, might matter more to those who worry that sex selection will result in large-scale shifts in the gender ratio of a population.

The possibility of widespread son preference in the United States has come to the fore with noninvasive prenatal testing for fetal sex (clinically referred to as prenatal screening because it is almost but not yet 100 percent accurate). PRENDA, for example, cites "a growing sex determination niche industry" that "market[s] low-cost commercial products, widely advertised and available, that aid in sex determination of an unborn child without the aid of medical professionals."[149] New prenatal screening can determine the fetus's sex in the first trimester of pregnancy.[150] This noninvasive genetic test depends not on an ultrasound image or amniocentesis but on a small blood sample collected from a pregnant woman after ten weeks of pregnancy.[151] These prenatal tests have already entered clinical and commercial use, and, in the near future, private companies will market sex determination kits directly to consumers, who will return a blood sample from the prospective mother to a company or laboratory.[152] Most clinicians and scientists writing about noninvasive prenatal screening believe it will revolutionize prenatal care.[153] Articles in medical journals analyzing technologies for prenatal selection of nonmedical characteristics predict that abortion based on fetal sex (or any nonmedical characteristic) will increase with the introduction of noninvasive testing.[154]

Reproductive rights organizations and writings supportive of U.S. abortion rights, however, have not offered an analysis of noninvasive testing's effect on pregnant women's decision making. The reproductive rights movement appears to wrestle with the possibility that some women will abort female fetuses after using new tests, some will take advantage of prenatal technologies to pick fetal characteristics, and some will face coercion when doing so. There are few feminist explanations for why inexpensive ultrasounds in India and China are a clear pathway to son preference and new noninvasive screening in the United States is not.

The purpose of explaining demographic studies and the emergence of noninvasive testing is not to take a side in a debate over the incidence of sex selection or on whether the practice more often than not manifests as son preference. Rather, spotlighting that each side has credible evidence demonstrates that sex selection could be an issue that U.S. reproductive rights advocates helped expose in other places and from which they cannot now hide at home. The same is true for the states' interests in upholding bans, which mimic feminist claims about cultural practices in other countries and could provide shields against constitutional attacks on the sex-selective abortion bans in U.S. courts. Neither the liberal feminist vision of sex selection as discrimination nor the dominance feminist narrative of violence confronts U.S. exceptionalism or what a sex-selection ban might look like in practice. On the latter point, existing laws and new markets in the United States are shaping prenatal testing and abortion access as this chapter is being written. The final section asks in what conversations—about the enforcement of a ban, the markets for buying sex determination services, and the stakes of other movements—reproductive rights advocacy might engage.

Missing Conversations

The responses of the U.S. reproductive rights movement to the issue of sex selection—its prevalence and constitutionality—have not dampened the legislative enthusiasm for abortion restrictions. Those responses may not be persuasive to the public or to courts, but they are predictable when viewed in light of the two feminist approaches to son preference mapped out in the previous sections.

First, responses rooted in U.S. constitutional rights make sense in light of the international campaign for reproductive rights. The liberal feminist project is an absolutist stance on abortion rights: if the goal is to expand abortion permission under law, terminations previability should never be encumbered by a reason-based ban, even if the ban is directed at sex selection. At the same time, liberal feminist claims to autonomy and equality that support abortion rights also condemn son preference, and this tension resurfaces in national debates about sex-selective abortion. Like their international counterparts, reproductive rights supporters face the dilemma of either seeming complicit in the practice of son preference or allowing anti-abortion legislation to undermine abortion rights.[155] Again, the threat to abortion rights in the United States is serious. Anti-abortion advocates are committed to their own abolitionist strategies in opposing all or nearly all abortions. And because U.S. feminists have committed substantial energy to establishing a right and then expecting it to deliver, they appear taken off guard when facing the contradictions of rights-based strategies.

Second, the argument that sex selection does not happen very often in the United States entrenches a variant of U.S. exceptionalism. At the international level but not in the United States, feminists of all stripes support some legal efforts to curb son preference, and the dominance feminist position is to label sex selection, as PRENDA does, a "harmful cultural and traditional practice."[156] Liberal feminist reproductive rights advocates rely on demographic studies and birth ratios to counter U.S. anti-abortion legislation, but their positions on sex-selective abortion in other countries, where it is a "real" problem, is not necessarily consistent. PRENDA and bills like it shine a light on this exceptionalism, and liberal feminists have not found a compelling answer for why evidence of sex selection in their country would be so different from that in others.

To date, responses to bills like PRENDA do not take seriously what a sex-selective abortion ban might actually achieve in the United States. Now that a number of states have bans on the books, the next section asks what the reproductive rights movement can expect. If the movement wanted to thwart further laws and demonstrate the foolishness or destructiveness of a ban, what strategies would be convincing? One place to start is to ask how sex-selective abortion bans might be enforced. This concluding section first considers the challenges and costs of enforcing a sex-selective abortion ban, and then considers feminist conflicts with two movements that also have stakes in sex selection—namely, campaigns for disability rights and critiques from feminists of the global South. These conflicts are products of the long-standing alliances of feminists within the fields of international human rights, which postcolonial theorists have problematized, and population control, which disability rights advocates have resisted for promoting eugenic policies. Taking and wielding power in both fields were victories for reproductive rights activists. But the legacies of those victories have costs for constituencies that view differently the roles of sexism and coercion.

Enforcement

Enforcement of a sex-selection ban in the United States, as elsewhere, will be difficult. But enforcement is possible. Enacting onerous regulation or making abortion or sex determination more expensive could overcome enforcement problems. As a result, some women will benefit and others will suffer because any ban, even with state resources dedicated to its success, will apply inconsistently across the population of pregnant women. This section briefly discusses those costs and benefits by assessing what hurdles states face in enforcing sex selection bans.

First, because providers do not typically vet women's purposes for terminating pregnancies, any effective reason-based abortion ban requires a system for inspecting women's reasons.[157] Current laws do not require clinics, at least for now, to administer lie detector tests in order to scrutinize patients' reasons for seeking prenatal diagnosis or for terminations. A pregnant woman could test for fetal sex in one health care facility and then have an abortion at another clinic. There is no communication between facilities or among physicians, although a temporarily enjoined statute in Arkansas would require such communication by instructing abortion providers to investigate their patients' medical histories.

At present, even with a ban on the books, many women seeking sex-selective terminations will go undetected.[158] The passage of state bans may be symbolic victories for the anti-abortion movement; those laws could make little practical difference to women's abortion access. Reproductive rights organizations seem to bank on the possibility that sex selection will be hard to catch. The American Congress of Obstetricians and Gynecologists, for example, has taken this position—sex selection is troubling as a sexist practice, but little can be done to stop it, and abortion restrictions are not the answer.[159]

Next, the piecemeal regulation of prenatal testing also makes sex selection difficult to monitor. Physicians and genetic counselors are the access points to prenatal sex determination. These health care providers decide what testing results to relate to their patients, and they decide the timing and often the content of genetic counseling.

The introduction of easy-to-administer noninvasive tests gives obstetricians financial incentives to offer new prenatal tests and attendant counseling. Reproductive choice rhetoric supports this development, too, by justifying the market for sex determination. When asked about offering sex determination specifically through noninvasive testing, providers explain their services in terms of women's right to reproductive autonomy: if their patients ask for a test, they have a right to it.[160] If the current system for prenatal testing holds, sex determination early in pregnancy will become easy and remain private (and potentially widely affordable depending on the development of the technology). Moreover, the introduction of self-use sex determination in the form of at-home testing kits will further complicate the relationship between abortion services and prenatal sex testing. A woman who returns a blood sample to a laboratory or receives online or mailed results need never visit a physician for sex determination services, and she could misrepresent her reason for seeking a termination after testing.

States also could pass laws or build systems that attempt to close these holes in enforcement. In the United States, laws controlling clinical information and relationships would be departures from the consumer-driven arena of prenatal screening; states (and the federal government) generally have left decisions to test, what to test for, and how to act on results to the patient.[161] But, again, laws attempting to control the information given to pregnant women and to impose restrictions on prenatal testing or counseling are imaginable. States could, for instance, bar any communication about the sex of the fetus unless patients have a medically valid reason unrelated to son preference, such as a sex-linked genetically transmissible disease.[162] In the same vein, state governments could try to impose restrictions or reporting requirements on physicians offering prenatal tests, the companies that sell testing kits, or the laboratories that determine results. In most states, abortion providers are restrained by informed-consent rules, which could serve as models for policies governing sex determination tests.[163] Obstetricians who provide prenatal screening would then have even fewer incentives to provide abortion care if they are subject to additional practice constraints.[164]

And given that sex-selective abortion laws usually punish providers, just a few cases of providers losing their licenses or facing imprisonment would prompt some abortion providers to more closely interrogate patients as to their reasons for termination or to stop offering any type of sex determination service. Abortion services would be further stigmatized and marginalized.[165] The ability to gain access to abortion services is already marked by inequalities—women who can travel, who can afford the procedure, and who can take time off from work have less difficulty obtaining terminations.[166] Even if prenatal sex determination was untouched by law reform, women's abortion options would be limited nonetheless because of cost and logistical impediments. This is constantly shifting ground, and the anti-abortion strategies of tomorrow are difficult to predict in detail. What seems certain, though, is that legislative attempts to police women seeking abortion and to punish providers offering services will continue.

If enforcement were only somewhat effective, sex-selection laws would put some women at a greater disadvantage than others; in some cases, women might benefit from a ban. Women who might experience familial or community pressure to terminate pregnancies could use a ban as a buffer between their decision and their communities, family members, or partners. At the same time, understanding the law is also an advantage, and those unlikely to be familiar with how bans work (those new to the country, for example) will be vulnerable. Some women will seek sex-selective abortion regardless of what the law says. A ban could drive sex determination into markets operating outside or at the periphery of law, and women relying on extralegal services may have limited resources or information.

Some pregnant women will want to abort female fetuses because they believe the birth of a boy is more valuable than the birth of a girl, perhaps sharing the attitudes of male superiority that liberal and dominance feminists reject. Or they could have any number of reasons, such as family balancing or gaining power over family members later in life (as a future mother-in-law might).[167] When governments lifted abortion restrictions in Pakistan and in the Philippines, commentators remarked: "It was in no way foreseen that autonomous, empowered women would deliberately enforce abortion against their own gender group."[168] This outcome is recognizable when pregnant women are viewed as actors, not as victims or morally superior decision makers.[169]

Movement Conflicts

Liberal and dominance feminist reactions to sex selection can be at odds with the priorities of groups invested in representing constituencies affected by sex-selective abortion. To take two examples, liberal feminist politics on this issue can alienate disability rights advocates, and dominance feminist accounts of son preference can fall into traps that postcolonial feminism has sought to expose and deconstruct. And these conflicts are in part legacies of feminists' involvement in the population control movement and in human rights campaigns.

Those advocating on behalf of persons with disabilities are suspicious of technologies that permit parents to select fetal characteristics prenatally.[170] Disability rights advocates have argued that deselection of genetic characteristics (such as aborting a fetus with a discovered disability) has expressive and practical consequences that lead to dehumanization for those living with disabilities.[171] At present, however, feminist writings on disability rights are typically anti-ban and pro-information, encouraging potential parents to learn about raising children with disabilities.[172] This is a testament to the influence of the U.S. reproductive rights movement, which tied support for abortion rights to support for women's rights. But with the introduction of noninvasive prenatal genetic tests, combined with research that reveals the erasure of newborns with certain disabilities, this position increasingly is under stress. For example, studies show a dwindling number of persons born with Down syndrome, in part because of the combination of abortion and the use of noninvasive prenatal testing (for single-gene disorders) described in this chapter.[173] Other populations with genetic conditions discovered prenatally may also be disappearing but have not attracted the same attention or advocacy as Down syndrome has.

The market in the United States for prenatal testing—for an increasing number of medical and nonmedical fetal characteristics—could exacerbate a conflict between protecting unencumbered abortion decisions and viewing some abortion decisions as problematic. Reproductive rights advocates are loathe, for all the reasons discussed, to accept an abortion restriction based on fetal disability, even if such terminations seem to have eugenic overtones. And disability rights advocates point to laws that allow pregnancy termination because of fetal impairment as proof of the pressure that law exerts on women to abort fetuses with certain prenatal diagnoses.[174] This is a long-standing tension. While feminist interventions in the population movement (described in the first section) disrupted some of the goals of population control, feminist involvement also took for granted that abortion laws would influence population growth and, more importantly, shape population characteristics.

The cost for the U.S. reproductive rights movement could be a deepening alliance between disability rights projects and conservative, anti-abortion politics. In the first half of 2017, five states have considered bills that banned abortion based on any fetal diagnosis,[175] and North Dakota, in 2014, enacted a law that prohibits all terminations based on diagnosis of "genetic abnormality or a potential for a genetic abnormality."[176] Outside of bans, groups such as Americans

United for Life and disability rights organizations might find common cause in policies that regulate the information learned from prenatal testing and dictate ethics training and licensing for genetic counselors.[177] As the previous section contemplates, strict informed consent or disclosure standards for noninvasive prenatal testing may be on the way. [178]

Critiques by postcolonial feminists of violence narratives have picked up on this tension, but from a perspective that is critical of dominance feminist framings of sex selection as abusive. Postcolonial feminists have argued that sex-selection bans paint abortion decisions based on fetal sex as inherently coercive, but frame abortions because of fetal disability as legitimate, autonomous decisions. Geography and power frame these characterizations: women in the global North make the "accepted" choice about disability, whereas women in the global South deselect fetal characteristics, like sex, because of a lack of agency.[179] If these characterizations "make sense" it is because they rely on stereotypes about the differences between women in the global North and women in the global South. Moreover, the commonsense nature of such depictions demonstrates the extent to which dominance feminist advocacy around harmful cultural practices has taken hold. It is what Deckha described as "the parade of (bodily) horrors relating to non-Western women that Westerners, including Western feminists, have historically used to demonstrate the supposed inherent misogyny and gender backwardness of non-Western cultures."[180]

In this vein, postcolonial feminists have questioned the dominance, as well as the liberal, feminist urge to universalize sexism and to problematize culture. The mainstream position on sex selection, which can straddle both nondiscrimination and violence narratives, blames sex-selective abortion on an all-powerful, monolithic culture that manifests in countries' various legal permissions and requirements. Sex selection is a phenomenon always tied to male domination and female subordination—discrimination or subjugation that is the same for all women, the world over.[181] Sital Kalantry complicates this position:

> Explanations for sex selection that focus only on culture fail to recognize that the contextual factors (such as economic opportunities for women, a system of support for senior citizens, and fertility patterns) influence sex selection practices as well. The discourse on sex-selective abortion bans also imagines culture as fixed rather than dynamic and

changing both in India and among Indian American immigrant communities.[182]

The impulse to universalize patriarchy oversimplifies sex selection as inevitably a form of gender violence affecting individuals and society as a whole. But demographic changes are hard to predict, and there are various possibilities for how sex selection might shape society or women's and men's status beyond "rampant demographic masculinization." To take one hypothetical, in the United States, a gender imbalance that favors men over women might not necessarily result in women's subordination. Scholars, mostly outside feminist circles, have argued that more men than women could promote a higher status for women.[183] In the United States, existing legal protections and cultural norms that advance women's empowerment and equality might protect a smaller population of women and help them obtain a greater share of societal resources. These advantages would stratify across lines of class, location, race, and any number of characteristics; not all women would reap rewards of supply and demand, and some women may suffer exploitation.[184] With a scarcity of women, marriage decisions and gender roles would shift, too, at least for some and likely with the most pronounced gains for privileged women.[185] Those possibilities, contrary to culture and coercion explanations of sex selection, depend on influences that are not wholly about what the law says or about men dominating women.[186]

Human rights law, which has absorbed the campaign against gender violence as a priority, has helped justify an understanding of sex selection as cultural coercion. On the one hand, human rights have been a key tool for abortion law reform, and violence explanations for sex selection appear in human rights law texts. On the other hand, as pressed by those critical of feminist interventions in "harmful cultural or traditional practices," human rights approaches can undermine context and locality by casting all women as the victims of culture.[187] A cost to the U.S. reproductive rights movement is that an agenda aligned with a "developing world perspective" is an aspiration and often not a reality.[188] Without skepticism of what human rights can accomplish, the reproductive rights movement can be accused of acting with "imperialist feminism"—exporting women's rights to other parts of the world and ignoring the consequences of absolutism or criminalization at home.[189]

Conclusion

This chapter describes the international campaign for abortion rights and the feminist arguments against sex selection that have traveled back to the United States. Its purpose in describing feminist responses to son preference is to query how the U.S. reproductive rights movement might take stock of the consequences of its advocacy strategies. Feminist interventions have succeeded when they marry the goal of abortion permission to human rights or to population control. But feminist arguments might inadequately question rights-based strategies, influence the provision of prenatal health care, or engage with the criticisms of actors in other fields. What would the approach to sex selection in the United States look like if feminists engaged as governors—weighing conflicting aims and norms from the position of policymakers? Those are questions this chapter does not try to answer. They are questions, however, at the heart of GF, when feminists who wield power assess what their legal strategies accomplish for the women they seek to speak for or whose needs they intend to address.

Notes

1. Liberal feminists argue that women have legal rights to terminate pregnancies so that they can succeed in workplaces, shed stereotypes, and have larger shares of societal resources. As this chapter argues, liberal feminism was the first and central discourse to register internationally. Reva B. Siegel, "The Constitutionalization of Abortion," in *The Oxford Handbook of Comparative Constitutional Law*, ed. Michel Rosenfeld and András Sajó (Oxford: Oxford University Press, 2012), 1057–78. Earlier versions of this chapter's arguments, although with a different focus and conclusion, appear in Rachel Rebouché, "Testing Sex," *University of Richmond Law Review* 49 (2015): 519–77, and in Rachel Rebouché, "Abortion Rights as Human Rights," *Social and Studies* 25 (2016): 765–82.

2. Mindy Jane Roseman and Laura Reichenbach, *Global Reproductive Health and Rights: Reflecting on the ICPD*, ed. Mindy Jane Roseman and Laura Reichenbach (Philadelphia: University of Pennsylvania Press, 2009), 17–18 (citing the work of Charlotte Bunch and Rebecca Cook).

3. This chapter refers to "reproductive rights" advocates, because that has been the central discourse for U.S. abortion rights. A "reproductive justice" perspective

urges that reproductive rights have been too focused on legal permission for abortion. Reproductive justice aims to address a broader spectrum of reproductive decision making and health care services (birth practices, treatment of incarcerated pregnant women, or assisted reproductive technologies, for example). Joan C. Chrisler, "Introduction: A Global Approach to Reproductive Justice—Psychosocial and Legal Aspects and Implications," *William and Mary Journal of Women and the Law* 20, no. 1 (2013): 3.

4. Sital Kalantry, "Sex Selection in the United States and India: A Contextualist Feminist Approach," *UCLA Journal of International Law and Foreign Affairs* 18, no. 1 (2013): 75–76.

5. For instance, the Center for Reproductive Rights, a leading nonprofit in the United States, refers to a human rights framework to make arguments in the domestic context. See, e.g., Center for Reproductive Rights, *Defending Human Rights: Abortion Providers Facing Threats, Restrictions, and Harassment* (New York: Center for Reproductive Rights, 2009), http://reproductiverights.org/sites/crr.civicactions .net/files/documents/DefendingHumanRights_0.pdf.

6. "A preponderance of males go[es] beyond the sadness experienced by the men unable to find mates or spouses. These harms include decreased political power of females as well as the return of the notion that women should resume their traditional family roles and should retain their virginity for marriage. In total, the effects of a population imbalance are likely to be extremely negative for women and affect all of society." Rachel E. Remaley, "'The Original Sexist Sin': Regulating Preconception Sex Selection Technology," *Health Matrix* 10, no. 2 (2013): 279.

7. Mara Hvistendahl, *Unnatural Selection: Choosing Boys over Girls, and the Consequences of a World Full of Men* (New York: PublicAffairs, 2011), 151.

8. Few self-proclaimed feminists are anti-abortion, but the position does exist; see, for instance, the nonprofit group Feminists for Life. And there are many nonfeminist arguments for abortion. But virtually all pro-abortion advocates today have feminist commitments. Their main and chief concerns are the autonomy, equality, and privacy rights for pregnant women. Though abortion rights supporters in the United States divide over what rights and values are the most important, they see their mission as an explicitly woman-centered one. Rickie Solinger, *Reproductive Politics: What Everyone Needs to Know* (Oxford: Oxford University Press, 2013), 1–6.

9. Roe v. Wade, 410 U.S. 113 (1973).

10. Gonzales v. Carhart, 550 U.S. 124 (2007). In 2016, the U.S. Supreme Court decided a case that could revive the undue burden test established under *Casey*. In striking down a law requiring abortion clinics to become ambulatory surgical centers and physicians to have admitting privileges, the Supreme Court held that the undue burden standard requires lower courts to balance the benefits and burdens imposed by an abortion restriction that purports to protect women's health. Whole Woman's Health v. Hellerstedt, 136 S.Ct. 2292, 2309-20 (2016).

11. United Nations, "Report of the International Conference on Population and Development," Cairo, Egypt, September 5–13, 1994, Principle 4, U.N. Doc. A/ CONF.171/13/Rev.1. See also The World Bank, *World Development Report 2012: Gender Equality and Development* (Washington, D.C.: The World Bank, 2011), 24, http://siteresources.worldbank.org/INTWDR2012/Resources/7778105-129969996 8583/7786210-1315936222006/Complete-Report.pdf.

12. UN feminist attention has historically focused on the increasing availability of ultrasound technology for sex determination and on birth ratios in China, India, and South Korea that indicated an unnatural number of male births. World Health Organization et al., *Preventing Gender-Biased Sex Selection: An Interagency Statement OHCHR, UNFPA, UNICEF, UN Women and WHO* (Geneva, Switzerland: World Health Organization, 2011), http://www.who.int/reproductivehealth/publications /gender_rights/9789241501460/en/.

13. Ibid.

14. Hvistendahl, *Unnatural Selection*, 146.

15. Roseman and Reichenbach, *Global Reproductive Health and Rights*, 9.

16. *Confronting the Legacies of Population Control: Historical Perspectives on the Global Spread of Sex-Selective Abortion, Before the Sub-comm. on Africa, Global Health, Global Human Rights, and International Organizations of the H. Comm. on Foreign Affairs*, 113th Cong. 39 (2013) (statement of Matthew Connelly, Professor of History, Columbia University), 3–4.

17. Hvistendahl, *Unnatural Selection*, 32. The population control agenda appealed to both those with Left political commitments and those with Right political commitments. Conservative thinkers focused on stemming the spread of communism, and progressive leftists focused on addressing hunger and poverty. Michelle Goldberg argues that although progressive and conservative movements came together over issues of population control, they later fell apart because of disagreements about women's rights to control fertility and to sexual expression. Michelle Goldberg, *The Means of Reproduction: Sex, Power, and the Future of the World* (New York: Penguin Books, 2009), 7–8.

18. Rachel Sullivan Robinson, "UNFPA in Context: An Institutional History" (background paper, Center for Global Development Working Group on UNFPA's Leaderships Transition, October 2010), 1, 6, http://www.cgdev.org/doc/UNFPA-in -Context.pdf.

19. The United States was the largest contributor to the UNFPA for the first decade of its existence. Chad M. Gerson, "Toward an International Standard of Abortion Rights: Two Obstacles," *Chicago Journal of International Law* 5, no. 2 (2005): 760.

20. Reed Boland, "The Environment, Population, and Women's Human Rights," *Environmental Law* 27, no. 4 (1997): 1137–167. Mary Ziegler explains the complicated relationship between population control and the abortion rights movement in the United States. Mary Ziegler, "The Framing of a Right to Choose: Roe v. Wade and the Changing Debate on Abortion Law," *Law and History Review* 27, no. 2 (2009): 281.

21. Hester Eisenstein, *Feminism Seduced: How Global Elites Use Women's Labor and Ideas to Exploit the World* (Boulder, Colo.: Paradigm Publishers, 2009), 89. In describing early autonomy and equality-driven arguments, Reva Siegel cites the 1969 speech of Betty Friedan, president of the National Organization for Women. Friedan called for legal abortion because "the right of woman to control her reproductive process must be established as a basic and valuable human civil right not to be denied or abridged by the state." Betty Friedan, "Abortion: A Woman's Civil Right" (speech, First National Conference on Abortion Laws, February 1969), in Reva B. Siegel, "Dignity and Sexuality: Claims on Dignity in Transnational Debates over Abortion and Same-Sex Marriage," *International Journal of Constitutional Law* 10, no. 2 (2012): 358.

22. Roseman and Reichenbach describe how the UNFPA's focus on women's empowerment was a bargain struck by UN leaders and feminist activists; both bureaucrats and advocates saw campaigns for women's rights to terminate pregnancies as practical and efficient means to curb population growth. Roseman and Reichenbach, *Global Reproductive Health and Rights,* 12.

23. Historian Matthew Connelly argued before a 2013 U.S. congressional hearing, "American scientists, aid officials, and activists played leading roles . . . promot[ing] sex-selective abortion as a potential solution to what they saw as the population explosion. It is precisely because the United States took [an early] leading role in advocating population control worldwide that we cannot pretend that we have no responsibility for the consequences." Connelly, *Confronting the Legacies of Population Control.*

24. For example, the UNFPA established the Office of the Senior Coordinator for International Women's Issues (now the Office of Global Women's Issues).

25. Dorothy L. Hodgson, ed., *Gender and Culture at the Limit of Rights* (Philadelphia: University of Pennsylvania Press, 2011), 118.

26. Timothy E. Wirth, "Address to Citizens of Cairo" (speech, Trusteeship Council Chamber, Cairo, Egypt, March 30, 1994). In the 1990s, feminists also became prominent leaders in the U.S. Agency for International Development (USAID), and the USAID created the Office of the Coordinator for Gender Equality and Women's Empowerment.

27. Roseman and Reichenbach, *Global Reproductive Health and Rights,* 17. See also Rhonda Copelon, "Remarks of Rhonda Copelon," *American University Law Review* 44, no. 4 (1995): 1253; Christina Zampas and Jamie M. Gher, "Abortion as a Human Right—International and Regional Standards," *Human Rights Law Review* 8, no. 2 (2008): 252.

28. Nadine Taub, "International Conference on Population and Development," *Issue Papers on World Conferences,* no. 1 (Washington, D.C.: American Society of International Law, 1994). Taub notes how women's rights advocates helped draft the ICPD's guiding principles, such as Principle 4 on "advancing of gender equality and equity and the empowerment of women, and the elimination of all kinds of violence against women."

29. Roseman and Reichenbach, *Global Reproductive Health and Rights,* 17–18.

30. United Nations, "Report of the International Conference on Population and Development."

31. Adrienne Germain and Theresa Kim, *Expanding Access to Abortion: Strategies for Action* (New York: International Women's Health Coalition, 1998), 3–4, 6, https://iwhc.org/resources/expanding-access-safe-abortion-strategies-action/; Marge Berer, "The Cairo Compromise on Abortion and Its Consequences," in *Reproductive Health and Human Rights: The Way Forward,* ed. Mindy Jane Roseman and Laura Reichenbach (Philadelphia: University of Pennsylvania Press, 2009), 156–57. Advocates have described the ICPD's compromise as "cost[ing] women their lives, as well as their health." Rebecca Firestone, Laura Reichenbach, and Mindy Roseman, "Conclusion: Conceptual Successes and Operational Challenges to ICPD: Global Reproductive Health and Rights Moving Forward," in Roseman and Reichenbach, *Reproductive Health and Human Rights,* 223.

32. "In the light of paragraph 8.25 of the Programme of Action of the International Conference on Population and Development, . . . [states should] consider reviewing laws containing punitive measures against women who have undergone illegal abortions." United Nations Fourth World Conference on Women, "Report of the Fourth World Conf. on Women," Beijing, China, September 4–15, 1995, ¶ 106(k), U.N. Doc. A/Conf. 177/20 (October 17, 1995).

33. In 1984, the Reagan administration issued an executive order that prohibited recipients of U.S. foreign aid, such as women's rights NGOs outside the United States, from performing abortions (except in cases of rape or incest or when the woman's life was threatened), providing counseling or referral for abortion, or lobbying for liberalized abortion laws. Democratic presidents have repealed this funding restriction and Republican presidents have reinstated it. Barbara B. Crane and Jennifer Dusenberry, "Power and Politics in International Funding for Reproductive Health: The US Global Gag Rule," *Reproductive Health Matters* 12, no. 24 (2004): 128–37.

34. Berer, "The Cairo Compromise on Abortion," 158. Berer discusses the efforts of Latin American governments to strengthen their family planning programs and to engage in a debate on abortion law reform.

35. United Nations Commission on the Elimination of Discrimination against Women, General Recommendation no. 24, Women and Health (Article 12) U.N. Doc. A/54/38/Rev.1, chapter I, at 31(c) (20th Sess., 1999).

36. Dr. Nafis Sadik, the executive director of the United Nations Population Fund, used the phrase in her Fourth World Conference on Women address: "The concept of reproductive rights did not spring from one group or one country. It is neither neo-colonialist nor unethical. It is a universal concept, which reflects the experience of thousands of women and men in countries all over the world. Reproductive rights are human rights." Rhonda Copelon, "Remarks of Rhonda Copelon," 1253–55.

37. United Nations, First Session of the Regional Conference on Population and Development in Latin America and the Caribbean, Montevideo Consensus on Population and Development Priority Action 42, U.N. Doc. LC/L.3697 (Montevideo, Uruguay, August 12–15, 2013) (published September 23, 2013).

38. Iqbal Shaha, Elisabeth Åhmana, and Nuriye Ortaylib, "Access to Safe Abortion: Progress and Challenges since the 1994 International Conference on Population and Development (ICPD)," *Contraception* 90, no. 6 (background paper #3, ICPD Beyond 2014 Expert Meeting on Women's Health—Rights, Empowerment, and Social Determinants, Mexico City, September 30–October 2, 2014): 19. doi:10.1016/j .contraception.2014.04.004.

39. For example, a World Bank report draws a connection between access to legal abortion and narrowing the gender gap in employment. The World Bank, *World Development Report 2012: Gender Equality and Development* (Washington, D.C.: The World Bank, 2011), 348, http://siteresources.worldbank.org/INTWDR2012 /Resources/7778105-1299699968583/7786210-1315936222006/Complete-Report.pdf.

40. Rebecca Cook and Bernard Dickens, "Human Rights Dynamics of Abortion Law Reform," *Human Rights Quarterly* 25, no. 1 (2003): 2–3. See also Martha Davis, "Abortion Access in the Global Marketplace," *North Carolina Law Review* 88, no. 5 (2010): 1657, 1674; Christina Zampas and Jamie M. Gher, "Abortion as a Human

Right: International and Regional Standards," *Human Rights Law Review* 8, no. 2 (2008): 255.

41. Sally Engle Merry, "Human Rights and Transnational Culture: Regulating Gender Violence through Global Law," *Osgoode Hall Law Journal* 44, no. 1 (2003): 56; David Kennedy, "The International Human Rights Regime: Still Part of the Problem?," in *Examining Critical Perspectives on Human Rights*, ed. Rob Dickinson et al. (Cambridge: Cambridge University Press, 2013), 20.

42. Rachel Rebouché, "Reproducing Rights," *University of California, Irvine Law Review* 6 (forthcoming). The question courts tend to resolve is how to mediate competing rights-based considerations between the human rights of pregnant women and the human rights of fetuses, with the latter usually losing to the former unless national law recognizes a fetal right to life.

43. Julia L. Ernst, Laura Katzive, and Erica Smock, "The Global Pattern of U.S. Initiatives Curtailing Women's Reproductive Rights: A Perspective on the Increasingly Anti-choice Mosaic," *University of Pennsylvania Journal of Constitutional Law* 6, no. 4 (2004): 752. Ernst, Katzive, and Smock write: "Grounding a woman's right to choose abortion in the guarantees protected by the U.S. Constitution, the U.S. Supreme Court offered a rights-based conceptual framework that has influenced constitutional decisions in the courts of other nations and has been read into the protections of international human rights treaties." *Roe v. Wade* has been a model and antimodel for other countries' abortion laws. Rachel Rebouché, "The Limits of Reproductive Rights in Improving Women's Health," *Alabama Law Review* 63, no. 1 (2011): 14–20.

44. For example, modern courts all over the world consistently rely on *Roe v. Wade* when upholding new abortion permissions or striking down restrictive penal codes. Rachel Rebouché, "Comparative Pragmatism," *Maryland Law Review* 72 (2012): 85.

45. Joan C. Chrisler, "A Global Approach to Reproductive Justice—Psychosocial and Legal Aspects and Implications," *William and Mary Journal of Women and the Law* 20, no. 1 (2013): 2.

46. Harris v. McRae, 448 U.S. 297 (1980) (holding that states participating in Medicaid did not have to pay for Medicaid patients' medically necessary abortions).

47. Zakiya Luna and Kristin Luker notice that many U.S. organizations and advocates have rebranded themselves as "reproductive justice" rather than "reproductive rights," although they question whether advocates' strategies, which retain a focus on abortion rights, have truly changed. Zakiya Luna and Kristin Luker, "Reproductive Justice," *Annual Review of Law and Social Science* 9 (2013): 343.

48. Rebouché, "Reproducing Rights." Chrisler writes that "reproductive rights," as compared to "reproductive justice," "fits best the situation of relatively privileged women in Western, industrialized nations." Chrisler, "A Global Approach to Reproductive Justice," 2.

49. See Wesley N. Hohfeld, "Fundamental Legal Conceptions as Applied in Judicial Reasoning," *Yale Law Journal* 26, no. 8 (1917): 710.

50. Both progressive and conservative political groups have long criticized sex selection. Feminists supportive of abortion rights and conservatives opposed to abortion criticized the UNFPA for complicity with purportedly coercive abortions of

typically female fetuses in China under the now-repealed one-child policy. Hvisten-dahl, *Unnatural Selection,* 153 (citing the Population and Family Planning Law of the People's Republic of China [December 29, 2001] [unofficial translation], codify-ing the 1979 policy).

51. UN Women, *Handbook for Legislation on Violence against Women: "Harmful Practices" against Women* (New York: United Nations Press, 2012), 4.

52. "The *only* way to achieve long-lasting social change on issues of gender bias, especially sex-selective practices, is through working to fundamentally shift attitudes and culture at the community level and to comprehensively address the underlying issues that propagate inequity." *India's Missing Girls, Before the Subcomm. on Africa, Global Health, Global Human Rights, & International Organizations of the H. Comm. on Foreign Affairs,* 113th Cong. 39 (2013) (statement of Mallika Dutt, President and Chief Executive Officer, Breakthrough).

53. World Health Organization et al., *Preventing Gender-Biased Sex Selection,* 7.

54. Ibid.

55. In materials explaining a discrimination approach, it is not clear whether community education or political awareness campaigns work; infrequently are fac-tors other than sexism considered in what shapes procreative decisions.

56. Hvistendahl, *Unnatural Selection,* 152–53.

57. April L. Cherry, "A Feminist Understanding of Sex-Selective Abortion: Solely a Matter of Choice?," *Wisconsin Women's Law Journal* 10, no. 2 (1995): 206–7.

58. Mary Anne Warren, *Gendercide: The Implications of Sex Selection* (Totowa, N.J.: Rowman & Allanheld, 1985), 104. See also Rosalind P. Petchesky, *Abortion and Woman's Choice: The State, Sexuality, and Reproductive Freedom* (New York: Long-man, 1984).

59. A recent example is the advocacy of anti-abortion groups before the UN Hu-man Rights Council (formerly the Human Rights Committee), which gathered public views on a new General Comment on the right to life under Article 6 of the Interna-tional Covenant on Civil and Political Rights. Human Rights Committee, "Human Rights Committee Discusses Draft General Comment on the Right to Life," July 14, 2015, http://www.ohchr.org/EN/NewsEvents/Pages/DisplayNews.

60. Mara Hvistendahl recounts an interview with a UNFPA officer who stated, "How do you hold onto this discrimination tag and at the same time talk about safe abortion and access to it?" Hvistendahl, *Unnatural Selection,* 150.

61. Ibid., 151.

62. United Nations Fourth World Conference on Women, "Platform for Action," Beijing, China, September 1995, D.1, ¶ 15.

63. United Nations Fourth World Conference on Women, "Report of the Fourth World Conf. on Women."

64. United Nations Department of Public Information, "Women and Violence: Kinds of Violence against Women," DPI/1772/HR (February 1996), http://www.womenaid.org/press/info/violence/womenviolence.html.

65. See, e.g., United Nations Department of Economic & Social Affairs, Division for the Advancement of Women (UN Women), "Supplement to the Handbook for Legislation on Violence against Women: 'Harmful Practices' against Women," at 1, ST/ESA/331 (2011), http://www.un.org/womenwatch/daw/vaw/handbook/Supplement-to-Handbook-English.pdf.

66. Vardit Ravitsky, "Is Gender Selection of a Fetus Ethical?," *CNN*, August 16, 2011, http://www.cnn.com/2011/OPINION/08/15/ravitsky.gender.selection/.

67. See, e.g., *India's Missing Girls, Before the S. Comm. on Africa, Global Health, Global Human Rights, and International Organizations*, 113th Cong. 3–4 (2013) (Testimony of Jill McElya, J.D., Vice President of Invisible Girl Project). The hearing testimony recounts stories of women in India forced by family members to abort because the fetus was female.

68. Catharine A. MacKinnon, "Reflections on Sex Equality under Law," *Yale Law Journal* 100, no. 5 (1991): 1317n157.

69. Cherry, "A Feminist Understanding of Sex-Selective Abortion," 219.

70. Ibid., 155.

71. Christine Overall, "The Implications of Sex Selection" (review of *Gendercide*, by Mary Anne Warren), *Canadian Journal of Philosophy* 17, no. 3 (1987): 683.

72. Ibid., 683–92.

73. "Abortion is violence . . . It is the offspring, and will continue to be the accuser of a more pervasive and prevalent violence, the violence of rapism." Adrienne Rich, *Of Woman Born: Motherhood as Experience and Institution* (New York: Norton, 1976). See also Catharine A. MacKinnon, *Toward a Feminist Theory of State* (Cambridge, Mass.: Harvard University Press, 1989), 184–85.

74. See, e.g., Jack M. Balkin, ed., *What Roe v. Wade Should Have Said: The Nation's Top Legal Experts Rewrite America's Most Controversial Decision* (New York: New York University Press, 2007).

75. Robin West, "From Choice to Reproductive Justice: De-constitutionalizing Abortion," *Yale Law Journal* 118, no. 7 (2009): 1409.

76. MacKinnon, "Reflections on Sex Equality under Law," 1317n157.

77. Hvistendahl, *Unnatural Selection*, 7.

78. Isabelle Attané and Christophe Z. Guilmoto, "Introduction," in *Watering the Neighbour's Garden: The Growing Demographic Female Deficit in Asia*, ed. Isabelle Attané and Christophe Z. Guilmoto (Paris: Committee for International Cooperation in National Research in Demography, 2007), 3; Hvistendahl, *Unnatural Selection*, 15–16.

79. United States Department of State, "Country Narratives," *Trafficking in Persons Report 2013* (2013): 131, http://www.state.gov/j/tip/rls/tiprpt/2013/.

80. Council of Europe, Parliamentary Assembly, Resolution 1829, "Prenatal Sex Selection," ¶ 7, October 3, 2011, http://assembly.coe.int/nw/xml/XRef/Xref-XM L2HTML-en.asp?fileid=18020&lang=en.

81. Cherry, "A Feminist Understanding of Sex-Selective Abortion," 221–22.

82. *India's Missing Girls, Before the S. Comm. on Africa, Global Health, Global Human Rights, and International Organizations*, 113th Cong. 3–4 (2013) (statement of Sabu M. George, researcher and member of India's Campaign against Sex Selection).

83. Attané and Guilmoto, *Watering the Neighbour's Garden*, 1, quoted in Hvistendahl, *Unnatural Selection*, 17.

84. See, for example, Catharine A. MacKinnon, "Women's September 11th: Rethinking the International Law of Conflict," *Harvard International Law Journal* 47, no. 1 (2006): 1, 2.

85. Council of Europe, Resolution 1829, ¶ 8.7.

86. Ibid.

87. Wybo Dondorp et al., "ESHRE Task Force on Ethics and Law 20: Sex Selection for Non-medical Reasons," *Human Reproduction* 28, no. 6 (2013): 1448, 1450.

88. In 1996, the UN reported that "genetic testing for sex selection has become a booming business, especially in [India]'s northern regions. Indian gender-detection clinics drew protests from women's groups after the appearance of advertisements suggesting that it was better to spend $38 now to terminate a female foetus than $3,800 later on her dowry." United Nations Department of Public Information DPI/1772/HR. Indian women's rights advocates reacted by calling for a ban: "For [the Bombay Women's Center], it's the survival of women that's at stake. The social implications of sex selection are disastrous." Siddhivinayak S. Hirve, "Abortion Law, Policy, and Services in India: A Critical Review," *Reproductive Health Matters* 12, no. 24 (2004): 114. What they won was a law that bans sex determination. Pre-Natal Diagnostic Techniques (Regulation and Prevention of Misuse) Amendment Act, No. 14 of 2003, India Code (2003). Feminist and other advocacy groups brought a public interest litigation petition asking courts to enforce the act. The Supreme Court of India issued opinions in 2001 and 2003 denouncing the practice of sex-selective abortion and highlighting the problems of prohibiting sex determination. CEHAT v. Union of India, A.I.R. 2003 S.C. 3309; CEHAT v. Union of India (2001) 3 S.C.R. 534. In response, the legislature passed the Pre-conception and Pre-natal Diagnostic Techniques Act, which included stricter penalties for sex determination and further delineated the prohibited uses of ultrasounds.

89. Maneesha Deckha, "(Not) Reproducing the Cultural, Racial, and Embodied Other: A Feminist Response to Canada's Partial Ban on Sex Selection," *University of California Los Angeles Women's Law Journal* 16, no. 1 (2007): 8. Sex selection as a culturally harmful practice sits very comfortably with colonialist depictions of "orientalism." Edward W. Said, *Orientalism* (New York: Vintage Books, 1979), 3. Said defined "orientalism as a Western style for dominating, restructuring, or having authority over the Orient." Ibid.

90. Critiques of the dominance feminist position on sex selection—that feminists seek to upend cultural practices as "outsiders" who "change community by force" and enact a type of "cultural imperialism"—are difficult if not impossible to find in UN reports and in international human rights documents. Deckha, "(Not) Reproducing the Cultural, Racial, and Embodied Other," 1; see also Gail Weiss, "Sex-Selective Abortion: A Relational Approach," *Hypatia* 10, no. 1 (1995): 202, 212–13.

91. For example, in 2013, North Dakota legislators cited Hvistendahl's book *Unnatural Selection* and the argument that 160 million women are missing. Nick Smith, "Abortion Bills Kick Up Debate," *Bismarck Tribune,* March 12, 2013.

92. Marian V. Liautaud, "Genocide in Shades of Pink," *Christianity Today* 56 (December 2012): 32; Celeste McGovern, "New Prenatal Testing Could Drastically Increase Abortion Rate," *National Catholic Register,* June 25, 2012, http://www.ncregister.com/daily-news/new-prenatal-testing-could-drastically-increase-abortion-rate.

93. 18 Pa. Cons. Stat. Ann. § 3204(c) (1982) ("No abortion which is sought solely because of the sex of the unborn child shall be deemed a necessary abortion."); 720 Ill. Comp. Stat. Ann. 510/6-(8) (1975) (enjoined before viability).

94. Seven states have sex-selection bans in effect—Arizona, Pennsylvania, Oklahoma, North Dakota, North Carolina, South Dakota, and Kansas. Okla. Stat. tit. 63, § 1-731.2(B) (2012); 18 Pa. Cons. Stat. Ann. § 3204(c) (West 2012); Ariz. Rev. Stat. Ann. § 13-3603.02 (2013); H.B. 2253, 2013 Leg., Reg. Sess. (Kan. 2013); H.R. 1305, 63d Leg. Assemb., Reg. Sess. (N.D. 2013); S.D. Codified Laws § 34-23A (2014). At the time of writing, sex selection laws are not in effect in Arkansas (temporary injunction), Illinois (permanent injunction for previable abortions), and Indiana (permanent injunction). Ark. Code Ann. § 20-16-1804 (2017); 720 Ill. Comp. Stat. 510/6(8) (2012); Ind. Code Ann. § 16-34-4-5 (2016).

95. Susan B. Anthony and Frederick Douglass Prenatal Nondiscrimination Act, H.R. 1822, 111th Cong. (2009); Susan B. Anthony and Frederick Douglass Prenatal Nondiscrimination Act of 2011, H.R. 3541, 112th Cong. (2011). Sital Kalantry notes that PRENDA was reintroduced in 2012, 2015, 2016, and 2017. Sital Kalantry, *Women's Human Rights and Migration: Sex-Selective Abortion Law in the United States and India* (Philadelphia: University of Pennsylvania Press, 2017), 74.

96. PRENDA, § 250(a)-(b). Note that PRENDA also prohibits race-based abortions, which I address elsewhere (see, e.g., Rebouché, "Testing Sex," 521–22).

97. Ibid., § 2(a)(1)(A).

98. Ibid., § 2(a)(1)(L)(i).

99. Ibid., § 2(a)(1)(L)(ii–iii). PRENDA states that homicide is the most common cause of death of pregnant women.

100. "Pre-natal sex selection and sex-selective abortions are forms of discrimination against women and are symptomatic of the devalued status of women in society." World Health Organization et al., *Preventing Gender-Biased Sex Selection*.

101. PRENDA, § 2(a)(1)(H). PRENDA notes that the United States led a delegation at the UN Commission session condemning sex-selective abortion.

102. Ibid., § 2(a)(1)(I); Amartya Sen, "More Than 100 Million Women Are Missing," *New York Review of Books*, December 20, 1990, http://www.nybooks.com/articles/archives/1990/dec/20/more-than-100-million-women-are-missing/. Sen noted the paradox that son preference persists even at a moment when economic development in varying countries should be improving the lives of women and girls.

103. PRENDA, § 2(a)(1)(M).

104. Lauren Vogel, "Sex-Selective Abortions: No Simple Solution," *Canadian Medical Association Journal* 184, no. 3 (2012): 286.

105. PRENDA, § 2(a)(1)(E)–(F).

106. Ibid., § 2(a)(1)(J).

107. Ibid.

108. Ratna Kapur, "The Tragedy of Victimization Rhetoric: Resurrecting the 'Native' Subject in International/Post-Colonial Feminist Legal Politics," *Harvard Human Rights Journal* 15, no. 2 (2002): 1, 6.

109. Mohapatra writes, "In the United States, PRENDA and the sex-selective state laws seem more concerned with weakening a general right to choose rather than a sincere commitment to gender equality." Seema Mohapatra, "Global Legal Responses to Prenatal Gender Identification and Sex Selection," *Nevada Law Journal* 13, no. 3 (2013): 720. Hvistendahl notes reproductive rights organizations try to "dodge" the issue of sex-selective abortion. Hvistendahl, *Unnatural Selection*, 150.

110. For example, the Center for Reproductive Rights (CRR) has argued that PRENDA is a "dangerous and unconstitutional attack on access to health services." Center for Reproductive Rights, *2013 Mid-Year Report 3* (New York: Center for Reproductive Rights, 2013). Legal scholars also argue that constitutional privacy rights protect the practice of sex-selective abortion; few academics have disagreed. See, e.g., John A. Robertson, "Abortion and Technology: Sonograms, Fetal Pain, Viability, and Early Prenatal Diagnosis," *University of Pennsylvania Journal of Constitutional Law* 14, no. 2 (2011): 374. Compare Radhika Rao, "Equal Liberty: Assisted Reproductive Technology and Reproductive Equality," *George Washington Law Review* 76, no. 6 (2008): 1457. Rao argues that there may not be a constitutional right to sex-selective abortion, and "if the government chose to enforce a policy against sex-selection not by banning certain abortions, but rather by prohibiting prenatal testing to obtain information regarding the sex of the fetus, such a law would likely be constitutional." Ibid.

111. Planned Parenthood of S.E. Pa. v. Casey, 505 U.S. 833, 844–46, 872–76 (1992). An undue burden is "a state regulation [that] has the purpose or effect of placing a substantial obstacle in the path of a woman seeking an abortion of a nonviable fetus." Ibid., 877.

112. According to Kalantry, protecting abortion rights has been "the driving force in the mainstream liberal feminist movement in the United States." Kalantry, "Sex Selection in the United States and India," 75–76. Kalantry cites Tabitha Powledge: "To make it illegal to use prenatal diagnostic techniques for sex choice is to nibble away at our hard-won reproductive control, control that I think most of us believe is the absolute rock-bottom minimum goal we have got to keep achieved before we can achieve anything else." Tabitha M. Powledge, "Unnatural Selection: On Choosing Children's Sex," in *The Custom-Made Child? Women-Centered Perspectives,* ed. Helen B. Holmes et al. (New York: Humana Press, 1981), 193, 197.

113. Gonzales v. Carhart, 550 U.S. 124, 136–37, 168 (2007).

114. Ibid., 159.

115. PRENDA § 2(a)(1)(L)(iii).

116. Ibid., § 2(a)(1)(M). Arguments about postabortion regret and poor mental health consequences are contested and are prominent in U.S. anti-abortion strategies. Reva B. Siegel, "The New Politics of Abortion: An Equality Analysis of Woman-Protective Abortion Restrictions," *University of Illinois Law Review* 2007, no. 3 (2007): 1014.

117. Jeannie Suk Gersen argues the "legal discourse of abortion trauma grows out of ideas about psychological trauma that have become pervasively familiar in the law through the rise of feminism." Jeannie Suk, "The Trajectory of Trauma: Bodies and Minds of Abortion Discourse," *Columbia Law Review* 110, no. 5 (2010): 1193.

118. MacKinnon, "Reflections on Sex Equality under Law," 1317n157.

119. Justice Ginsburg, writing in dissent, remarked on the majority's anti-abortion language: "Throughout, the opinion refers to obstetrician-gynecologists and surgeons who perform abortions not by the titles of their medical specialties, but by the pejorative label 'abortion doctor.' " *Gonzales,* 550 U.S. at 186–87.

120. Ibid., 159–60.

121. Ronald Dworkin wrote of the *Gonzales* opinion, "If we understand Kennedy's opinion as intended to bolster the strength of the state interest in previable life then the opinion is much more radical than he lets on. It begins to undo the

well-established precedent that the state may not prohibit previable abortions and opens the door to future bans of previable abortion procedures based on visceral concerns about the sensibilities of the community and the medical profession." Ronald Dworkin, "The Court & Abortion: Worse Than You Think," *New York Review of Books,* May 31, 2007, 21.

122. Amy Swanson, Amy J. Sehnert, and Sucheta Bhatt, "Non-invasive Prenatal Testing: Technologies, Clinical Assays, and Implementation Strategies for Women's Healthcare Practitioners," *Current Genetic Medical Report* 1, no. 2 (2013): 114.

123. *Gonzales,* 550 U.S. at 160.

124. PRENDA, § 2(a)(1)(P).

125. Ibid. § 2(k)(10). PRENDA cites a working paper of the President's Council on Bioethics. Ibid. See also Michael Specter, "The Gene Factory," *New Yorker,* January 6, 2014, 34.

126. Dov Fox, "Interest Creep," *George Washington Law Review* 82, no, 2 (2014): 60. Fox argues that there is no precedent protecting fetuses under the Equal Protection Clause of the Fourteenth Amendment.

127. Amitai Etzioni, "Sex Control, Science, and Society," *Science* 161, no. 3846 (1968): 1109. Etzioni states, "Interracial and interclass tensions are likely to be intensified because some groups, lower classes and minorities specifically, seem to be more male oriented than the rest of the society." Ibid.

128. In a review of materials on the relationship between trafficking and son preference, I did not find evidence that the two practices were linked and only found commentary that predicted "how bad the male surplus will be." For example, Hvistendahl states: "Historically, societies in which men substantially outnumber women are not nice places to live. Often they are unstable. Sometimes they are violent." Hvistendahl, *Unnatural Selection,* 15. The leading demographer on the issue, Christophe Guilmoto, predicts "trouble in the marriage market," but both he and Hvistendahl offer anecdotal accounts of trafficking and bride buying. Ibid.

129. As noted in chapter 2 of this book, it is also part of a cultural feminist agenda to assert that women contribute distinct perspectives and participate in society in gender-defined ways. See Martha Chamallas, *Introduction to Feminist Legal Theory* (New York: Aspen Publishers, 2003), 53; Eva Brems, "Enemies or Allies? Feminism and Cultural Relativism as Dissident Voices in Human Rights Discourse," *Human Rights Quarterly* 19, no. 1 (1997): 136, 140.

130. A 1993 decision on the constitutionality of Germany's abortion law, issued by the Federal Constitutional Court of Germany, mentions the United States once, arguing that the lack of criminal restraints on abortion in the United States provides no legal means of curbing practices like sex selection. Bundesverfassungsgericht [BVerfG] [Federal Constitutional Court], May 28, 1993, 88 Entscheidungen des Bundesverfassungsgerichts [BVerfGE] at 122.

131. "State Policies in Brief: Abortion Bans in Cases of Sex or Race Selection or Genetic Anomaly," Guttmacher Institute, January 1, 2016, http://www.guttmacher .org/statecenter/spibs/spib_SRSGAAB.pdf; "State Policies in Brief: Abortion for Sex Selection Banned," Guttmacher Institute, August 1, 2017, https://www.gutt macher.org/state-policy.

132. Sneha Barot, "A Problem-and-Solution Mismatch," *Guttmacher Policy Review* 15, no. 2 (2002): 21. See also Katie McDonough, "Congressional Republicans

Try to Exploit India's 'Missing Girls' for Anti-choice Propaganda," *Salon,* September 16, 2013, http://www.salon.com/2013/09/16/congressional_republicans_try_to _exploit_indias_missing_girls_for_anti_choice_propaganda/.

133. NARAL wrote for the hearing, "But while sex-selective abortion may be an issue in various parts of the world, there is no data that it is a prevalent practice in the U.S." *Hearing on H.R. 3541 Before the Subcomm. on the Constitution of the H. Comm. on the Judiciary,* 112th Cong. app. A (2011): 187. The CRR argued, "In the United States as a whole, son preference is not a problem, and the data on the general population reflect this reality . . . To the extent that son preference exists in the United States, it is not a general problem, but exists only in a few communities . . . The impact of this limited son preference is negligible on the country as a whole." Ibid., 200. The National Asian Pacific American Women's Forum (NAPAWF) offered as evidence that populations of women suspected of son preference are less than 2 percent of the population. Ibid., 68.

134. The ACLU Reproductive Freedom Project and NAPAWF unsuccessfully challenged an Arizona law's ban on race-based abortions. ACLU, "Ninth Circuit Rules Women Have No Standing to Challenge Law That Forces Doctors to Racially Profile," December 16, 2015, https://www.aclu.org/news/court-dismisses-challenge -racist-arizona-abortion-ban. In 2016, however, Planned Parenthood and the ACLU won a temporary injunction of the Indiana sex selection ban. Emma Green, "Indiana Tried to Raise Ethical Issues to Abortion, But Will Probably Fail," *The Atlantic,* July 1, 2016, https://www.theatlantic.com/politics/archive/2016/07/indiana-tried-to -raise-ethical-challenges-to-abortion-but-will-probably-fail/489746/. And, in 2017, the ACLU and CRR won a temporary injunction of an Arkansas law that banned sex-selective abortion and required abortion providers to review the medical records of a patient's entire pregnancy history to vet the patient's reasons for termination. Christina Cauterucci, "Judge Blocks Arkansas Law That Could Have Forced Women to Notify Their Rapists of Abortions," *Slate,* July 31, 2017, http://www.slate.com /blogs/xx_factor/2017/07/31/judge_blocks_arkansas_law_that_could_have_made _women_notify_their_rapists.html.

135. Michael D. Hinds, "Federal Judge Blocks a New Anti-abortion Law in Pennsylvania," *New York Times,* January 12, 1990, http://www.nytimes.com/1990/01/12 /us/federal-judge-blocks-a-new-anti-abortion-law-in-pennsylvania.html.

136. Carole J. Peterson, "Reproductive Justice, Public Policy, and Abortion on the Basis of Fetal Impairment: Lessons from International Human Rights Law and the Potential Impact of the Convention on the Rights of Persons with Disabilities," *Journal of Law and Health* 28, no. 1 (2015): 131.

137. Erin Gloria Ryan, "Terribly Dumb Sting Operation Claims It Captures Planned Parenthood Endorsing Sex-Selective Abortion," *Jezebel,* May 29, 2012, http://jezebel.com/5913918/can-anti+choice-rascals-prove-planned-parenthood -endorses-sex+selective-abortion; Laura Bassett, "Planned Parenthood Sting Caught on Video, Released by Anti-abortion Activists (Video)," *Huffington Post Politics,* May 29, 2012, http://www.huffingtonpost.com/2012/05/29/planned-parenthood -video_n_1552672.html; Leslie Kantor and Carolyn Westhoff, "New Secret Hoax Campaign Another Tactic in the Wars over Safe Abortion Care and Women's Rights," *RH Reality Check,* April 23, 2012, http://rhrealitycheck.org/article/2012/04/23/secret -hoax-campaign-is-another-abortion-wars-tactic/.

138. "Sex-Selection in America Part 1," *Protect Our Girls,* May 29, 2012, http://protectourgirls.com/transcript-of-video/.

139. Planned Parenthood Federation of America (PPFA) issued the statement: "It is critical that we help the public understand the importance of providing non-judgmental, confidential care even when faced with difficult questions about deeply troubling issues such as sex selection motivated by gender bias." Planned Parenthood Federation of America (PPFA), press release, May 30, 2012 (on file with author). Given that Texas does not ban sex-selective abortion and PPFA does not deny women abortions based on the reason given, it is not clear what the "proper protocol" for PPFA employees should be. Ibid.

140. Most patients appear to use sex determination tests to have an equal number of sons and daughters, although it is clear that some fertility services, for example, target specific cultural groups that may favor sons to daughters. Sujatha Jesudason and Susannah Baruch, "Sex Selection: What Role for Providers," *Contraception* 86 (2012): 598.

141. One study compared sex ratios of "Blacks, Chinese, Filipinos, Asian Indians, and Koreans relative to Whites, while also comparing the sex ratio by order of birth in families with multiple children. The data suggests an occurrence of prenatal sex selection in Chinese, Asian Indian, and Korean families with 3 children or more." James F. X. Egan et al., "Distortions of Sex Ratios at Birth in the United States: Evidence of Prenatal Gender Selection," *Prenatal Diagnosis* 31 (2011): 560. doi:10.1002/pd.2747. A 2008 study documents skewed sex ratios among children born to parents with Chinese, Korean, or Indian ancestry in several states. The study similarly found that while the sex ratio for firstborn children was normal, subsequent children were much more likely to be male if there was no previous male child. Douglas Almond and Lena Edlund, "Son-Biased Sex Ratios in the 2000 United States Census," *Proceedings of the National Academy of Sciences* 105, no. 15 (2008): 5681.

142. Sunita Puri, Vincanne Adams, Susan Ivey, and Robert D. Nachtigall, "'There Is Such a Thing as Too Many Daughters, but Not Too Many Sons': A Qualitative Study of Son Preference and Fetal Sex Selection among Indian Immigrants in the United States," *Social Science and Medicine* 72, no. 2 (2011): 1169. doi: 10.1016/j.socscimed.2011.01.027.

143. Ibid.

144. For example, the UN and other international agencies have called for more and better data on the prevalence of sex selection—studies on what factors influence parents' decisions and why. World Health Organization et al., *Preventing Gender-Biased Sex Selection,* 8.

145. Barot, "A Problem-and-Solution Mismatch," 15. Sex selection occurs with assisted reproductive technology because patients can test embryos cultivated by in vitro fertilization (IVF) before implantation in the uterus. Parents can discard nonimplanted embryos or "selectively reduce" implanted embryos for any number of reasons, including gender. Judith F. Daar, "ART and the Search for Perfectionism: On Selecting Gender, Genes, and Gametes," *Journal Gender, Race, and Justice* 9 (2005): 249–50. The literature on physician experiences suggests that some IVF patients ask to select for fetal sex. Richard R. Sharp et al., "Moral Attitudes and

Beliefs among Couples Pursuing PGD for Sex Selection," *Reproductive Bio Medicine Online* 21 (2010): 845. doi:10.1016/j.rbmo.2010.09.009.

146. The University of Chicago International Human Rights Clinic, National Asian Pacific American Women's Forum, and Advancing New Standards in Reproductive Health, "Replacing Myths with Facts: Sex-Selective Abortion Laws in the United States," 2014, 15–17, https://ihrclinic.uchicago.edu/page/replacing-myths-facts -sex-selective-abortion-laws-united-states.

147. Osagie K. Obasogie declares that "between numerous newspaper and magazine articles, a report by the World Health Organization, and Mara Hvistendahl's new book *Unnatural Selection,* it is safe to declare this the 'Summer of Sex Selection' given widespread attention to the topic." Obasogie, "Are Skewed Sex Ratios in America's Future?," *Biopolitical Times,* June 30, 2011, http://www.biopolitical times.org/article.php?id=5775. See also Sujatha Jesudason and Anat Shenker-Osorio, "Sex Selection in America: Why It Persists and How We Can Change It," *Atlantic,* May 31, 2012, http://www.theatlantic.com/politics/archive/2012/05/sex-selection-in -america-why-it-persists-and-how-we-can-change-it/257864/.

148. The relevance of *how many* women are affected by a law has been the subject of U.S. abortion jurisprudence. The Supreme Court, in *Planned Parenthood of S.E. Pa. v. Casey,* rejected the state's argument that a spousal notification requirement was not an undue burden because "only one percent of the women who obtain abortions" were affected by the requirement. *Casey,* 505 U.S. at 894.

149. PRENDA, § 2(a)(1)(C).

150. For an analysis of noninvasive prenatal screening and fetal sex determination, see Rebouché, "Testing Sex," 519–25.

151. The *Journal of the American Medical Association* published a meta-analysis of fifty-seven studies on noninvasive testing for fetal sex, describing high levels of accuracy for the new tests. Stephanie A. Devaney et al., "Noninvasive Fetal Sex Determination Using Cell-Free Fetal DNA: A Systematic Review and Meta-analysis," *Journal of the American Medical Association* 306 (2011): 631–33. doi:10.1001/jama.2011.1114. See also Melissa Hill et al., "Non-invasive Prenatal Determination of Fetal Sex: Translating Research into Clinical Practice," *Clinical Genetics* 80, no. 1 (2010): 70. doi:10.1111/j.1399–0004.2010.01533.x.

152. See Ashwin Agarwal et al., "Commercial Landscape of Noninvasive Prenatal Testing in the United States," *Prenatal Diagnosis* 33, no. 6 (2013): 521. doi:10.1002/pd.4101.

153. Henry T. Greely, "Get Ready for the Flood of Fetal Gene Screening," *Nature* 469 (2011): 289. doi:10.1038/469289a.

154. Hill et al., "Non-invasive Prenatal Determination of Fetal Sex," 70.

155. Peterson, "Reproductive Justice, Public Policy, and Abortion on the Basis of Fetal Impairment," 121, 130.

156. Indian women's rights groups, for example, will not defend a right to abortion for any reason. Reporting on a meeting of Indian women's rights groups on the issue of sex-selective abortion, Filipovic reports: "No member of the meeting, according to Ipas, defended or supported sex-selective abortion . . . [and] positive messaging around safe, legal abortion is still nowhere near as widespread as warnings about the illegality of sex-selective abortion." Jill Filipovic, "The Unintended

Consequences of India's War on Sex Selection," *World Policy Journal* 33, no. 1 (2016): 78. doi:10.1215/07402775-3545954.

157. Lynne M. Kohm, "Sex Selection Abortion and the Boomerang Effect of a Woman's Right to Choose: A Paradox of the Skeptics," *William and Mary Journal of Women and the Law* 4, no. 1 (1997): 120.

158. U.S. state legislators increasingly want to know women's reasons for abortion. Currently, fifteen states require physicians to record a reason before performing an abortion, and all fifteen ask whether the abortion was performed because of a diagnosed fetal characteristic. "State Policies in Brief: Abortion Reporting Requirements," Guttmacher Institute, February 1, 2014, http://www.guttmacher.org/statecenter/spibs/spib_ARR.pdf. See also Elizabeth Nash et al., "Laws Affecting Reproductive Health and Rights: State Policy Trends in the First Quarter of 2017," Guttmacher Institute, April 12, 2017, https://www.guttmacher.org/article/2017/04/laws-affecting-reproductive-health-and-rights-state-policy-trends-first-quarter-2017.

159. "The Committee on Ethics supports the practice of offering patients procedures for the purpose of preventing serious sex-linked genetic diseases. However, the committee opposes meeting requests for sex selection for personal and family reasons, including family balancing, because of the concern that such requests may ultimately support sexist practices . . . Because a patient is entitled to obtain personal medical information, including information about the sex of her fetus, it will sometimes be impossible for health care professionals to avoid unwitting participation in sex selection." American College of Obstetricians and Gynecologists Committee on Ethics, "Sex Selection," *Obstetrics and Gynecology* 109 (2007): 1.

160. Sunita Puri and Robert D. Nachtigall, "The Ethics of Sex Selection: A Comparison of the Attitudes and Experiences of Primary Care Physicians and Physician Providers of Clinical Sex Selection Services," *Fertility and Sterility* 93, no, 7 (2010): 2111. doi:10.1016/j.fertnstert.2009.02.053.

161. Rachel Rebouché and Karen Rothenberg, "Mixed Messages: The Intersection of Prenatal Genetic Testing and Abortion," *Howard Law Journal* 53, no. 3 (2012): 992–98.

162. The prohibition of ultrasound (or other technologies) to determine fetal sex in India reportedly has chilled second-trimester abortion services because providers suspect women's motives for second-trimester terminations. Filipovic, "The Unintended Consequences of India's War on Sex Selection," 72.

163. Rebouché and Rothenberg, "Mixed Messages," 992.

164. Lori Freedman, *Willing and Unable: Doctors' Constraints in Abortion Care* (Nashville, Tenn.: Vanderbilt University Press, 2010), 37–59.

165. Complementing criminal tools, public education campaigns might focus on sending the message to pregnant women that sex selection is immoral and illegal.

166. Patients seeking prenatal genetic screening typically have higher incomes and education levels; they usually are educated and have better access to information about the genetic characteristics of potential children. Peter A. Benn and Audrey R. Chapman, "Ethical Challenges in Providing Non-invasive Prenatal

Diagnosis," *Current Opinion in Obstetrics & Gynecology* 22 (2010): 129; Bernard Dickens, "Ethical and Legal Aspects of Noninvasive Prenatal Genetic Diagnosis," *International Law Journal of Gynecology and Obstetrics* 124, no. 2 (2014): 183.

167. Filipovic, "The Unintended Consequences of India's War on Sex Selection," 75.

168. See Sarah Ditum, "Why Women Have a Right to Sex-Selective Abortion," *The Guardian*, September 19, 2013.

169. Kalantry makes this point in her book on sex selection in the United States and India, arguing that it is inaccurate to attribute all sex selection to culture and to coercion. Kalantry, *Women's Human Rights and Migration*, 8.

170. Hvistendahl, *Unnatural Selection*, 152–53 (describing the long history of the UNFPA avoiding the issue of sex selection in support of permissive abortion laws).

171. Adrienne Asch, "Disability Equality and Prenatal Testing: Contradictory or Compatible?," *Florida State University Law Review* 30, no. 2 (2002): 339; Deborah Pergament, "What Does Choice Really Mean? Prenatal Testing, Disability, and Special Education without Illusions," *Health Matrix* 23, no. 1 (2013): 56–57; Alicia Ouellette, "Intersections in Reproduction: Perspectives on Abortion and Assisted Reproductive Technologies: Selection against Disability: Abortion, ART, and Access," *Journal of Law, Medicine, and Ethics* 43, no. 2 (2015): 211.

172. Asch, "Disability Equality and Prenatal Testing," 339; Martha A. Field, "Killing 'the Handicapped'—Before and after Birth," *Harvard Women's Law Journal* 16, no. 2 (1993): 110; Mary Crossley and Lois Shepherd, "Genes and Disability: Questions at the Crossroads," *Florida State University Law Review* 30, no. 2 (2003): xi.

173. Ouellette, "Intersections in Reproduction," 212.

174. Debates leading up to the Convention on the Rights of Persons with Disabilities (CRPD) reflected concerns about how to address the social, clinical, and legal pressures that women face to abort disabled fetuses. During the CRPD drafting process, a working group recommended a "right to life" section, which was not included in the final text. A draft provision suggested that states revisit laws permitting abortion because of prenatal diagnosis. The language was omitted after protests from reproductive rights advocates. Peterson, "Reproductive Justice, Public Policy, and Abortion on the Basis of Fetal Impairment," 130, 150.

175. "Genetic Anomalies Abortion Ban," *Rewire*, http://data.rhrealitycheck.org /law-topic/genetic-anomalies-abortion-ban/; Nash et al., "Laws Affecting Reproductive Health and Rights."

176. H.B. 1305, § 2(1)(b), 63d Leg. Assemb. (N.D. 2013).

177. Anti-abortion laws increasingly focus on prenatal genetic counseling. In March 2014, Virginia enacted a law requiring licensing for genetic counselors and permitting counselors to refuse services that "conflict[] with the counselor's deeply-held moral or religious beliefs." Refusal "shall not form the basis for any claim of damages or for any disciplinary or recriminatory action against the genetic counselor, provided the genetic counselor informs the patient that he will not participate in such counseling and offers to direct the patient to the

online directory of licensed genetic counselors." Va. Code Ann. § 54.1-2957.21 (2014).

178. Rebouché and Rothenberg, "Mixed Messages," 992.

179. Deckha, "(Not) Reproducing the Cultural, Racial, and Embodied Other," 22–23; Cyra Choudhury, "Exporting Subjects: Globalizing Family Law Progress through International Human Rights," *Michigan Journal of International Law* 32, no. 2 (2011): 323.

180. Deckha, "(Not) Reproducing the Cultural, Racial, and Embodied Other," 8.

181. Kalantry writes that too often advocates assume that just because a practice has discriminatory implications and meanings in one country, it has the same implications and meanings in another. Kalantry, *Women's Human Rights and Migration*, 2.

182. Ibid., 8.

183. Gary Becker made this argument: a scarcity of women will mean that their value will increase and will prompt better treatment from parents and partners. His description of the "market" for women, in which there are more men than women, attracted rebuttals by feminists. Gary Becker, "Is Sex Selection of Births Undesirable?," *The Becker-Posner Blog,* February 12, 2007, http://www.becker -posner-blog.com/2007/02/is-sex-selection-of-births-undesirablebecker.html.

184. For marriage trends in the United States, which are changing based on income, race, age, geography, and other factors, see June Carbone and Naomi Cahn, *Marriage Markets: How Inequality Is Remaking the American Family* (New York: Oxford University Press, 2014), 107.

185. A blog in China caused outrage because its author proposed polyandry as the way to solve the gender imbalance and to give women bargaining power in intimate relationships. Didi Kirsten Tatlow, "Not Enough Women in China? Let Men Share a Wife, an Economist Suggests Polyandry in China," *Sinosphere* (blog), *New York Times,* October 26, 2015, http://sinosphere.blogs.nytimes.com/2015/10/26/china -polyandry-gender-ratio-bachelors/. For another iteration of a supply-demand argument, see Richard Posner's economic justifications for polygamy and son preference in some cultural contexts. Richard A. Posner, *Sex and Reason* (Cambridge, Mass.: Harvard University Press, 1992), 143–44.

186. South Korea banned sex-selective abortions and the number of girls born increased. The UNFPA attributed South Korea's success not to the ban but to changes in culture based on the "Love Your Daughters" media campaign. Woojin Chung and Monica Das Gupta questioned explanations that looked to "culture" generally and that ignored changes in the South Korean agricultural economy. Woojin Chung and Monica Das Gupta, "The Decline of Sex Preference in South Korea: The Roles of Development and Public Policy," *Population and Development Review* 33, no. 4 (2007): 777–78.

187. As argued by Uma Narayan, feminist campaigns against harmful cultural practices can stereotype women in the global South as "dupes of patriarchy." Uma Narayan, "Minds of Their Own: Choices, Autonomy, Cultural Practices, and Other Women," in *A Mind of One's Own: Feminist Essays on Reason and Objectivity,* ed. Louise M. Antony and Charlotte E. Witt (Boulder, Colo.: Westview Press, 2002), 418.

188. Chrisler, "A Global Approach to Reproductive Justice," 2.

189. Kalantry, "Sex Selection in the United States and India," 78. Choudhury writes, "Transnational collaborations must make space for subaltern agents to speak and act. If they do not, they risk disempowering poor women further and failing to reach the potential of feminist transnational advocacy." Choudhury, "Exporting Subjects," 323.

Distribution and Decision

Assessing Governance Feminism

JANET HALLEY

We have argued in the Preface to this book that as long as GF exists, feminists who wish to embrace it or who struggle with it should do so in what Max Weber called an ethic of responsibility.[1] There are many ways to do that. Here we offer one of them—doing a distributional analysis. The chief advantage of distributional analysis is that it is oriented not to the symbolic "norm announcing" function of law and legal institutions but to their distributional consequences. It asks of any particular element of governance: *what distributions does it leave in place, and what distributions does it shift?* Attempting to see distributions enables one to imagine *re*distributions. And that is where the ethic of responsibility engages. Once you see and imagine them, you can now ask: *Do you think they are good or bad?*

Doing a distributional analysis is a classic mode of work in critical legal studies (CLS).[2] Though it follows many of the steps of standard utility-maximizing welfare economics, it rejects the market-affirming premises that permeate that intellectual protocol and instead traces its roots back to Marx, through legal realism, and into the flowering of CLS in the 1980s and 1990s. Here, I set forth not a full theoretical statement of the motives and practices that have seemed to various laborers in this vineyard to help them trace distribution and imagine how to reshape it,[3] but a short how-to manual with theoretical backing brought in as sparely as possible to clarify the argument.[4]

You can do a distributional analysis in your mind while walking to an important meeting where you play a femocrat role or via a highly abbreviated e-mail huddle with allies; you can make it the form and substance of a long book. Basically, you are trying to identify the consequences of introducing a change in the status quo and then deciding whether they are "worth it." In this chapter, I elaborate three ideal, typical "steps" in a full-blown, completely elaborated distributional analysis, two of which have several substeps. Articulating even one of the substeps can be a major contribution.

Separating Is from Ought

If you want to know what the law *really is,* teaches Oliver Wendell Holmes, imagine it not suffused through the hazy filter of its moral justification but from the beady-eyed perspective of the bad man: the man who wants to maximize his gains and minimize his losses and who wants to know what the legal system will do—actually *do,* not just promise to do—to reward, help, hinder, block, fine, or imprison him.[5] What the legal system will actually do is, in this view, *what the law is.*

Holmes's attitude toward the bad man is hotly contested: he is the father of legal realism, and very diverse children claim his patrimony. The CLS reading detects no suggestion that Holmes aimed to affirm the bad man as a normative legal actor, an exemplar, a person we are permitted by realist legal theory to *be,* or the everyman whom lawmakers try and fail to control. The bad man, instead, is an imaginary standpoint: *looking at law the way he would look at it* allows one to *see* a particular legal order not for its vaunted merits but *as what it does.*

One aspect of this move, for Holmes, was peeling law apart from morality. Karl Llewellyn later called this "separating is from ought";[6] pushing one's own moral lenses to one side, to return to *later,* when the hard job of detached description is done. It is a very hard ethical discipline. The effort is to see the whole thing, not just the parts you already love and resent.

Identifying the Struggle and the Players

As David Kennedy puts it, the distributions achieved in social life are produced through struggle.[7] All the places GF emerges are such sites of struggle. To envision that struggle, he urges, we should think not of institutions like states and political parties but of *people with projects.*[8]

It is possible to think of the transaction you are concerned about either as a game with many players or as a zone of human concern marked by convergence and conflict. You can think of the various people involved in the game, in the struggle, as players, as stakeholders, as the end users of the legal system. Let us look at prostitution. Who besides the prostitute and the customer is involved? Do we see landlords? Madams? Pimps? Police? Clients? Johns? Brothels with institutional structures of their own? Neighbors? Communities? What about the husbands or boyfriends of the sex workers, or the wives of the clients? Does anyone have children to support? How do they interact among themselves? What are they seeking? What strategies do they follow, and why do they think those steps will lead them closer to their goals?

Envisioning people with projects makes it easier to stay attentive when players in struggle identify costs and benefits in surprising ways, as they often do. Here, again, we find a deviation from standard welfare economics: critical distributional analysis makes no assumption that goods are commensurable, zero-sum, or reducible to a single yardstick like "the dollar" or even "value." In sex, some are masochists: they seek suffering. In market exchange, some love to be benefactors: they tip big. Everyone is partly, if not mostly, crazy. Market rationality does not *begin* to capture the range of motives, desires, and aversions. To follow our sex markets example, some sex workers come into "the life" through force, or force of circumstances, and often underage. Collapsing the entire sex worker population under the rubric "underage victims of systematic rape" misses the fact that even those sex workers—to the extent that they had any opportunities for exit that they did not take—are in a different position later on, and have a very different profile of desires and goals than they did when they first began to trade sex for compensation. Equating all sex workers as sex slaves aggregates street sex workers, brothel-based workers, workers who become pimps or madams over time, and escorts: but a distributional analysis would be interested in the fact that any robust sex market differentiates. And it goes deeper than that: the affective life of a single sex worker is complex, irreducible to formulae about trauma and posttraumatic stress disorder. Would it be possible for a feminist to engage sympathetically with the prostitute's clients as people with projects? With the pimp or the madam? With the trafficker? These would be acts of imagination that could significantly expand the distributional analysis.

Identifying the Surplus at Stake

Now that you have the players, you can begin to think about the price each of them pays to be part of the struggle, and the gains they hope to capture by staying in it.

In the tradition of distributional analysis that Duncan Kennedy draws from Richard Ricardo and Karl Marx and through legal realism and CLS,[9] this analysis starts by identifying not the injury—the violence, the discrimination, the harm—in a given setting but the *surplus* it generates. What gain in human welfare—quantifiable like profits or nonquantifiable like pleasure or prestige—does a given struggle produce?[10]

This step alone radically departs from liberal and neoliberal assumptions about what an economy is and what the law does to help and hurt people engaged with each other in economic exchange. Liberal and neoliberal economic theory—both based on neoclassical economics—assumes that free-market exchanges motivated by individual preferences and unhampered by transaction costs leave all players better off. But Marxist economic theory posits that market exchanges produce a *surplus*—value over and above the bare costs of production—that can be appropriated by players with superior social power.[11] Liberal and neoliberal economic theory starts with an assumption that the distributions of the market are fair; redistribution under these circumstances is an appropriation needing a strong policy justification. It systematically denies even the existence of a surplus. But the latter sees the surplus as up for grabs, normatively, no matter where it actually ends up in exchanges among market actors. A distributional analysis that starts by identifying the surplus therefore posits from the start a normative question about the justice of its distribution, and thus the possibility of normatively justifiable redistribution.

This set of inconsistent assumptions then conditions the possibilities for law. Under liberal and neoliberal assumptions, legal intervention is justifiable only when business as usual goes awry. Call it John Stuart Mill's harm principle;[12] call it the will theory;[13] call it the freedom/force distinction;[14] call it political and civil emancipation.[15] The basic liberal idea is that people are and should be free until they interfere with the freedom of others, coerce others, harm others, or step into the sphere of action properly allocated to others. Then and only then can the state justifiably step in and restrict their freedom. In a freedom of contract regime, this means that trades are fair as long as they are not formed through force, fraud, or coercion. In a regime premised on the idea that employers and service providers are market-rational actors who seek the "right" gain from trade in every encounter with workers and customers, discrimination is a wrong because it robs transactions of their rationality.[16] Both of these approaches *take for granted the baseline distribution that the players would have gotten absent the harm or the force.* Suing a corporation for discrimination is seeking restoration of that presumed-market-rational deal. As Shamir argues in chapter 5, prosecuting a labor broker for trafficking effectively ratifies the legitimacy of all the labor deals made in the system that respect the contract freedom of the worker. Starting a distributional analysis by identifying the surplus, however, assumes that *all the social goods at stake in an exchange are distributed in the game and are normatively open to redistribution.*

However beneficial antidiscrimination law may be in strengthening the bargaining position of members of disadvantaged groups, there is no reason to adopt its freedom/force paradigm or its harm principle for analyzing complex distributional interactions, and good reason to suspect that exploitation of superior social power, subtended by law, will be exposed to view if we assume that a surplus is at play. Identifying the surplus thus involves framing the whole transaction, not just the act of violence or discrimination that may mar it. Identifying the surplus assumes that market transactions can achieve bad distributions—horribly unfair, immiserating, and exploitative ones—even when they are punctiliously free of force, fraud, or coercion; of legally recognized harm; and of discrimination. All the corporation's profits, all the allure of its stock on the stock exchanges, all its contracts with suppliers, all the wages and benefits, even all the fun, security, and résumé enhancement people enjoy by working for it, come within the frame.

A word on the frame. You cannot frame everything in. How far out do you look for players? In our sex work example, do you want to include the wives of customers?[17] How deep into the psyche do you want to go to find surprising forms of surplus? Any distributional analysis done with limited time and resources is subject to the depth/breadth trade-off: the deeper you go, the less broad your coverage will be, and vice versa. But the frame has to make sense to be a good fit with the political and intellectual problem that motivates the analysis in the first place. Ideally, your intended audience will recognize the frame as a fair way to divide the world into a small part that you are paying attention to and the infinitude of the rest, that vast zone you must leave out. This is an inductive and political question. Getting the frame right enough is part of the challenge.

One thing that does not make sense, ever, is to frame in only the losers. What are they losing, exactly? Who are they losing *to*? How triumphal are the winners in that transaction, and what do they lose to other, even more powerful players? Can you see them as losers too, by shifting the frame to include more of their struggle? Why were all these people in the game in the first place? It almost always makes sense to attend to local knowledge: if the sex workers think of and use their brothel not as a sweatshop or a prison but as a household—sharing daily chores and raising children there—you might want to try imagining it that way too.

But above all, you have now identified the surplus. How does it get distributed? Let us go back to our prostitution example. What are the goods sought by the people engaged in this particular form of human struggle? You could stop at monetary rewards; sorting that out would be a major contribution. But there is so much else at stake. Some sex workers value the entrepreneurial form of the labor, the flexible schedules, and the ability (if they have it) to limit their clientele to repeat players; others value the opportunity to work in a more cash-rich economic setting than they can find in their home country, even if they have to be among the lowest-paid workers and do the most dangerous work; others are fleeing from something close to starvation or homelessness and find sex work to be a step up. Sometimes their only realistic alternatives to sex work in the labor markets available to them are actually, in their view, more immiserating. The surplus sought by their customers is equally diverse: some seek to have sex that degrades and harms their partners, some intend rape, some are violent, and some like to conjoin sex with subordination. But others seek connection, the whole range of pleasures that come with sex minus a deep or domestic relationship; others seek danger; and others are ashamed of what they are doing and pursue commercial sex almost in a masochistic frenzy.

Many so-called pimps and madams are vicious exploiters, but others are not. Most of them have ended up as petty managers in a dangerous underworld sector not because they are full of power but because they lack it. Some of them are just eking by. Identifying the surplus is a work of imagination, just as seeing the law from the point of view of the bad man is an act of imagination. What do *these people with projects* see as a good they could extract from the struggle?

Bargaining in the Shadow of the Law — That Is, in the Shadow of the Background Rules

We imagine all the players in the struggle not so much governed by law as *conditioned* by it. They bargain with the other players not "under" the law but in its shadow, in the predictive range of their individual and collective guesses about what the law might do if X, Y, or Z happens. Following Lewis Kornhauser and Robert Mnookin, we call this bargaining in the shadow of the law.[18]

There will almost always be some glamorous, ideologically saturated legal rules that people focus on when debating a distributional system. These foreground rules will often be constitutional rights or crimes: freedom of contract / right to work; the crime of prostitution; trafficking as force, fraud, or coercion. They are not even half the story, however. Each of the player types has a deep field of background rules that condition its play.

Bargaining in the shadow of the background rules is a much more dynamic, crazily complex thing than determining whether a contract was free or forced or whether an employment contract was denied "because of sex." All but the most absolutely dominated and enslaved find material to work with in the background rules; rules can come in and out of importance depending on the state of play and its imagined trajectory; players have highly differing estimates of the costs and benefits of using various legally enabled strategies.

The legal theory classic that underlies Kornhauser and Mnookin's formulation is Robert Hale's 1923 article "Coercion and Distribution in a Supposedly Noncoercive State."[19] For Hale, the super-glamorous foreground rule was the U.S. Supreme Court's holding, in *Lochner v. New York*[20] and related cases, that the Due Process Clause of the Constitution required the Supreme Court to uphold the freedom of contract: the right of contracting parties to determine, without state interference, the terms of their agreement. In the *Lochner* case itself, this meant that a statute limiting the number of hours that bakers could be required to work—a statute that had been unanimously adopted by the New York legislature—was unconstitutional. All eyes were on this constitutional holding as the Supreme Court repeatedly blocked efforts by the legislative branch to regulate market exchange, often, as in *Lochner,* to protect the weaker party. But Hale moved to the background rules, specifically the rules of property, as the key to understanding the social encounter of the factory owner and the worker. And there, he argued, the liberal pairing of freedom (good) with coercion (bad) implied in the theory of freedom of contract was simply inapplicable: *all* contracts entered into by *all* parties—weak and strong—were coerced when their opponents in struggle used their law-endowed power to walk away from any particular deal. The property owner had a lot more of this power and could refuse to deal with the propertyless man up to and beyond the point where the latter starved. Property rules allowing property owners to refuse access to their property—whether it be a bag of peanuts, a plot of land to grow food on, the material needed to make a broom to sell, or a factory with shop-floor jobs on offer—gave them coercive power over the propertyless man seeking to relieve his hunger. Any deal he made with them was coerced. But the propertyless man had counter-coercive power endowed by the same body of law: he could refuse to work for this or that factory owner and drive up the wage all of them had to offer to obtain his labor. Any deal the factory owner made with its workers was also coerced.[21] Hale here follows Holmes and paves the way to Llewelyn in separating "is" from "ought," by demoralizing concepts fundamental to liberalism in order to see more clearly the operation of law in conditioning social bargaining.

Hale concludes: "The distribution of income . . . depends on the relative power of coercion which the different members of the community can exert against one another."[22] Doing a distributional analysis can enable you to analyze market interactions without requiring you to ratify neoliberal fantasies about free choice and universal agency or dominance feminist presumptions that the weaker party is abject. In this work, we assume that almost everyone has choices, and that almost all of those choices are constrained. Absolute dominations are surely possible, but are not ubiquitous or even frequent. Following

Hale, we see the systems in which surpluses are generated and power circulated as pervasively coercive, though differentially so, for everybody.[23] Everybody in them is trying hard to restrict the range of motion of other players and to use law to hold that range narrow. It is the distribution, not the fact that it is produced through pervasive coercion and counter-coercion, that provides the nexus of moral concern.

One thing that classic liberal analysis leaves out—as did Ricardo and Marx—but is crucial in any critical realist practice is the possibility that some or all of the players will actually break the rules.[24] The prostitutes in a legal brothel—bound by contracts to work in exchange for pay and unprotected by legal unionization—can nevertheless go on strike and force the madam to provide more security or to share more of the take with them. Tenants angry about the landlord's threats to exercise his legal rights can burn the tenement down.[25] The police can look the other way or take bribes.

Or the players can turn rules that look, on the face of it, like a problem for them into bargaining advantages. Legal rules *in action* are not simple; for instance, not only do duties often follow rights, but players can "flip" rights into duties and vice versa. Among Amanda Chong's migrant brides in Singapore, for instance, one woman turned her husband's sex-discriminatory monopoly over marital property rights, with its corresponding duty to pay the household bills, to her advantage by being a bad homemaker wife. It was her job to keep the books, and she stopped paying his monthly bills. Her husband promptly fell into debt, her bargaining power soared proportionately, and he had to drop his mistress to both save money and restore domestic peace.

Both illegality and perverse benefits converge when trafficking enforcement pushes prostitution underground, where it repeatedly morphs into a more dangerous and smaller enterprise that is also more profitable for some of the players. This is surely what Elizabeth Bernstein shows in her ethnographic comparison of end-demand regulation in Sweden and legalization in the Netherlands.[26] The Swedish sex market shrank, went underground, became concentrated with illegal immigrant workers, and became less safe for those workers. But making prostitution legal also distributes costs as well as benefits. As Bernstein also shows, legalization in the Netherlands brought regulation, which not only put sex workers onto social insurance but also priced small prostitution enterprises out of the market. Be prepared for paradoxes.

For sex workers at any given moment in the struggle, the key background rules can be landlord/tenant law, land use law, public transportation, access to social security, health care, banking and credit, a minor's incapacity to contract, social media facilities, and immigration law—even the rules governing the job they would be doing if they were not doing this one—domestic labor perhaps, or work in a kitchen or nursing home. Can the sex worker get a driver's license? The answer to that may lie in their probationary status with the misdemeanor court. Can he, she, or they get identification papers that match his, her, or their gender? The answer to that may depend on a struggle in the court of last appeal. Can he, she, or they use online communications to work directly with customers, and eliminate the madam and the pimp—and their background rules—entirely? The answer to that may lie in the bargaining power struggle over Backpage between dominance feminists and Craigslist. Pay attention to the permissions that emerge from the definitional limits of the law and from nonenforcement: the sex worker is not entitled to them—in Hohfeldian terms they are "no-rights"—but they are nevertheless legal permissions to act.[27] Do the same for the sex worker's clients and for any brokers he, she, or they works with.

Now, pull it all together: who is playing, with what tools, including what legal background rules, in pursuit of what fragment of the surplus, at what cost, and with what success? You can never describe it all. You have to typify. Underground markets will systematically defeat precision and even vague hunches. Your so-called information is only as good as the ideologies you used to make and collect it. But if you put your description forward modestly and with the appropriate provisos, you can do a lot better to assess a situation by describing its distributional consequences than by uttering slogans like "end demand" and "free the slaves."

Imagining It Otherwise

By now the advantages of postponing ought should be coming into view. It makes no sense to be against the deployment of power in these systems: everyone is doing it. And it makes no sense to determine in advance who is winning and who is losing until you know who is playing, with what tools, in pursuit of what fragment of the surplus, at what cost, and with what success.

It is also premature to decide who you are *for* until you have some sense of the distribution. It is not just unintended consequences, though that is a very important form of surprise in this process. You can acknowledge that rules that have been good for middle-class women in developed economies might backfire for poor women there or for women being entrepreneurialized in the developing world. The analytic can also shift your object of moral concern. You can think that the entrepreneurialization of women is good or bad because it empowers or exploits them, but find yourself worrying with new intensity that the fates of the men they love are rapidly declining.

Doing a distributional analysis discloses the large and tiny rules, buried deep in the background assumptions of a liberal legal order, that condition bargaining power. As a result, many more law reform targets come into view. For Hale, this meant that law reform projects that redistributed the social powers endowed by the rules of property became fair game. For example, the control that an industry accumulates to determine the activities of its workers can be distributed elsewhere:

> To take this control by law from the owner of the plant and to vest it in public officials or in a guild or in a union organization elected by the workers would neither add to nor subtract from the constraint which is exercised with the aid of the government. It would merely transfer the constraining power to a different set of persons. It might result in greater or in less actual power of free initiative all round, but this sort of freedom is not to be confused with the "freedom" which means absence of governmental constraint.[28]

Doing a distributional analysis thus opens up for challenge the deep background assumptions built into the rules of the game.

The options for change are equivocal in their operation, of course: you can do harm as well as good by keeping them as well as by changing them. Many small rules are softer targets than the highly ideologized foreground rules, where doctrinal impasses—war, or truce in an ongoing war—sediment themselves into seemingly permanent patterns. They can be ticked in various directions, to influence various distributions, in incremental and major ways; small changes can concatenate into so many ever-larger ones until the overall system is transformed, for good or for ill.[29] It can be more revolutionary to work on the small rules than to issue thumping denunciations.

But summing up the distributional analysis is where ought really begins. By that we do not mean deontological morality deducing commands from principles of human dignity. We mean increasing the equality of the distribution of income and other social goods in a world where inequality is both vast and growing. We mean redistribution by changing the rules of the game. We are, in short, leftists.

Doing a distributional analysis can be good for feminists confronting the myriad dilemmas posed by the entrance of feminism into governance. Some forms of feminism now have some control over some rules and some enforcement decisions: denying this strikes us as irresponsible. But affirming it does not require feminists to assume they are somehow to be glorified for everything good and blamed for everything bad that happens in the wake of their reforms. The users of the legal system play a huge role in determining the outcomes, as do, of course, the liberalism, neoliberalism, religious conservatism, and carceralism with which so many feminist reforms have gone to bed. Feminists following the surplus can reassess their achievements, repoliticize internal feminist debates about them, invent and tailor new goals, and live as responsible governors. In Max Weber's term, they can opt out of an ethic of absolute ends and adopt an ethic of responsibility.[30]

Deciding how and even where to do this is a daunting task. Take Shamir's story of how Israel transformed its prostitution market in response to U.S. anti-trafficking reputational sanctions. By the conclusion of this campaign, the Eastern European migrant sex workers were all repatriated, the shelters were mostly empty, and the prostitution segment of the sex sector was back in the hands of Israeli sex workers. Good or bad? Hard to say. It is possible that the migrant workers were better off now—but they could also be much worse off. It is possible that the Israeli sex workers demand, and get, a safer, more remunerative operation than the system needed to provide the migrants. Is that good, in that sex work is now more profitable for them, or bad, in that it is more attractive than ever despite its social stigma and aspects of illegality? It is possible that Israel's catastrophic love affair with border control has been intensified by this "success" story. Our sense is that morals alone will not help you pick among these visions of the outcome, that you need politics as well, and that feminist politics alone will not get you all the way to a decision. But an ethic of responsibility can directly confront, rather than blindspot, the challenge of that indeterminacy.

Doing a distributional analysis can pave the way for engagement. But it makes *enchanted* engagement much harder. Now you can see that to help your friends you might have to hurt some group of even less well-off players; that not all players enjoying more bargaining power than your friends are evil dominators (some of them may have merely a different, slightly higher-ranking but similarly precarious perch in an asymmetric game); and that you can befriend a group without completely understanding its own investment in the game and misconstrue what the people in it think is their best outcome. You cannot intervene while keeping your hands clean.

The temptation at this point is to wait for more information or work harder on your justifications. These can be exactly the right reactions to moments of doubt, uncertainty, and ignorance. But if you wait forever for these blessings, you run the risk that they will never fully materialize. Indeed, they are very unlikely to. Your information is not merely partial; its very constitution as information is an achievement of ideological precommitments that are invisibly baked into the facts. You are not a god of knowledge capable of rising entirely above this enmeshment of knowledge with power. And the minute you think your justifications fully warrant what you plan to do, you become a danger to society: you are now a zealot who will stop at nothing.

We believe, instead, that the information and the justifications are indeterminate not only for those who admit it but also for those who do not, and that it is more responsible to admit it. You have to leap to decide. The great goal we have for GF is that its participants take this leap *while* maintaining a critical analysis of it. We envision feminists as decisionists, both as actors and as analysts:

> If the decisionist is a responsible actor, and time has run out at the same time "the law" has, then she accepts that she will just have to "do it" on the basis of intuition rather than with a "warrant." The decisionist as analyst, on the other hand, wants to talk about how we can understand decisions that are underdetermined by the discourse that is supposed to guide them. This inquiry into the intelligibility of the indeterminate can have either a normative or a descriptive focus—either on making

ethical sense of underdetermined action, or figuring out how the existence of denied lacunae in normative systems modifies their operation
as normative facts (internalized by actors) in the world.[31]

Whether disenchanted critical engagement takes the form of action
or analysis, it consistently involves making decisions—large and
small—under conditions of indeterminacy. Responsible governance is
not perfect governance; rather, it is critically engaged governance.

Notes

1. Max Weber, "Politics as a Vocation," in *The Vocation Lectures,* ed. David
Owen and Tracy B. Strong, trans. Rodney Livingstone (Indianapolis: Hackett Publishing Company, 2004), 83. For a discussion, see the Preface, xiv–xvi.
2. See, e.g., Duncan Kennedy, "Sexual Abuse, Sexy Dressing, and the Eroticiza-
tion of Domination," in *Sexy Dressing, Etc.* (Cambridge, Mass.: Harvard University
Press, 1993): 126–213; Amanda Wei-Zhen Chong, "Migrant Brides in Singapore:
Women Strategizing within Family, Market, and State," *Harvard Journal of Law and
Gender* 37, no. 2 (2014): 331–405; Prabha Kotiswaran, "Born unto Brothels—Toward
a Legal Ethnography of Sex Work in an Indian Red-Light Area," *Law and Social
Inquiry* 33, no. 3 (2008): 579–629; Benjamin E. Apple, "Mapping Fracking: An Anal-
ysis of Law, Power, and Regional Distribution in the United States," *Harvard Envi-
ronmental Law Review* 38, no. 1 (2014): 217–44; Hila Shamir, "The State of Care:
Rethinking the Distributive Effects of Familial Care Policies in Liberal Welfare
States," *American Journal of Comparative Law* 58, no. 4 (2010): 953–86; Philomila
Tsoukala, "Gary Becker, Legal Feminism, and the Costs of Moralizing Care," *Columbia
Journal of Gender and Law* 16, no. 2 (2007): 357–428; Havva G. Guney-Ruebenacker,
"An Islamic Legal Realist Critique of the Traditional Theory of Slavery, Marriage,
and Divorce in Islamic Law" (S.J.D. diss., Harvard Law School, 2011).
3. For a more thorough theoretical statement than I attempt here, see David
Kennedy, "Law and the Global Dynamics of Distribution," in *A World of Struggle:
How Power, Law, and Expertise Shape Global Political Economy* (Princeton, N.J.:
Princeton University Press, 2016), 171–217.
4. For another, similar effort to present the effort stepwise, see Kennedy, "Struggle:
Toward a Cartography of Engagement," in *A World of Struggle,* 54–86.
5. Oliver Wendell Holmes, "The Path of the Law," *Harvard Law Review* 110, no.
5 (1997): 991–1009 (a centennial reprinting of an address delivered by Justice Holmes
in 1897 and originally printed in the *Harvard Law Review* that same year).
6. Karl N. Llewellyn, "Some Realism about Realism—Responding to Dean
Pound," *Harvard Law Review* 44, no. 8 (1931): 1222–64.
7. Kennedy, "Struggle," 59.
8. Ibid., 66–69.
9. Duncan Kennedy, "Analyzing Distribution: Ricardo, Marx, CLS" (unpub-
lished manuscript, March 12, 2013), Microsoft Word file.

10. Kennedy, "Law and the Global Dynamics of Distribution."

11. Richard D. Wolff and Stephen A. Resnick, *Contending Economic Theories: Neoclassical, Keynesian, and Marxian* (Cambridge, Mass.: MIT Press, 2012), 27–28.

12. John Stuart Mill, *On Liberty* (London: J. W. Parker and Son, 1859).

13. Duncan Kennedy, "Three Globalizations of Law and Legal Thought: 1850–2000," in *The New Law and Economic Development: A Critical Appraisal,* ed. David M. Trubek and Alvaro Santos (Cambridge: Cambridge University Press, 2006), 19–73.

14. For a discussion, see chapter 2, 28–29.

15. Karl Marx, "On the Jewish Question," in *The Marx-Engels Reader,* 2nd ed., ed. Robert C. Tucker (New York: W. W. Norton & Company, 1978), 26–52.

16. Mark Kelman and Gillian Lester, "Ideology and Entitlement," in *Left Legalism / Left Critique,* ed. Wendy Brown and Janet Halley (Durham, N.C.: Duke University Press, 2002), 134–77.

17. Prabha Kotiswaran, "Wives and Whores: Prospects for a Feminist Theory of Redistribution," in *Sexuality and the Law: Feminist Engagements,* ed. Vanessa E. Munro and Carl F. Stychin (London: Routledge-Cavendish, 2007), 283–303.

18. Lewis Kornhauser and Robert H. Mnookin, "Bargaining in the Shadow of the Law: The Case of Divorce," *Yale Law Journal* 88, no. 5 (1979): 950–97.

19. Robert L. Hale, "Coercion and Distribution in a Supposedly Non-coercive State," *Political Science Quarterly* 38, no. 3 (1923): 470–94.

20. Lochner v. New York, 198 U.S. 45 (1905).

21. Hale, "Coercion and Distribution," 470–79.

22. Ibid., 478.

23. Ibid., 470–94.

24. Kennedy, "Analyzing Distribution," 32–33.

25. Ibid., 34. This is Duncan Kennedy's example—vividly real in the agricultural land contracts he describes.

26. Elizabeth Bernstein, "The State, Sexuality, and the Market," in *Temporarily Yours: Intimacy, Authenticity, and the Commerce of Sex* (Chicago: Chicago University Press, 2007): 142-66.

27. Wesley Newcomb Hohfeld, "Some Fundamental Legal Conceptions as Applied in Judicial Reasoning," *Yale Law Journal* 23, no. 1 (1913): 30.

28. Hale, "Coercion and Distribution," 478.

29. Kennedy, "Analyzing Distribution," 39–43.

30. Weber, "Politics as a Vocation."

31. Duncan Kennedy, "A Semiotics of Critique," *Cardozo Law Review* 22, no. 4 (2001): 1163. For Kennedy's discussion of the tradition of decisionism that he derives from Nietzsche, Schmitt, Sartre, and Camus, see ibid., 1161–69.

Acknowledgments

This book, *Governance Feminism: An Introduction,* and its sequel, *Governance Feminism: Notes from the Field,* gather conversations and labors spanning almost fifteen years. We owe many thanks to all our coworkers, interlocutors, contributors, and resisters.

We owe special thanks to a few people who have organized with us, written with us, criticized our drafts, broken bread with us, and labored in the vineyard of feminist law reform with us over these many years. They include Libby Adler, Aziza Ahmed, Elizabeth Bartholet, Karen Engle, David Kennedy, Duncan Kennedy, Jeannie Suk Gersen, and Chantal Thomas. Without their clear-eyed critical and activist energies, we would have lost our way in this project dozens of times.

We particularly want to note our gratitude, admiration, and love for Helen Reece, who joined the project midway into its development and died, so young, before we brought it to fruition. Helen exemplified the courage, honesty, and willingness to engage—even when intense political pressure threatened to shut down the space for internal critique—that we think are needed by all of us who seek to participate as responsible feminist governors. We dedicate this book to Helen in thanks and in mourning.

This has been a remarkably interlocutory process, built over a series of conferences that we organized in Cambridge and Dighton, Massachusetts; London; and Tel Aviv over our many years' effort to figure out what was happening to governance as some feminists and feminist ideas entered it, and what was happening inside feminism as this shift in its capacities evolved. Those who inspired us and helped us on sex, sexuality, gender, and the family include Lila Abu-Lughod, Libby Adler, Aziza Ahmed, Helena Alviar Garcia, Elizabeth Bernstein, Mary Anne Case, Cyra Choudhury, Janie Chuang, Amy J. Cohen, Dan Danielsen, Adrienne Davis, Karen Engle, Pascale Fournier, Anne T. Gallagher, Jacob Gersen, Leigh Goodmark, Aeyal Gross, Aya Gruber, Rema Hammami, Vanja Hamzić, Isabel Cristina Jaramillo Sierra, Nkatha Kabira, Lisa Kelly, David Kennedy, Duncan Kennedy, Karen Knop, Gillian Lester, Maleiha Malik, Sally Engle Merry, Kate Mogulescu, Vasuki Nesiah, Diane Otto, Helen Reece, Annelise Riles, Kerry Rittich, Darren Rosenblum, Jeannie Suk Gersen, Chantal Thomas, and Mariana Valverde. As we tested the idea of governmentality against various theoretical and actual framings of the state, we learned much from Raanan Alexandrovitch, Ori Aronson, Ritu Birla, Yishai Blank, Talia Fisher, Aeyal Gross, Daphna Hacker, Kevin Kolben, Roy Kreitner, Orly Lobel, Doreen Lustig, Zina Miller, Guy Mundlak, Adi Ophir, Issachar Rosen-Zvi, Gila Stopler, Yofi Tirosh, Dana Weiss, Neta Ziv, and Raef Zreik. Hester Eisenstein and Marian Sawer generously updated us on the Australian femocrats. We gained immensely from the outside reviews contributed by Kristin Bumiller and an anonymous reviewer and from the comments on earlier drafts from Karen Engle, Duncan Kennedy, Kerry Rittich, and Holger Spamann.

All of us have learned so much from exchanges with our students at Harvard Law School; the Dickson Poon School of Law, King's College London; the School of Oriental and African Studies, London; the University of Florida Levin College of Law; Temple University Beasley School of Law; the Tel Aviv University Buchmann Faculty of Law; and the University of California at Berkeley. Shamir's spring 2015 course on Governance Feminism at UC Berkeley provided a particularly timely and intense laboratory for ideas that appear in these books. Thanks to all our students for their critical passion for social justice.

In conferences large and small we have benefited from opportunities to explore the implications of Governance Feminism, and we want to thank the many generous institutional sponsors of these events. Support for the initial exploratory mini-conference "Governance Feminism?," held in Cambridge, Massachusetts, in March 2006, was provided by the Harvard Law School Program on Law and Social Thought. We also thank the Minerva Center for Human Rights and the Paula Goldberg Fund for International Law at the Tel Aviv University Buchmann Faculty of Law, the Program on Law and Social Thought at Harvard Law School, and the University of Florida Levin College of Law for sponsoring our conference "Governance without a State? Governmentality in a Global World," held in June 2012 at the Tel-Aviv University Buchmann Faculty of Law, and our study tours of East Jerusalem (led by Ir Amim) and of Hebron (led by Breaking the Silence) in connection with that conference. We particularly thank Zina Miller and Rob Blecher for help in organizing those events. We thank the Dickson Poon School of Law, King's College London, for supporting and housing the "International Workshop on Governance Feminism" in May 2014, and the Law and Society Association for including the panel "Governance Feminism" in its 2015 annual meeting in Seattle, Washington.

We thank the Rosalinde and Arthur Gilbert Foundation's Israel Studies Colloquium; the Stanford Law School Law and Humanities Workshop; the Berkeley Institute for Jewish Law and Israel Studies Colloquium; the Tel-Aviv University Faculty of Law Faculty Workshop; the College of Law and Business (Ramat Gan) Faculty Workshop; the Law, Globalization, and the Transnational Sphere Project at the Minerva Center for Human Rights at Tel-Aviv University; the International Law Workshop at Tel-Aviv University for inviting Shamir to present her chapter in this book; and the Harvard Law School Faculty Workshop for inviting Halley to present Part I and the Conclusion of this book. Kotiswaran is grateful to the Jindal Global Law School; the Centre for South Asian Studies, University of Toronto; and the Centre for Women's Development Studies and the Centre for the Study of Law and Governance, Jawaharlal Nehru University, for opportunities to present her chapter in their respective seminar series. She also thanks the organizers of the Law and Social Sciences Network Conference for hosting a Consent Roundtable, where she shared the key arguments of her chapter. She is also grateful to Brenna Bhandar for organizing the Workshop on Taking Account of Postcolonial Legal Theory, at the School of Law at Queen Mary University of London, where Kotiswaran presented her chapter. Finally, we thank the Temple University Beasley School of Law Faculty Colloquium, the University of Richmond School of Law Emroch Faculty Colloquy Series, the Vulnerability and the Human Condition Workshop on Reproduction and

Sexuality, the Southeastern Association of Law Schools 2013 Annual Conference, and Northeastern Law Workshop on Sexuality and Reproduction for inviting Rebouché to present her chapter.

The Harvard Law School Institute for Global Law and Policy (IGLP) has been a steadfast supporter, providing funds for the conference "Reproduction and Sex in Contemporary Governmentalities: Governance Feminism and Its Others," held at Dighton, Massachusetts, September 2011, and for "Governance Feminism: A Writer's Workshop," at which contributors to both books presented works in progress, held at Harvard Law School, January 2015. We are also grateful to the IGLP for including the panels "Governance Feminism: Sex, Reproduction, and the Family" and "Rethinking 20 Years of Feminist Law Reform on Sexual Violence" in its June 2013 conference, and for staging "Roundtable on Governance Feminism" in its June 2015 conference at Harvard Law School.

Indeed, we have benefited so much from all these conversations that it is important to note that all errors of fact and judgment remain our own.

We have also benefited from many forms of institutional support. Kotiswaran in particular is grateful for a Leverhulme Trust Prize (Award Number PLP-2014-387), and Shamir to the Israel Science Foundation (Grant No. 1697/15); this support enabled them to dive deeply into the political and legal events that they analyze in their chapters.

Richard W. Morrison, our first editor at the University of Minnesota Press, and now at Fordham University Press, gave us crucial advice at the outset of our work toward these books; and our new editor, Jason Weidemann, has been a steadying force ever since he stepped into the role. The librarians at all of our schools—Harvard Law School; the Dickson Poon School of Law, King's College London; the School of Oriental and African Studies, London; the University of Florida Levin College of Law; Temple University Beasley School of Law; the Tel-Aviv University Buchmann Faculty of Law; and the University of California at Berkeley—have been stalwarts as we sought materials from all over the world. Terry Cyr, Michal Locker-Eshed, Caitlin Harrington, and Gemma Noyce provided support for every aspect of our work on this project, from teaching to conferences to research to coordinating incoming manuscripts. We were so lucky to have the stellar research and editing assistance of Beanka Chiang, Theo Cornetta, Sarah M. Deibler, Daniel Fishelovich, James Glowacki, Kelsey Grimes, Laura Lazaro Cabrera, Karin Rotenberg, and Sharon Salinas.

Above all, we thank critically engaged feminists around the world who inspired this project and whose work we hope these books will strengthen.

Index

abortion bans: reason-based, 210, 211, 213, 219, 221–22, 227–29, 245n134, 248nn158–59; of sex selection, 203–4, 218–19, 225–26, 231–32

abortion rights, 235n21, 237n39; dominance feminists' resistance to, 203, 213–33; GF's engagement with, xvii, 15, 201; liberal feminists' arguments for, 202–3, 210, 213–33, 243n112. *See also* fetuses, rights of; human rights; reproductive rights

abortions: laws against, 201, 237nn32–34, 244n130, 248n158, 249n174; previability, 201, 219, 220, 221, 225, 243–44n121; race-based, 245n134; safe, 239n60; Supreme Court rulings, 26–27, 40, 209–10; and trauma, 243nn116–17; U.S. federal funding for, 237n33, 238n46; as violence against women, 214, 240n73. See also *Gonzales v. Carhart* (2007); *Planned Parenthood of Southeastern Pennsylvania v. Casey* (1992); *Roe v. Wade* (1973); sex-selective abortions

acid attacks, India, 97, 98, 111–12, 130, 138–39n84, 220

ACLU Reproductive Freedom Project, 245n134

Adler (Chief Judge), 192n70

adultery, 146n210

aggravated rape, 98, 101, 113, 116–17, 118–19, 122. *See also* power rape; rape

aggravated sexual assault, 92, 94, 97, 138n77, 139n87, 140n105. *See also* sexual assault

Agnes, Flavia, 94–95, 109

Agustín, Laura M., 135n18

Ailes, Roger, 12

All-India Democratic Women's Association (AIDWA), 137n68

Ambai (C. S. Lakshmi), story by, 133

American Congress of Obstetricians and Gynecologists, on sex selection, 227

Americans United for Life, 230–31

Amir, Menahem, 189n31

Amnesty International, on sex trafficking in Israel, 158–59, 163

anti-abortion movement, U.S., xvii, 211, 216–26, 227. *See also* abortion bans

Anti-Prostitution Loyalty Oath (APLO), 44

anti-trafficking campaigns, 10, 14, 80, 135n18, 193n80. *See also* trafficking

275

Israeli anti-trafficking campaigns, 174–84; of legal changes, 113; separating is from ought, 254, 260, 262–63, 264; of sex work markets, 255–56, 258–59, 262

divorce, x, 10–11, 147n220, 147n222; in India, xviii, 93, 124–27

domestic violence, xviii, 8–9, 21n24, 66, 109, 121, 138n82, 213. *See also* Protection of Women from Domestic Violence Act of 2005 (PWDVA, India); violence against women

dominance feminism, 25, 31–39; and anti-human trafficking campaigns, xvi, xvii, xix, 14, 156, 162–63, 166–84; assistance to trafficking victims, 166–69, 170–74; liberal feminism's relationship with, xix–xx, 29, 34, 39–44, 47, 213–14; presumptions of, 260–61; resistance to abortion rights by, 203, 213–33; sex selection opposed by, xix, 202, 212, 219–25, 231; U.S., xvii, 161; use of term, 76. *See also* neo-abolitionist feminism

dominance feminism, Israel: anti-trafficking campaign, xvi, 114, 156, 162–63, 166–84; collaboration with the state, 150

domination, male, xiii, 231; female subordination and, 32–33, 34, 36–37, 60–61; prostitution as, 37–38, 158; in and as sexuality, 34, 35–36. *See also* men

dowries / dowry deaths, 126, 146n211, 211, 212, 241n88. *See also* marriage

dual systems theory, 106, 142n130. *See also* intersectionality, theory of

Dworkin, Ronald, 243–44n121

Echols, Alice, xiii, 32, 36
economic dominance, 96, 97, 139n87
economic theories. *See* capitalism; distributional analysis; Marxism
Ecuador, Bedford's essay on, 65, 67–68

Egypt, Israel's border with, 154, 155, 184, 195–96n114

Eisenstein, Hester, 62–63, 64–65

emancipation: feminist project of, x–xi, xii, 32–33, 34, 36; political/civil, 256–57; social movements seeking, 57

employment: equal access to, 11–13, 30, 34, 237n39; sexual harassment in, 75–76, 109, 121–23

end-demand legislation: Israel, 150, 155, 163, 165, 173–74, 184–85; Sweden, 197n132, 261; U.S., 9, 40. *See also* johns, criminalization of

England, conditional consent standard in, 120

entryism, use of term, 62

equality, as liberal feminism ideal, 25–31. *See also* gender: equality/inequality in; socially redistributive equality; substantive equality

Equal Rights Amendment, xiii, 13

essentialism, 35; strategic, 58, 59

ethic of absolute ends, 264

ethic of conviction, xiv–xv

ethic of responsibility, xiv, xv–xvi, xx, 5, 56, 253, 264–65

Etzioni, Amitai, 244n127

exploitation, 46, 109, 257; class, xiii, 32, 35–36, 44–47, 142n130; labor, 32, 152–53, 170, 181–83, 185; rehabilitation package for victims of, 149–50, 154, 163; sexual, 37, 44, 152, 185, 214–15; of sex workers, xix, 163–64, 173–76, 180; of women, xix, 37, 175, 214, 232. *See also* forced labor; slavery

family, 34, 105, 106, 199, 214; hetero-patriarchal, 82–83; market and, 10–13, 38, 66–67; pressure on women from, 114, 122, 216, 223, 229, 240n67; rape by members of, 98, 118–19, 120–21, 124, 126. *See also* children; parenthood

family planning, 205–6, 207, 212, 237n34, 248n159

intact dilation and evacuation (intact D&E), 219, 220. *See also* abortions
Inter-ministerial Committee to Formulate Policy on the Issue of Human Trafficking (Israel), 190–91n54
International Commission of Jurists, Yogyakarta Principles, 47–48n1
International Conference on Population (1984), 205
International Convention on Population and Development (ICPD) Programme of Action (1994), 236n28, 236n31; on abortion rights, 204, 206–7, 208–9
International Covenant on Civil and Political Rights, 239n59
International Criminal Court (ICC), 23, 41
International Criminal Tribunal for the Former Yugoslavia (ICTY), 42
International Planned Parenthood Foundation, feminist-aligned politics of, 206
intersectionality, theory of, 104, 106, 132, 142n131. *See also* dual systems theory
Interventions for Support, Healing, and Awareness (India), 137n68
Isha L'Isha ("Woman to Woman") feminist center (Israel), 161, 190n138, 192n65
Israel: dominance feminist activism in, 14; Egyptian border, 154, 155, 184, 185–86, 195–96n114; immigrant prostitution in, xvii, xix; Palestinian citizens of, 187n18. *See also* anti-trafficking campaigns, Israel; borders, Israel; immigration, to Israel; Knesset; labor market, Israel; migrant sex workers, Israel; prostitution, Israel
Israel Penal Code: abolitionist approach to prostitution, 171–72; criminalization of trafficking under, 166, 169; provisions relating to prostitution, 157–58, 159–60, 190n42

Jaising, Indira, 109, 122, 140n111
Jeannette Rankin Brigade, xiii
Jews: favored over non-Jewish migrants, 177, 178; migration to Israel, 145n199, 150, 153–55, 177, 181, 183, 199n145
John, Maya, 104–7, 130, 132, 141–42n128, 142nn130–31
johns, criminalization of, 9, 150, 165, 173. *See also* brothels, Israel; madams; prostitution
justice: abstract, 33; gap in, 83, 111–12; gender, 14, 41–43, 108–9; injustice and, 10, 24, 34; redistributive, 256; reforming, 61; reproductive, 210, 233–34n3, 238nn47–48; retributive, 84; social, 26

Kalantry, Sital, 231–32, 243n112, 249n169, 250n181
Kandaswamy, Meena, 133
Kannabiran, Kalpana, 87
Kapur, Ratna, 146n202
Kariv, Yifat, 197n131
Kennedy, Anthony (U.S. Supreme Court Justice), 219–20, 243–44n121
Kennedy, David, 18, 254–55
Kennedy, Duncan, 83, 112–13, 256
Kenya: criminalization of sexual violence in, 21n24; 2010 constitution, 14
Khanna, Akshay, 148n244
Kishwar, Madhu, 112, 144n168
Knesset: bills prohibiting prostitution, 158, 160, 192n74, 197n131; Committee on the Status of Women, 162, 191n63; members, 161, 166; NGO lobbying in, 161, 168
Kornhauser, Lewis, 259
Kotiswaran, Prabha, xvi–xvii, xviii, xx, 14–15, 216
Krishnaswamy, Sudhir, 106
Kuchik case (Israel), 163–64

labor market, Israel, 153–54; trafficking into, 161, 167, 172–73, 176, 179, 180, 181–83. *See also* exploitation: labor

Janet Halley is the Royall Professor of Law at Harvard Law School. She has a PhD in English from UCLA and a JD from Yale Law School. She is author of *Split Decisions: How and Why to Take a Break from Feminism* and *Don't: A Reader's Guide to the Military's Anti-Gay Policy*. She coedited *Left Legalism / Left Critique* with Wendy Brown and *After Sex? New Writing since Queer Theory* with Andrew Parker, and edited *Critical Directions in Comparative Family Law*, a special issue of *American Journal of Comparative Law*.

Prabha Kotiswaran is reader in law and social justice at the Dickson Poon School of Law, King's College London. She has a BA, LLB from the National Law School of India University, Bangalore, and an LLM and an SJD from Harvard Law School. She researches criminal law, transnational criminal law, sociology of law, postcolonial theory, and feminist legal theory. She is author of *Dangerous Sex, Invisible Labor: Sex Work and the Law in India* (winner of the 2012 SLSA-Hart Prize for Early Career Academics). She edited *Sex Work* and *Revisiting the Law and Governance of Trafficking, Forced Labor and Modern Slavery*, and coedited *Towards an Economic Sociology of Law* with Diamond Ashiagbor and Amanda Perry-Kessaris.

Rachel Rebouché is a professor of law at Temple University Beasley School of Law. She teaches family law, health care law, and comparative family law with a focus on reproductive health and reproductive justice. She earned an LLM from Queen's University, Belfast, and a JD from Harvard Law School. She is coauthor of a leading casebook on U.S. family law, and she is writing a book on international reproductive rights and editing a collection of essays on family law cases rewritten from a feminist perspective.

Hila Shamir is an associate professor at Buchmann Faculty of Law, Tel Aviv University. She earned an LLM and an SJD from Harvard Law School and an LLB from Tel Aviv University Faculty of Law. She teaches and researches employment, labor, immigration, and welfare law, with a focus on issues of gender equality, informal work, human trafficking, and welfare state privatization.